THE CITY & GUILDS TEXTBOOK

LEVEL 2 DIPLOMA IN

HEALTH AND SOCIAL CARE

SIOBHAN MACLEAN
ROB HARRISON
MELANIE BRIDGE
ELIZABETH GELHARD

About City & Guilds

City & Guilds is the UK's leading provider of vocational qualifications, offering over 500 awards across a wide range of industries, and progressing from entry level to the highest levels of professional achievement. With over 8500 centres in 100 countries, City & Guilds is recognised by employers worldwide for providing qualifications that offer proof of the skills they need to get the job done.

Equal opportunities

City & Guilds fully supports the principle of equal opportunities and we are committed to satisfying this principle in all our activities and published material. A copy of our equal opportunities policy statement is available on the City & Guilds website.

Copyright

First edition 2015
ISBN 978 0 85193 274 3

Commissioning Manager Charlie Evans
Senior Content Project Manager Claire Owen
Senior Production Editor Natalie Griffith

Cover design by Select Typesetters Ltd
Typeset by Integra Software Services Pvt., Ltd
Printed in the UK by Cambrian Printers Ltd

British Library Cataloguing in Publication Data

A catalogue record for this book is available from the British Library.

Publications

For information about or to order City & Guilds support materials, contact 0844 534 0000 or centresupport@cityandguilds.com. You can find more information about the materials we have available at www.cityandguilds.com/publications.

Every effort has been made to ensure that the information contained in this publication is true and correct at the time of going to press. However, City & Guilds' products and services are subject to continuous development and improvement and the right is reserved to change products and services from time to time. City & Guilds cannot accept liability for loss or damage arising from the use of information in this publication.

City & Guilds
1 Giltspur Street
London EC1A 9DD

0844 543 0033
www.cityandguilds.com
publishingfeedback@cityandguilds.com

THE CITY & GUILDS TEXTBOOK
LEVEL 2 D
HEA
SOC

CONTENTS

ABOUT THE AUTHORS

SIOBHAN MACLEAN

I started working in social care in a voluntary capacity when I was still at school, and since I was 18 I have worked in a variety of social care settings. I qualified as a social worker in 1990 and have since worked in a variety of service settings. I have a strong commitment to person-centred practice and to respecting the expertise of the people that social care seeks to support. I have written a number of publications for health and social care workers, many of them with Rob, and am committed to making the knowledge base accessible to busy practitioners.

ROB HARRISON

I began my work in this field as a volunteer, and have continued in a variety of voluntary roles to this day. I have worked in a range of services since 1996, primarily in the voluntary sector. Recently, I have managed advocacy services and services for carers. I am passionate about ensuring that the knowledge base is accessible across the profession, and about the ways in which the personalisation agenda can lead to better outcomes for service users and their carers.

MELANIE BRIDGE

Melanie Bridge has worked in health and social care for 32 years. With experience that includes working as a home care organiser and as a qualified social worker within an adult care team, she is currently a senior practitioner within an integrated locality team with additional specialisms of qualified Best Interests Assessor and Practice Educator.

ELIZABETH GELHARD

Elizabeth Gelhard spent 18 years nursing followed by over 20 years managing education and training organisations in the health and social care sector. She now works as a self-employed writer, trainer and therapist.

FOREWORD

Working with people in any capacity is always interesting. Working with people who are in need of care or support is also a great privilege.

With nearly 2 million people now working in social care, and with the Government expressing its commitment to making health and social care a priority in coming years, there has never been a more exciting time to work in the sector.

Whether you are new to health and social care or whether you have been working in the sector for some time, you will be working with people at times of need and often at crisis points in their lives, and what you do to support people can make a real difference to their lives. The *way* you carry out your work is what will make the real difference. People who receive health and social care services from professionals who provide care and support with compassion really feel the difference. Working in this way is both a challenge and a joy – you will receive so much satisfaction from your work.

HOW TO USE THIS TEXTBOOK

Welcome to your City & Guilds Level 2 Diploma in Health and Social Care textbook. It is designed to guide you through your Level 2 qualification and be a useful reference for you throughout your career.

Each chapter covers a unit from the 4222 Level 2 qualification and also provides additional information.

Throughout this textbook you will see the following features:

KEY POINT

- Medical models emphasise people's needs, deficits and 'treatments'.
- Social models are about access to resources and people's rights.

KEY POINT These are particularly useful hints that may assist in you in revision for your tests or to help you remember something important.

Key term 

Holistic means looking at the whole picture.

KEY TERM Words in colour in the text are explained in the margin to aid your understanding. They also appear in the glossary at the back of the book.

CASE STUDY

Oma works with people with learning disabilities. She is working with George, a young man who lives at home with his parents. George tells Oma that he wants to leave school and go to college, but his parents have said that he has to stay at school. He has told his teacher, who also said that George is better off at school. George says he keeps rowing with his mum and he is getting cross with his family. His sister left school when she was 16, and he is 17 and he says he is being treated like a baby. When Oma visits George at home she notices that there is a very strained atmosphere between George and his parents.

- What should Oma do?
- Why?

CASE STUDIES Useful, down-to-earth examples describing situations you may encounter in your work. There are usually questions at the end to help you shape your own thinking.

REFLECT

Consider a time when you have had to challenge somebody at work. This does not have to have been over a massive issue, or anything which led to an escalation of the issue. It might have been quite an informal challenge to a person over their use of language, or to somebody making fun of another person without thinking about how upsetting this could be.

- How did you challenge?
- Why did you decide to challenge?
- How did it feel to challenge?
- What worked well, and what would you do again in a similar situation?
- What would you do differently?
- What support might you need if this occurred again, or if the other person did not respond to the challenge you made?

REFLECT Questions to encourage you to think more deeply about the topic you are studying.

RESEARCH

What are your service's policy and procedure in relation to:

- handling of information?
- confidentiality?
- access to recording systems?
- service user access to files?

RESEARCH Useful pointers to finding out more about the subject you are studying.

APPLICATION OF SKILLS

Identifying appropriate communication with service users

Mrs Akabogu has dementia. Communication can be problematic because she is experiencing intermittent memory loss.

- How would you identify the most appropriate methods of communication to use with Mrs Akabogu?
- What methods do you think you might be able to use to maximise communication with Mrs Akabogu?

Mr Thompson has a hearing impairment. He does have a hearing aid, but doesn't always use it.

- Why might Mr Thompson not always use his hearing aid?
- How might you get over this?
- How would you investigate the best way to communicate with Mr Thompson?

APPLICATION OF SKILLS These are contexualised questions designed to develop your thinking and provoke further reflection on the skills you will need in your everyday work.

ACKNOWLEDGEMENTS

City & Guilds would like to sincerely thank the following.

For invaluable subject knowledge and expertise
Geraldine Donworth, Debbie Matthewson and Paul Robottom.

Picture credits
Every effort has been made to acknowledge all copyright holders as below and the publishers will, if notified, correct any errors in future editions.

Front cover: Shutterstock © Lisa S.

Alamy © Chris Rout p355; © Disability Images p494; © Image Source p91; © Image Source Plus p223; © John Hopkins p178; © Paula Solloway p257, p313; © Pauline Cutler p451; **Care Images.com** p23, p39, p69, p78, p107, p326, p333, p336, p351, p374, p378, p383, p463, p465, p470, p479, p488, p490, p496; © Dee Welch p347, p353; © John Edler p52, p317, p337; © Marc Morris p341; **City & Guilds** p1, p16, p26; **Crown copyright** p364, © Crown copyright material is reproduced with the permission of the Controller of HMSO and Queen's Printer for Scotland; **KJA-artists.com** p36, p54; **Living Made Easy** p375, p376; **Science Photo Library** © Nancy Kedersha p452; © Pasieka p449; **Shutterstock** © aastock p33; © AdrianNunez p255; © Africa Studio p397, p403; © albund p403; © Alexander Image p219; © Alexander Raths p59, p111, p116, p146, p308, p331, p361, p432; © Alsu p323; © Ammentorp Photography p231; © Ammit Jack p272; © Ana Bokan p318; © andras_csontos p46; © andreasnikolas p199; © Andrey_Kuzmin p366; © Andrey_Popov p398, p412; © Anna Lurye p128; © Antonov Roman p57; © AR Images p352; © auremar p285; © ayzek p218; © Barry Barnes p180; © Bashutskyy p414; © Bevan Goldswain p25; © bikeriderlondon p198, p248, p284, p301, p395, p396; © Blend images p51; © BlueRingMedia p450; © Bob Orsillo p402; © Bobkeenan Photography p92; © Brian A Jackson p30, p105, p238; © Brian Eichhorn p455; © CandyBox Images p174; © Catalin Petolea p300; © Cheryl E. Davis p268; © ConstantinosZ p171; © corund p37, p487; © Cosmin Manci p427; © Creatista p5; © DeiMosz p475; © Deklofenak p367; © Denise Lett p460; © De Visu p344; © diem p311; © Digital Genetics p155; © Djomas p439; © Dmitrijs Dmitrijevs p276; © DNF Style p70; © dotshock p130; © dreamerve p356; © Dziewul p265; © EcoPrint p147; © Edouard Coleman p180; © ElenaGaak p362; © Ensuper p204; © eurobanks p89; © ffolas p433; © Flashon Studio p240; © Fotoluminate LLC p382, p384; © Fulop Zsolt p256; © GlebStock p165; © Goodluz p102; © Grandpa p270; © graphixmania p100; © gresei p77; © gyn9037 p76; © Huntstock.com p177; © hxdbzxy p114, p389, p435, p477; © Iakov Filimonov p290, p313; © iko p42; © ILYA AKINSHIN p368; © InesBazdar p468; © Irina Rogova p34; © JPagetRFPhotos p395; © James Steidl p9; © jdwfoto p65; © Jasmin Awad p71; © Jenny Sturm p292, p295; © Jezper p424, p426; © Joe Gough, p82; © joesayhello p371; © John Abbate p37; © John Lumb p187; © jps p135; © Kamira p121; © Karuka p423; © Kenneth Man p387; © Knorre p426; © Kostenko Maxim p458; © kostudio p295; © Kristo-Gothard Hunor p138; © Ksenia Palimski p10; © kurhan p179; © Kzenon p175; © LeventeGyori p370; © Lighthunter p153; © linerpics p294; © Lisa F. Young p274; © LoloStock p134; © Loskutnikov p209; © Luis Santos p201, p443; © mangostock p62; © Marcin Balcerzak p30; © mariakraynova p438; © Mark William Richardson p186; © Maryna Pleshkun p168; © Mega Pixel p102; © michaeljung p31, p56; © Mikko Lemola p390; © Miriam Doerr p462; © MJTH p214; © molaruso p37; © Monkey Business Images p5, p40, p72, p82, p86, p88, p112, p132, p207, p230, p237, p242, p279, p358, p379; © mykeyruna p74; © nata-lunata p440; © Nattesha p113; © oblong1 p180; © Nerthuz p450; © Ocskay Bence p162; © Odua Images p441; © Olaru Radian-Alexandru p157; © Oleg Golonev p125; © Olesya Feketa p206; © Olha Afanasieva p370; © ollyy p15, p67, p324; © OPOLIA p432; © OPOLJA p251,p329; © Pachanatt Plysri p202; © Paul Vasarhelyi p457; © Pavel L Photo and Video p57; © Phasut Warapisit p395; © Phil.Tinkler p407; © photastic p63, p119; © Photobac p214; © Photographee.eu p287; © photomak p283; © Piotr Marcinski p376; © pockygallery p188; © Poprotskiy Alexey p73; © Pressmaster p38, p137, p193; © privilege p332; © Prixel Creative p115; © Pupes p266; © ra2studio p268; © racorn p247, p280; © RAGMA IMAGES p160; © RazoomGame p216; © Rido p52, p355; © RioPatuca p448; © Rob Byron p20; © Rob Marmion p18; © Robert Kneschke p163, p189, p253, p294, p320; © Rommel Canlas p220; © SARAPON p172; © Sebastian Crocker p37; © Serg64 p363; © SFC p396; © sharpshutter p27, p38; © SnowWhiteimages p45, p299; © spaxiax p242; © Stepan Kapl p97; © Stock Avalanche p328; © StockCube p158; © stockyimages p94, p305, p441; © Stuart Miles p260; © Talashow p180; © terekhov igor p160; ©theerasakj p349; © Thomas Bethge p211; © Titova Irina p37; © tiveryluck p50; © Tomas Jasinskis p182; © veronchick84 p180; © vgstudio p63; © Victor Naumik p95; © Volodymyr Baleha p260; © Vucicevic Milos p263; © Warren Goldswain p225, p278, p322; © wavebreakmedia p129, p167, p395; © William Perugini p230; © Winston Link p151; © woe p397; © XiXinXing p385; © Yaromir p8; © zimmytws p8.

Siobhan
Whilst I was working on this publication I had some health problems and spent a few weeks in hospital. I was extremely well cared for and would like to thank all the nurses and healthcare assistants who supported me during that difficult time. I would particularly like to thank Jude, a healthcare support worker who was working towards her Level 2 QCF. I learnt a great deal from you all.

Rob
My thanks to all the people I have worked with over the years who have all taught me everything I know. I really do hope that readers of this book find it useful, whatever stage of their career they are at.

CHAPTER 1

The role of the health and social care worker

As a professional in the field of health and social care, you need to be clear about your role, its boundaries and the purpose of your work and working relationships. This chapter covers this in detail, as well as some of the key issues surrounding partnership working, which is a feature that is increasing in importance in all areas of health and social care work.

Links to other chapters

This is the first chapter in the book for a good reason – you need to understand your role in order to carry out your work effectively. This chapter will assist you in all aspects of your work, but there are particular links to communicating effectively and to working in ways which promote equality and inclusion.

DID YOU KNOW?

- There are around 1.63 million people working in adult social care in England.
- Almost half of the workforce are in full-time posts.
- 23% of the workforce work for recipients of direct payments.
- 36% are employed in residential care.
- 45% in domiciliary care.
- 5% in day services.
- 14% in community services.
- 78% of the workforce are in direct care roles.
- The average age of a worker starting in social care is 35.

(Skills for Care 2012)

UNDERSTANDING WORKING RELATIONSHIPS IN HEALTH AND SOCIAL CARE

To really understand working relationships in health and social care, you need to recognise the differences between working relationships and relationships in your personal life.

TYPES OF RELATIONSHIPS

Everyone who has a job of any kind has two distinct types of relationships.

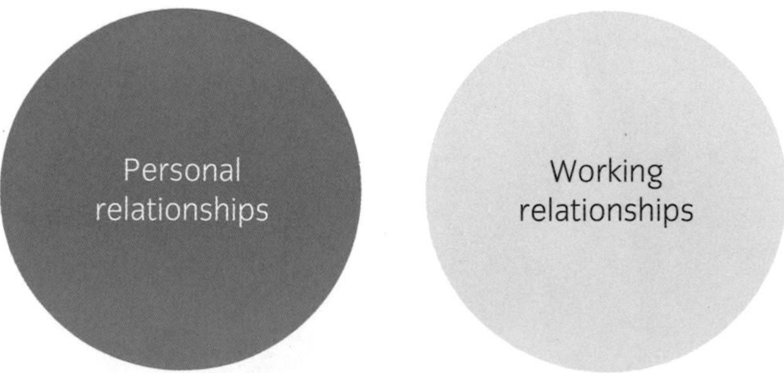

- Being paid brings responsibilities with it (for example, to follow your job description, to do your job according to the duty of care in this particular field of work, and to work according to national legislation and your employer's codes, policies and **procedures**). For example, if a friend tells you something you could choose to gossip about it (though you wouldn't be a very good friend). However, if a person tells you something as part of a working relationship you need to uphold professional confidentiality.
- When you are employed, you represent your employer/agency to everyone you come into contact with, so you need to be mindful of this and think about your employer's reputation as a responsible provider of services to people.

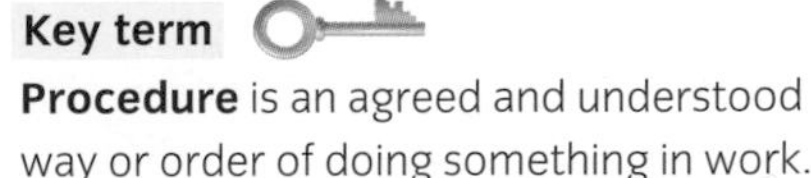

Procedure is an agreed and understood way or order of doing something in work.

Relationships with service users are different from all of the other relationships discussed above, because these relationships involve power imbalance. This concept is explored more in Chapter 3, and is critical to consider for the following reasons:

- Service users rely on workers (ie you) in order to have their basic or other needs met.
- People do not choose to have their needs met by others, so you have a duty of care to them. This involves doing your job to the best of your ability, safeguarding them, respecting their uniqueness and worth as a person, maintaining their dignity and promoting their independence.
- Even if you do not feel powerful in relation to the service user, they are likely to perceive you as having power in the relationship because you are a worker.
- You may hold societal power over them (as discussed in detail in Chapter 3) because of your age, race, gender, (lack of) disability and so on.

Therefore, in order to be an effective professional in this field of work you need to:

- understand possible power imbalances
- understand your role in relation to service users
- understand and apply professional values to your practice
- understand how your professional relationships differ from your personal ones, especially those relationships with service users
- reflect on your own practice
- listen to service users in respect of the quality of care they receive.

ARE HEALTH AND SOCIAL CARE WORKERS THE FRIENDS OF SERVICE USERS?

Service users may feel that health and social care workers are extended family or friends. This can be for a number of reasons:

- Staff are friendly towards service users.
- Staff can learn a lot about service users' personal problems and may be instrumental in addressing or resolving these problems.
- Staff can support service users in social activities.
- There can be contact through touch between staff and service users.
- Service users may spend more time with staff than with family and friends.

Increasingly, the importance of maintaining professional boundaries is being recognised and emphasised.

The following factors make the relationship between a staff member and a service user professional rather than one of family or friendship:

- Confidentiality – there are two aspects to this:
  - Health and social care workers may have to discuss personal details of service users with colleagues and record information in files.
  - Health and social care workers cannot discuss other service users or colleagues with a service user.
- Health and social care workers are paid to be there.
- The relationship is not reciprocal in that staff may know a lot about a service user but the service user may know little about a staff member.
- Health and social care workers are required to observe various organisational and policy rules, for example, service users not visiting homes of staff.
- Health and social care workers are open to formal complaint from a service user; staff are accountable to a manager for their conduct with a service user.
- Health and social care workers must be positive towards service users and there is an expectation that they will work with individuals they would not choose to socialise with.
- Health and social care workers have the right to leave their work behind them at the end of each work day.
- Health and social care workers are required to adhere to person-centred plans, care/support plans.
- Health and social care workers should not give advice, only information.

THE IMPORTANCE OF PROFESSIONAL BOUNDARIES

In a professional relationship, you can be friendly with a service user but you are not a service user's friend. You should be clear about the limits of your role as a health and social care worker. Working within **professional boundaries** keeps you focused on the work you are doing with a service user. Without boundaries, you risk overstepping your responsibilities, duties and working outside of safe practice.

Key term

Professional boundaries, in work settings, determine what we will and will not do, and what is appropriate in our relationships with service users and other people – and what is not.

What could indicate poor boundaries?

Poor boundaries can be indicated by a range of situations:

- A worker and a service user call each other friends and interact outside of the working environment.
- Valuable gifts are exchanged between worker and service user.
- A worker shares personal information with the service user.
- A worker finds themselves discussing the service user and their circumstances with their family and friends.
- A worker has discussions with the service user about other workers or service users.

What are the consequences of poor boundaries?

Poor boundaries lead to poor practice, in a number of ways:

- Without professional boundaries the health and social care worker may not provide appropriate services to the service user. A worker without clear boundaries could over-identify with a service user, and this will make it difficult for them to provide the objectivity that health and social care workers need.
- If you do not maintain professional boundaries, you may find yourself acting in an inappropriate manner – this might put you and the service user at risk.
- Professionals with poor boundaries often work outside of set policies and procedures, which leaves them open to allegations and without the support of their employer.

CASE STUDY

Mary is a home care worker. She visits service users in their own homes to offer support in line with their care plans. Mary has been working with Mr Hamlin for some time. Mr Hamlin is a widower and has no surviving family members; the only son he had died in infancy. Mr Hamlin is particularly lonely and often talks to Mary about this. Mary feels really sorry for Mr Hamlin and starts to visit him outside of her working hours. She enjoys sharing stories about her family and showing Mr Hamlin photos.

Mary is excited about becoming a grandmother for the first time and when the baby is born she shows photos to Mr Hamlin. Mr Hamlin gives Mary £20 for the baby's saving account. He is insistent that Mary accepts the money and says it makes him happy to give this to her. Mary accepts the gift, although she knows it is against policy, because she doesn't want Mr Hamlin to be upset. During a review with his social worker Mr Hamlin tells the social worker about how well he gets on with Mary and how happy he was about her becoming a grandma. The social worker talks to Mr Hamlin for a while about this and finds out about Mr Hamlin's gift to Mary. He contacts the care agency to raise a formal complaint about Mary.

- In what ways are Mary's boundaries poor?
- Why might she have acted the way she has?
- What might the social worker's concerns be?

REFLECT

- What different working relationships do you have?
- How do your work relationships differ from your personal ones?

RESEARCH

Ask your supervisor what policies and procedures relate to working relationships, and particularly professional boundaries. Ensure that you are fully aware of these boundaries so you can work within them at all times.

APPLICATION OF SKILLS

Would you?

Thinking through the boundaries you have in your relationships with service users and the research you have carried out on policies and procedures, consider the following questions.

- If you saw a service user in town when you were out shopping, would you stop to chat to them?
- When in a service user's home, would you have a cup of tea? What about a piece of cake?
- Would you tell a service user about your family? How much would you tell them? For example, if your partner had lost their job, would you tell a service user?
- Would you invite a service user to a celebration – such as your wedding or birthday party?
- If a service user was struggling to get their clothes cleaned, would you take their laundry home and do it when you do your own laundry?
- If a service user asked you to become a 'friend' on a social networking site, would you accept the request?
- Would you accept a birthday card or gift from a service user?
- Would you send a birthday card to a service user?

For each question, think about:

- Would you do this?
- If so, why?
- If not, why not?
- If it 'depends', what does it depend upon?

You could talk some of these examples through with your colleagues and your manager. It is interesting to see how different workers might have different boundaries – and it is also important to be aware of the boundaries your employing organisation expects you to have.

WORKING IN WAYS THAT ARE AGREED WITH THE EMPLOYER

It is vital that health and social care workers work in the ways required by their employer. If a health and social care worker works outside of these agreed ways of working, they are in danger of not being supported by their employer should something go wrong. Therefore it is important that you understand the scope of your role and that you work within this agreed scope.

Key terms

Job description describes the day-to-day tasks and responsibilities of a job.

Person specification goes through the criteria (skills, knowledge, experience, values and qualifications) that you need in order to do your job. These may either be 'essential' or 'desirable'.

Key terms

Policy in health and social care is a written statement explaining the service or agency's expected approach to an issue, area of practice, or key aspects of people's work. Policies can be local and/or national.

Procedure is an agreed and understood way or order of doing something in work.

THE SCOPE OF YOUR JOB ROLE

When you apply for any job in health and social care, you are likely to have seen the job advertised somewhere, and submitted an application before being interviewed. When you were shortlisted for interview for your current job (and every other job you have had in the past) your application will have been assessed against the **job description** and, in many cases, against a **person specification** for that role.

The job description and person specification are key documents that provide the beginning of the scope of your job role. **Policies**, **procedures**, legislation and codes of practice complete the scope of your role once you are employed.

Think of the scope of your job role as a building which you do not go outside of – the foundations are made up of the value base of health and social care; the walls are made up of your job description and the person specification, along with policies and procedures; and the roof is the law that you need to work within.

Policies are usually written and formal. Meanwhile, procedures can be:

- presented in writing, or in a flow chart or other format
- formal
- informal – an informal procedure would be something which workers understand they follow in the work setting, but which is not necessarily written out, eg a way in which people are expected to greet and sign visitors in to the organisation or health and social care setting.

Policies and procedures will differ between service settings, but they will always reflect the law and the employer's responsibilities to both staff and service users. Health and social care workers need to have a working knowledge of their agency's policies and procedures in order to carry out their responsibilities.

ADHERING TO THE AGREED SCOPE OF YOUR ROLE

It is important to adhere to the scope of your job role because:

- the level of responsibility you have will be defined in the scope
- others will hold other duties and responsibilities which support your role, and which complement it – workers in other roles will have different levels of responsibility and will have been measured against different criteria when they got their jobs
- doing so keeps service users safe, and ensures that the right workers are in the right post, and that the right person carries out the right tasks to meet the service user's individual needs.

Going beyond the scope of your job role can be dangerous and inappropriate because:

- there could be employer **liabilities** and insurance implications
- there could be safeguarding implications for the people you work with
- other people may be more skilled and more experienced, and therefore more effective, in certain areas of work
- there may be a procedural, ethical or legal duty for certain workers to undertake certain tasks
- there could be consequences for you in terms of your own reputation for competence, and potentially for your current (and future) employment.

Key term 

Liability is a legal responsibility. Employers can be legally responsible for action carried out by an employee. Individuals can also have legal responsibilities.

Knowing your own boundaries, and understanding and adhering to those of your job role, are essential for good practice in this field of work.

RESEARCH

- What does your job description and person specification say about your job role?
- When were they last reviewed?
- Do they reflect the actual job you do?

REFLECT

Why do you think it is important to adhere to the scope of your job role?

ACCESSING FULL AND UP-TO-DATE DETAILS OF AGREED WAYS OF WORKING

It is important that you keep yourself up to date with the agreed ways of working in your organisation. Central to this is ensuring that you are familiar with the policies and procedures of your employer.

Policies are statements which define the agency's position on key issues, as well as some detail on how this stance should be implemented in practice. Most health and social care employers will have set policies on the following:

- safeguarding
- health and safety
- **equality** and diversity
- confidentiality and information sharing
- recruitment and selection of workers
- training and development
- bullying and harassment
- whistleblowing
- environmental policy
- grievance and disciplinary policy.

Key term

Equality is about treating people in a way that ensures that they are not placed at a disadvantage to others.

As stated earlier, procedures are more about how things are expected to be done at work. Procedures can cover a wide range of tasks, including:

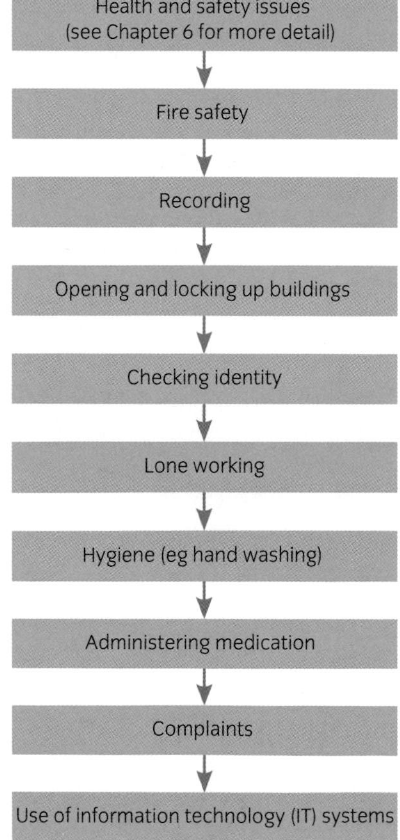

It is your employer's duty to provide you with copies of all of the above when you start a job (or give you the tools and time to research them for yourself). It is also your employer's duty to notify you of any changes that may occur to these. It is your duty to make sure you read up on any changes, stay up to date and implement agreed ways of working in your work setting.

IMPLEMENTING AGREED WAYS OF WORKING

When there is a procedure in place in health and social care, this is because either:

- there has to be a set way of doing something (ie for legal reasons)

or

- this is felt to be (or has been shown by evidence to be) the best way of achieving a task.

Your duty of care means that you have to follow procedures to keep people safe and ensure their needs are met. Also, your contractual obligations mean that you have to follow your employer's policies and procedures.

If you feel that a policy or procedure does not reflect actual practices in your work setting, part of your duty of care means you either have to change your practices and follow procedure more closely, or flag to your manager that the procedure needs to be changed or improved.

REFLECT

- How do you work in agreed ways in your work setting?
- Are there any procedures which you feel could be improved in your work setting in order to meet service users' needs better? What would you change and why?

KEY POINT

Codes of practice and conduct

Whilst individual organisations often have their own code of practice or code of conduct, health and social care workers should also follow the codes developed in their own countries. For Scotland, the Scottish Social Services Council has a Code of Practice for Social Service Workers whilst in Wales the Care Council Wales has a Code of Practice for Social Care Workers. In England, the Code of Conduct for Healthcare Support Workers and Adult Social Care Workers applies.

FOLLOWING AGREED WAYS OF WORKING – WHAT DOES THE CODE OF CONDUCT SAY?

The Code of Conduct for Healthcare Support Workers and Adult Social Care Workers in England 2013 makes clear that you need to be accountable, and that you must do the following:

- Be honest with yourself and others about what you can do, recognise your abilities and the limitations of your competence and only carry out or delegate those tasks agreed in your job description and for which you are competent.
- Always behave and present yourself in a way that does not call into question your suitability to work in a health and social care environment.
- Be able to justify and be accountable for your actions or omissions – what you fail to do.
- Always ask your supervisor or employer for guidance if you do not feel adequately prepared to carry out any aspect of your work, or if you are unsure how to effectively deliver a task.
- Tell your supervisor or employer about any issues that might affect your ability to do your job competently and safely. If you do not feel competent to carry out an activity you must report this.
- Honour your work commitments, agreements and arrangements, and be reliable, dependable and trustworthy.
- Comply with your employer's agreed ways of working.

CASE STUDY

Mkosi starts work in a domiciliary care agency. She is looking forward to working in the care field as she has always enjoyed supporting her friends and neighbours. Mkosi anticipates that the main aspect of her job will be chatting to people and seeing what help they want her to provide. On her first day she is introduced to a range of policies and procedures, and the process of care planning and following care plans is explained to her. At first Mkosi is a little taken aback by all the paperwork – but after shadowing some other care workers during her induction she recognises the value of procedures in ensuring that everyone followed the same practices.

- Why might Mkosi have started work with a misunderstanding of the role of a **domiciliary care worker**?
- How important was her **induction**, and why?

Key terms 

Domiciliary care worker is a person who provides care to people who live independently.

Induction is training to introduce an employee to a new role or organisation.

WORKING IN PARTNERSHIP WITH OTHERS

Partnership working means working closely with others. Being able to work effectively in partnership with service users and their family members as well as a wide range of other agencies and professionals is an essential skill for everyone in health and social care.

Working in partnership with service users and their family members is a key theme throughout this book, and involves everyone:

- communicating effectively
- working in a person-centred way
- promoting the principles of **active participation** and self-directed support.

Key term 

Active participation is about people being involved in their own care, as opposed to being a 'recipient' of that care (ie it is about something being done *with* someone rather than something being done *to* someone). Active participation also means that people take part in the activities of daily and independent life as much as possible.

This section will focus on the issues of working in partnership with other professionals. Some of the skills you will use to work in partnership with service users and their family members are central to good practice for working in partnership with other professionals, too. However, some of the challenges in working with people from other settings, services, professional backgrounds and agencies involve other skills, as well as your communication and interpersonal skills.

WORKING RELATIONSHIPS IN HEALTH AND SOCIAL CARE SETTINGS

A health and social care worker has working relationships with managers, supervisors, colleagues and other agencies as well as with users of services and their relatives.

As a health and social care worker you should work to a shared set of values. The values of social care are also defined in detail in Chapter 3. These values inform a common understanding of the role of a health and social care worker. Your role is:

- communicating with people
- understanding (assessing) and meeting people's needs
- respecting differences and promoting equality and **inclusion** for people who may otherwise be excluded from accessing resources
- empowering people and enabling the maximum possible independence for them
- keeping accurate and up-to-date records
- working in partnership with other agencies
- keeping people healthy and safe, and maintaining a safe working environment for yourself and for others.

Key term

Inclusion is the word used to describe the opposite of social exclusion. It is where action is taken to address the effects of discrimination, and to strive towards preventing or ideally eliminating oppression.

Your working relationships with other people should be based on this common understanding and shared set of values. Working with others is sometimes challenging, but all relationships in life can be challenging at times.

Unlike other fields of work, in health and social care your conduct outside of work usually has to reflect a commitment to the values of your profession too, and a serious failure outside work to adhere to the standards expected can affect your employment. For example, workers in health and social care could lose their employment if convicted of certain offences, or if their conduct was seen to damage the reputation of their employer.

WORKING WITH OTHERS

Working in health and social care involves working with other people. Although many health and social care workers work alone in an individual's home, they are still part of a wider care team. Working with others can be a source of great support, and of professional satisfaction. It can also be a source of stress and one of the harder things about the health and social care role, as people's views and approaches may be very different.

Some key ways of working with others are linked to principles of good care practice.

Listen to other people's viewpoints

There is not always just one way of doing things, and getting the best **outcome** can be far more important than how you get there. The exceptions to this are often connected with health and safety (where the only way of doing something can be determined by legislation), safeguarding, and where procedures and policies prescribe a set way of doing a task and show the employer's expectations of consistency and best practice.

Key term
Outcomes are what people want to achieve.

Respect differences

We are all different, and different professionals may have different ways of looking at things. This is to be valued – sometimes other people can see something that you don't. They might have ideas that wouldn't have occurred to you. The fact that different professionals might approach a situation differently is one of the main benefits of working together. Look for areas of common ground, as this will help to minimise differences.

Be open to trying out new ideas

In health and social care taking an open-minded approach is really important – not least when working with others.

Say if you have got something wrong

Everyone gets things wrong sometimes. If you don't say anything, this may reflect badly on you as people respect those who are open and admit when they have got something wrong. You are also more likely to be able to learn from these experiences if you are open and if you reflect on them afterwards.

Praise people for doing a good job

If you think someone has done a good job or has had a good idea, tell them.

Support others in the way you hope they would support you

If someone is particularly pressured they may need a little help and support from their colleagues. People might need to swap shifts or might need a little advice. Think about the way you would like to be supported – and be as supportive as you can to others.

In summary

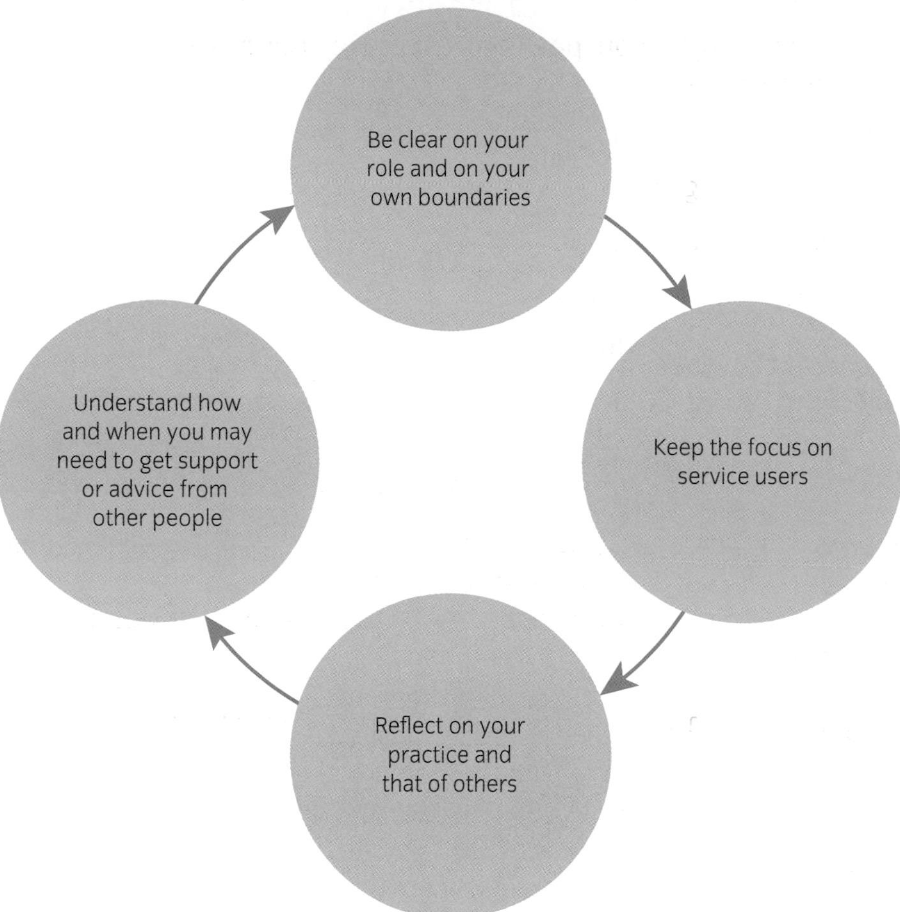

RELATIONSHIPS WITH PROFESSIONALS

When working with other professionals, health and social care workers have various responsibilities and boundaries that they must recognise.

The responsibilities include:

- working in partnership
- sharing information appropriately
- sharing decision making appropriately
- respecting the particular role and contribution of other professionals
- respecting alternative viewpoints
- continuing to work positively even when there are disagreements.

The boundaries of the relationship include:

- not passing on information inappropriately
- not overstepping the boundaries of others' roles
- not expecting personal help
- not accepting gifts.

TENSIONS IN WORKING RELATIONSHIPS

Even within one service, work setting or agency, working relationships can become strained for a range of reasons. The following is not an exhaustive list by any means, but indicates some of the possible causes of tension in working relationships:

- differences in values between two workers (despite the common values of the field of work, we are all still different)
- resource constraints
- stress
- differences in point of view towards a conflict or dilemma
- differences in approach to work practices
- safeguarding issues
- whistleblowing (where one colleague raises a concern about another person's work)
- health issues which may make us unwell and/or tense
- different understandings of what an agreed procedure or practice is for the service
- clash of personalities.

WORKING RELATIONSHIPS – WHAT DOES THE CODE OF CONDUCT SAY?

The Code of Conduct for Healthcare Support Workers and Adult Social Care Workers in England 2013 makes clear that you need to develop professional relationships in your work, and that you must:

- establish and maintain clear and appropriate professional boundaries in your relationships with people who use health and care services, carers and colleagues at all times
- never accept any offers of loans, gifts, benefits or hospitality from anyone you are supporting or anyone close to them, which may be seen to compromise your position.

CASE STUDY

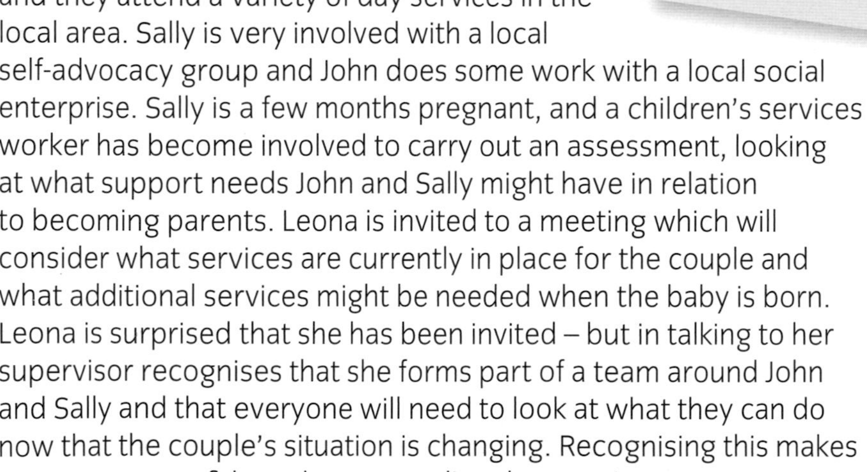

Leona works as a support worker with a housing association. She is working with John and Sally, who are married. They have learning disabilities and live in their own home. Leona provides support to John and Sally in managing their tenancy and in managing their money. John and Sally also receive support from a social worker and they attend a variety of day services in the local area. Sally is very involved with a local self-advocacy group and John does some work with a local social enterprise. Sally is a few months pregnant, and a children's services worker has become involved to carry out an assessment, looking at what support needs John and Sally might have in relation to becoming parents. Leona is invited to a meeting which will consider what services are currently in place for the couple and what additional services might be needed when the baby is born. Leona is surprised that she has been invited – but in talking to her supervisor recognises that she forms part of a team around John and Sally and that everyone will need to look at what they can do now that the couple's situation is changing. Recognising this makes Leona more confident about attending the meeting.

- Why is it important for Leona to attend the meeting?
- Who else should be at the meeting, and why?

WORKING IN PARTNERSHIP WITH OTHER PROFESSIONALS

The agenda for ensuring that all professionals work well together is at the heart of all government policy in health and social care work. The idea of a range of professionals forming a 'team around the service user' is one which is key to providing person-centred services to vulnerable service users which truly meet their individual needs. Most people who have contact with health and social care workers have contact with a range of different professionals and therefore as a health and social care worker you will need to work with professionals from different agencies and organisations.

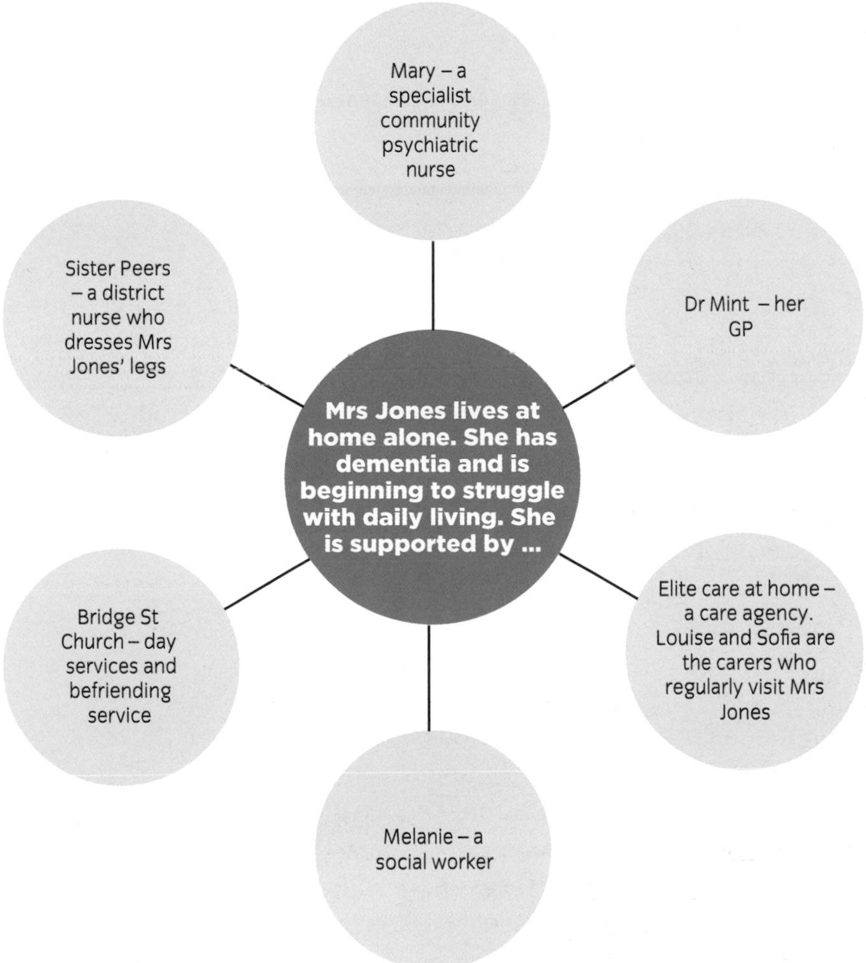

Most people receive support from a number of workers and services. In this example Louise and Sofia are part of a wider care team.

BENEFITS OF WORKING IN PARTNERSHIP WITH OTHER AGENCIES

There are a range of benefits to working in partnership with other professionals and other agencies, which might include the following.

Being able to 'tap into' resources which other agencies hold

Not only does this lead to better outcomes for service users, but it means that people can access specialist help from the right people at the right time.

Being able to use a single assessment process

This reduces the need for people to have to keep repeating their 'story' to different professionals.

Being able to be clear about services' roles and responsibilities

Effective partnership working needs all workers to be clear about the roles and responsibilities of other professionals. This means that workers need to be clear about the boundaries of their own roles, so that this can be communicated to service users and other agencies. It also means that people working in health and social care need to be clear on the roles of others (occupational therapists, district nurses, community psychiatric nurses, social workers, etc), so that when a team is formed to provide support to a service user everyone knows:

- who is doing what
- when
- where
- why
- what each professional can and cannot offer.

Being clear in this way means that service users can also feel confident in understanding why so many people may be involved in their lives. It also means that service users can be supported to understand what may be expected of them when it comes to supporting themselves in line with the principles of active participation and self-directed support.

Being able to put into place effective and safe practices towards confidentiality and information sharing

Where multiple agencies and workers are involved in a service user's care, it is vital that good practice towards confidentiality is agreed and maintained. This is essential, as working together usually means that certain information needs to be shared so that effective care and support can be offered. At the same time, it is a service user's legal and moral right to know which information is shared, with whom, and the purpose of this sharing of knowledge about them.

Growing in confidence in professional knowledge and expertise

Working with others enables health and social care staff to learn, develop their skills and knowledge and feel confident about their own role.

THE CHALLENGES OF PARTNERSHIP WORKING

Despite the various benefits to partnership working in health and social care, there are a number of challenges to effective partnership working. These can include:

Organisational culture

All organisations have their own values and **culture**. An organisation's culture is about:

- the people who work there, their beliefs, values and standards
- its policies, procedures and expectations
- its environment and how the organisation and workers present themselves to others outside of the organisation
- the way in which people (staff and service users) feel *about* the organisation or service
- the way in which people (staff and service users) feel valued *by* the organisation or service.

Key term

Culture refers to what people do and why they do it. All individuals have a culture which is shaped by their beliefs, their background and any groups which they belong to. Organisations also have a culture which is often shaped by the organisation's leaders.

The concept of organisational culture applies to agencies, to professional roles and to individual teams. This can mean that tensions arise where people from different professional cultures are expected to work together. There may be several factors which create difficulties:

- lack of a mutual understanding around the roles and boundaries of other professional roles
- stereotyping of other agencies and professionals (eg social workers just want to close cases, district nurses don't take enough time with the person, etc)
- issues surrounding leadership – managers need to be committed to the ideals of partnership working and communicate this consistently, as well as challenging stereotyping of other agencies
- factors within teams or services creating pressures at certain times which lead professionals to 'shut down' and work in an insular way (eg when facing change, redundancy or high workloads).

Status issues and perceptions of other roles

The value and status of some professions and workers in relation to other professions can cause problems. Tension can arise in decision making, as certain professionals have more status granted them within society than others. This can be made apparent by differences in length of training, pay and by actions which accord some individuals more status. The obvious example of this is GPs – how many of us have found it hard to question decisions and actions taken by the GP because they are seen as so powerful? Similarly, this can apply to health and social care workers on a professional level, as it can feel hard to challenge other agencies' views about a service user's needs.

Learning how to challenge others constructively

All relationships involve differences of opinion at some point. However, health and social care workers need particular sensitivity when challenging other agencies' views, decisions and actions. It is a difficult task to challenge other workers' decisions without it seeming like a reflection on their professional judgement. Being able to do this is a core skill in all professional practice in all fields. Sometimes personalities may clash, or another worker may simply not be in the right frame of mind to hear a challenge which is made. Therefore, health and social care workers must be able to plan, weigh up and carry out the best way of making challenges in order to achieve the desired outcomes for an individual service user.

Protectiveness of jobs

Sometimes working in partnership can be difficult because other professionals might perceive unintended threats to their own jobs and status. One of the key skills in partnership working involves the ability to consider the other person's standpoint, and their pressures and their anxieties, in the same way as with service users. Workers too can feel threatened by other people coming into the picture and offering support which they may feel is part of their job to deliver. The ability to share this openly can be a core skill for those working in health and social care, particularly when a relationship is new or already feels strained. Openness can achieve great change though, as other professionals may respond well to someone taking the time to find out what the barriers are to partnerships from their point of view. In this way shared solutions can be created so that closer partnership working can be achieved, although this can be an ongoing struggle in trying to form shared visions with some individuals.

CASE STUDY

Amanda is a home care worker. Many of the people she supports are recently discharged from hospital and require support at home during their recovery. Amanda sometimes finds this challenging. She feels that sometimes the people she supports are discharged from hospital before they are ready. She feels that when people are discharged too early it affects how much she can do with them to support them in developing their independence.

Amanda talks to her manager about what can be done about this. Amanda and her manager arrange to meet with the discharge coordinator from the local hospital to discuss the concerns. The meeting is really useful, as the discharge coordinator talks about the support that can be provided by occupational therapists and district nurses and Amanda feels that she is recognised as a key part of the discharge planning team.

- Was Amanda right to share her concerns with her manager?
- Why is it important for Amanda to be aware of the role of different professionals in the hospital discharge process?

WAYS OF WORKING THAT CAN HELP IMPROVE PARTNERSHIP WORKING

Partnership working can be improved in various different ways:

- by understanding the meaning and purpose of partnership working
- by recognising the benefits of partnership working
- by being committed to working in partnership – recognising the way that it can improve outcomes for service users
- by managers and senior managers agreeing joint working protocols, which include detail on how disagreement will be resolved
- by spending time with other professionals, and those working in partner agencies and disciplines
- by understanding the challenges to partnership working
- by developing skills in dealing with conflict
- by attending joint training events
- by shadowing colleagues from other agencies
- by attending multi-agency meetings and listening to partners' views about an issue, a person's needs, or solutions to barriers

Increasingly teams may be co-located in buildings, which can help partnership working, as people get to know each other informally as well as seeing on a day-to-day level how partners work.

As with all good health and social care practice, listening to partners, respecting difference and focusing on the service user are the key skills to ensure partnership working is improved.

PARTNERSHIP WORKING – WHAT DOES THE CODE OF CONDUCT SAY?

The importance of effective partnership working is recognised in the Code of Conduct for Healthcare Support Workers and Adult Social Care Workers in England 2013, which states that you must:

- understand and value your contribution and the vital part you play in your team
- recognise and respect the roles and expertise of your colleagues both in the team and from other agencies and disciplines, and work in partnership with them
- work openly and cooperatively with colleagues, including those from other disciplines and agencies, and treat them with respect
- work openly and cooperatively with people who use health and care services and their families or carers and treat them with respect.

ACCESSING SUPPORT AND ADVICE ABOUT PARTNERSHIP WORKING

Knowing how and when to access support for the challenges which partnership working can bring is important.

When

- When the above strategies have been tried but the tension remains in the relationship.
- When there are ethical dilemmas which may need someone else's input (see also Chapter 4).
- When there may need to be an escalation of a specific issue, or a use of joint working protocols.

How

- Usually workers would contact their immediate line manager for support, advice and information.
- If they were not available, there may be a duty system for managerial support in some settings.

- Some issues may need escalating to more senior managers.
- Support may be available from employee assistance helplines, unions, or from other agencies.

At all times, whenever there are issues in partnership working, and when additional support or advice is needed, keep the service user as the focus.

REFLECT

- Which agencies and other professionals do you work in partnership with in your role and work setting?
- What do you see as being the benefits of partnership working?
- What do you see as the tensions in partnership working?
- How would you resolve issues in your work setting? Have you had any experience of challenges within partnerships? If so, what worked in resolving these challenges, and what did not work so well?

RESEARCH

- Does your service or employer have any formal partnership agreements, or joint working protocols (either formally agreed in writing, or informal expectations about how partnership working will be conducted)?
- If not, are there any areas where you feel this could be helpful, and could improve outcomes for service users?

RESOLVING CONFLICT

Health and social care workers at all levels regularly find themselves in situations of conflict with others. This is particularly likely to occur in situations where they are working in partnership with others, which is why resolving conflicts is covered in this chapter. However, it is important to remember that being able to work with others and resolve conflict is an important skill in all aspects of health and social care work.

Conflict: positive or negative?

Experience shows that health and social care workers often view conflict negatively. However, this can create difficulties in terms of conflict responses. In itself, conflict is neither positive nor negative – it is the way that conflict is managed and its consequences which make it either positive or negative.

Conflict can be a positive force, in that it:

- enables a person to become aware of problems in a relationship
- serves as catalyst for learning and positive change
- energises and motivates people to deal with immediate problems
- can stimulate interest and curiosity
- relieves minor tensions and can be liberating
- creates more creative approaches to decision making
- promotes self-awareness
- clears the air of unexpressed resentment.

What might create conflict?

There are five main sources of conflict:

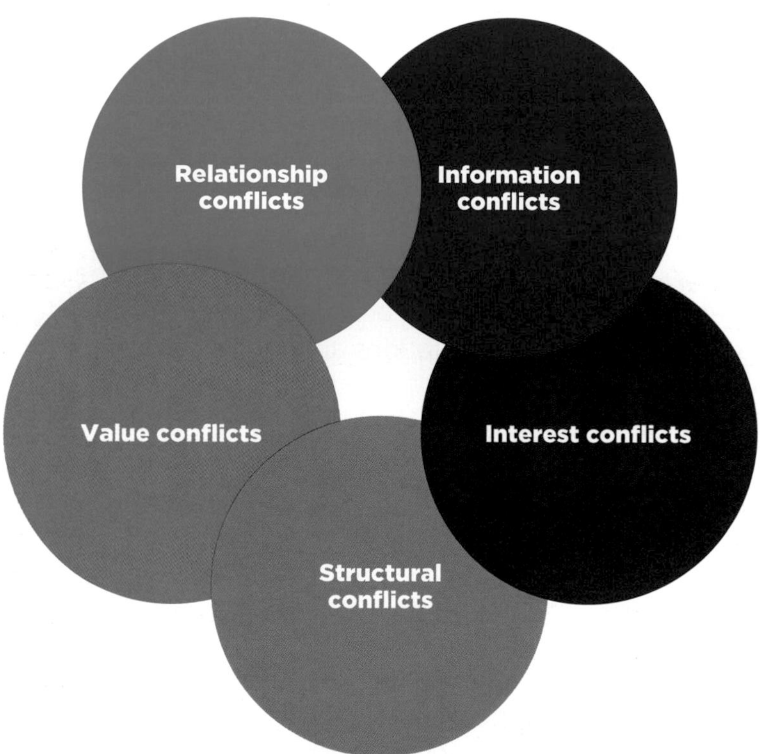

Relationship conflicts

When we think about conflict, conflicts between people or relationship-based conflicts are generally the first thing that comes to mind. Relationship conflicts can occur because of:

- poor communication
- strong negative emotions
- misperceptions or **stereotypes**
- repetitive negative behaviours.

Key term

Stereotype is a generalised idea about a group of people.

Information conflicts

Essentially, information conficts arise where information is the source of the conflict. They might occur when:

- people lack the information necessary to make decisions
- people are misinformed
- there is a disagreement about which information is relevant
- there is conflicting information.

Interest conflicts

Interest conflicts are caused by competition between needs which may be seen as incompatible with each other. Conflicts of interest result when one or more of the parties believes that in order to satisfy their needs, the needs and interests of another person must be sacrificed or are less of a priority than their own.

Structural conflicts

Structural conflicts are caused by forces external to the people in dispute. Often they are related to the way in which institutions and society are constructed. Issues such as limited physical resources, geographical constraints (distance or proximity), time (too little or too much) and organisational changes can make structural conflict seem like a crisis. It can be helpful to assist parties in conflict to appreciate the external forces and constraints which have an impact, as an understanding that a conflict has an external source can bring people together to jointly address the imposed difficulties.

Value conflicts

Value conflicts are caused by differences in people's value systems; however, differing value systems do not necessarily cause conflict. Value conflicts arise only when people attempt to force one set of values on others or lay claim to exclusive value systems that do not allow for different beliefs. Value conflicts can create internal conflicts for health and social care workers – for example, where their personal values conflict with the professional values of social care or where organisational values conflict with professional values.

It can be useful when trying to resolve conflict to first of all analyse where the conflict is coming from. Understanding whether a conflict is based on relationships or information, for example, is a good starting point for resolving the conflict.

Conflict resolution: stages, skills and attitudes

Resolving conflict involves the following.

Communication

When you are in a situation of potential conflict with another person, you need to avoid adopting an adversarial and defensive approach. The

initial task is to have an attitude where you want yourself and the person who is in dispute with you to benefit from any shared decision (win/win).

To do this, the starting point is to find out what each party's needs are. Skills required include supportive questioning (to identify the other person's needs), effective listening and the ability to communicate your own needs. In communicating your own needs you should be assertive and use the 'I' word without expectations of what the other person should do. Conflict resolution needs to recognise that the person could be very angry with you. Approaches include:

- not defending yourself at first, as this can antagonise the other person
- dealing with their emotions; acknowledge that you recognise that they are angry
- acknowledging their perspective; you do not need to agree with them but you do need to understand them.

Following this process should help the person to calm down.

One of the key elements of conflict resolution is attitude:

- there must be an openness to recognising the benefit of differences
- there must be a willingness to adapt or trade for mutual benefit
- there must be a view that the difficulty is to be addressed, and not the person
- disagreements or potential conflicts must not be seen as a problem, but as an opportunity to engage with the other person.

Negotiation

Once the needs of each individual have been expressed, the next stage is negotiation. As part of this, the focus must remain on the issue. Where possible, acknowledge common ground. If it appears to be a big problem, can it be broken down?

If negotiations get heated:

- manage your own emotions
- let barbed comments go without responding to them
- have a break, but agree when to resume.

In seeking a solution:

- make a trial proposal
- suggest a trade – 'I will do this if you do that'
- make an agreement temporary or time limited, so that agreements can be reviewed.

Mediation

If it is not possible to reach a win/win situation, it may be necessary to go for mediation.

A **mediator** requires various skills and conditions, including:

- being explicit that mutual benefit is the aim
- having a clear sense that both parties are willing to address the problem
- enabling each party to express themselves, and checking that they understand each other
- an ability to encourage suggestions (the mediator should avoid making their own suggestions)
- discouraging personal comments or behaviours that could be provocative (name calling, ignoring, threats, belittlement, etc).

Key term

Mediator is a person who intervenes in situations of conflict.

Resolution

Be clear about the agreement that has been made. It is easy for two people to leave a conflict situation with each having a different understanding of what has been agreed.

CASE STUDY

Oma works with people with learning disabilities. She is working with George, a young man who lives at home with his parents. George tells Oma that he wants to leave school and go to college, but his parents have said that he has to stay at school. He has told his teacher, who also said that George is better off at school. George says he keeps rowing with his mum and he is getting cross with his family. His sister left school when she was 16, and he is 17 and he says he is being treated like a baby. When Oma visits George at home she notices that there is a very strained atmosphere between George and his parents.

- What should Oma do?
- Why?

ACCESSING SUPPORT AND ADVICE ABOUT RESOLVING CONFLICTS

Knowing how and when to access support when you face conflict situations is important.

When

- When you face a conflict which you feel cannot easily be resolved.
- When there are a range of conflicts which may need someone else's input.
- When there may need to be an escalation of a specific issue, or a use of joint working protocols.

How

- Usually workers would contact their immediate line manager for support, advice and information.
- If they were not available, there may be a duty system for managerial support in some settings.
- Some issues may need escalating to more senior managers.

At all times, whenever there are conflict issues, and when additional support or advice is needed, keep the service user as the focus.

REFLECT

Identify a situation in which you have faced conflict at work.

- What was the conflict about?
- How did you handle it?
- Could you have improved your response to this situation? How?
- If a similar situation were to occur again, how would you deal with it?

Before going to the next chapter, take some time to consider:

- what you see as the main differences between your working and personal relationships
- what you think about the quality of your working relationships/work
- how you could improve your working relationships
- whether you fully understand the scope of your job role
- how good you think you are at resolving conflicts at work
- how you could improve your skills in working with conflict – how will you do this?

CHAPTER 2

Introduction to communication in health and social care

Communication is a core skill in all health and social care practice. Many people think that communication skills are 'natural' – that a person is either a good communicator or they are not. However, communication skills can be learned, and they can certainly be developed. This chapter ensures that you understand how to communicate effectively with service users you care for, as well as colleagues and other professionals, and how to overcome the barriers to communication that you might face.

Links to other chapters

The other skills which you will need to work in health and social care cannot be developed unless you have good skills in communication. Specific aspects of health and social care practice are covered in the other chapters of this book. In order to be able to carry these out you will need to be able to communicate effectively. Therefore the knowledge covered in this chapter will be useful to you in completing all the units of the Diploma.

WHY IS COMMUNICATION IMPORTANT IN THE WORK SETTING?

In order to understand the importance of communication at work, you need to understand:

- what we mean by 'communication'
- why people communicate
- how people communicate
- the way in which communication impacts on your work.

WHAT IS COMMUNICATION?

This might seem a very basic question, but as you work through this chapter you will find that there is a lot more to communication than you might first think.

Communication is a two-way process which is affected by the environment in which the communication takes place. So communication is never straightforward – it is never about one individual, but always about relationships, specific needs and environments.

Even newborn babies can communicate effectively:

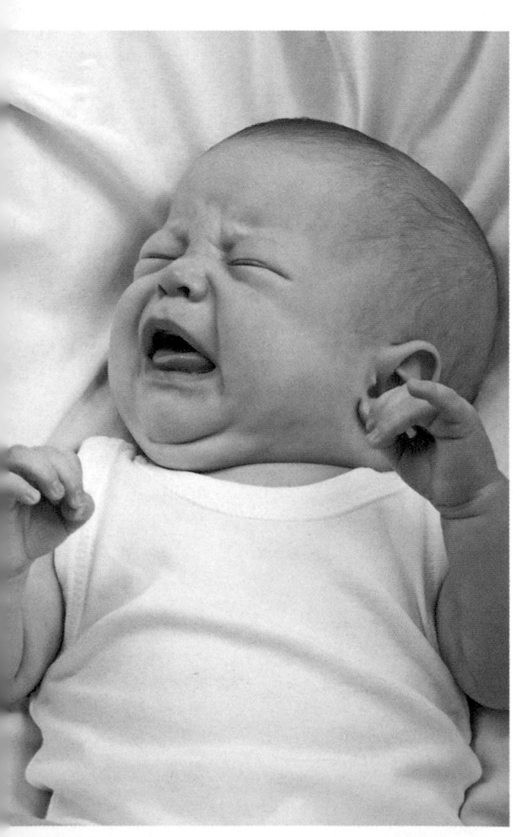

- because their needs are unmet (for food, warmth, comfort, affection or a nappy needing changing)
- because they want to be stimulated
- because of fear or loneliness.

Many new parents will tell you that they quickly learn the different ways their baby cries – enabling them to understand the difference between a baby that is hungry and one that wants attention.

COMMUNICATION AS A TWO-WAY PROCESS

Perhaps the most important aspect of communication is that it is a two-way process. It is about giving and receiving a message. If you are alone – there is no one to see you, no one to hear you and your 'communication' is not being picked up by anyone – effectively there is no communication.

Communication, as you will see in other parts of this chapter, is as much about the listening to and receiving of information from another person as it is about whatever we are trying to communicate to them. In order to relate to other people as individuals, we need to be considerate of their communication styles, preferences and needs, and ensure that our own communication enables them to communicate with us.

Communication is about:

- understanding other people's needs and wishes
- letting people know that you have heard and understood them
- being honest and open about what you can and cannot do to meet those needs and wishes
- on its most basic level, 'getting on' with people – ie treating them with respect and dignity, as an individual and as an equal.

This is why good communication at work builds effective relationships with colleagues and service users, and why barriers to communication have to be overcome to aid effective mutual understanding.

WHY DO PEOPLE COMMUNICATE?

There are four main reasons people communicate.

Instrumental communication

We communicate in order to:

- ask for something
- refuse something
- choose something
- tell someone what we need or want.

Informative communication

We communicate in order to:

- obtain information
- give another person information.
- describe something

Expressive communication

We communicate in order to:

- express our thoughts or feelings
- shares ideas.

Social communication

We communicate in order to:

- attract attention
- build relationships.
- maintain relationships

HOW DO PEOPLE COMMUNICATE?

As discussed, communication is a two-way process. To give a message or receive a message you can use a wide range of communication methods.

Non-verbal communication	Verbal communication
Eye contact	Vocabulary
Touch	Tone of voice
Physical gestures	Pitch
Body language	Volume
Behaviour	Speed

Verbal communication

Vocabulary

The words you use when communicating with service users are important – are they words that service users can understand? Are they words which show respect? The vocabulary you use is certainly important; however, research indicates that the words we use are less important than other aspects of communication in conveying or understanding our needs. Only a small proportion of communication is conveyed by the words we use, with more being communicated by the tone, volume and pitch of the voice and even more in the form of body language.

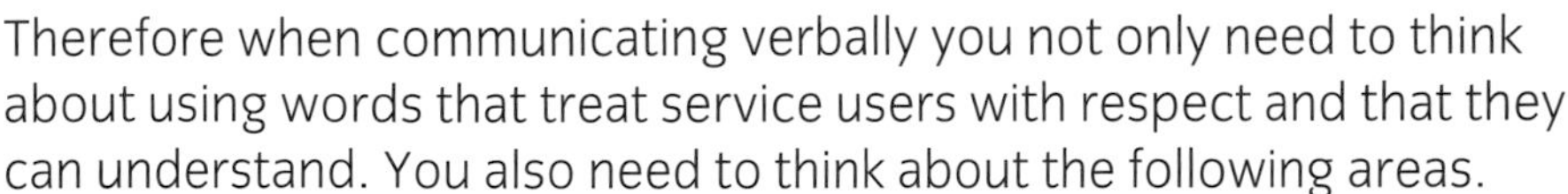

Therefore when communicating verbally you not only need to think about using words that treat service users with respect and that they can understand. You also need to think about the following areas.

Speed

The speed at which someone talks is very significant. It might indicate someone's emotional state – for example, fast speech is associated with anger or excitement, while slow speech can be associated with tiredness or a low mood. The speed at which someone speaks can also be interpreted in a range of ways – for example, slow speech can suggest a lack of interest.

Tone

People are often not aware of the tone of their own voice (how their voice sounds to others). However, it is important for health and social care staff to develop this awareness, as tone of voice has a significant impact on communication.

Pitch

Pitch refers to how high or low your voice is. It is important to be aware of the pitch of your voice, as this can communicate a great deal. For example, sometimes people raise the pitch of their voice when talking to children – so if the pitch of your voice is too high, this could be seen as patronising.

It is worth changing the pitch of your voice so that it is not always the same – this can help to maintain people's interest in what you are saying.

Volume

How loudly or softly we speak has a very significant impact on communication. For example, loud speech can indicate anger or aggression and yet many health and social care staff raise the volume of their voice when talking to service users.

Register

The 'register' of speech refers to how formal or informal it is. You will already be aware that people change the formality of their speech depending on the situation they are in.

Non-verbal communication

Body language (also known as non-verbal communication) refers to the messages given out by body actions and movements rather than words. Body language is an important part of the communication process. As the saying goes, 'actions speak louder than words'. Usually verbal and non-verbal communications are in agreement (eg someone saying 'I am happy' and smiling) but at times they may contradict each other (eg someone saying 'I am happy' while they look positively sad). If you only listen to a person's words and don't observe their body language, you may fail to understand the true meaning of their communication.

Body language

Body language is not just about how we hold and move our bodies. It also includes a range of other things:

- how we position our bodies
- what gestures we use
- our closeness to and the space between us and other people, and how this changes
- our facial expressions
- how we use our eyes – how our eyes move and focus, and whether we maintain eye contact with others.

It is important to recognise that the way body language is seen differs greatly – especially in terms of age and culture. For example, eye contact is seen as respectful and demonstrating listening in some cultures, while in others it is seen as rude. In some cultures people like to shake hands, kiss both cheeks or bow when they meet someone, while others prefer not to make physical contact at all.

Behaviour as a method of communication

Everything we do is communicating something. We even communicate in some way in our sleep – when you are asleep you are communicating that you are tired or that you are bored. Very often people behave in certain ways to communicate something to another person. It is important that when you see someone behaving in a certain way you ask yourself what they are trying to communicate to you. Recognising that all behaviour is a form of communication is an important starting point in promoting effective communication.

The use of touch in communication

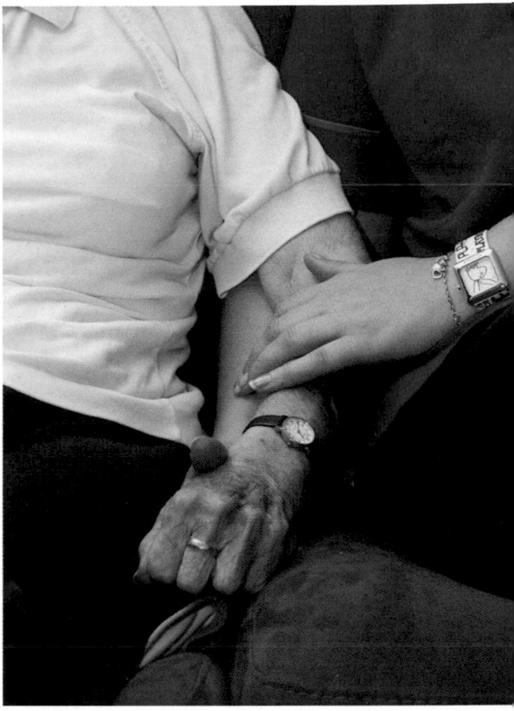

Touch is a very powerful form of non-verbal communication. Think about the way that you might experience touch yourself – when someone you know well touches you, you might feel comforted and safe, but when someone you don't know touches you, you might feel vulnerable and threatened.

When used appropriately, touch can be a very positive form of communication. Touch can:

- provide comfort and reassurance when someone is distressed, making them feel safe and secure
- show respect
- calm someone who is agitated.

However, when used indiscriminately, touch can:

- invade privacy, making people feel vulnerable
- embarrass people
- undermine trust
- be a form of harassment.

You can see that this is a sensitive area. The best approach is to keep touch to a minimum, because it can easily be experienced as threatening, inappropriate or uncomfortable – especially for a service user who may already be feeling vulnerable. If a health and social care worker needs to touch someone as part of the care process, they should explain what they are doing and always ask permission. Failure to ask permission and obtain **consent** is an intrusion and an abuse of power.

Key term 
Consent is when a person consents to something when they are making an informed decision or giving informed permission.

EFFECTIVE COMMUNICATION AFFECTS ALL ASPECTS OF YOUR WORK

Good communication is essential to good care.

In health and social care settings, communication occurs:

- between individual workers and individual service users
- between individual workers and groups of service users
- within groups of service users
- between team members
- within staff groups
- between staff members and managers

- between staff members, managers and partner agencies
- between service users and their carers, family and friends
- between staff and a service user's carers, family and friends.

A breakdown in communication can lead to misunderstandings and worse. For example, a failure between staff to communicate about a service user's care plan could have serious consequences for the service user's health.

THE IMPORTANCE OF OBSERVING REACTIONS

Observing a person's reactions when you are communicating with them is an essential aspect of effective listening. People often think of listening as something that you do with your ears – however, this only helps in terms of 'hearing' verbal communication. However, as we have covered, communication is about far more than words, so we need to *listen* to far more than words. To listen effectively you need to listen to what a service user is saying and note the following.

How the person is speaking

You can tell a great deal from the way someone speaks. For example, as discussed, if someone is speaking quickly they may be excited or anxious, and if someone is using a monotonous tone they may be feeling low. It is important not to make assumptions, though. Always check out your views, for example, by asking, 'It sounds as though you are happy about that?' By making the statement a question, it is likely that the service user will let you know how they feel.

A person's body language

Observe the whole person, but be aware that body language is culturally specific. In some cultures avoiding eye contact can be seen as ignorant, while in others making eye contact can be seen as offensive. However, it is probably safe to assume that if someone is smiling they are happy.

A person's behaviour

Some behaviours such as crying and aggression can communicate a great deal. However you need to listen to the 'whole person' to be clear exactly what the behaviour is communicating. For example, people can cry tears of either joy or sadness.

When you communicate with someone, they usually respond not only by using words, but by using body language. Sensitive observation is an essential aspect of listening. Observing reactions is about taking notice of all aspects of a person's verbal and non-verbal communication. Sometimes a service user's reaction to your words will show you that they haven't heard you or that they haven't understood you. You will then know that you need to try again, perhaps by speaking more slowly and clearly this time or, if necessary, by using a different method, for example, by writing down what you want to say it the service user is hard of hearing. You may sometimes need to ask for help, for example, if the service user can't understand you because they don't speak the same language as you.

Listen to:

- what a service user says
- how they say it
- their body language – through visual observation.

CASE STUDY

Maria is helping Janet to wash on a Friday morning, and chatting with her as usual. She asks Janet if she is looking forward to the weekend when she will be visiting her son. Maria knows that Janet always enjoys these visits. Her son picks her up on a Saturday evening and then brings her back to her sheltered home on Sunday after lunch. Janet says that she is looking forward to it, but there is something in her tone of voice and facial expression that suggests she isn't happy. Her tone of voice is flat, she isn't smiling and she doesn't look at Maria when she replies. Maria is surprised. Why would Janet not really be looking forward to the visit? She asks Janet if she is worried about something. Janet hesitates then explains to Maria that it is her friend Eleanor's 90th birthday party on Saturday afternoon, and she will miss it because of the visit to her son. Maria is relieved that it is nothing more serious, but she understands how important this is to Janet. Maria encourages Janet to call her son and ask him to pick her up a little later than usual so that she can attend the party. Janet calls him and he is more than happy to pick her up at the later time.

- Why might Janet feel worried about this issue?
- How would you act if you were in Maria's role?

For communication to work, there must be reasons, means and opportunities:

The reasons (why we communicate):

- **Instrumental** – to make choices
- **Informative** – to give information
- **Expressive** – to express feelings
- **Social** – to build relationships

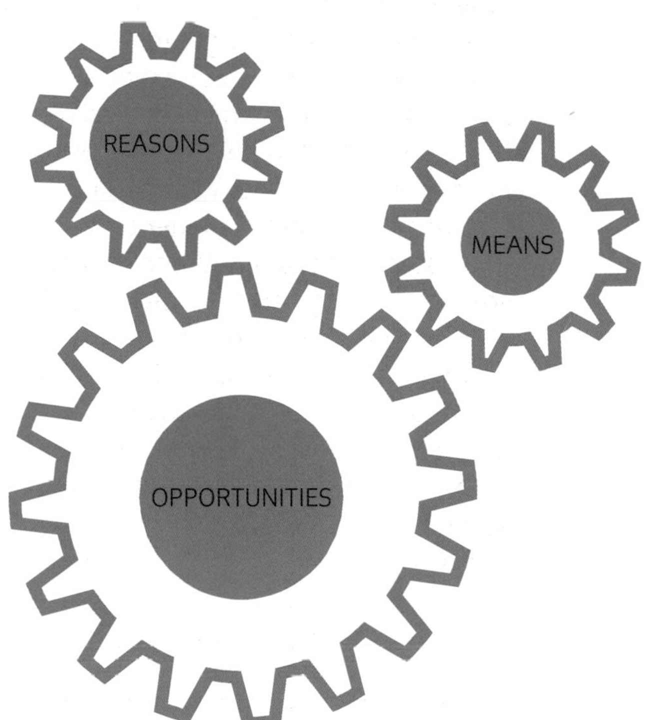

The means (how we communicate):

- Signs
- Speech
- Symbols
- Volume
- Writing
- Inflection
- Tone
- Technology
- Fluency
- Pointing
- Gestures
- Body language
- Facial expression
- Behaviour

Opportunities to communicate – where, when and with whom:

- Someone to communicate with
- Time
- Place
- Shared interests
- Shared language

MEETING COMMUNICATION AND LANGUAGE NEEDS, WISHES AND PREFERENCES

Everyone has their own preferred methods of communication. Within health and social care work, it is the worker's role to know about the needs and preferences of the people they are there to support. You therefore need to be competent to establish *how* each service user communicates, and *what* they want to communicate about their needs and wishes.

Some of this is like a detective task, as you cannot assume that every service user communicates in the same way. Sometimes when people have similar issues, they may communicate differently and want different things.

FINDING OUT NEEDS, WISHES AND PREFERENCES

There are several possible ways to find out a service user's communication and language needs, wishes and preferences.

- *Ask them*. This is the most important thing that any health and social care worker can do. If they are not able to tell you, try one of the following.
- *Ask someone who knows them well*. Possibly a family member, or another professional
- *Read their notes*. These might provide you with some information about the most effective form of communication to use with a service user. Occasionally, there may even be an assessment report by a communication therapist (sometimes referred to as a speech and language therapist).
- *Try different methods of communication and review what response you get.* Sometimes it is a matter of trial and error. Try a method, and if it doesn't work, try something else.

A service user's communication needs are a key element of their care and support needs, and the person's preferred communication method and any specific communication needs should be recorded in their care plan. Periodically the service user's communication needs should be reviewed, as with any other aspect of their support needs, and they should be re-assessed as necessary. A review may need to consider advice from relatives of the service user or from a specialist, such as a doctor or a communication therapist.

CASE STUDY

Parminder lives in Foxgloves Care Home. The most important event of her week is on Tuesday evenings, when her granddaughter Kate comes to visit. Although Parminder has recently been having mild memory problems, she always knows when it is Tuesday as she has her daily newspaper to remind her of the day and date. One week Kate phones Foxgloves to say that she is performing in a concert that Tuesday but she will come on Wednesday instead. Helen, the care worker who takes the call, tells Parminder straight away that Kate will come a day later than usual. Helen is new to Foxgloves and doesn't know Parminder, but she has read her notes. Unfortunately, the notes have not been updated for some time and do not mention that Parminder is now prone to forgetfulness. By Tuesday evening Parminder has completely forgotten that Kate isn't coming and becomes very worried and upset.

- How could Parminder's distress have been avoided or reduced?
- Whose responsibility is it to ensure that notes are updated?
- Whose responsibility would it have been to make sure Helen knew all she needed to know about Parminder's needs, as well as those of other residents?

REFLECT

How do you establish the communication and language needs of the service users you work with?

APPLICATION OF SKILLS

Identifying appropriate communication with service users

Mrs Akabogu has dementia. Communication can be problematic because she is experiencing intermittent memory loss.

- How would you identify the most appropriate methods of communication to use with Mrs Akabogu?
- What methods do you think you might be able to use to maximise communication with Mrs Akabogu?

Mr Thompson has a hearing impairment. He does have a hearing aid, but doesn't always use it.

- Why might Mr Thompson not always use his hearing aid?
- How might you get over this?
- How would you investigate the best way to communicate with Mr Thompson?

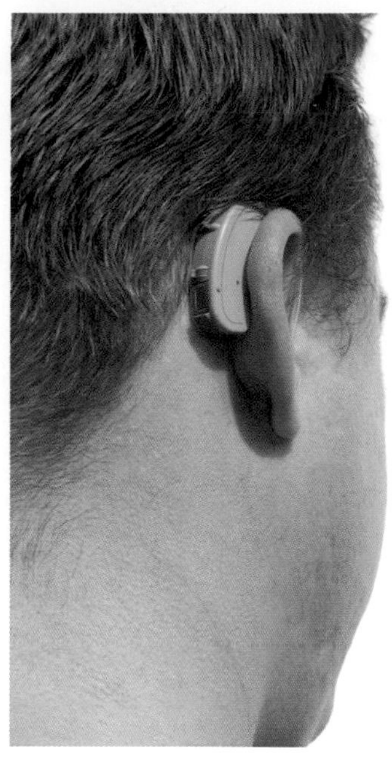

DEMONSTRATING COMMUNICATION METHODS THAT MEET SERVICE USERS' NEEDS, WISHES AND PREFERENCES

Essentially you need to establish what a service user's communication needs, wishes and preferences are – and then make use of a variety of communication methods to meet them. Draw on a whole range of communication methods, including those covered in this chapter.

To facilitate the communication process, consider the following issues before starting to communicate:

- Consider any specific communication needs; is there anything written in the service user's file or care plan relating to communication? Also, is there anything to consider relating to their culture?
- Consider what the aim of the interaction is and what you want to achieve – for example, to successfully complete a care task.
- Consider the perspective of the service user you are about to help.
- What will the information or task mean to the service user? Is it of a particularly sensitive or personal nature? Think about how you would feel in their position.
- How does the service user appear to you at the moment? Are they already distressed, tired, unwell or anxious?
- Does the service user present any behaviour which is seen as challenging?

HOW AND WHEN SHOULD YOU SEEK ADVICE ABOUT COMMUNICATION?

There will be times when you feel that you are not communicating as well as you should be with someone. There may even be times when you feel you are not communicating at all. Sometimes this may be just a temporary problem, for example, if a service user is ill, but as soon as you have any longer-term communication difficulties it is very important that you seek advice from others. You may be able to get help from the service user's family or friends, or you may need to consult your manager or other colleagues.

COMMUNICATION – WHAT DOES THE CODE OF CONDUCT SAY?

The vital importance of effective communication in health and social care is recognised in the Code of Conduct for Healthcare Support Workers and Adult Social Care Workers in England 2013, which states that you must:

- communicate respectfully with people who use health and social care services and their carers in an open, accurate, effective, straightforward and confidential way
- communicate effectively and consult with your colleagues as appropriate
- recognise both the extent and the limits of your role, knowledge and competence when communicating with people who use health and social care services, carers and colleagues.

REDUCING BARRIERS TO COMMUNICATION

A number of things can get in the way of effective communication – these are often referred to as barriers to communication. Essentially all these barriers come down to two areas – problems relating to the message being given or problems relating to the message being received. This again shows how communication is always a two-way process.

Problems with the message being given can include the following:

- it may be difficult to understand because of jargon
- it might contain too much information
- it might be distorted, perhaps by being passed through too many people
- verbal and non-verbal messages may not agree
- the message might be given inappropriately, eg aggressively
- there might be cultural differences between the person giving the message and the person receiving the message.

Problems with the message being received can vary, but usually fall into the following categories:

- environmental barriers
- clinical barriers
- emotional barriers
- attitudinal barriers
- bureaucratic barriers.

ENVIRONMENTAL BARRIERS

The environment you are in can affect communication, both in terms of being able to pass on a message or being able to receive a message. For example:

- In noisy surroundings, people may not be able to hear what is being said, or even be able to formulate a message to pass on ('It's so noisy I can't even think!').
- Poor lighting could be a barrier, particularly when service users use lip reading, and also if facial expressions cannot be seen properly.
- In environments that are not private, people may not raise certain issues which they see as very personal.
- If people are not comfortable (for example, if they are too hot or too cold) this will effect the quality of communication taking place.
- The formality of the environment needs to be matched to the communication method. For example, a service user may feel inhibited and unable to communicate informally in a very formal environment. The furniture could be rearranged, where possible, to suit the situation.

REFLECT

- What environmental barriers do you face in terms of communication?
- What control do you have in your work role around these barriers?

CLINICAL BARRIERS

According to the Royal College of Speech and Language Therapists, there are a range of clinical barriers to effective communication, including:

- genetic or medical conditions
- trauma
- mental health problems
- learning difficulties or disabilities
- speech problems (clarity, stammering, etc)
- voice problems (lack of voice, low volume or hyper-nasality – this is where the speech sound is made primarily through the person's nose)
- fluency problems (processing the delivery and receipt of language)

- use of different languages, or of specific accents, dialects or jargons within a language
- psychologically based communication disorders
- poor or underdeveloped social skills
- lack of problem-solving skills
- literacy issues or dyslexia.

When considering specific clinical issues and the barriers that can be created, it is vital that staff do not blame the service user for the communication barrier, but that they look at how the barriers can be overcome.

Working in a **holistic** way, and recognising the individual needs of service users, means that any specific barriers should be addressed – but always remember that it is *not* the service user that is the barrier. Any difficulties faced in terms of communication can be as much about the staff member having a limited understanding and having a very rigid approach to communication.

Key term 

Holistic means looking at the whole picture.

EMOTIONAL BARRIERS

A range of emotions can have an impact on communication.

Embarrassment

If someone is embarrassed about an issue they may avoid discussing it.

Stress/Distress

It can be hard to communicate if you are feeling stressed or distressed.

Anxiety

If people are particularly anxious, they may find communication difficult. Having to communicate certain issues can create anxiety in itself.

Shock/Anger

People can be shocked or angry about what they are hearing. This may result in a person not listening effectively.

Other feelings can have significant impact on communication, for example:

- fear
- powerlessness
- nervousness
- lack of confidence
- lack of **self-esteem**.

Key term

Self-esteem is about how we feel about or value ourselves.

ATTITUDINAL BARRIERS

Negative or unhelpful attitudes can be a significant barrier to good communication. Where people have negative attitudes towards the person or people they are communicating with, it is likely that the quality of communication will suffer. For example, the following attitudes will create barriers to good communication:

- **prejudice**
- lack of respect
- arrogance
- lack of interest.

Key term

Prejudice is where an individual makes a judgement based on either inadequate or inaccurate information that leads to the development of irrational preferences. One of the main features of prejudice is rigidity or inflexibility of ideas. This means that new information may not have an impact on prejudicial views.

The barriers created by attitudes are often referred to by staff in terms of service users (eg 'He's got a real attitude problem towards authority figures'). However, it is important to recognise that attitudinal barriers often lie with staff. Statements like this are not helpful when describing a situation or a person's reaction to it, and when workers display attitudinal barriers in these ways, the situation or issue can often be made worse.

BUREAUCRATIC BARRIERS

Bureaucratic barriers can include:

- issues around the pressure of the work that people have to undertake
- lack of staffing
- lack of support from managers or colleagues
- being allocated insufficient time to perform tasks
- not being provided with the right resources in the workplace to communicate and engage service users.

All of these are challenging issues for busy and under-resourced services to grapple with, and communication can often be adversely affected by these sorts of barriers within services and systems. However, tackling these barriers, challenging poor practices in services and maintaining dignity and respect for service users' individuality and communication needs are paramount in good care practice.

ADDRESSING COMMUNICATION BARRIERS

Where there are barriers to communication, people might use alternative methods. For example, if you have ever been out in a very busy environment, you probably found that you adapted and communicated with your friends using gestures.

In health and social care people might use a range of alternative communication methods.

Objects of reference

This means using an object or a picture to indicate what the service user wants. The service user could pick up a cup to indicate that they would like a hot drink, for example, or could use a picture or symbol to indicate this. A particular object or picture may have a specific meaning for that individual which may not be immediately apparent, and this is where observations, together with feedback from others, will be especially helpful.

Touch

This might involve the service user using a tap on the arm to obtain your attention or guiding you to indicate what they need. In this way, a service user might guide you to a room where they want to be or show you something of interest.

Behaviour, gestures and movement

This communication method can be used by many people. Behaviour that may be labelled as challenging or difficult may in fact be much more about a service user communicating some aspect of their needs.

Sounds

If service users have relatively few or no words, they may use other sounds to indicate what they want. The meaning of some sounds may well be obvious, such as laughter or shouts of joy or pleasure. As with the use of objects of reference and touch, the association made with some sounds will be specific to that individual.

Smell

Where other senses are impaired, the sense of smell may take on added significance and some service users may, for example, sniff different types of foods and toiletries to make their choice.

Drawing

Some service users may prefer you to make a drawing to indicate what choices are available or what may be taking place. Symbols are often used when communicating with service users to help understanding.

Writing

Some service users may prefer to write rather than speak. This may be the case if their speech is temporarily impaired due to illness, or it may help them to clarify what they mean.

Technological aids

A wide range of technology is available to assist communication, including:

- voice-assisted software
- hearing aids
- tablets and smart devices
- devices where service users can point with their eyes to letters or words to be understood.

Service users might also use mobile phones and the internet to communicate. Texting, emailing, mobile phones and new technologies add a rapidly evolving layer to the means and methods by which we can communicate with service users, and also to how they engage with others in society.

CASE STUDY

Tom has become increasingly hard of hearing with age, and finds this embarrassing. He wears invisible hearing aids, which help to some extent, but he doesn't like other people to know just how difficult he finds it to hear what they are saying. His new care worker, Jean, has a very soft voice and Tom can hardly hear her at all. He doesn't like to ask her to speak up, so he just pretends that he can hear her and nods or shakes his head when she looks as if she is expecting an answer. Jean is surprised by some of his responses because they don't seem appropriate. She soon realises that she is failing to communicate well with Tom and guesses what the problem might be. 'People have told me that my voice is rather quiet. Do you think I should turn the volume up?' she asks Tom, already speaking in a much louder tone. Tom smiles with relief. 'That might be a good idea,' he says. After that the two of them communicate very well. Jean is new to caring and has learned an important lesson.

- Have you had any experiences similar to Jean's?
- What might have been the outcome if Jean hadn't asked the question she asked of Tom?

ENSURING THAT YOUR COMMUNICATION HAS BEEN UNDERSTOOD

It is essential that every time you communicate with someone they understand what you mean. This applies equally to service users you are caring for, their families and friends and the people you work with.

Sometimes it will be obvious that your words have not been understood. For example, the person you are talking to may look confused or perhaps respond to a question with an inappropriate answer. On other occasions it won't be so obvious. For example, the person may smile and nod their head as if in agreement with you, even though they haven't heard you properly. This could be because they have hearing difficulties but find it embarrassing to ask other people to repeat themselves. To ensure that someone has understood your communication, make sure you observe their reactions fully.

Often asking a question can help you check whether communication has been understood. Questions are a vital part of the communication process. While we all ask questions at different times, sometimes to be effective as health and social care practitioners people need to learn how to ask questions effectively.

In addition to helping ensure that communication has been understood, questions can be useful to gather information, to help understand situations and to develop trust. However, incorrect use of questions can lead to a total breakdown in effective communication.

TYPES OF QUESTIONS

There are three main types of questions.

Question type	Example
Open	'What's your favourite drink?'
Closed	'Is tea your favourite drink?'
Leading	'Tea is your favourite drink, isn't it?'

Open questions

Open questions ask the speaker to think about their answer and give more information.

Open questions demonstrate an interest in a person because the questioner has effectively said 'tell me more – I'm interested'.

Open questions encourage people to think about the answer they are giving, and the answer often gives a range of information to the questioner, allowing the conversation to develop further.

Closed questions

Closed questions allow for limited responses (usually a 'yes' or 'no' answer).

Closed questions are not that helpful in gaining further information, because the response is limited. However, they can be useful to gain specific basic information where the speaker regularly goes off the subject, or where an open question could be confusing for the service user. They can also be used to end a conversation.

Asking closed questions can be frustrating both for the person asking and the person answering a question – it can be much more straightforward to ask a simple open question. For example, in this scenario, lots of closed questions didn't get the desired result (an answer), whereas one open question did.

If you ask someone 'did you understand that?' they may well say 'yes' but later it may appear that they didn't. So be aware that using closed questions isn't always the best way to ensure that your communication has been understood – use your observation and **active listening** skills to ensure that someone understands your communication.

As communication is a two-way process, you will also sometimes need to demonstrate that you have understood what others are communicating to you. In situations where you feel that you may have problems understanding what someone is communicating to you, the best approach is to listen carefully, then summarise what you believe to have been said to the person.

Key term

Active listening is a key skill in health and social care, and involves ensuring that the service user knows you are working to understand what they are communicating. Active listening can be conveyed by your body language, nodding, eye contact, and by your summarising what the service user has said to check that you have fully understood them.

REFLECT

Consider occasions when other people have found you difficult to understand. What factors influenced this? Was it your accent, words used, dialect, tone, non-verbal communication or factors around the other person's needs being unmet? How could (or did) you adapt your own communication in order to clarify misunderstandings?

OVERCOMING BARRIERS TO EFFECTIVE COMMUNICATION

There are a number of factors that can assist in overcoming barriers to communication. These factors can be general or specific.

GENERAL FACTORS THAT AID COMMUNICATION

Knowing the person

Knowing a person means we are more likely to understand them and what they are trying to convey. Asking for advice from colleagues who know the service user can be helpful and speed up your own learning, and that is why you should not feel embarrassed about asking colleagues. If you spend time with people you will soon get to know them, and will then be asked by new staff for advice and support regarding how best to communicate with an individual.

Not overloading the person with information

Especially when a service user is new to a service or situation, they may find that too much information is given to them. Consider what they need to know at each stage to progress to the next stage.

Using points of reference the person is familiar with

A service user may better understand something that is about to happen if you can draw on a similar experience they have already had.

Checking understanding

Check with the service user to be sure they have understood you – don't rely on asking 'do you understand what I've said?'. Most of us would answer 'yes' whether we have understood or not. Invite the person to ask questions to clarify understanding.

Demonstrating a task or action

It may be beneficial for you to model some tasks. In a personal care situation in a bathroom, before the service user does anything, it may be helpful for you to show the movements expected of the service user using any relevant grab rails. This will be particularly helpful because each staff member will do things differently with different service users.

If you are assisting a service user to learn or re-learn an independence skill, demonstrating that task could be a stronger form of communication compared with just describing what is expected.

SPECIFIC FACTORS THAT AID COMMUNICATION

Communication is always individual. However, there are some basic guidelines in terms of overcoming the barriers to communicating with different groups of people which can be helpful for everyone to know. Although the following guidelines make reference to specific needs and certain conditions, good practice in communication is generic and the guidelines may provide pointers that are relevant to other service users, whatever their individual needs.

Communicating with service users with a hearing impairment

The following guidelines may help in promoting effective communication with service users who have a hearing impairment:

- Never assume that a person only hears what they want to hear. There may be differences in hearing at different times, and service users may be able to hear some people better than others.
- Show somebody with a hearing impairment what you would like them do, rather than telling them.
- Use gestures, signs, pictures or photographs.
- Make sure service users can see you when you are talking to them, and never cover your mouth, as this will prevent lip reading.

- It is tempting to raise your voice when speaking to a service user with a hearing impairment. However, remember not to shout, as this can distort speech sounds (and if the person wears a hearing aid it can really hurt).
- If a service user has a hearing aid, ensure that it is correctly used and maintained.
- Avoid background noise like the TV or radio.
- Ensure that service users have access to any necessary equipment (eg minicom).
- Help service users make use of subtitles to watch the TV.
- Speak clearly, naturally and slowly, and make sure that your non-verbal communication is in line with what you are saying.
- When you need to repeat something, do so with patience – do not get exasperated.
- It can be helpful to ask the person with whom you are talking to tell you what they heard – it might be very different to what you said.
- If the service user uses British Sign Language (BSL), get an interpreter.

Communicating with service users with a visual impairment

The following guidelines may help to promote effective communication with service users who have a visual impairment:

- Make sure service users can hear you coming towards them, and introduce yourself verbally. If the person has poor hearing they may be able to sense you by smell or touch.
- Tell the person that you are leaving when you are going to depart.
- Touch service users in a way that is respectful; firm yet gentle. Remember that touching a person without warning from behind is very threatening.
- Be careful that you do not block a service user's light.
- Always consult the service user when their environment changes.
- Give as much information and explanation as possible, so the service user knows what to expect.
- Ensure that service users are not isolated from conversations and/or activities.
- Describe objects and events to service users to ensure they feel included.

Communicating with service users from a different cultural background

Communication techniques should be flexible in order to respect different cultural needs. The following guide provides key suggestions for communicating with service users from a different cultural background to your own:

- There is no 'standard' form of address (eg 'Mr ...', or the use of a first name). It is down to individual choice how different service users would like to be referred to. The best way is to ask individuals what they would prefer to be called.
- The term 'Christian name' should not be used, as people may not be Christians. Use 'first name' or 'forename' instead.
- The use of tactile introductions, such as shaking hands, may be unacceptable in some cultures.
- Confirm with the service user that they are comfortable with your way of communication.
- Respect differences. You need to understand that a person's diversity may affect a whole host of things, including accent, dialect, slang and non-verbal communication. Find out as much as you can about the service user's background and the effects this may have on communication.

Communicating with service users whose first language isn't English

Where a service user is not fluent in English, you will need to adapt your communication. The following pointers may be helpful:

- Speak clearly but not too loudly.
- Pace your communication. If you speak too quickly service users may not understand, but if you speak too slowly this can be patronising and it may be difficult to understand the whole sentence.
- Use clear language. When someone is from a different cultural background to your own, they may not be familiar with culturally specific sayings (eg 'I've got a frog in my throat' or 'it's raining cats and dogs').
- Use pictures and symbols.
- Pronounce names correctly.
- Check and rephrase as you go along.
- Provide written information in the service user's home language to back up other communication.
- Get a trained interpreter to help if possible (do not use family, friends or especially children to enable this, as this can be inappropriate).

Communicating with service users with a learning disability

- Use Makaton if the service user uses Makaton. (Makaton is a sign language used in learning disability services.)
- Use pictures and images or any communication aid the service user normally uses, eg a Bliss board. Bliss is a symbolic communication system. Often boards are developed which contain key symbols that the person will use to communicate.
- Give the service user time to express themselves.
- Be prepared to 'read' their behaviour.
- Don't try to anticipate what they are trying to communicate.
- Encourage the service user to express themselves by letting them know that their opinions and choices are valued by you.

Communicating with service users with dementia

- Use objects and pictures to communicate messages.
- Talk about one thing at a time.
- Be prepared for unexpected responses.
- Be sensitive to the fact that there are some times that are better than others.
- Repeat messages without showing impatience, and certainly don't treat service users like children.
- Don't get into argumentative situations.
- Use nostalgia/reminiscence.
- Use music.

Communicating with service users who have had a stroke

- Use drawings, pictures and objects, and let the service user use them.
- Use music and stories to keep up the service user's interest and motivation.
- Remember that most people who have had strokes have their mental abilities unimpaired; it is offensive to discuss them as if they cannot think for themselves.
- Give the service user time.
- Consider simplifying questions so they can be answered with a 'yes' or 'no'.

REFLECT

- What do you see as the main barriers to effective communication in your work practice?
- How can you overcome these in order to communicate with service users effectively?
- How do you support other staff and relevant people to understand and overcome the potential barriers?

SOURCES OF INFORMATION, SUPPORT AND SERVICES ENABLING MORE EFFECTIVE COMMUNICATION

It may be important to access specific additional support or services in order to enable individual service users to communicate effectively. These could include:

- people who know the service user well already, such as friends and family
- colleagues or your manager.

It may also mean external services:

- interpreting or translation services
- **advocacy** services
- speech and language therapy assessments, services and resources
- occupational therapy assessments and services.

Key term

Advocacy is speaking for or on behalf of someone.

USING INTERPRETERS

Service users who do not speak English as a first language may need the support of an interpreter. In certain circumstances, family or friends can act as interpreters. However, there are important disadvantages to this:

- Service users receiving care may not want members of their family or community to know personal details and information.
- Service users may feel disempowered (ie that others have more power than they do over their life) and they may feel that their control and choice may be adversely affected. This can be a particular issue if the family member or friend is seen to overpower the service user, or if there are concerns that they may not truly represent the service user's views and choices

- Interpreting is a task that requires great skill in remaining objective and translating information in a completely neutral manner. Professional interpreters receive specific training in these issues.
- In rare circumstances, family or friends may be actually perpetrating abuse against the service user receiving care.

When you work with an interpreter, communication is clearly affected because instead of being a two-way process, communication becomes a three-way process. Therefore, perhaps the most important thing for a health and social care worker to consider when working with an interpreter is to ensure that they still build a relationship with the service user. Health and social care workers will also need to think about their relationship with the interpreter. They will need to be clear with the interpreter about roles and negotiate expectations around working together to facilitate effective communication with the service user.

Many care workers believe that their communication skills will not be used when working with an interpreter, because the communication will be managed by the interpreter. However, your professional skills will be more vital than ever. You will need to maintain good eye contact with both the service user and the interpreter. Listening skills will be very important – you will need to listen to what the interpreter is saying as well as attending to the non-verbal communication of the interpreter and the service user. Using an interpreter adds another layer to listening.

ADVOCACY

The word advocacy means 'speaking for or on behalf of'. There are several different kinds of advocacy.

Self-advocacy

Self-advocacy is about service users speaking up for themselves. A commitment to self-advocacy entails enabling and empowering service users to act on their own behalf.

Peer advocacy

In peer advocacy the advocate shares a similar perspective to the service user. For example, a person with learning disabilities supports another person with learning disabilities to get their views across.

Independent advocacy

This is where either a volunteer or a paid employee of an advocacy service takes on the role of the advocate for the service user.

The role of an advocate demands skill, and is different from that of a health and social care worker. Advocates can help in situations where:

- it is difficult for others to understand the service user's means of communicating
- the service user is not happy with the service they are receiving and wishes to complain
- supporters such as family, friends, paid carers or health and social care professionals disagree about how to support the service user or with the service user's point of view
- a significant change has taken place in relation to the service user: this may be in relation to their health or wellbeing, or as a result of a major life change.

An advocate will initially work with the service user to understand the way they communicate and to find out what is important to them so that they can represent them in a variety of situations. They will usually go to a meeting alongside the service user they are supporting, and must always be clear about representing the service user's point of view even if the advocate believes that this may not be in the service user's interests. The aim of the advocate is to empower the service user by making sure that their views and interests are heard. The advocate will try to obtain permission from the service user to represent their views and to contact others who may be able to help.

Non-instructed advocacy

This is where the service user is unable to put their views across, perhaps because of profound disability or very advanced dementia, and usually lacks the **capacity** or ability to make decisions. Just as with the other forms of advocacy, the advocate will work hard to form a strong relationship with the service user, to learn about their preferences and to do their best to represent their interests. Chapter 4 looks at issues around the Mental Capacity Act 2005 which are relevant in situations where advocacy is needed.

Key term

Capacity is about whether someone is physically or mentally able to do something.

CASE STUDY

John is attending a review of Mr Wilder's future needs, chaired by a social worker. John has been working with Mr Wilder for over six weeks and his involvement is about to cease. The social worker asks Mr Wilder 'do you wash yourself in the morning?' to which Mr Wilder replies 'no'. She goes on to ask other similarly closed questions to which Mr Wilder can only answer 'yes' or 'no'. John observes that Mr Wilder starts looking at the floor and doesn't make eye contact with anyone in the meeting. John feels that the people at the review are not getting a full picture of Mr Wilder's needs, and he would like Mr Wilder to feel more involved, so he asks follow-up open questions such as 'how do you wash in the morning?'. These questions lead to everyone gaining much more useful information about Mr Wilder's needs, and Mr Wilder starts to engage in the meeting, making eye contact with people and talking about his situation more fully.

- How might Mr Wilder feel about the way the social worker was communicating with him?
- Have you had experiences which are similar to this in your work role?

CONFIDENTIALITY AT WORK

Health and social care workers must have an understanding of confidentiality and be able to implement this in their practice. This requires knowledge of what confidentiality entails and what dilemmas it might create.

WHAT IS CONFIDENTIALITY?

Confidentiality is a very important aspect of practice in health and social care. However, it is often misunderstood, in that people think confidentiality is about keeping information secret. Confidentiality is rather about keeping information within a service and sharing it only on a need-to-know basis. When someone shares information with you it is confidential, but that doesn't mean it is secret – it means that the information should only be shared with your manager and others responsible for providing care to the service user.

The right to confidentiality is important to all of us, and especially to service users accessing health and social care services. This is because highly sensitive and personal information about service users becomes known to a number of people who hold a position of power over their lives.

Establishing clear boundaries around confidentiality within a service is vital. Confidentiality enables service users to have a sense of trust in professionals and a sense of control over their life and the service they receive.

As a worker in health and social care, you will need to be able to:

- explain the idea of confidentiality to service users, relatives, and other professionals
- understand and uphold your own boundaries around confidentiality
- understand, express and adhere to your service or agency's policies and procedures around confidentiality.

Aspects of confidentiality are covered in more detail in Chapter 7. The key principles are that, as much as possible (in terms of consent, capacity and safeguarding), service users should always know:

- what information you are sharing
- who you are sharing it with
- why you are sharing it.

DEMONSTRATING CONFIDENTIALITY IN LINE WITH AGREED WAYS OF WORKING

It is vital for health and social care workers to demonstrate a commitment to confidentiality. This can be done in a range of ways:

- *Transparency*. Users of services have the right to know that records are kept, that information about their needs is known (and who knows it), and when and why information may need to be shared with other people.
- *Role-modelling*. If someone gossips about one member of staff to another, or makes jokes about a service user or their circumstances, they are showing a lack of respect for the service user and for confidentiality. Health and social care workers should role-model effective practice in terms of confidentiality in all of their work.
- *Following policy*. Services should have an effective confidentiality policy in place which makes the responsibilities of staff clear and which adheres to the Data Protection Act 1998.

- *Taking action*. If care workers breach confidentiality, you should take appropriate action. For example, if you hear other workers effectively 'gossiping' about a service user in a break, you should challenge this.
- *Ensuring the security of information*. Make sure that lockable cabinets are available (and used) for the storage of personal information. For electronic records, services and agencies should have robust systems in place controlling access to and security of these records (see also Chapter 7).

Confidentiality must be maintained in:

- written communication about service users
- storage of written records
- the way buildings and care environments are accessed and organised
- verbal communications within a care team
- communication with individual service users about other service users (where services are accessed by groups of people)
- communication by members of a care team with other agencies and professionals, so that nothing is shared which is not pertinent to the service user's care plan and which the other agency does not need to know
- communication by workers with family members and other carers
- communication by workers with their own friends and family outside of their work.

It is important that workers only know information that is relevant to supporting the service users they work with. Health and social care workers do not have a right to know everything about a service user. It is also vital that health and social care workers realise that the information which they receive is given to them because they are professionals or members of a staff team, and that such information must remain confidential within the care team responsible for each individual service user.

Where a care team supports a service user, it is important that information is shared in order for everyone to work in a consistent way to meet that person's needs. However, when information is shared within one agency or even between agencies, this information remains confidential. The fact that it has been shared does not mean it can be shared further – the obligation to maintain confidentiality is shared just as much as the information itself.

The consequences of not maintaining confidentiality in everyday communications are extremely significant for you as a professional, for your employer, agency or service, and most importantly, for the dignity and rights of the service users.

APPLICATION OF SKILLS

Confidentiality dilemmas

- The mother of a man who receives support from your service comes to attend a meeting. She is in her seventies, and often talks to staff. After the meeting, when you are alone with her, she tearfully tells you that her son was illegitimate. What do you do?
- You are in town with a woman service user you support. While in the post office you meet, by chance, a colleague. He asks you about the financial situation of another service user you support. What do you do?
- One of your colleagues tells you that she has just heard that a service user you work with was married four times and had several children by different men. She tells you that she is surprised at what she describes as the service user's 'colourful background', as the service user seems so quiet. She goes on to say that the other staff will never believe it when she tells them. What do you do? Why?

WHEN TO PASS ON CONFIDENTIAL INFORMATION

There is the potential for significant tension between maintaining confidentiality and disclosing concerns – particularly in relation to safeguarding. This is covered in more depth in Chapter 5.

Remember the following, when there are concerns about a service user's safety:

- *Check*. Check out your concerns and maintain your observations, as well as checking with the service user (without investigating) how they are feeling.
- *Record*. As always, good practice in recording is part of good practice generally, but this is especially important when recording concerns about a service user's wellbeing.
- *Report*. You cannot keep something to yourself if someone is being harmed by another service user. You should always report concerns, first to your managers (according to service policies and procedures), and take action if required, even where this may mean going against the service user's wishes in relation to confidentiality.

- *Explain*. If you do need to pass information on to another agency or service user, it is important that the service user knows:
  - what you are doing
  - why you are doing it
  - what will happen next
  - who else might learn the information that was previously confidential
  - that you are there to support them
  - that they have done the right thing in telling you (in the event of a disclosure of abuse)
  - that they still have rights (eg to access records, or to complain).

CASE STUDY

Linda, a care worker, was visiting Michael in his own home. She visited him every day to help him get up and dressed in the morning. On this particular occasion Michael, who was normally calm and cheerful, seemed agitated. Linda asked him what was wrong. He explained that he had opened several letters telling him that bills had not been paid. The gas company was threatening to cut off his supply because the bill hadn't been paid for a number of months. His niece, Sara, was supposed to pay his bills for him. He also added that after Sara had visited last time, £50 had gone missing from the old teapot where he kept it. Michael asked Linda not to mention this to anyone else, but Linda was very concerned and, after giving the matter some thought, she decided to talk to her manager. Her manager said that she was right to bring this to her attention and that, if necessary, she would involve the police because it was possible that Sara had committed a criminal offence.

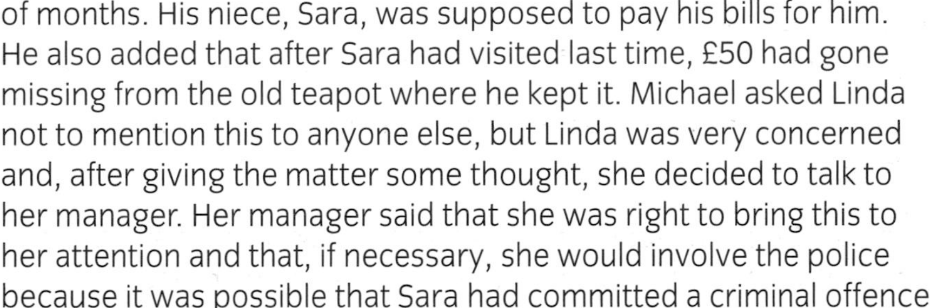

- Was Linda right to talk to her manager? Why?
- What should Linda do next?
- How might Michael feel?
- What should Linda do next when communicating with him?

SEEKING ADVICE ABOUT CONFIDENTIALITY

It is important that the service users you support are able to trust you. They may share information with you and expect you to keep it secret, and they have a right to expect confidentiality. However, on rare occasions someone might share information with you that you don't think that you should keep to yourself. For example, a service user might tell you about a situation which involves abuse.

Support when dealing with these issues is available from a variety of sources, including:

- your manager
- the Local Authority in the area where you work (and potentially its legal department if relevant and necessary)
- training courses
- regulatory and inspection bodies.

You should always discuss any situation where there are concerns about maintaining confidentiality or where you need to share information with others outside of your work setting with your supervisor or line manager.

Before going to the next chapter, take some time to consider:

- what you think your main strengths are in terms of communicating at work
- what communication skills you would like to improve
- what strategies you might use to improve these skills
- what main barriers you face to communicating effectively
- how you can reduce these barriers.

CHAPTER 3

Introduction to equality and inclusion in health and social care

Good practice in health and social care is based on a number of basic principles which are often seen as 'the values' of the profession. One of the core values is the need for health and social care workers to promote equality and inclusion in all aspects of their work. The knowledge within this chapter is therefore central to all practice in working with users of health and social care services.

Links to other units

The values of health and social care are introduced in Chapter 8. The unit covered by this chapter should be addressed in every aspect of work with every service user. Therefore the knowledge covered in this chapter is linked to every unit of the Diploma.

RECOGNISING THE IMPORTANCE OF DIVERSITY, EQUALITY AND INCLUSION

The three key concepts of diversity, equality and inclusion are part of the value base of health and social care work, as covered in Chapter 8. You need to be able to express what the words diversity, equality and inclusion mean in order to show that you recognise the importance of these ideas within all heath and social care work.

While the concepts of equality and inclusion are very closely linked, it is important to understand a number of key concepts in order to promote them both.

DIVERSITY

Diversity is essentially about difference. Difference should be valued and celebrated. The world would be very dull if we were all the same.

Promoting diversity is about taking the fact that we are all different and saying that this is a good thing, and should be seen as so by everybody.

Within all health and social care settings there will be a rich mixture of people from a variety of backgrounds and cultures. This diversity should be celebrated and reflected within the service.

EQUALITY

Being committed to equality is often misunderstood as being about 'treating everyone the same'. Instead, equality builds on diversity and recognises that we are *not* all 'the same'. Equality should be seen as offering the framework within which individuals and employers can show their commitment to promoting equality and treating people as they deserve to be treated – in accordance with their rights, allowing for choices and individuality, and with due respect.

INCLUSION

Key term

Discrimination is where someone is treated less favourably than another person.

Inclusion is about challenging **discrimination**, ensuring that all people feel valued and included, and respecting diversity.

It may be that a service user cannot access their entitlement to a service, education, employment or cultural resources because of the following:

- language barriers
- physical barriers (eg they cannot get in the building where the service is offered because it is not accessible)
- cultural barriers.

If this is the case then services need to find ways of ensuring that their provision *can* be accessed, rather than accepting the existence of such barriers and allowing the potential service user to continue experiencing a lack of opportunity.

Inclusion focuses on the fact that people have the right to access resources and services without being discriminated against. Those in charge of providing resources have a responsibility to ensure that their provision can be accessed.

DISCRIMINATION

Discrimination is where someone is treated less favourably than another person because they are 'different'. Most people will have been discriminated against in some way, at some stage of their lives. However, it is widely accepted that some groups of people are more likely to experience discrimination than others – for example, black people, women, older people and people with disabilities. Some of the main forms of discrimination which have been identified in British society are outlined here.

Ageism

This describes the way that older people can be discriminated against. It is based on the prejudiced belief that older people are inferior to younger people.

Disabilism/Ablism

This is the term used to describe people with disabilities experiencing discrimination and **oppression**, as a result of the prejudiced belief that not having a disability makes people superior.

Key term 

Oppression refers to negative treatment of people. The word comes from the Latin 'opprinere' which means to flatten or to squash out of shape.

Heterosexism

This describes the way that gay people are discriminated against. It is based on the prejudiced belief that only heterosexual relationships are 'normal' and therefore valid.

Racism

This describes the way that people are discriminated against because of their race. It is based on the prejudiced belief that people of some races are superior to others.

Sexism

This describes the way in which people are oppressed based on their gender. It is based on the prejudiced belief that one sex is superior to another. In British society the word sexism is usually used to describe the way that women are discriminated against.

Homophobia

This is a set of negative attitudes and feelings towards homosexual people, which may give rise to discriminatory behaviour.

Key term 

Drug is any substance which when taken into the body affects the way that the body functions.

These categories are by no means exhaustive – other examples of groups that are particularly vulnerable to oppression include people who are homeless, people who use **drugs**, asylum seekers, people who have mental health problems, people with long-term health conditions... and the list goes on.

TYPES OF DISCRIMINATION

It is commonly accepted that there are three main types of discrimination.

Individual discrimination

This is where the actions and attitudes (often unconscious) of individuals towards people from excluded groups support and sustain a broader social pattern of discrimination.

For example, a man may believe that women should be responsible for all household chores and childcare. The way this man acts towards women will sustain the broader view of women in society.

Institutional discrimination

This is where institutions (for example, schools, employers, churches and residential services) reflect the structure of the society they serve. By doing this, they maintain a set of rules, procedures and practices which perpetuate discrimination against excluded groups.

An example might be a secondary school English course where all the books chosen to read have central male characters but only minor female characters. This will reinforce society's view that men are more important or interesting than women.

Another example might be an organisation in which 75% of the workforce are women but 75% of the managers are men. This could convey the idea that men are more important and are the key decision makers. Both of these are clear examples of institutional sexism.

Key term

Local Authorities are local government organisations which operate local services such as schools and refuge collection.

These issues have recently been successfully challenged in **Local Authorities** and in the area of equal pay for female employees. The Stephen Lawrence enquiry in 1993 also described the Metropolitan Police as harbouring institutional racism, as well as structural discrimination.

Structural discrimination

This is where organisations and institutions work together, with the effect that a structural or societal system of discrimination is generated and sustained.

For example, residential care services generally have an accepted weekly costing that funding bodies (such as social services) are willing to pay. Above this cost, senior managers will need to agree the funding.

The accepted weekly cost of older people's residential care is the lowest of all. The accepted weekly cost of residential care for adults with a learning disability and adults with mental health problems is higher. The accepted weekly cost of children's residential care is higher still. This illustrates one kind of structural inequality.

It is important to note that individual, institutional and structural kinds of discrimination are very closely linked. After all, institutions are made up of a number of individuals. Therefore, individual beliefs and actions will have a profound impact on organisations, institutions and society as a whole. The key to the difference, however, is that where the discrimination is carried out by one or two people this is individual discrimination. Where the root of the discrimination is in an organisation this is institutional discrimination. When discrimination is endemic across a number of organisations, this becomes structural discrimination.

HOW DOES DISCRIMINATION OCCUR IN THE WORK SETTING?

Discrimination may occur deliberately or inadvertently (ie in a way which may be unintentional, but which can still have the same negative impact).

Deliberate discrimination occurs when a person or organisation intentionally treats someone unfairly because of their difference. They know that their words or actions will be experienced by people as discrimination and that they are likely to cause distress. For example:

- using language that is offensive and demonstrates prejudice
- only appointing women to care worker roles because of the belief that they are better at caring than men
- refusing to allow gay people to share a room because of the belief that gay relationships are 'wrong'.

Inadvertent discrimination occurs when a person or organisation unintentionally treats someone unfairly because of their difference. They do not realise that their words or actions will be experienced by people as discrimination. In the case of organisations, they may have policies and procedures that are inadvertently discriminatory. Examples of inadvertent discrimination include:

- failing to realise that providing written information only in English for people in a multicultural community discriminates against those who do not speak English
- using terms such as 'love' and 'dear' when talking to older people without understanding that this can be seen as patronising
- ignoring someone in a wheelchair and speaking to the person accompanying them because of a failure to understand that someone with a physical disability can speak for themselves.

CASE STUDY

Lu Qian cares for Jim in his own home and visits him daily. Jim has had a stroke and although he has recovered quite well, he does have difficulty with his speech – it can be quite hard to understand what he is saying. Jim's wife Martha is usually in the room when Lu Qian visits Jim. At first Lu Qian addresses all of her conversation, including questions about Jim's care, to Martha, but after a while she begins to question her own behaviour. She realises that she is discriminating against Jim because of his disability. It takes him some effort to express his own needs and Lu Qian has to make an effort as well to understand him, but they can have a conversation. Lu Qian decides to change her behaviour and instead of talking to Martha she looks directly at Jim and speaks directly to him. Occasionally Martha helps out, but by listening to Jim talk regularly, Lu Qian soon finds that she can understand Jim much better than she could at first. She also notices that Jim is now much happier to see her when she comes to visit. Lu Qian's discrimination was inadvertent as she didn't have any intention of showing prejudice towards Jim, but it had a negative impact on him.

- How does Lu Qian discriminate against Jim?
- Have you ever realised that you are discriminating against someone? What did you do?

HOW CAN PRACTICES THAT SUPPORT EQUALITY AND INCLUSION REDUCE DISCRIMINATION?

Best practice in health and social care promotes equality and inclusion, and therefore reduces the likelihood of discrimination. Examples of the range of practices which support equality and inclusion include the following:

- Enabling accessibility, by ensuring that service users can access the right provision to meet their needs and preferences, whether this is within your own service setting, or around you, by supporting a service user to access another resource.
- Ensuring that service users can access advocates when necessary or when significant decisions are being taken.
- Working positively to include relatives, friends and carers of service users.

- Updating the service's decor to ensure the images are positive and inclusive, and that the messages displayed show that service users are important.
- Looking at events and promotional activities (where possible and appropriate) in order to celebrate achievement and to enable services and local communities to interact with each other (as opposed to the service operating in isolation from its community setting).
- Providing events or guest speakers to enable learning around different faiths, cultures, languages and people's differences.
- Providing materials such as books, magazines and DVDs that meet the language and cultural needs of service users.
- Ensuring that complaints are actively responded to.
- Talking to service users directly (not those accompanying them) and always assuming when you meet them for the first time that they have the capacity to understand and respond to you.
- Treating everyone with the same dignity and respect that you would want to be shown yourself.

APPLICATION OF SKILLS

Understanding how good practice supports equality and inclusion

Good practice supports equality and inclusion in a range of ways. The following table is part completed. What else can you include?

Practice	How this supports equality and inclusion and reduces the risk of discrimination
Effective listening	This shows respect and helps a health and social care worker to really understand a service user and develop an understanding of beliefs, culture and preferences so that their needs can be better met.
Good communication	A health and social care worker with effective communication skills can ensure that a service user feels respected and included in decisions about their care.
Empathy and compassion	This means developing an understanding of a service user's experiences and how these might make them feel, and working in a compassionate way to promote inclusion and equality.
Challenging discrimination	
What other skills can you identify?	

DID YOU KNOW?

The Equality Measurement Framework (EMF) published by the Equality and Human Rights Commission highlights that:

- black people are less likely than any other group to feel they are treated with respect
- younger people are more likely to feel that diversity is a good thing and one which is to be enjoyed and celebrated
- there are specific barriers for older lesbian, gay, bisexual and transgender people (LGBT) people in accessing social care services
- mixed-race Britons are the fastest growing minority group in the UK
- many people with disabilities experience violence and hostility on a daily basis in their communities
- gypsies and travelling communities face specific barriers and have a life expectancy that is 10 years lower than non-travelling people.

WORKING IN AN INCLUSIVE WAY

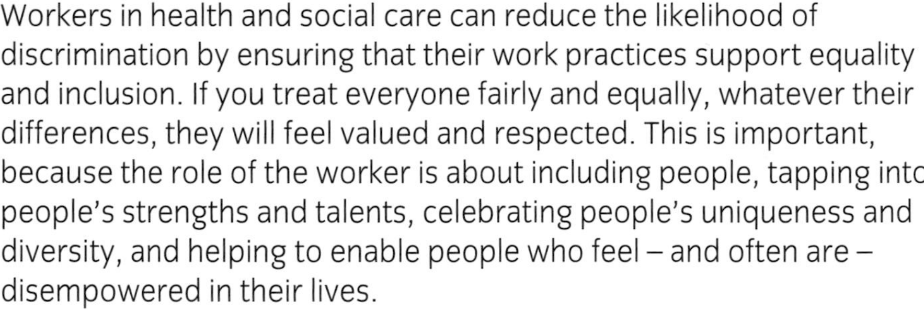

Workers in health and social care can reduce the likelihood of discrimination by ensuring that their work practices support equality and inclusion. If you treat everyone fairly and equally, whatever their differences, they will feel valued and respected. This is important, because the role of the worker is about including people, tapping into people's strengths and talents, celebrating people's uniqueness and diversity, and helping to enable people who feel – and often are – disempowered in their lives.

To work in an inclusive way health and social care workers need to incorporate their understanding of equality and diversity into every aspect of their practice.

HOW DO LEGISLATION AND CODES OF PRACTICE APPLY TO YOUR WORK ROLE?

In the UK we have a history of legislation designed to ensure that discrimination on certain grounds is unlawful. It is important to know about this legislation and to develop an understanding of the way in which this applies to your work setting. It is also important to have a clear understanding of the legislative framework in order to enhance your own practice in terms of challenging oppression. However, be aware that good practice is way ahead of the minimum legal requirements.

The two main Acts of Parliament which relate to promoting equality, diversity and inclusion are the Equality Act 2010 and the Human Rights Act 1998.

If you think of inclusive practice as a bag of tools, then the legal framework is one tool to aid your practice. There are two other good reasons to be aware of what the law says in this area – first, you are required to work within the law. Second, you need to be aware of what action could be taken if any of the people you work with have been discriminated against and wish to take legal action.

THE EQUALITY ACT 2010

As the legal framework around equality and discrimination in the UK developed after the 1970s, we were left with a complex and fragmented legal framework in this area. The idea of the Equality Act 2010 was to provide what is described by the government as a new 'cross-cutting' legislative framework to promote equality for all. It was designed to simplify and strengthen the legal framework.

The Act covers nine protected characteristics which cannot be used as a reason to discriminate against someone:

- age
- disability
- gender reassignment
- marriage and civil partnership
- pregnancy and maternity
- race
- religion or belief
- sex
- sexual orientation.

The Act outlines seven different types of discrimination:

- *Direct discrimination.* Where someone is treated less favourably than another person because of a protected characteristic.
- *Associative discrimination.* This is direct discrimination against someone because they are associated with another person who possesses a protected characteristic.
- *Discrimination by perception.* This is direct discrimination against someone because others think that they possess a particular protected characteristic. They do not necessarily have to possess the characteristic, just be perceived to.

Key term

Single equality duty was introduced by the Equality Act 2010. It is imposed on all public bodies when they are making plans and strategic decisions. The single equality duty means that services need to be targeted at people who are disadvantaged, instead of at groups who have specific characteristics in common. This focuses the duty of those planning services on to the goal of equality itself. The single equality duty tasks public bodies to:

- eliminate discrimination
- advance equality of opportunity
- foster good relations.

Key terms

Intersectional multiple discrimination is where a person experiences discrimination because they belong to a number of groups which may be treated less favourably than others. Where discrimination is 'intersectional', this means that the person's different identities interact in such a way that it is impossible to separate them out from each other. The person's whole experience of being treated differently is not because of one aspect of their uniqueness, but it is about how their *differences* (plural) intersect with each other.

Exclusion describes a situation where people face discrimination on many levels and are effectively 'excluded from society' – that is where they have no voice and are not recognised in their society.

- *Indirect discrimination.* This can occur when you have a rule or policy that applies to everyone but disadvantages a person with a particular protected characteristic.
- *Harassment.* This is behaviour that is deemed offensive by the recipient. Employees can now complain of the behaviour they find offensive even if it is not directed at them.
- *Harassment by a third party.* Employers are potentially liable for the harassment of their staff or customers by people they don't themselves employ, ie a contractor.
- *Victimisation.* This occurs when someone is treated badly because they have made or supported a complaint or grievance under this legislation.

The Act puts a new '**single equality duty**' on all public bodies when they are making strategic decisions, for example, new policies. The single equality duty means targeting services at people who are disadvantaged, so the real essence of this legislation is that it recognises that a person can experience several types of disadvantage at once. This makes sense. A single equality duty means that the focus is on the goal of equality, rather than a label or characteristic of a person or group of people. After all, if you are a black gay man with a disability who is discriminated against at work, why should you have to pinpoint the aspect of self that is being discriminated against?

This gives rise to the concept of '**intersectional multiple discrimination**'. This is where there is discrimination against two or more such characteristics at the same time. This is all very new, and for employers and Local Authorities, very complicated. It remains to be seen how it will work in practice, and we can anticipate much of that practice being thrashed out in the courts to create case law.

How does this legislation apply in health and social care work?

The Equality Act 2010 is important to health and social care in that:

- service users are likely to experience (or have experienced) discrimination on the basis of their difference or the difficulty they may have in accessing the resources they need
- all services have duties to promote equality under this legislation
- as a professional, you have an individual duty to promote equality and inclusion
- you need to be able to understand what the law says about discrimination and equality in order to be able to challenge discrimination and **exclusion** effectively.

REFLECT

How do you meet the requirements of the Equality Act in your practice?

THE HUMAN RIGHTS ACT 1998

The Human Rights Act 1998 came into force in October 2000. It embodies, in effect, the European Convention on Human Rights.

Listed in Schedule 1 of the Act are various rights. These include:

- *Article 2*. Everyone's right to life shall be protected by law.
- *Article 3*. No one shall be subjected to ... degrading ... treatment.
- *Article 5*. Everyone has the right to liberty and security of person.
- *Article 8*. Everyone has the right to respect for his private and family life and his correspondence.
- *Article 9*. Everyone has the right to freedom of thought, conscience and religion.
- *Article 12*. Men and women of marriageable age have the right to marry and to found a family.
- *Article 14*. The enjoyment of these rights and freedoms set forth in this Convention shall be secured without discrimination on any ground.

COMMISSION FOR EQUALITY AND HUMAN RIGHTS (CEHR)

The Commission for Equality and Human Rights was established by the Equality Act 2006. It has a general duty to encourage and support the development of a society in which:

- people's ability to achieve their potential is not limited by prejudice or discrimination
- there is respect for and protection of each individual's human rights
- there is respect for the dignity and worth of each individual
- each individual has an equal opportunity to participate in society
- there is mutual respect between groups based on understanding and valuing of diversity and on shared respect for equality and human rights.

The CEHR is to pursue these objectives by:

- promoting equality of opportunity and diversity
- enforcing anti-discriminatory legislation
- promoting awareness, understanding and protection of human rights.

The CEHR has the power to:

- issue codes of practice to assist organisations to comply with legislation
- initiate inquiries and investigations
- issue notices requiring people to comply with anti-discriminatory legislation
- assist individuals to take legal proceedings where anti-discriminatory legislation appears to have been violated.

EQUALITY AND INCLUSION – WHAT DOES THE CODE OF CONDUCT SAY?

The Code of Conduct for Healthcare Support Workers and Adult Social Care Workers in England 2013 makes clear that you need to uphold and promote equality, diversity and inclusion. To do so, it states that you must:

- respect the individuality and diversity of service users, their carers and your colleagues
- not discriminate or condone discrimination against service users, their carers or your colleagues
- promote equal opportunities for service users and their carers
- report any concerns regarding equality, diversity and inclusion to a senior member of staff as soon as possible.

INTERACTING WITH SERVICE USERS IN A WAY THAT DEMONSTRATES RESPECT

Following best practice in health and social care and ensuring that your practice supports equality and inclusion should mean that you interact with service users in a way which demonstrates respect for beliefs, culture and values. This is also an essential aspect of person-centred practice, which is covered in detail in Chapter 9.

Understanding culture

Culture is an aspect of identity where there can be significant diversity. Culture is based on a number of things shared with others, such as language, shared history, beliefs, attitudes, celebrations, musical taste, dress, diet and many other things. Culture is basically about a shared understanding. Cultures are neither inferior nor superior to each other – they are just *different*. It is important to recognise too that cultures are dynamic and constantly changing.

The term 'culture' incorporates concepts around differences between people's faiths, race/ethnicity and identity. However, it is a broader concept, as cultural diversity (difference) is not only created by these factors, but is also influenced by the folowing:

- *Generational difference*. Experience, identity and preference can be based on people's ages. Consider how different your musical preferences, use of speech and language, sense of humour or identity might be from those of your own parents or grandparents.
- *Differences based on geographical location or between local communities*. Consider how towns in the UK which are 10 miles apart can feel very different culturally, and how areas within one town can have their own identity – these are aspects of culture.
- *Differences in beliefs (as opposed to faith)*. People believe different things about what is right or wrong, about how life should be conducted, and about what is important in life.

It is also important to recognise that culture is an aspect of a person's identity. It is not their 'whole' identity and it does not act as an indicator of how a person will behave and what they will believe. Everyone will choose which aspects of their cultural identity they will 'own' and which they will not. As such, each person has a unique approach to their culture – leading to a complexity in the way in which culture affects people's individual needs.

It is vital that health and social care workers do not make assumptions based on a service user's culture. Culture does not mean uniformity and we still need to treat people as unique individuals. For example, we could say that 'English culture' involves:

- eating fish and chips or Sunday roast
- attending Church of England services
- monogamous relationships
- wearing business suits.

This would lead us to believe that all English people wear business suits, are in life-long monogamous relationships, attend church every Sunday and eat fish and chips in the week and roast dinners on Sunday. Clearly this is not the case.

People working in health and social care settings should be well aware that making assumptions is dangerous. Making assumptions about what people might eat or wear because of a basic understanding of cultural norms can be misleading. A good general rule is that you should never make assumptions about service users.

The experience of service users from different backgrounds may differ radically from the cultural background of any member of staff. Cultural beliefs and practices may also vary between generations and within a racial group. Certain cultural beliefs may be shared with others from the same background and others may not. The final collection therefore is completely unique to each and every individual.

CASE STUDY

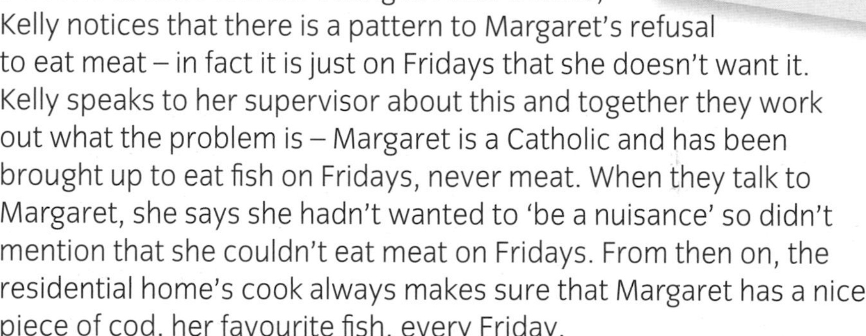

Kelly works in a residential home for older people. She regularly helps out at lunchtimes. One of the residents, Margaret, usually enjoys her meals. She particularly likes meat dishes, but on some occasions Kelly notices that Margaret leaves her meat on her plate. Kelly tries to encourage Margaret to finish her food, but she won't, saying that she doesn't feel like eating it. After a while, Kelly notices that there is a pattern to Margaret's refusal to eat meat – in fact it is just on Fridays that she doesn't want it. Kelly speaks to her supervisor about this and together they work out what the problem is – Margaret is a Catholic and has been brought up to eat fish on Fridays, never meat. When they talk to Margaret, she says she hadn't wanted to 'be a nuisance' so didn't mention that she couldn't eat meat on Fridays. From then on, the residential home's cook always makes sure that Margaret has a nice piece of cod, her favourite fish, every Friday.

CHALLENGING DISCRIMINATION IN A WAY THAT ENCOURAGES CHANGE

A key part of promoting equality and inclusion is challenging discrimination. Sometimes people aren't comfortable with the term 'challenging' because they might be unsure about what 'challenging' means and how workers can challenge effectively.

Whenever you come across a situation which you feel you want (or indeed, need) to challenge, you need to ask the following:

- Why challenge?
- What are you challenging?
- Who are you challenging?
- How should you challenge?

and

- When should you challenge?

You may need to challenge other workers, or you may need to challenge service users or their family members.

Why challenge?

It is important to challenge poor practice and discriminatory behaviour, because we all have a commitment to promote good practice. Through challenging we are able to ask questions about practice that would otherwise remain unasked. We can make positive changes and we can ensure that others adopt a challenging approach.

The purpose of challenging someone else, whether this is a service user, a colleague or another professional, should always be to promote change, or to enable more effective and inclusive practice to take place.

In a healthy, positive and inclusive working culture, challenging should be seen as:

- positive
- constructive
- enabling mutual learning
- respectful

- a way of improving practice
- a way of enabling inclusion and continuous improvement around this key issue.

Sadly, in many working environments, this can still be difficult to achieve as people may feel worried about challenging others, about how the other person may receive the challenge, or about not being supported sufficiently by their employer.

Key term

Whistleblowing policy is where a colleague raises a concern about another person's work or wider practices in an organisation.

If people feel really concerned about someone else's working practice, and they have tried to challenge this and it has not promoted change, their duty of care to service users may mean they are required to take this challenge further. This is why agencies should have a **whistleblowing policy** in place, and this policy should detail what support is available to workers who do escalate challenges in this way.

What is the challenge?

The person who is making the challenge should be clear about exactly what is being challenged. They must:

- listen to the other person
- examine the issue
- think about the context

and

- make the links with institutional oppression and structural forces (by thinking 'Why does the person think like this?', 'What might make them think it is OK to say this in this particular way?', 'What is the service's expectations around use of acceptable language?', etc).

By working in this way, you can avoid making challenging personally threatening.

Who is being challenged?

You must always consider the person being challenged. You should never avoid challenging because of the individual concerned, but clearly you will need to alter the focus and content of your challenge based on the understanding and experiences of the individual. You should think about communication in terms of the person who is being challenged.

How should the challenge be given?

You should choose the right way of challenging, and you will need to put thought into this. As a starting point, consider the following.

Understanding

There could be a difference in understanding between you and the person you are challenging.

Values

There may be a difference between what is important to you and what is important to the person you are challenging.

Styles

There may well be a difference in the way in which you do things and the way the other person does things. That does not necessarily mean that the other person's way of doing something is bad practice.

Opinions

There will be differences in opinion between you and the person you are challenging.

If you bear all of the above in mind when deciding *how* to challenge, your approach is much more likely to be effective. In addition, it is important to choose the least confrontational way of challenging someone.

When should you challenge?

This is very closely linked to *how* to challenge. Is it appropriate to challenge at the time, or later?

Consequences of challenging

In addition to considering the questions outlined above, you need to think about the consequences of any challenge both in terms of yourself and the person being challenged. You should also think about the needs of the person harmed by the poor practice, the oppression, etc. They may need support, too.

REFLECT

Consider a time when you have had to challenge somebody at work. This does not have to have been over a massive issue, or anything which led to an escalation of the issue. It might have been quite an informal challenge to a person over their use of language, or to somebody making fun of another person without thinking about how upsetting this could be.

- How did you challenge?
- Why did you decide to challenge?
- How did it feel to challenge?
- What worked well, and what would you do again in a similar situation?
- What would you do differently?
- What support might you need if this occurred again, or if the other person did not respond to the challenge you made?

APPLICATION OF SKILLS

Challenging discrimination

Stan is an older man with dementia. One staff member in particular always talks to Stan very loudly and simply. They never explain to Stan what they are doing as they assume that he won't understand.

- Should you challenge this?
- Why? How?

Seema has recently moved into the residential service where you work. Seema does not like to sit in the main lounge where very often 'classic films' are shown. A colleague says that Seema is 'a typical Asian woman who likes to keep herself to herself'.

- Should you challenge this?
- Why? How?

Alfred Moore refuses to have a male care worker assist him, as he says 'any man who wants to do a woman's job must be a poof'.

- Should you challenge this?
- Why? How?

The cycle of discrimination – promoting inclusive practice is about breaking this negative cycle.

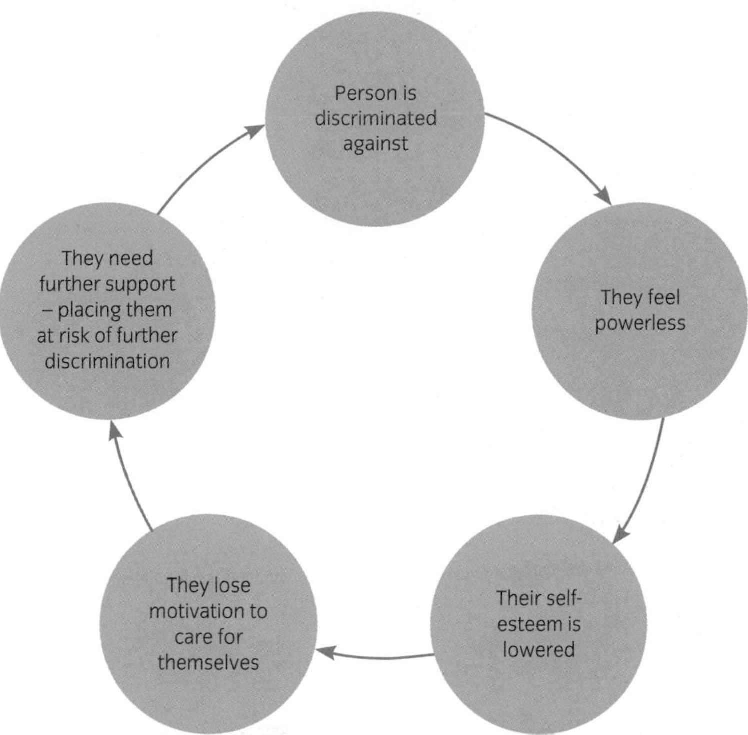

ACCESSING INFORMATION, ADVICE AND SUPPORT ABOUT DIVERSITY, EQUALITY AND INCLUSION

Although you may be committed to working in an inclusive way, there may be times when you need additional help to ensure that service users do not experience any form of discrimination. This could be, for example, if you are caring for a person from a cultural background that you know little about and you need to find out more about their cultural practices.

WHERE CAN YOU FIND INFORMATION, ADVICE AND SUPPORT?

A range of information and advice is available on diversity, equality and inclusion.

Information at work

Your organisation should have an equality and diversity policy that will explain how staff are expected to practise in a way that supports diversity, equality and inclusion. For more specific information on a particular issue, your supervisor or colleagues may be able to help.

If you are caring for someone who has a cultural background that you know little about, perhaps you have a colleague from the same cultural background as the service user and they could support you to ensure that you are meeting the service user's cultural needs. If not, your supervisor or colleagues may know of a local source of information, such as a cultural centre or community club.

Relatives and friends are another good source of information. They will know the service user best, and will be able help you with issues that relate to diversity, equality and inclusion. They will want to support you in ensuring that the person is treated fairly and without discrimination.

Don't forget that in some cases, the best source of information will be service users themselves. As long as you are sensitive when you are asking questions that relate to diversity, equality and inclusion, and make it clear that the reason for your questions is to avoid discrimination, most people will be happy to share information about their particular needs.

Information in the local community

Information about diversity, equality and inclusion will be available at the following places:

- libraries
- Citizens Advice Bureaus
- law centres

- welfare rights centres
- local support groups, such as groups for gay people, people with dementia, mental health problems or learning disabilities.

The internet

You can also find plenty of information on the internet about diversity, equality and inclusion. Useful websites include the following:

- Equality and Human Rights Commission
- Citizens Advice Bureau
- National and local support groups.

WHEN SHOULD YOU ACCESS INFORMATION, ADVICE AND SUPPORT

You should access information, advice and support about diversity, equality and inclusion as soon as you have any concerns about any of the service users you are caring for. If you think that someone is being discriminated against, you need to offer them support as soon as you possibly can.

CASE STUDY

Ben provides care for a number of refugees. The people he works with have experienced traumatic events in their own countries, and some have had endured severe hardship in order to leave and start a new life in the UK. Unfortunately, some of the refugees have experienced discrimination since they have been in the UK, not only from members of the public, but also from institutions, such as benefits agencies, that are supposed to support them. Ben is determined to ensure that he promotes equality, diversity and inclusion in his work. He knows that by understanding as much as he can about the experience of refugees and by being well informed about their rights in the UK he can do the best for the people he works with. To get the information he needed, Ben looks at the website of the Refugee Council. He also visits a local refugee centre so that he can help the people he worked with to make connections in the community.

Before going to the next chapter, take some time to consider:

- what you see as the main ways that people you work with may be discriminated against
- what you need to do to promote equality and inclusion in your work
- what challenges you face in promoting equality and diversity
- whether you fully understand the legal framework of equality
- how you could improve your skills in this area.

CHAPTER 4

Introduction to duty of care in health and social care

At the centre of health and social care work is a duty of care. Implementing the duty of care is basically about being a professional care worker.

This chapter considers what is meant by the term 'duty of care' and addresses some of the dilemmas that can occur when delivering this duty for and with service users.

Links with other chapters

The duty of care applies to all aspects of your work, so this chapter links to every unit you will complete for your Diploma. There are particular links with Chapters 3 and 5. There are also clear links between the issues of risk covered in this chapter and in Chapter 6.

UNDERSTANDING THE DUTY OF CARE

The duty of care underpins all work in health and social care. It is about:

- putting the needs of service users first
- making sure that service users' needs are met
- treating service users with respect, and respecting their rights
- working in service users' best interests
- promoting service users' independence, and empowering them
- supporting service users to keep themselves safe
- ensuring that service users are listened to
- carrying out your job competently
- doing your job to the best of your ability
- meeting legal requirements.

The government defines the duty of care as:

'An obligation placed on an individual requiring that they exercise a reasonable standard of care while doing something (or possibly omitting to do something) that could foreseeably harm others.'

(Department of Health 2007)

Meanwhile, Unison says:

'"Duty of care" is a phrase used to describe the obligations implicit in your role as a health or social care worker. As a health or social care worker you owe a duty of care to your patients/service users, your colleagues, your employer, yourself and the public interest. Everyone has a duty of care – it is not something that you can opt out of.'

(Unison 2012)

This makes clear that your duty of care is an obligation – it is something you owe the service users you work with, and it is their right to receive the best possible care when they access services. The duty of care is a legal concept – when workers do not follow it there can be serious consequences.

The concept of a duty of care can apply outside of health and social care settings, too. If someone trips over a paving stone, they can argue that the Local Authority has not met its obligations to them. The ever-increasing frequency of legal action being taken as a result of negligence is an example of how people exercise their rights when they feel that organisations have not met their duty of care.

REFLECT

- What does the phrase 'duty of care' mean to you?
- What does it mean for your role at work?

HOW DOES THE DUTY OF CARE AFFECT YOUR OWN WORK ROLE?

The duty of care which you have is vital in supporting service users effectively, keeping them safe and ensuring that their rights are not contravened or ignored.

Your duty of care involves:

- providing care in a safe and compassionate way
- taking responsibility for what you do
- being able to explain why you have done something in a particular way
- upholding people's right to feel safe from harm and abuse
- promoting people's right to be treated with dignity and respect
- following policies and procedures
- ensuring that service users are supported to take risks in a way that respects their individuality
- you meeting your duty to liaise with other professionals when you are concerned about a service user's safety or welfare
- your duty to put service users' 'best interests' at the heart of your work.

REFLECT

How does the duty of care apply when you are:

- providing personal care?
- communicating with relatives and friends of individuals?
- conducting your health and safety responsibilities at work?
- recording your work?
- working with colleagues?

YOUR EMPLOYER'S DUTY OF CARE

While you have a duty of care to the service users you support, your employer has a duty of care to you. They have a duty to ensure your health and safety, and to provide you with any necessary training and appropriate equipment. To ensure that they uphold this duty of care your employer will have a number of policies and procedures in place. They will also have policies relating to how you can complain and what you can do if you feel they are failing in their duty of care towards you – grievance procedures, for example.

CASE STUDY

Alison has been transferred from a day service to a home care service, following changes in the provision of care in the local area. She is asked to go and assist a service user, as the regular care worker is off sick. Alison checks the notes and sees that this service user needs help with using a hoist. Alison has not been trained to use a hoist, as this was not required in her previous role. Alison is keen to impress in her new workplace but recognises that she has a duty of care to the service user and that her employer has a duty of care towards her. She explains to her manager that she is not able to use a hoist. The manager apologises and says he made an assumption that since Alison is a very experienced worker she would have experienced the use of hoists. He arranges for a different worker to assist the service user and make arrangements for Alison to receive the necessary training so that she can assist service users with hoists in the future. Alison is pleased that she raised the issue and recognises that both she and her manager have met their duty of care.

- What might have happened if Alison had not been honest with her manager?
- How has Alison worked in line with the duty of care she has?

DUTY OF CARE CONFLICTS AND DILEMMAS

The duty of care for service users in health and social care settings can create a range of conflicts or dilemmas for workers. This is because:

- upholding people's rights is complex
- rights are balanced with responsibilities
- what one person wants might be in conflict with what another person wants
- what people want is not always what is best for them.

Conflicts and dilemmas generally occur where:

- there is an issue concerning rights and responsibilities
- there is conflict between different people holding different views about a situation
- there are different values (perhaps there is a conflict between a worker's personal and professional values) – this is covered in detail on pages 29–30
- a solution is not clear-cut or obvious
- every possible alternative in a situation would lead to an undesirable outcome for a service user
- there are concerns about the risks that a situation might pose.

CONFLICTS AND DILEMMAS RELATING TO RIGHTS AND RESPONSIBILITIES

Often dilemmas arise where there is a conflict over upholding service users' rights in practice.

Closely tied to rights are responsibilities that the person enjoying those rights has an obligation to observe. Various rights and responsibilities are listed in brief in the following table. The table is not exhaustive, but gives you an idea of some of the responsibilities that follow from exercising rights.

Individual rights	Responsibilities
To life	To respect the right of others to life
Freedom of movement	Not to infringe the rights of anyone else
Freedom of speech	To be prepared to hear what others say in response; not to say anything that incites hatred or violence
Freedom of association	To seek to be with those who also want to be with you
To make decisions that affect own life	To acknowledge and face any reasonable and likely consequences of a decision
To practise religious beliefs	Not to infringe the same right of anyone else
To have sex	To ensure it is a mutual decision and to be aware of possible consequences, eg sexually transmitted diseases
To get married	To be aware of the nature of the commitment and intend to uphold your promise
To be treated with dignity and respect	To treat others in the same way
To be treated fairly and equally	To treat others fairly and equally
To be protected from unnecessary risk of harm, neglect, abuse, etc	Not to subject others to harm, abuse, etc, and not to place oneself in situations where there is unnecessary risk of harm or abuse
To medical treatment based on clinical need	To provide relevant information to medical staff
To take risks	To accept the consequences that could reasonably be expected to follow
To privacy	Not to infringe same right of anyone else

TENSIONS WITHIN RIGHTS AND RESPONSIBILITIES

There can easily be potential conflicts when considering rights and responsibilities, and these can take one of several forms.

Tension between a person's own rights and responsibilities

It may be that there are times when a person's rights conflict with their responsibilities. For example, a person may have the right to smoke, but they also have the responsibility not to endanger others. In situations where a person smokes irresponsibly there is a danger of fire, eg as a result of a person smoking in bed and falling asleep as they smoke.

Tension between different people's rights and responsibilities

In any shared living or recreational environment, tensions between people will arise. For example, one person's right to pursue their own interest can conflict with another person's right to do something different in the same place at the same time. A very basic example of this could be an argument between people about what television channel to watch.

At times the duty of care can be in conflict with upholding the rights of the service users you care for. This may be because of some of the tensions between rights and responsibilities covered previously.

You need to be very clear about how you would answer the question 'When should rights be overridden?' This is a difficult but vital question. The key answer is to do with **risk**, and relates to situations in which exercising a particular right may place someone in danger. Essentially, this applies in two main ways:

- *Danger to others.* No one has the right to violate or infringe the rights of someone else. If a person is acting in a way that intrudes on someone else's rights (eg hitting them), then action needs to be taken.
- *Danger to self.* Certain actions can place people at risk. Examples may include self-harm or smoking in bed (which may also pose a danger to others).

It is vital, if someone's rights are restricted (because of a danger to themselves or others), that you explain the reasons to them clearly. When service users are unclear about boundaries or rights they may be left confused and frustrated. Explaining any restrictions clearly is a key part of your duty of care.

Key term

Risk is the likelihood that a hazard will actually cause harm.

APPLICATION OF SKILLS

Doing the 'right thing'

Alton has learning disabilities. He lives in a residential home and has attended a day service for many years. He is unable to speak, but recently has appeared unwell while at the day service and has vomited on occasion, so he then goes home. This is happening increasingly frequently, but the home manager has asked if Alton can stay at the day service even if he vomits, because of the drain on staff hours and because he must do something during the day.

- What are the concerns about rights here?
- How can Alton's rights be upheld?

Mr Singh always insists on accompanying his wife for appointments with the doctor. She has limited understanding of the English language, but indicates to you that she would prefer not to have her husband present. Mr Singh is insistent that it is appropriate that he **chaperone** his wife and act as interpreter.

Key term

Chaperone means to accompany. Most commonly a chaperone accompanies a person during a medical treatment or examination.

- What are the concerns about rights here?
- How can Mrs Singh's rights be upheld?

Mrs Gable has smoked for over 40 years. Her doctor has said she must stop, so her daughter stops bringing her cigarettes when she visits her in the residential home where she lives. Mrs Gable pleads with staff to buy cigarettes for her and she has now started to take cigarettes from other people.

- What are the concerns about rights here?
- How can Mrs Gable's rights be upheld?

RISK – CREATING MAJOR DILEMMAS

Concerns about risks often cause dilemmas and uncertainty for health and social care workers in terms of implementing their duty of care.

Risk assessment is covered in detail on pages 270–272 and again on pages 412–414. However, it is worth exploring how people understand risk in health and social care here, as this is closely related to the dilemmas and conflicts that health and social care workers often face in relation to their duty of care.

Approaches to risk

In health and social care services the main approaches to risk can be categorised as follows.

Risk elimination

This approach seeks to eliminate risks. It is rare to be able to completely eliminate risks – but if there is the risk of someone falling over a rug, for instance, the rug can be removed and this would then be an example of risk elimination.

Risk reduction

This approach seeks to reduce risks, or the likelihood of identified risks occurring. An example might be that someone is at risk from trailing wires, so the wires are contained in some way. (This would reduce the likelihood of harm occurring.)

Risk minimisation

This approach is often referred to as harm minimisation. Essentially, this approach is about minimising the potential impact of the risk. An example might be the use of assistive technology – such as a sensor pad which indicates when someone has got out of bed.

Risk management

This approach recognises that risk is a part of life and seeks to manage the risks rather than attempting to eliminate them – perhaps using a combination of the other approaches to risk.

Risk-averse approaches

A number of health and social care services are seen as having a 'risk-averse' culture. That is, they seek to adopt a risk elimination rather than a risk management approach. It is widely recognised that services have in the past often been too protective of people.

The table below shows the key differences between risk elimination and risk management.

	Risk elimination	Risk management
How risks are defined	Risk is viewed as wholly negative; it is seen only as a danger or a threat	Risk is viewed as potentially positive – balancing risks and benefits is part of life; it is part of a service user's development, encouraging them to become self-determining and personally responsible
Priority principles	Emphasis on professional responsibility and accountability	Encourages self-determination, equality and inclusion
Practice priorities	Emphasis on identification (assessment scales) and elimination (procedural, legalistic)	Encourages partnership working, active support and empowerment

Recognising the dignity of risk

It is now accepted that the attempt to eliminate all risk undermines service users' dignity and rights and inhibits opportunities for personal development and growth.

The answer to over-protection is not to ignore risks but to work in partnership to support service users to take measured reasonable risks.

Reasonable risk

The concept of 'reasonable risk' is important. Health and safety legislation often refers to what would be 'reasonable', and the expected actions of a 'reasonable person'. One of the difficulties in determining what constitutes a reasonable risk is that sometimes our view is coloured by our own anxieties about a person's safety and our attitude towards risk in our own lives. The Department of Health states the following:

'Because of perceptions of risk which may or may not be real, a person might be prevented from doing things which most people take for granted. So perceived risk must be tested and assessed against the likely benefits of taking an active part in the community, learning new skills and gaining confidence.'

(Department of Health 2007)

Decisions about 'reasonable' risk must never be taken in isolation – what seems reasonable to one person may be unreasonable to another. People's personal values, for example, will have a significant impact on their view of risk, which demonstrates the importance of being clear about professional and organisational values.

A risk enablement culture

If a health and social care worker works to the principles of active support, as described in Chapter 10, they will be well on the way to promoting a positive culture in relation to risk.

Taking some risks is a daily occurrence for everyone and is necessary if people are to take a full and active part in their communities. Government guidance makes this clear:

'The possibility of risk is an inevitable consequence of empowered people taking decisions about their own lives.'

(Department of Health 2007)

Most people are able to balance risk against possible benefits and will take any necessary precautions to help minimise risk. However, it may not be quite as easy for service users to achieve this balance for themselves. This is where support will be required. It is where the key dilemmas will occur and where getting the balance right is perhaps most difficult. Sometimes when providing support, health and social care workers can be anxious to eliminate any identified risk of harm, which can mean that a decision is made that a particular choice cannot be supported. As discussed in Chapter 9, this should only occur in extreme circumstances and where risk assessments clearly indicate the reasons why the person's choice cannot be supported.

REFLECT

- What dilemmas have you faced in managing the balancing act between rights and risks?
- How did you promote balance?
- Could you have dealt with this situation differently? How?
- If a similar situation were to occur again, what would you do? Why?

Getting the balance right

Effective practice in working with risk within care environments is about balance. It is vital that the duty of care is not used as a reason to deny the dignity of risk taking.

WHEN EMPLOYERS' INSTRUCTIONS CONFLICT WITH THE DUTY OF CARE

Unison (2012) points out that a health and social care worker may be placed in a difficult position when they are asked to do something by their employer which they feel conflicts with their duty of care. As examples, Unison cites situations in which:

- an instruction is unlawful, eg in relation to health and safety law
- an instruction is clearly unsafe, eg if it could compromise an individual's wellbeing
- an instruction is insufficiently direct – for example, different managers giving conflicting instructions.

Where you consider there to be a conflict between what your employer is asking of you and your duty of care, you must raise this with your manager. If the situation is not clarified or resolved, you should consider whether to follow whistleblowing procedures. The Public Interest Disclosure Act (1998) will provide protection if you have followed your organisation's whistleblowing policy.

Public Interest Disclosure Act 1998

This is often referred to as the 'whistleblowers' legislation', and was implemented in July 1999. This Act gives significant statutory protection to employees who disclose malpractice reasonably and responsibly in the public interest and are victimised as a result. If an employee is victimised or dismissed for this disclosure they can make a claim for compensation to an industrial tribunal. There is no cap to the amount that can be awarded.

While it is not a statutory requirement, there is an expectation that organisations will establish their own whistleblowing policy and guidelines. These guidelines should:

- clearly indicate how staff can raise concerns about malpractice
- make a clear organisational commitment to take concerns seriously and to protect people from victimisation
- designate a senior manager with specific responsibility for addressing concerns in confidence which need to be handled outside the usual management chain.

Staff receive the full protection of the Act if they seek to disclose malpractice responsibly, ie by following the organisation's whistleblowing policy or guidelines.

CASE STUDY

Shola has just started working in a residential home. He becomes aware that staff are falsifying records about the restraint of service users and he is concerned about this. He talks to his supervisor, who says that this is common practice – and it is what he must do too – as there have been complaints from relatives in the past about restraints, so it is better to simply not record incidents. Shola feels very concerned about what to do and researches the organisation's whistleblowing policy so that he can alert the relevant people to what is happening.

- Why is Shola right to research the organisation's whistleblowing policy?
- What would you do if you were in Shola's position?

GETTING SUPPORT AND ADVICE ABOUT CONFLICTS AND DILEMMAS

It is important that professionals in health and social care know when to ask for help, and do not see needing support or advice as a sign of weakness. This is especially critical where there are dilemmas, as quite often there are no 'rights' or 'wrongs' in these situations, and a sound decision can only be made by sharing knowledge and information, and talking with others.

Potential sources of support and information about how to respond to dilemmas include:

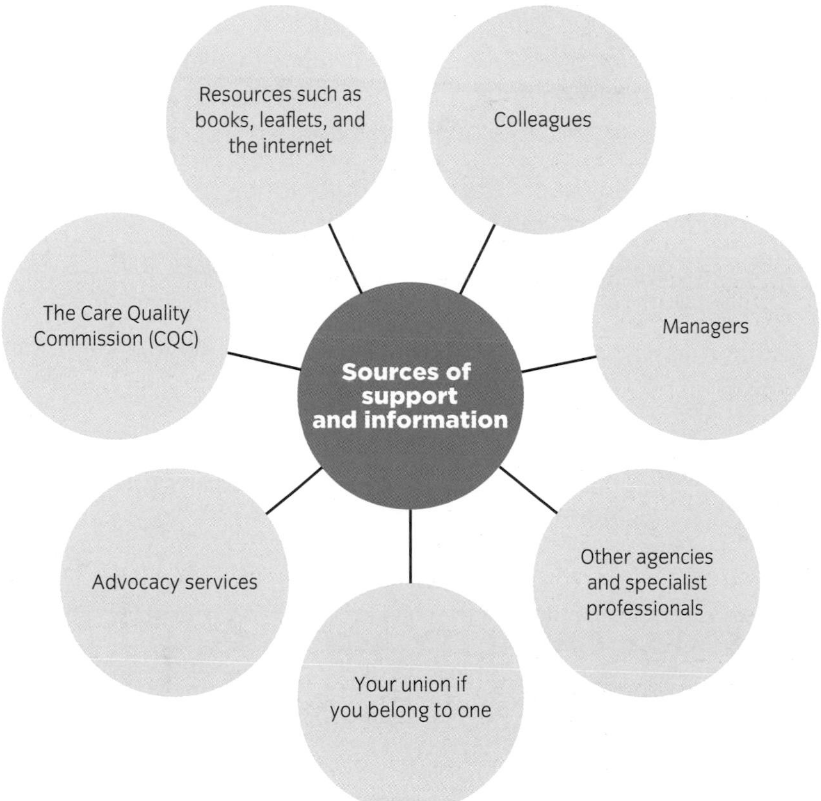

REFLECT

How would you access support, advice and information where you face a duty of care dilemma?

BEST INTEREST DECISIONS

All decisions on dilemmas and conflicts must be made in line with best interest principles.

What are best interests?

The idea of people's 'best interests' is critical in health and social care work, and it is a term which is used frequently in all fields. The following are key when considering best interests:

- It is important not to make assumptions about what is in someone's best interests. Decisions about best interests should be based on evidence, knowledge of the individual and a deep understanding of risk and safeguarding practice.
- Decisions about best interests should not be made in isolation – considering best interests needs to involve discussion between a range of different professionals working in conjunction with the service user and their family.
- What is in someone's best interests is not always what they want.
- Your duty of care involves explaining best interest decisions when this is an issue, and evidencing the reasons for your decision making.

THE MENTAL CAPACITY ACT 2005

This Act represented a fundamental change for adult services, and is particularly relevant to this chapter.

Where the Mental Capacity Act broke new ground was that it departed from the idea that an assessment of capacity is made on a once-and-for-all basis and affects all other decisions that the person makes. It recognises that the ability to be able to make rational decisions may vary for a variety of reasons and according to the complexity of what is being asked of the person.

The Mental Capacity Act has five core principles:

1 A person must be assumed to have capacity unless it is established that they lack capacity.

2 A person must not be treated as unable to make a decision unless all practicable steps to help them to make the decision have been taken.

3 A person must not be treated as unable to make a decision just because they make an unwise decision.

4 Any decision made or act carried out on behalf of a person must be in their best interests.

5 Before a decision is made or an act is carried out, consideration must be given about how this can be achieved in a way which is least restrictive of the person's rights and freedoms.

COMPLAINTS PROCEDURES

An effective complaints procedure is essential for service users, but it can also be helpful for health and social care workers in that it can:

- emphasise the need for a high-quality service provision
- identify areas of poor practice
- support staff to develop their practice
- clarify misunderstandings
- bring attention to lack of resources
- improve practice.

It is therefore important that health and social care professionals do not view complaints procedures negatively or as a threat. A good-quality complaints procedure is a positive attribute to a service. It will encourage service users to participate more fully in the service and have more control over the care they receive.

However, service users often experience problems in making use of complaints procedures.

Some of the difficulties experienced in putting a complaints policy into effect can be caused by the following factors.

LACK OF ACCESSIBILITY

A complaints system may exist in the form of a paper document in a Policy Manual, for example, but it can only be a living document if those who may need to use it are aware of it and understand how they can use it. Therefore, health and social care services should:

- refer to the complaints policy in any brochures or explanatory information that they give people when they begin receiving the service
- ensure that relatives and other people who are important in the lives of the service users are aware of the policy, together with who they might need to raise a complaint with and how to do so

- ensure that the policy is available in different formats depending on the service users' needs; for example, on an audio tape or in a larger font for people with impaired vision.

Happless Care, Complaints Procedure

As part of our commitment to improving all our Care Services, any person wishing to make a complaint may do so, following the procedure outlined below:

1. Please make your complaint using form C7.0000.bd.XIX.
2. If your complaint is made on behalf of a relative, then please use form C7,0090.SS.XXXX (part A) only. Parts C and D should only be completed if your relative incurred any financial loss in relation to the complaint, but no personal injury.
3. If personal injury was incurred, please complete parts D, supplemented by form C3.0010...S. (ignoring part B).
4. Forms are available from floor 40, Bleak Tower, Middle of Nowhere. Please collect by hand.
5. Please collect the appropriate form prior to the incident in question.
6. Please return the form promptly, making sure all 50 questions are answered in full, with supporting evidence from your GP and other referee.
7. Please complete your full name and address, and include a photograph of yourself and/or your loved one. This is to ensure that members of staff can be absolutely clear about who is making a nuisance of themselves.
8. Please obtain a receipt of postage, though a Microchip trace may be the only means of ensuring the complaint will not get completely and entirely lost.
9. If you do not have any response within 12 months of making your complaint, please complete form ZZ.23,000,SSI.
10. Forms are available in a variety of languages, though it is doubtful if these can be found anywhere at all.

"HAPPY TO HELP"

(Basnett and Maclean 2000)

Clearly this complaints procedure is an example of very poor practice in accessibility.

NEGATIVE POWER BALANCE

- Although individual members of staff may not feel as if they are especially powerful in their own right, they will be perceived by service users as being more powerful than they are. For this reason, service users may find it more difficult to raise concerns if they have them.
- Service users may feel that they do not have much control over their own lives. This could be because they may require assistance in many aspects of their lives, and they are dependent on health and care workers to enable them to access the community.

- Service users and their family members may be afraid to raise a complaint in case they lose the service. They may feel no one will listen or they may find it difficult to act assertively.
- Service users and their families may feel that they don't want to 'cause any trouble' or fear that there will be consequences for them if they make a complaint.

For these reasons, health and social care professionals need to:

- recognise power differentials and work with them effectively
- ensure that service users are empowered by the service
- promote a positive culture of support which welcomes comments and complaints about the service provided.

SERVICE USERS' PAST NEGATIVE EXPERIENCES

- Past experiences of 'care' (perhaps in long-stay institutions where they may have had even less control and many elements of daily life were directed by staff) may mean that service users have low expectations of service provision.
- Memories of institutional care and behaviour patterns learned in this environment are often very difficult to shift, even many decades later, and you may see this in behaviours such as a reluctance to raise complaints or expectations.

THE NEED TO COMBAT STAFF DEFENSIVENESS

One of the most difficult elements to establish in a healthy complaints policy is a positive culture.

One difficulty is that there is a fear that a complaint will inevitably lead to disciplinary action being taken and could lead to a person losing their job. In some organisations where staff experience the organisational culture as being this negative, they may have grounds for thinking in this way.

This feeling can also come about because employees habitually regard a complaint as reflecting solely on their own work. It is preferable for everyone in a service to share the understanding that complaints need to be dealt with as a reflection on the service as a whole, rather than any specific worker's failing.

REFLECT

- Are you aware of the complaints procedure in your workplace?
- How do you ensure that service users are aware of the procedure, and that they receive any support they might need to complain when they are not satisfied with their care?

WHY DO SERVICE USERS COMPLAIN?

Service users may complain for a variety of reasons, including the following:

- They are not receiving a service which they feel entitled to.
- The service they are receiving is not what they expected it to be.
- The service they have the right to access is inaccessible to them.
- They feel they have been treated unfairly or without sufficient respect.
- They have not been informed about their rights.
- They are unsafe, or feel that they are.
- They feel that an individual staff member's duty of care or that of a service is not being met.

RESPONDING EFFECTIVELY TO COMPLAINTS

When responding to complaints, the most important thing is to follow the procedure and policy of your service setting. This is likely to involve the following steps:

- *Provide information.* Service users should be informed about what the service's procedure on complaints says, both when they begin to access a service, and regularly after this. Service users need information about what is happening to their complaint when they have made one. They also need information about their rights (eg to an advocate or other support).
- *Provide support.* As a general rule, people do not want to complain and do not 'enjoy' complaining. People do so because they feel unhappy, aggrieved or unfairly treated. Your duty of care involves respecting people, and supporting them through difficult situations.
- *Provide access to advocacy.* Ensure that the service user knows about advocacy services which are available to them, and explain what an advocate does if they do not know this already. Service users often have the right to an advocate, and this can be especially useful if they are making a complaint.

- *Use good active listening skills.* People have the right to be listened to, and your skills in listening effectively when a service user is unhappy about an issue are critical.
- *Record the complaint.* Make sure you use the appropriate paperwork.
- *Do something with the complaint.* It might sound obvious, but this is essential, as is telling the person what you are doing, what will happen next, and who will get back to them to inform them of the outcome of their complaint where this is possible.
- *Handle the complaint with sensitivity.* If the complaint is about another worker, consider how you will handle this with sensitivity, and take any appropriate action to make sure that managers are aware as soon as you can.
- *Maintain respect.* If the complaint is about you, maintain your respect for the person in how you handle this information and in your future work with them.
- *Respect the person's right to confidentiality.* If someone shares their complaint with you, you should not talk to colleagues or anyone else apart from your manager(s) about it.

UNDERSTANDING PROCEDURES FOR HANDLING COMPLAINTS

Although the specific policies and procedures for handling complaints will be individual to each agency, service or employer, there are a few common elements of effective complaints procedures.

Usually, a complaints procedure has three or four stages.

Stage one – informal or local resolution

The complaint is looked at by a manager, who discusses with the complainant what they would like to see happen (eg an apology or a change of worker). The matter is resolved to the complainant's satisfaction and the complaint is recorded, but no formal investigation is completed.

Stage two – a formal complaint which is handled within the service

This is where a formal investigation takes place, either by an immediate manager, or by a senior manager, or by someone who is independent from the service being complained about. Interviews may take place with the complainant (which is where an advocate can be extremely helpful), any witnesses and the person who is being complained about (if the complaint is about an individual). The outcome of the complaint may be shared with the complainant, as long as the confidentiality of anyone who has been complained about is respected.

Stage three – the complaint is examined

If the person making the complaint is not satisfied with the outcome of stage two, the next stage may involve either:

- an independent person who is commissioned to come in and examine the complaint

or

- a panel of managers looking in more detail at the complaint.

Stage four – external involvement

Within Local Authority complaints procedures, the final stage is usually where the complainant asks the Local Authority ombudsman to look at how their complaint has been handled.

Some complaints may also be referred directly to the Care Quality Commission, in which case their procedures would be followed. Up-to-date versions of these are best found by contacting CQC directly, or researching them on the CQC website.

KEY POINTS

Here is a summary of the key issues surrounding complaints procedures:

- It is vital that complaints procedures are clear and transparent so that service users (and their representatives or advocates) can access them and make effective use of them.
- If an agency or service has a complaints procedure, it must expect complaints. Workers should be able to pick up on situations where a service user or family member is unhappy about a matter and, if possible, the worker should try to resolve the problem.
- If the concerns raised are outside an individual worker's control, they will need to convey how it is important that a comments or complaints form is filled in. The worker can also help the service user and their family members to complete the form.

COMPLAINTS – WHAT DOES THE CODE OF CONDUCT SAY?

The importance of responding effectively to complaints is recognised in the Code of Conduct for Healthcare Support Workers and Adult Social Care Workers in England 2013, which states that you must:

- always take comments and complaints seriously
- respond to them in line with agreed ways of working and
- inform a senior member of staff.

RESEARCH

- Read your organisation's complaints procedure.
- What does it say about how you should respond to a complaint?

CASE STUDY

Louise has mental health problems. She lives at home with her parents, who are getting older and have care needs of their own. Louise is admitted to hospital and her parents feel that she cannot return home, as they are struggling to provide the care she needs. The hospital staff identify that Louise would benefit from moving into a flat of her own with support from a care agency. However, they are unable to locate accommodation for Louise as there is a long waiting list. Louise is therefore moved into a residential care home. Louise feels that her independence is being affected and she talks to her parents about making a complaint about the move she has made. Her parents advise her not to 'rock the boat' because they feel she is better off in the home than she was in the hospital. They tell Louise 'everyone has been lovely – we shouldn't complain as it might get someone into trouble'.

- Why might Louise be reluctant to complain?
- What might happen if she does complain?

SERIOUS FAILURES IN HEALTH AND SOCIAL CARE PRACTICE

Care and Compassion? was published in 2011. It is a report by the Health Service Ombudsman for England (Ann Abraham) detailing 10 investigations into NHS care of older people carried out by the Ombudsman during 2009 and 2010. The report shows how many health staff failed in their duty of care to patients, and highlights:

- a lack of dignity, sensitivity, compassion and professionalism
- an attitude which fails to recognise humanity and individuality
- an apparent indifference of staff to deplorable standards of care
- a failing in the most basic standards of care.

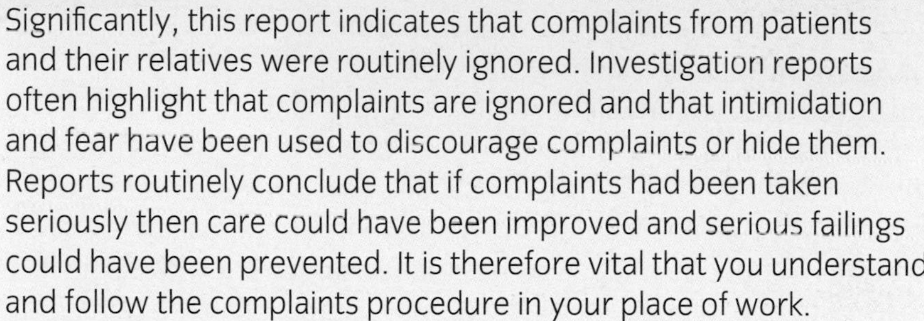

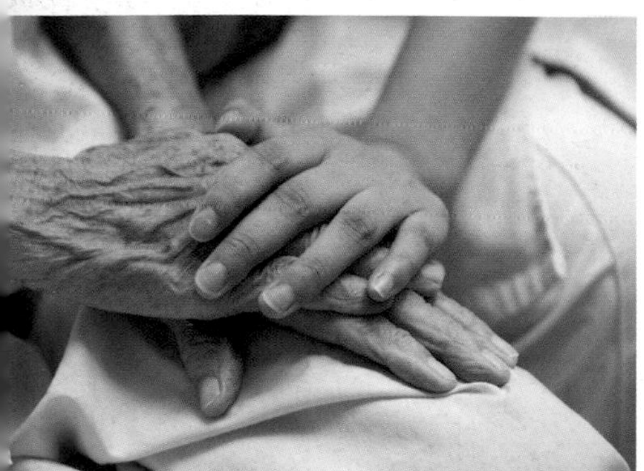

Significantly, this report indicates that complaints from patients and their relatives were routinely ignored. Investigation reports often highlight that complaints are ignored and that intimidation and fear have been used to discourage complaints or hide them. Reports routinely conclude that if complaints had been taken seriously then care could have been improved and serious failings could have been prevented. It is therefore vital that you understand and follow the complaints procedure in your place of work.

Refer to Chapter 5 for information on the Winterbourne and Stafford hospital enquiries.

Before going to the next chapter take some time to consider:

- what you see as your duty of care
- what dilemmas you face in carrying out your duty of care
- what you can do to solve these dilemmas
- how you should respond to complaints
- what you have learned from working through this chapter.

CHAPTER 5

Principles of safeguarding and protection in health and social care

Safeguarding and protection are key aspects of every health and social care worker's role. Perhaps because they are so often used in the same sentence, the concepts of safeguarding and protection are often confused. Safeguarding refers to holistic practices which uphold rights and promote the safety of service users, predominantly through implementing good care practices. Protection refers to specific actions which may be taken where there are concerns about an individual being at risk of abuse.

Links to other chapters

As stated previously, safeguarding is an essential aspect of a health and social care worker's role, and therefore this chapter links with the content of many of the other chapters in this book. There are particular links to Chapter 1, which covers aspects of working together with other professionals in detail, and with Chapter 4. In addition, many of the practices covered in other chapters are the best practices to prevent abuse – for example, active support and person-centered approaches.

UNDERSTANDING ABUSE

Understanding abuse and neglect is the first step in effective safeguarding practice. All health and social care workers need to develop their understanding in this area for the following main reasons:

- Service users have a fundamental right to be free from abuse and the fear of abuse.
- Care staff involved in intimate aspects of a person's life are in a position to identify suspicions of abuse.
- Care staff may be part of a support package and care plan designed to monitor and reduce the risk of abuse.
- Disturbingly, much abuse actually stems from the care environment itself. Professional care workers need to be aware of, and be able to respond to, the complex reasons for this.

Media coverage of abuse tends to focus mainly on the abuse of children. Perhaps because of this and the distasteful nature of abuse, many people do not recognise the extent of abuse in the lives of vulnerable adults. The abuse of vulnerable adults tends to be a hidden and ignored problem in our society, despite the fact that there have been several recent high-profile cases showing its extent.

WHAT IS ABUSE?

In 2000 the government issued *No Secrets*. This is a guidance document on the development of policies to protect adults at risk of abuse. This guidance recognised that abuse can be defined in many ways, but states that the starting point for any definition should be as follows:

'Abuse is a violation of an individual's human rights and civil rights by any other person or persons.'

(Department of Health and Home Office 2000)

The guidance goes on to explain that abuse can:

- be a single act or repeated acts
- take a number of forms
- occur when a vulnerable person is forced to do something which they do not (or cannot) consent to
- occur in any relationship.

In understanding abuse and neglect it is important to understand the key terms **commission** and **omission**.

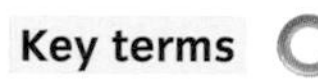

Key terms

Commission is where something is done where the person understands the implications of what they are doing. For example, hitting someone would be an act of commission.

Omission is where something is not done (accidentally or on purpose). For example, not providing an adequate standard of care for a service user would be an act of omission.

RECOGNISING THE FORMS AND SIGNS OF ABUSE

Abuse is often divided into different forms or types. It is important to recognise that while understanding abuse in terms of the different forms it may take can be useful, people may experience more than one type of abuse at a time. For example, physical abuse is often accompanied by threats and abusive comments, which means that the person is not only physically but also emotionally abused.

Abuse can be categorised into the following forms:

- physical abuse – which can include self-harm
- sexual abuse
- emotional/psychological abuse
- financial abuse
- institutional abuse
- neglect – either by self or others.

Physical abuse

Physical abuse includes any action that causes or is intended to cause physical harm to another, for example, kicking, punching, pushing, slapping, scalding, burning or biting. Most physical abuse would come within the remit of criminal law. However, particularly when dealing with vulnerable people, 'rough handling' and deliberately poor administration of care tasks (such as lack of physical sensitivity when handling dressings and catheters, or lack of sensitivity and concern when helping someone to eat) would also constitute physical abuse.

EXAMPLE

John has been caring for his father Arnold for some time and is finding this ever more stressful. Arnold is becoming more confused and has a tendency to repeat the same questions again and again. John has become increasingly irritated by Arnold's repetition and he is finding his father more and more demanding. John returned from a bad day at work and, when his father started repeating the same question over and over again, he hit Arnold.

Signs of physical abuse may include:

- various injuries which may not tally with the explanation given
- repeated injuries
- explanations for injuries that change over time, or are over-elaborate

- physical evidence of injuries, bruises, etc which have been acquired at different points in time
- injuries such as cigarette burns, fingertip bruising or bites
- inappropriate clothing intended to cover injuries
- unwillingness to undress or show parts of the body where there may be injury
- reaction to a particular person or people of a particular gender
- changes in appetite and weight
- anxiety
- agitation
- distress/tearfulness.

Sexual abuse

Sexual abuse includes any sexual act carried out against a person's wishes, or when that person is unable to consent. This would include rape, touching sexual parts of the body, inserting objects into sexual organs, forcing the person to perform sexual acts or filming or photographing a person against their will for sexual purposes.

Sexual abuse can be categorised into contact and non-contact abuse:

- Non-contact sexual abuse can include any sexual abuse where physical contact does not take place, eg sexual harassment, teasing, the taking of photos, the showing of pornography against a person's will, etc.
- Contact sexual abuse is abuse where physical contact takes place, eg touching of the breasts, genitals, mouth, etc; masturbation, of one or both persons; or penetration of the mouth, vagina or anus by a penis or other object.

EXAMPLE

Richard forces Alison, who has a severe learning disability, to look at pornographic images on his phone. He finds her reaction amusing.

Signs of sexual abuse may include:

- injuries to genital areas or breasts that do not tally with explanations given
- repeated injury to the above
- repeated urinary or genital infections
- ripped or damaged clothing
- unexplained injury or bleeding from the anus or genitals

- unexplained discomfort or unwillingness to urinate or defecate
- overly sexualised behaviour
- sexually explicit drawings/artwork
- sudden, unexpected, behaviour changes
- avoidance of a certain person/people
- low self-esteem
- difficulties in relationships
- changes in eating patterns
- hints/comments.

Emotional/psychological abuse

This includes the use of words and actions as weapons against a vulnerable adult and does not necessarily encompass physical harm. Examples of emotional abuse include racist, homophobic or sexist taunts and discrimination, as well as shouting, abusive language, belittling, mocking, threatening or bullying.

Emotional abuse can also include removing sources of comfort and reassurance, encouraging disruption and unhappiness in a person's life or preventing participation in activities that are important to social and emotional wellbeing.

When someone is subjected to physical or sexual abuse or to neglect, there are always elements of emotional abuse inherent within this.

EXAMPLE

Miriam has a diagnosis of schizophrenia. She lives independently on a local housing estate. Miriam often wears clothing that is very colourful and does not match the weather, making her stand out. Other residents on the estate call her 'mad' and 'mental' and laugh at her appearance.

Signs of emotional abuse may include:

- anxiety
- sleeplessness
- reluctance to get up
- withdrawal and self-isolation
- anger
- distress/tearfulness
- fears and phobias
- low self-esteem

- comforting behaviour such as rocking
- weight loss or gain
- antisocial/destructive behaviour
- sudden changes in behaviour.

Financial abuse

This includes all issues surrounding the misuse of finances, property or belongings of a person, including:

- robbery and fraud
- spending of allowances or savings of a person against their will, or without their knowledge or informed consent
- misleading people about how their money will be spent, or the relevance of expenditure
- disposing of property against a person's will or without a person's knowledge
- displacing a person from their property.

EXAMPLE

Shortly before Christmas, Lena, a care assistant, agrees to go shopping for several residents to get their Christmas presents. She buys cheap presents for the residents and uses some of their money to do her own shopping.

Indications of financial abuse may include:

- unexplained withdrawals from savings accounts
- lack of finances to pay bills
- unexplained arrears or debts
- possessions going missing or being sold
- sudden and unexplained change in lifestyle
- unusual interest by another in an individual's finances.

Institutional abuse

Any of the types of abuse described above can and do occur within institutions. However, institutional abuse itself refers to the abusive practices and behaviours that can occur on a widespread basis within an institution, and that are considered 'acceptable'. Examples of institutional abuse include:

- uniform treatment of all service users
- possessions and clothes being used by anyone in the service

- service users being forced to follow routines that benefit the service and not the service user, eg set bedtimes
- expectations that staff can impose punishments or 'withhold privileges'.

EXAMPLE

Monica (a care assistant) has already assisted Mr Patel to have a shave using his electric razor, and he has gone to have his breakfast. Monica then goes to support first Mr Mathers and then Mr Gardner. Monica takes Mr Patel's electric razor and shaves both men before putting it back in Mr Patel's room. This is common practice in the service, as it saves time.

Signs of institutional abuse can be recognised in two different areas, as follows.

Signs in the individual service user:

- anxiety
- loss of confidence
- submissiveness
- low self-esteem
- weight loss, changes in appetite, etc
- difficulty in/anxiety about making independent decisions.

Signs in the environment:

- rigid routines and practices
- service users have a lack of choice
- dignity is not upheld
- the service is run to meet the needs of staff rather than service users
- poor standards of care
- family members and friends have restricted visiting access
- misuse of medication – for example, medication used to sedate people so that staff have a 'quiet shift'.

Neglect

Neglect can be divided into two types: direct and indirect.

Direct neglect is when a person knowingly and deliberately withholds something which should meet a person's essential needs. For example, direct neglect could involve the withholding of food, comfort or water from a service user.

Indirect neglect is where the perpetrator does not actively mean to cause harm, but is neglectful for other reasons. Indirect (or unintentional) neglect could be due to a worker having a lack of information about the implications of their actions, or a lack of awareness about alternative means of addressing an issue. An example of this could be where a service user is given the wrong medication because the worker does not have access to or look at their records.

Neglect can be carried out by the person themselves or by another person.

Self-neglect

Self-neglect describes a situation in which a service user neglects themselves. They may do so on purpose, or accidentally/unintentionally, without realising.

Self-neglect and active abuse (the abuse of an individual by a deliberate perpetrator) are very closely linked. For example, research indicates that almost half of cases of active abuse also involve the service user self-neglecting, and in cases where the service user is neglected by carers or staff teams almost two-thirds of the service users also self-neglect.

A whole range of behaviours constitute self-neglect. These include:

- not eating adequately
- not attending to personal **hygiene** tasks (eg not using the toilet appropriately, not bathing or washing)
- not changing clothing
- not taking medication
- not engaging with healthcare provision or not cooperating with health treatment, etc
- deliberate self-harm.

Key term
Hygiene is keeping yourself and your environment clean to maintain health.

Why does self-neglect occur?

There are many reasons why people neglect themselves. These can include:

- depression – people see no point in caring for themselves
- low self-esteem – people can have a poor view of themselves and therefore see no reason to care for themselves
- lack of motivation – people may have little to look forward to
- abuse – self-neglect may be a sign that a person has been abused
- control – if service users have little control over their life they may only be able to control their food intake, their personal hygiene, etc

and may therefore choose to exert their control by not caring for themselves

- mental health problems at that time
- confusion (possibly a temporary state) or dementia
- living alone and being isolated
- having alcohol or drug problems
- decreased physical abilities resulting in a loss of motivation
- decreased physical abilities due to general or specific health issues.

There are many dilemmas surrounding self-neglect. Since service users have a right to make choices, health and social care staff may allow a person to neglect themselves. However, staff have their 'duty of care' to consider and therefore need to address self-neglect. Where there are concerns about self-neglect, staff should discuss these as soon as possible with their line manager and strategies will need to be devised to deal with the neglect.

EXAMPLE

Daisy's husband died recently and she only has very infrequent contact with her grown-up children. Daisy has stopped taking care of herself and her home. She doesn't have any food in the house and hasn't eaten for several days. She does not get dressed most days and often does not even get out of bed.

Neglect by others

Neglect by others involves situations where people fail to attend to the key needs of people who are dependent on their support.

EXAMPLE

Mary has a number of support needs. Her neighbour Joan agrees to support her, and as part of this she manages Mary's money. Joan does not provide the necessary support for Mary, but she does not want Mary to receive support from services as this means that she will no longer be able to manage Mary's money (much of which she keeps for herself).

Signs of neglect

The signs of neglect will be very similar whether the neglect is self-neglect or neglect by others. They could include:

- anxiety
- physical appearance of neglect and unkemptness

- weight loss
- increased susceptibility to illness due to lack of warmth or nutrition
- submissiveness/lack of confidence
- low self-esteem
- unsanitary living conditions.

THE SIGNS AND SYMPTOMS OF ABUSE

In detailing the different types of abuse, we have indicated what signs and symptoms there may be. However, it is important to remember the following when considering the potential signs of abuse.

- Particular signs are not necessarily indicative of a particular form of abuse (as discussed in this chapter, there is a great deal of crossover in terms of the signs and symptoms of abuse).
- There may be other explanations for the symptoms. It is important not to jump to the conclusion that just because someone is displaying some of the symptoms of abuse that they have been abused. However, it is also important not to miss issues that could be indicators of abuse.

REFLECT

Define the following forms of abuse:

- physical abuse
- sexual abuse
- emotional/psychological abuse
- financial abuse
- institutional abuse
- self-neglect
- neglect by others.

What are the key signs and symptoms of each of the forms of abuse?

WHY ARE SOME PEOPLE MORE VULNERABLE TO ABUSE THAN OTHERS?

Media coverage of abuse tends to focus mainly on the abuse of children, although in recent years there have been some high-profile cases involving the abuse of adults. It is vital to remember that adults are also open to abuse, with some people being more at risk than others.

The government document *No Secrets* refers to a vulnerable adult as a person 'who is or may be in need of community care services by reason of mental or other disability, age or illness; and who is or may be unable to take care of him or herself, or unable to protect him or herself against significant harm or exploitation.'

In 2009 the government carried out a review of *No Secrets* which involved 12,000 people; 90% of the respondents felt that the definition of a 'vulnerable adult' needed to be revised, and there was a great deal of support for replacing the term 'vulnerable adult' with 'person at risk'. This same review made clear that some adults are more at risk of abuse than others.

Safeguarding Adults, published by the Association of Directors of Social Services in October 2005, identifies six aspects of people's lives which may indicate that they are more at risk of abuse:

1. *Social isolation and lack of inclusion.* In general, the more social contacts that an individual has, the more likely it is that others will notice if something is wrong. For example, if person does not attend college other students on the course may notice that he or she is missing, as might the friends of someone who usually joins in a lunch-club or similar activity. Being a member of a social network whether at work, in leisure activities or as a member of a church congregation will make that person just a little more noticeable and increase the possibility that someone will notice if the person is not their usual self.
2. *Dependency on others for essential needs.* This can include those who require support with shopping, personal care, finances and mobility and therefore includes the majority of service users. Paid support staff are sometimes the only people in the lives of service users, and although most staff working in the health and social care field are well intentioned, there are others who may take the opportunity to abuse their privileged access.
3. *Poor-quality policies and information.* Inadequate policies and procedures can leave service users unsure about what to do if they are the victim of abuse or suspect that it is occurring to others. This can result in a time delay before action is taken and, in the worst-case scenario, to nothing being done to protect the service user. One of the most shocking aspects of dealing with abuse is that

serial abusers will deliberately seek out organisations which they see as not having robust policies and procedures to protect adults at risk.

4 *Low standards becoming the norm.* In institutional services people may lose sight of what they should regard as acceptable and what they would not tolerate for themselves and their loved ones. Accepting low standards as the norm can happen where the setting is geographically or socially isolated. However, it can also be the case where resources are under strain, where there are staff shortages or where training has not been adequate.

5 *Domestic abuse being seen as the norm.* Health and social care workers may provide services to individuals in homes which they share with their families and so may develop concerns about domestic abuse. As more services are provided to people in their own homes, health and social care workers may become more aware of behaviour such as bullying within the home. This behaviour may have become accepted within the family, but it would be unacceptable within any other setting. It remains unacceptable in the home too, and should be addressed as it would be elsewhere. Violent, brutal or threatening behaviour within the home is as serious as a violent assault by a stranger.

6 *An unhealthy power balance.* Health and social care workers are in a position of significant power over service users. Where there is a lack of understanding of power or a deliberate misuse of this power, there is likely to be an abuse of power.

Other factors can also increase people's vulnerability to abuse. These include the following.

Loss and change

People may be particularly at risk at certain stages of their lives because of the impact of loss or change, such as:

- the onset of mental health problems
- acquiring a disability
- increasing frailty due to the ageing process
- inability of family members to continue to provide care
- loss of a partner or family member.

Low self-esteem

Key term

Self-image is about how we see or describe ourselves.

Self-esteem is the way in which we view ourselves. When a person is described as having a low self-esteem or poor **self-image** it basically means they 'feel bad' about themselves. Where someone has a 'healthy' self-esteem it means that they are confident and 'feel good' about themselves. Even though self-esteem is about our psychological wellbeing it can have a profound effect on our physical health.

It is important that care staff support service users to feel good about themselves. Service users are likely to have poor self-image and self-esteem, and they may feel dependent and even worthless. Negative feelings like these will then have a negative impact on the person's health and wellbeing. It will also leave them much more at risk of abuse and self-harm.

Communication differences

Where there are significant challenges in terms of communication, the risks of abuse increase. For example, a person with limited or no verbal communication may be especially vulnerable to abuse, not least because they may lack the means to disclose the abuse. This reinforces the need to listen to more than words and to develop effective methods of communication wherever there are differences in communication.

REFLECT

- In your work setting, what factors mean that individuals are more vulnerable to abuse?
- How do you and your service attempt to support individuals through periods of particular stress (eg loss and change), and how do you meet individual communication needs in order to keep people safe?

CASE STUDY

Mr Hall lives alone in the large house which he used to share with his wife. Mr Hall was a senior salesperson in a large business, which meant he travelled widely. He didn't make many friends in the local area as he was away from home so often. Mrs Hall did all the housework and Mr Hall wasn't responsible for shopping or cooking, and he lacks skills in these basic aspects of living. Mr and Mrs Hall had one daughter – who now lives in Australia. Shortly after Mr Hall retired he had a stroke which has impacted on his communication. His wife provided all of Mr Hall's daily care. Mrs Hall died suddenly a few months ago. Mr Hall's neighbour offered to provide support to Mr Hall in doing his shopping and cooking. However, his daughter is concerned that Mr Hall is very vulnerable to abuse and she contacts the local social services requesting that Mr Hall be 'put in a home'.

- What factors might make Mr Hall more vulnerable to being abused?
- What could be done to address these factors and to minimise the likelihood of Mr Hall being abused?

SAFEGUARDING

Safeguarding is defined by the government as:

'a range of activity aimed at upholding an adult's fundamental right to be safe. Being or feeling unsafe undermines our relationships and self-belief, and our ability to participate freely in communities and contribute to society. Safeguarding is of particular importance to people who, because of their situation or circumstances, are unable to keep themselves safe.'

(Department of Health 2010)

RESPONDING TO SUSPECTED OR ALLEGED ABUSE

If care staff understand the nature of harm and abuse and why it can occur, the likelihood of this happening is minimised. Likewise if service users, carers and the general public are more informed about danger, harm and abuse they will be more aware and risks will be reduced. However, abuse will still occur even with the best prevention strategies in place, and health and social care staff therefore need to know what to do when they suspect abuse is taking place.

HOW DO YOU KNOW THAT ABUSE IS OCCURRING?

Sometimes you will know that abuse is happening because someone will tell you that it is – or, rarely, because you actually see it happening. However, most of the time you will suspect that abuse is happening as you become aware that a person's behaviour is changing or you notice issues of concern occurring over a period of time. A service user may say things that appear out of place or their behaviour may change in a way that raises concern. The main skill lies in not jumping to a conclusion about whether abuse has occurred or not, but in 'listening' fully to what the person is communicating. However, it is equally important to recognise these signs as potential indicators of abuse.

The worst thing you can do is ignore the possibility that something could be the sign of abuse.

DISCLOSURES OF ABUSE

A significant amount of abuse is discovered because the victim declares that it is happening – often to someone they trust. A disclosure can take different forms.

Full disclosure

A full disclosure is where a victim tells a person directly that they are being abused. A full disclosure may be totally unexpected and come as a real surprise.

Partial disclosure

A partial disclosure is where the victim hints to a person that they are being abused. However, they may change the subject quickly and may seem reluctant to give details.

Indirect disclosure

An indirect disclosure is where the victim talks about abuse in a general sense or with regard to someone else. They may be looking for the person's response, and trying to find out how they would respond if the victim declared the abuse that they were experiencing.

WHAT SHOULD YOU DO IF YOU SUSPECT THAT SOMEONE IS BEING ABUSED?

Often people do not disclose abuse for a variety of reasons, including:

- fear of the abuser
- fear of not being believed
- communication barriers
- feelings of guilt
- confusion.

This means that health and social care workers need to be alert to the possibilities of abuse and need to be aware of the signs and symptoms of abuse.

Where there are suspicions of abuse, it may feel as if there are various pieces of a jigsaw that need to be put together to get a clear picture. Sometimes different people hold different pieces of the jigsaw, which can make it more difficult to put the pieces together.

Often, health and social care workers will have a significant amount of contact and time with service users. This gives workers the opportunity to:

- observe any changes (eg in a service user's appearance, behaviour, or responses to situations)
- spend time talking with service users and building up trust (which is what enables service users to disclose when abuse has occurred to them)
- observe changes in the presentation and behaviour of others (eg a service user's relatives or friends, or your own colleagues)
- reflect in supervision and discussions with managers (and other agencies) on these sorts of changes in order to put together the pieces of a 'safeguarding jigsaw'; sometimes, workers may have suspicions and no direct disclosure of abuse occurring, but by putting all of the pieces of information and observation together, a real need for action can be identified.

POTENTIAL INDICATORS OF ABUSE

Physical signs may include:

- injuries
- pain
- unexplained accidents
- infections.

Emotional signs may include:

- distress
- tearfulness
- anxiety
- fear
- agitation
- lack of self-worth
- low self-esteem
- compliance
- anger.

Health-related signs may include:

- changes in appetite and weight
- deterioration in health
- sleep disturbance.

Behavioural signs may include:

- any sudden changes in behaviour
- comfort behaviours such as rocking
- unusual responses to certain individuals or people of a particular gender
- wetting/soiling.

Environmental signs may include:

- rigid routines
- lack of choice
- staff demonstrating little concern for service users' dignity.

Other signs, such as:

- sudden lack of funds
- loss of possessions
- changes in communication
- hints or full disclosure.

Always remember that just because a person is displaying one or more of the signs of abuse it does not automatically mean that they are being abused.

ACTIONS TO TAKE IN CASES OF SUSPECTED ABUSE

Where you suspect that a service user is being abused, there are a number of things you should do. Your priorities should be as follows:

1 Ensure that the person is safe.
2 Preserve any evidence.
3 Record and report as soon as possible.
4 Follow up by ensuring that a referral has been made.

Ensuring that the person is safe

A service user's immediate safety is the first concern when there are actions to be taken to keep them safe. They key questions to ask are as follows:

- If the service user is due to be leaving the service that day, when is this taking place, where are they going, and will they be safe?
- If the service user won't be safe and the concern is about a risk in the place they are going to, discuss this with your manager, and stay with the service user until an agreement can be reached about where it is safe for them to go.
- If the service user is not due to be leaving that day (and potentially, the concern or risk to them is within your service setting), ensure that someone is with them, and agree how their immediate need for safety will be met with your manager.
- In any scenario, your duty of care means you cannot leave issues of immediate safety without full consideration, and you cannot leave the service user until you know:
  - that they will be safe when you do leave them
  - that the issue which has been raised is being dealt with
  - that there is support for the person after you have left them.

Healthcare emergencies where abuse is suspected

Should the service user be injured or unwell as a result of the incident, you should:

- give them first aid treatment (as long as you are trained to do so), but remember to inform the emergency services what you have done
- call an ambulance
- notify the police, who will arrange for a police surgeon to examine them

- follow organisational procedure and the policy for the Local Authority area
- preserve any evidence (see below).

Preserving evidence of abuse in the case of immediate reporting to the police

If a criminal offence such as assault or a sexual offence has been committed, the police will need to be notified. Who should do this will be indicated by local procedure.

The service user concerned is likely to be very distressed and may well want to have a bath or shower for reasons of cleanliness and because they feel 'dirty'. You will need to reassure the service user and comfort them until the police arrive. You will also need to explain to them what will be happening, as far as possible, which may not be easy, particularly if the person is distressed by the fact that the police are involved. Obviously, all of these conversations need to take place with the greatest sensitivity and you would need to explain to the service user why they may not be able to take a bath or shower.

Similarly, the service user may wish to change their clothes, but this must not take place until the police have arrived. Some service users may be unhappy and distressed about police involvement, as this may heighten any fears they may have about events spiralling out of their control, and it may also prompt fears of retribution by the abuser.

It is also important to ensure that the service user is not given anything to drink until the police arrive, as they may wish to take a swab from the person's mouth.

The scene of the incident should not be disturbed. Do not strip the bed, wash bedclothes or disturb any items in the room. Do not allow anyone else to go into the room until the police arrive.

If there are any tissues, condoms or other material contaminated by blood, semen or other body fluids either leave these in situ or, if this is not practical, put them in a clean envelope or glass.

Ensure that the person who has disclosed the possible abuse and the alleged abuser are kept apart – under no circumstances should one worker be supporting both people.

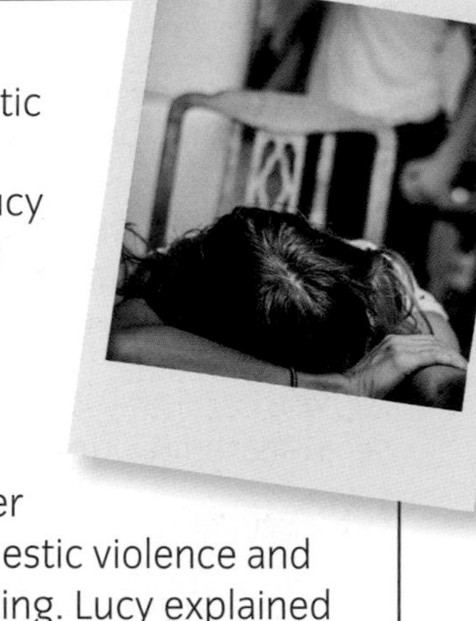

CASE STUDY

Rosie works as an outreach worker in a domestic violence service. Rosie visits Lucy at home as arranged. When she arrives at Lucy's home, Lucy is in a dressing gown and has clearly just had a shower. Rosie notices that the room is a mess, with clothes on the floor and a lamp tipped over – Lucy is normally very tidy. Lucy starts crying and tells Rosie that she invited a man back to her flat last night. He had listened to her talking about her previous experiences of domestic violence and had seemed very sympathetic and understanding. Lucy explained that as soon as they got back to the flat the man demanded sex and although Lucy asked him to leave he became violent and attacked her. Then she said that 'something terrible' happened. The man said that no one would believe Lucy as she had already been making 'accusations about other men'.

- What should Rosie do?
- Why?

Preventing 'contamination' of an investigation and any potential evidence

When a service user discloses abuse, health and social care workers need to think about not 'contaminating' evidence or hindering the investigation process. You should not stop someone recalling events, but you also need to keep in mind that it will be someone else's role – possibly the police's – to investigate and find out more information. To pursue too much detail at this stage risks compromising any subsequent investigation and could mean the service user being needlessly distressed by being asked the same questions again.

You will need to ensure that emotional and practical support is provided to the service user, who may have been the victim of the alleged abuse. You need to ensure that the organisation's procedures for dealing with abuse and your Local Authority's guidelines on protecting vulnerable adults are followed, and also that the appropriate personnel are notified according to your procedures.

Key term

Leading question is one which gives the person being asked a clear indication about the expected answer. For example, 'He hit you, didn't he?'

Preventing contamination of evidence is a key issue for health and social care workers. For example, if you suspect that abuse has been taking place and you ask a **leading question**, the potential evidence will be contaminated. So, if a health and social care worker asked something like 'He kicked you, didn't he?' or later said something like 'You're acting like this because of the abuse, aren't you?' this would make anything the service user said inadmissible in court. For this reason, it is clear how important careful recording and reporting are.

RECORDING SUSPICIONS

Recording potential signs and symptoms is important, as a picture can be built up to aid the detection of abuse.

Any abuse investigation will involve a consideration of any relevant recording. Indeed records can be used as evidence in legal proceedings, investigations and inspections.

It is important that all records follow principles of good recording (see Chapter 7). It is particularly important where there may be concerns about abuse.

PRINCIPLES OF RECORDING

- Recording should be in black ink.
- Recording should be legible. (It doesn't matter what the quality of the information is if it cannot be easily read by others. If your handwriting is poor, slow down when you write, as this may help.)
- If you make a mistake, do not use correction fluid. Cross out your mistake with a single line, ensuring that what you wrote can still be read. Initial the error. This is important because if the records are required, for whatever purpose, in the future, it is clear that they have not been falsified.
- Always attribute information being recorded to show where it came from. For example, if a service user's relative told you something, make this clear in the records. For example, 'Soriya's mother said that Soriya fell down and had a nosebleed yesterday' rather than 'Soriya fell and had a nosebleed yesterday'.
- Recording should be completed at the time and not several days later.
- Records should be dated, timed and signed by the person completing the record.
- All documentation should be objective. It should not contain information about the feelings, thoughts, instincts or assumptions of the staff member.
- Documentation should be fact based.
- Judgemental language must be avoided.

If you have concerns about abuse, or someone has made a disclosure to you about abuse, it is vital that the recording you complete follows these guidelines. If you are unsure, ask a senior worker or your manager to support you as you complete the record. Remember though that good recording should be usual practice.

WHAT SHOULD YOU DO IF SOMEONE ALLEGES THAT THEY ARE BEING ABUSED?

Responding to suspicions of abuse quickly is very important. As soon as you suspect that abuse is occurring you must report this to your line manager and get guidance on what to do next.

You should report any suspicions or concerns to your line manager immediately. If your manager is on leave or off shift, you must pass the information to whoever is responsible in their absence. *Do not* wait for your manager's return.

In reporting to your manager, you need to:

- keep the information factual
- tell your manager whether you have recorded any relevant information yet and where this is to be found
- ask your manager for guidance and ask them what will happen next.

When a service user discloses abuse, as well as passing the information on immediately, it is also important to record accurately what the service user said.

Any disclosure should be followed up with an investigation – which is almost always multi-agency. Investigations should *never* be undertaken by individual care staff. The way that the disclosure is handled and the recording and reporting of the disclosure will be vital in terms of the progress of any investigation.

Sensitive interpersonal skills are required in order to support a service user who discloses abuse (ie says that they are being abused). These skills include:

- believing the person
- showing concern
- listening effectively.

THE DOS AND DON'TS OF DISCLOSURE

If abuse is disclosed to you, you must:

- listen
- stay calm
- allow the service user to talk

- reassure the service user that they are doing the right thing by telling someone
- tell the service user that you believe them
- tell the service user that you need to pass this information on
- record accurately the date, time and place of the disclosure and what was said (using the service user's own words as far as possible)
- report the disclosure to your manager immediately.

You must not:

- ask any questions that may be 'leading' (see page 134)
- appear shocked, horrified, disgusted, etc
- pressurise the person
- ignore what you have been told
- promise to keep what you have been told a secret
- put opinions into your recording
- pass judgement on either the victim or the abuser
- confront the alleged abuser.

Recording disclosures

If a service user has disclosed abuse or the possibility of abuse, it is very important that a clear and accurate record is made of the disclosure. Making a note at the time will probably distract from the work of supporting the service user, and they may find this off-putting, but this must be done at the first possible opportunity.

If anyone who is involved with a disclosure is making notes for their own records, they must bear in mind that these may be needed for any subsequent investigation or for a court case. Any rough notes made at the time must therefore be placed in the service user's file.

Records should contain the following:

- the date, time and where the service user disclosed the information
- the date, time and place of the alleged incident disclosed by the service user, or witnessed
- the name of anyone else who was there when the alleged incident took place or anyone else who was present when the service user disclosed the information
- what the service user said in their own words
- any other information which is relevant to record, without going into unnecessary detail.

CASE STUDY

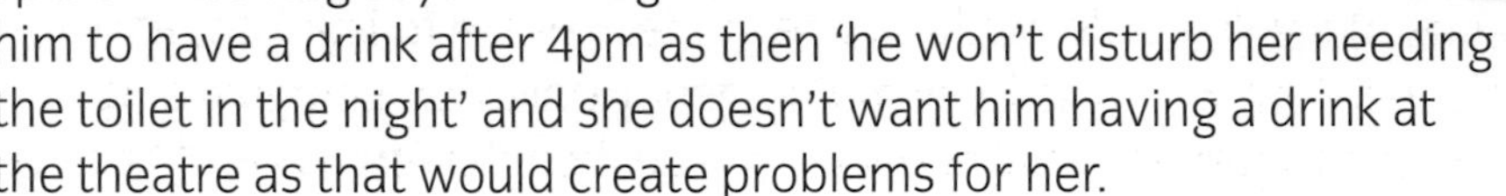

Karen works in a day service for older people. Reg attends the day service. Karen is organising a trip to the local pantomime at Christmas. It means that the service users will be back home much later than they normally are. Reg tells Karen that he would really like to go but his daughter said he can't – as she manages his money and with Christmas coming up 'there is no money to spare'. Also Reg says his daughter doesn't allow him to have a drink after 4pm as then 'he won't disturb her needing the toilet in the night' and she doesn't want him having a drink at the theatre as that would create problems for her.

- Is this a disclosure of abuse?
- What kind of disclosure?
- What should Karen do? Why?

SAFEGUARDING AND PROTECTION FROM ABUSE – NATIONAL AND LOCAL CONTEXT

There is a clear and extensive legal framework surrounding child protection. However, the legal basis for safeguarding adults from abuse is much less developed.

UNDERSTANDING THE LEGAL CONTEXT

The picture is very different across the United Kingdom. Scotland is the nation which is furthest ahead since it passed the Adult Support and Protection Act in 2007. This placed adult protection on a statutory footing. In England and Wales, the picture is much more patchy, where there is statutory guidance on the development and implementation of policies and procedures for the protection of adults at risk of abuse. In England this is called *No Secrets*, and it was published by the Department of Health and the Home Office in 2000. The Welsh guidance was published by the Welsh Assembly and the Home Office in the same year, and is called *In Safe Hands*.

No Secrets (2000)

This is guidance issued by the Department of Health in 2000; as such it does not have the full force of statute law. It is important for all health and social care staff to be aware that the government wants all agencies to take seriously and to respond as fully as possible to situations where vulnerable adults are being abused.

In *No Secrets* the Department of Health makes clear its expectations for individual providers of care to minimise the risk of abuse by:

- rigorous recruitment practices
- take-up of written references
- ensuring that all volunteers are subject to the same checks as paid staff.

Services are also to have in place guidelines detailing staff responsibilities and how they should respond to concerns about any abuse of a vulnerable adult. These guidelines are to link into, and be consistent with, the local multi-agency policy on safeguarding (bringing together social services, police, health services and provider services).

Provider services are also expected to ensure that service users, carers and the general public have accessible information detailing what abuse is, and how they can raise concerns and/or make a complaint.

Statement of Government Policy on Safeguarding: Department of Health 13 May 2011

This document sets out the government's policy on safeguarding vulnerable adults. It includes a statement of principles for use by Local Authority social services and housing, health, the police and other agencies for both developing and assessing the effectiveness of their local safeguarding arrangements.

This is a very useful document, setting out the key principles for organisations to benchmark their existing arrangements to see how they support this aim and to measure future improvements. A series of outcomes are set out as a starting point for assessing progress and the basis for locally agreed outcomes.

Safeguarding Adults Boards

As a result of the *No Secrets* guidance, Local Authorities have developed Safeguarding Adults Boards.

Safeguarding Adults Boards generally include members from local agencies engaged in health and social care, community groups and service users and carers.

The Social Care Institute for Excellence (2011a:20) states that Safeguarding Adults Boards have a strategic role to:

- determine local safeguarding policy
- oversee development and implementation of procedures
- raise public awareness
- ensure staff are trained

- monitor performance
- improve the quality of safeguarding practice.

THE *NO SECRETS* REVIEW

In 2009 the government reviewed *No Secrets*. The review involved 12,000 people and more than 68% of them supported bringing in safeguarding legislation. However, there were also arguments against legislation for safeguarding adults, including the following:

- much has been achieved in adult safeguarding without legislation, and improvements are felt to be likely to continue
- legislation will not necessarily lead to adult safeguarding becoming a priority
- the experience in Scotland should be studied over some years before conclusions are drawn
- some of the possible new legislative powers would extend the government's power over people's lives in a dangerous way
- the most effective safeguarding was when it became part of mainstream activity and was effectively part of the choice agenda.

(Department of Health 2009a:7)

FOUR KEY MESSAGES FROM THE REVIEW OF *NO SECRETS*

- Safeguarding must be built on empowerment – or listening to the victim's voice. Without this, safeguarding is experienced as safety at the expense of other qualities of life, such as self-determination and the right to family life.
- Everyone must help to empower individuals, but safeguarding decisions should be taken by the individual concerned. People wanted help with options, information and support. However, they wanted to retain control and make their own choices.
- Safeguarding adults is not like child protection. Adults do not want to be treated like children and do not want a system that was designed for children.
- The participation/representation of people who lack capacity is also important.

(Department of Health 2009a:5)

The Law Commission's review of adult social care law found that 'the existing framework for adult protection is neither systematic nor coordinated, reflecting the sporadic development of safeguarding policy over the last 25 years' (Gillen 2011:21).

What this means is that in England and Wales a kind of patchwork quilt of legislation exists – in that there is a great deal of legislation which relates to safeguarding adults from abuse. Some of the key legislation is outlined in the following table.

Legislation	What it covers
Family Law Act 1996	Makes arrangements for non-molestation orders to protect people from domestic abuse.
Youth Justice and Criminal Evidence Act 1999	Provides for special measures to be taken to support vulnerable people who are victims or witnesses to an offence.
Mental Capacity Act 2005	This introduced a new offence of ill-treatment or wilful neglect by any person who has the care of another person who lacks capacity or who the offender believes to lack capacity. A number of health and social care staff have been charged and imprisoned for this offence. Includes Deprivation of Liberty Safeguards.
Health and Social Care (Community Health and Standards) Act 2003	Although many of the provisions of this Act have been changed by the Health and Social Care Act 2008, Section 114 of the Act remains in place. This gave the government powers to issue and enforce regulations about the provision of complaints procedures in health and social care services.
Sexual Offences Act 2003	Defines 'consent' to a sexual act and outlines sexual offences clearly. Protects service users with a mental health problem or a learning disability from sexual exploitation by staff.
Domestic Violence Crime and Victims Act 2004	Makes it an offence to cause or allow the death of a vulnerable adult.
Fraud Act 2006	Created an offence to abuse a position of trust – can be used in situations of financial abuse.
Safeguarding Vulnerable Groups Act 2006	This Act set up a new system of vetting people who work with children, young people and vulnerable adults.
Forced Marriage (Civil Protection) Act 2007	Provides a range of civil remedies for the victims of forced marriage.
Health and Social Care Act 2008	Introduced wideranging changes to the regulation of health and social care services. Established the Care Quality Commission.

This demonstrates that the legislation which surrounds safeguarding adults from abuse is very complex. Legal advice should always be sought where there are any concerns.

SERVICE-SPECIFIC POLICIES AND PROCEDURES

All organisations providing health and social care services should have a policy relating specifically to safeguarding vulnerable adults – these may be referred to as POVA (Protection Of Vulnerable Adults) policies or safeguarding procedures. Health and social care staff must ensure that they are familiar with the policies which relate to their working environment.

LOCAL AUTHORITY POLICIES AND PROCEDURES

Every Local Authority in England and Wales will have locally specific policies, procedures and expectations for safeguarding adults. It is vital that you know about these in order to be able to work to local protocols and best practice, and to make the local links which you may need to access in the event of a safeguarding concern.

MULTI-AGENCY WORKING

Whenever a disclosure of abuse is made or there are suspicions of abuse, an investigation must take place. However, the responsibility for investigating situations does not lie with any one individual (even a senior manager). Alleged abuse must always be investigated in line with an agreed protocol.

Investigations will usually be multi-agency, because different agencies and individuals can offer a range of skills, knowledge about a specialist area (such as the law or medicine), different knowledge about the service user concerned, and different resources and means of support. It is this combined multi-agency approach that can offer a holistic approach both in detecting abuse and in formulating a way to best support and protect the vulnerable person.

The role of individual health and social care staff is limited in the investigation of abuse. Their role will be in contributing to the overall process of multi-agency investigation. Objective verbal and written communication, with vigilant regard for facts such as dates and times, will be the principal way in which health and social care staff contribute to the investigation of alleged abuse.

YOUR RESPONSIBILITIES

Care staff responsibilities in this area can be summarised by four points (ROCK):

- ***R**eport.* Always report any disclosure or concerns to your line manager immediately.
- ***O**bserve.* Make careful observations and record these accurately.
- ***C**are plan.* Be aware of a service user's care plan and work to it carefully. The care plan may contain specific information about reducing the risk of abuse (eg increased observation, restriction on certain visitors).
- ***K**nowledge.* Share any information and knowledge you have as necessary.

YOUR MANAGER'S RESPONSIBILITIES

A social care manager's responsibilities in relation to this area can be summarised by four points (CAMS):

- ***C**ollate.* Managers need to collate all the information which they receive from staff members and pass this on where necessary. It may be that individual staff don't have enough of the 'jigsaw', but that when the manager reviews what all staff are saying, they can recognise patterns of behaviour which may indicate abuse.
- ***A**dvise.* Managers should keep the service user and the staff team advised about the investigation process and progress (as far as confidentiality allows), and advise staff about their roles and the limits to them.
- ***M**onitor.* Managers should monitor the work of staff (for example, are they recording effectively?), and observe the service user themselves, if possible, to monitor the situation fully.
- ***S**upport.* Managers should support the service user as well as the staff working with the service user, who may find the situation distressing.

HOW DO DIFFERENT AGENCIES WORK TOGETHER?

Each agency involved has a specific role.

Local Authority social care services

Local Authorities have a key role in safeguarding adults where there are concerns about abuse. For example, they will:

- receive and manage safeguarding alerts
- coordinate adult protection investigations
- provide information and advice on safeguarding issues
- arrange and chair investigation meetings and case conferences.

Police

The police will usually be involved in investigations of abuse, and will always be involved (possibly taking the lead) where a crime is suspected. Their involvement will include:

- investigations
- gathering evidence
- pursuing criminal prosecution with the Crown Prosecution Service where relevant
- ensuring that vulnerable witnesses and vulnerable victims have access to appropriate support.

Health services

Health services, particularly doctors, will have a role in providing:

- medical treatment to people where necessary
- medical evidence.

SAFEGUARDING IS EVERYONE'S CONCERN

Despite the fact that some professionals and agencies have specific tasks in relation to safeguarding people from abuse, it is vital to recognise that safeguarding is a shared concern. Everyone has a responsibility to:

- work within their organisation's safeguarding policy and procedures
- liaise with other professionals where there are safeguarding concerns
- recognise and report the signs of abuse
- provide information and advice on safeguarding issues and support services
- work safely and report any unsafe working practices.

SERIOUS FAILURES TO PROTECT PEOPLE FROM ABUSE

There have been a variety of serious failures to protect people from abuse in both health and social care settings. Following such failures, inquiries are often set up to investigate the failings and to support people to 'learn the lessons' so that similar failings do not happen again.

It is a sad fact that in reviewing the reports into serious failures in health and social care over the last 20 years, many of the same issues arise again and again. This begs the question of when we *are* going to learn the lessons.

WINTERBOURNE VIEW

In late 2012 six workers from Winterbourne View, a private care home near Bristol, were jailed for abusing residents, following exposure by a BBC documentary. The *Panorama* programme in 2011 showed people being slapped, pinned under chairs and subjected to cold showers as punishment.

The people living in the home were subjected to appalling treatment and this exposure led to a high-profile public debate around the placement and treatment of adults with learning disabilities.

Key learning from the Serious Case Review into what happened at Winterbourne View highlights the following:

- There is a very negative perception of people with learning disabilities.
- The inspection of institutional care, and the **monitoring** of safeguarding notifications by Local Authorities is inadequate.
- There is a clear need for better planning and commissioning of services.
- Whistleblowing policies must be applied properly.
- Other forms of alert must exist.
- There needs to be an improvement in access to advocacy services.

Key term

Monitoring means keeping an eye on how something is working. Monitoring can either be done formally (on documentation, such as those prepared for review meetings), or informally (via conversation and observation).

MID STAFFORDSHIRE NHS FOUNDATION TRUST

The most in-depth inquiry in recent times into NHS failings concerned the Mid Staffordshire NHS Foundation Trust hospital in Stafford. A local pressure group of patients and relatives formed, calling themselves 'Cure the NHS', after identifying common concerns about the standard of care and treatment at the hospital. A lengthy and detailed public inquiry was held involving ministers, the Department of Health, the Care Quality Commission, the local Primary Care Trust and the West Midlands Strategic Health Authority.

The inquiry was overseen by Robert Francis QC, and his report in February 2013 made 18 recommendations for both the Trust and the government.

The evidence gathered by the inquiry shows clearly that for many patients the most basic elements of care were neglected. Calls for help to use the toilet were ignored and patients were left lying in soiled sheeting and sitting on commodes for hours, often feeling ashamed and afraid. Patients were left unwashed, at times for up to a month. Food and drinks were left out of the reach of patients and many were forced to rely on family members for help with eating. Staff failed to make basic observations and pain relief was provided late or in some cases not at all. The standards of hygiene at the hospital were well below the expected standard. Staff showed a general lack of compassion and poor standards were seen as the norm.

REFLECT

- Locate one of the reports highlighted above or research other serious failures in health and social care services.
- What 'lessons' can be learned from what went wrong?
- How might you use what you have learned to improve your own practice?

Where to find information and advice about your own role in safeguarding and protection

The organisation that you work for will have a safeguarding policy and procedures document that describes the responsibilities that all staff members have in relation to safeguarding. Responsibilities will differ according to the level of seniority. It is very important that you understand what your responsibilities are. Your manager will also be able to help you to understand your role.

There are National Occupational Standards that relate to safeguarding adults. These can be found at http://nos.ukces.org.uk/, and they explain what is expected of care workers.

SAFEGUARDING AND PROTECTION – WHAT DOES THE CODE OF CONDUCT SAY?

The importance of safeguarding in health and social care practice is recognised in the Code of Conduct for Healthcare Support Workers and Adult Social Care Workers in England 2013, which states that you must:

- always make sure that your actions or omissions do not harm a service user's health or wellbeing. You must never abuse, neglect, harm or exploit service users, their carers or your colleagues
- challenge and report dangerous, abusive, discriminatory or exploitative behaviour or practice
- always take comments and complaints seriously, respond to them in line with agreed ways of working and inform a senior member of staff
- always discuss issues of disclosure with a senior member of staff
- report any actions or omissions by yourself or colleagues that you feel may compromise the safety or care of service users and, if necessary, use whistleblowing procedures to report any suspected wrongdoing.

REDUCING THE LIKELIHOOD OF ABUSE

'You know, sometimes it feels like this. There I am standing by the shore of a swiftly flowing river and I hear the cry of a drowning man. So I jump into the river, put my arms around him, pull him to shore and apply artificial respiration. Just when he begins to breathe there is another cry for help. So, back in the river again, reaching, pulling, applying, breathing and then another yell. Again and again, without end, goes the sequence. You know I am so busy jumping in pulling them to shore, applying artificial respiration that I have no time to see who the hell is upstream pushing them all in'.

(Source unknown)

Prevention depends on accurately identifying why abuse occurs in the first place and then establishing work-based practices that aim to counter (and if possible eliminate) those factors.

As with all work in health and social care, best practice involves working proactively: in terms of abuse, this means working assertively to reduce the likelihood that abuse can occur.

If care staff understand the nature of abuse and why it can occur, the likelihood of this happening is minimised. Likewise if service users, carers and the general public are better informed about abuse they will be more aware and risks will be reduced.

Reducing the likelihood of abuse occurring is an important aspect of your role as a care worker. As the saying goes, 'prevention is better than cure'. Ensuring good care practice can be very effective in minimising the risks to service users.

'Safeguarding must be built on empowerment – or listening to the victim's voice. Without this, safeguarding is experienced as safety at the expense of other qualities of life, such as self-determination and the right to family life.'

(Department of Health 2009a:5)

HOW CAN PERSON-CENTRED PRACTICE REDUCE THE LIKELIHOOD OF ABUSE?

The likelihood of abuse occurring can be reduced (but not eliminated) by working in a person-centred way and with person-centred values at the heart of all practice (also see Chapter 9). Treating people with respect and dignity and working within the value base of health and social care increases people's self-esteem, and this in turn increases people's abilities to protect themselves and recognise and report abuse.

As well as respect and dignity, person-centred values include:

- individuality
- rights
- choice
- privacy
- independence
- partnership.

Involving service users in risk assessment is important (see Chapter 9). Services should also complete risk assessments for specific issues of concern for individuals, in a way which enables people to enjoy the dignity of taking risks, but which also ensures that risks have been fully considered in partnership with the individual. The following can help:

- encouraging active participation (see Chapters 10 and 11).
- encouraging good care practices which promote people's choices and rights – informing service users about their rights can empower them and reduce vulnerability (see Chapter 4).

Safeguarding is not something which workers do in isolation from the rest of their practice, or only in response to an incident or disclosure. It is something which cuts across all practice in health and social care, and which is an essential component of person-centred work. This is because:

- people with a voice (and who feel their voice is listened to) are more likely to say if they are being hurt or abused
- people with positive and supportive relationships around them are less likely to be vulnerable to abuse and will feel more confident that they will be listened to and believed if they are
- if people direct their own support, they are more likely to feel in control of their own lives (and therefore, to experience fewer feelings of powerlessness, vulnerability and isolation which increase the risk of abuse occurring)
- people who feel respected and important are more likely to complain if the high standards of care which they deserve are not met.

HOW DO POLICIES AND COMPLAINTS PROCEDURES REDUCE THE LIKELIHOOD OF ABUSE?

One of the ways in which health and social care services seek to reduce the risk of abuse occurring is through the development and implementation of policies and procedures that, if followed, markedly reduce the likelihood of abuse occurring in the first place. Examples of this include policies around the handling of service users' money. If this is followed by staff then service users' money and valuables should be protected, and if any allegations against staff were made then staff can produce evidence that they have acted professionally and responsibly.

This also explains why other policies have been developed, for example, policies relating to providing intimate personal care, risk assessment procedures, etc. A vital aspect of reducing the risk of abuse is therefore following all policies and guidelines carefully.

Ensuring that the service has a complaints procedure and that service users have the opportunity to complain can help to empower people, and therefore make them less vulnerable to abuse. Knowing that service users have access to an effective complaints procedure may also prevent potential perpetrators from abusing them.

An effective complaints procedure can also be helpful for health and social care workers in that it can:

- emphasise the need for a high-quality service provision
- identify areas of poor practice
- support staff to develop their practice
- clarify misunderstandings
- bring attention to lack of resources.

It is therefore important that health and social care professionals do not view complaints procedures negatively or as a threat. One difficulty can be that there is a fear that a complaint will inevitably lead to disciplinary action being taken and could lead to a person losing their job. In some organisations where the culture is quite negative or punitive, people may have grounds for thinking in this way.

This feeling can also come about because employees habitually regard a complaint as reflecting solely upon their own work. It is preferable that everyone in a service shares the understanding that complaints need to be dealt with as a reflection on the service as a whole, rather than any specific worker's failing.

Responding to complaints is covered in detail in Chapter 4.

REFLECT

In health and social care one of the best ways to prevent abuse and safeguard service users is to follow good care practices.

- What might these include? (Try to list three or four examples.)
- How might each of these be effective in preventing abuse and safeguarding people?

RECOGNISING AND REPORTING UNSAFE PRACTICES

This section should be cross-referenced with Chapters 4 and 7, on the duty of care and handling information. The need to keep safeguarding at the forefront in all aspects of health and social care practice means that it needs to be considered in everything you do in your role.

WHAT ARE UNSAFE PRACTICES?

Unsafe practices can include:

- poor working practices (either accepted practices within a service, or individual practices by workers which do not meet the expected standards)
- resource difficulties (where the resources are not available within a service to provide adequate or safe care practice)
- operational difficulties (eg where staff absence means that a service is not staffed according to a safe ratio).

HOW DO UNSAFE PRACTICES AFFECT THE WELLBEING OF SERVICE USERS?

If practices such as those outlined above take place within a service, service users are not going to receive a standard of care and support which:

- is individual to their needs
- is sufficient for their needs to be met
- respects their dignity and uniqueness
- is safe.

WHAT IS THE LEGAL FRAMEWORK SURROUNDING REPORTING UNSAFE PRACTICES?

Workers who identify and report unsafe practices are protected by thc law. Stating this does not make it easier to take action, but it is important that workers know about the legislative duty and protection in order for anyone to feel able to escalate issues appropriately.

PUBLIC INTEREST DISCLOSURE ACT 1998

This is often referred to as the 'whistleblowers' legislation', and was implemented in July 1999. This Act gives significant statutory protection to employees who disclose malpractice reasonably and responsibly in the public interest and are victimised as a result. If an employee is victimised or dismissed for this disclosure they can make a claim for compensation to an industrial tribunal. There is no cap to the amount that can be awarded.

While it is not a statutory requirement, there is an expectation that organisations will establish their own whistleblowing policy and guidelines. These guidelines should:

- clearly indicate how staff can raise concerns about malpractice
- make a clear organisational commitment to take concerns seriously and to protect people from victimisation
- designate a senior manager with specific responsibility for addressing concerns in confidence which need to be handled outside the usual management chain.

Staff receive the full protection of the Act if they seek to disclose malpractice responsibly, ie by following the organisation's whistleblowing policy or guidelines.

WHAT ACTIONS SHOULD BE TAKEN IF UNSAFE PRACTICES ARE IDENTIFIED?

Where unsafe practices are identified, you have a duty to report them. This forms part of your duty of care to those you support (see Chapter 4). Part of this duty as a professional in the field of health and social care means that:

- you cannot ignore practices that are unsafe and that impact on service users' rights and wellbeing
- you have to report concerns
- you should expect to justify your concerns with evidence, knowledge and understanding of the impact of unsafe practices.

WHAT ACTIONS SHOULD BE TAKEN IF NOTHING IS DONE IN RESPONSE TO REPORTING?

If you report a concern, identify a practice as unsafe in your service or inform your employer that a colleague's practice is unsafe or abusive, you should expect the person you inform to take action. It is reasonable that, where a colleague's practice has to be investigated, you may not get to know all of the detail of this investigation or its outcome (eg if a person were to be disciplined for a conduct issue at work). However, you should expect that:

- the person you tell records what you are concerned about and why
- the person should take your concerns seriously
- the person agrees with you what will happen in terms of feedback to you following this
- the person should identify sources of support (either internally or externally) and recognise that coming forward and sharing concerns is not easy to do.

If you have reported concerns and the above does not happen, or if you do not see change as a result of the action, there are other actions you may need to consider taking, such as:

- escalating the issue to the next level of management
- talking to your union
- notifying the Local Authority and/or police (in cases where someone is being abused, you would follow safeguarding procedures immediately anyway, as described elsewhere in this chapter)
- notifying the regulator (the Care Quality Commission).

SUMMARISING THE CONCERNS PROCESS

In Chapter 4 you explored the fact that your duty of care involves making any concerns you have clear and known. You should remember this concept in raising concerns about any aspect of practice.

The basic stages to raising concerns is as follows:

1 Raise concerns with your manager.

If nothing is done:

2 Raise the concerns with senior managers.

If nothing is done:

3 Raise concerns with whoever is in charge of the organisation (Director, Chief Executive, etc).

If nothing is done:

4 Raise concerns with the regulator (Care Quality Commission).

Keep a record of your concerns and the responses you have had at every stage of the process.

CASE STUDY

Sonia works in a residential service for older people. She is concerned that a number of her colleagues show a lack of compassion in supporting residents. She has recently noted that staff have started to use incontinence wear for residents who could use the toilet if they were given assistance. When she talks to her colleagues about this they say it's easier to use the incontinence wear than support residents to use the toilet and that some shifts are so short-staffed they have to put ease of work first.

- Should Sonia talk to anyone about her concerns?
- Why?
- What action should she take?

Before going to the next chapter, take some time to consider:

- what you know about the signs and symptoms of abuse
- how confident you are that you would be able to identify abuse
- whether you know what to do if you suspect that someone is being abused
- whether you understand the national and local context of safeguarding and protection from abuse
- how what you do at work reduces the likelihood of abuse
- how you would report unsafe practice, and why it is important that you do this.

CHAPTER 6

Contribute to health and safety in health and social care

Health and safety issues are important in all work settings and sectors. However, in health and social care settings you are working with people who have particular vulnerabilities and specific care needs, so this means that you need to be especially vigilant in relation to health and safety at work.

Links to other units

As health and safety underpins all work in health and social care the content of this chapter links to all the other chapters in the book. There are particular links with Chapters 5 and 7.

HEALTH AND SAFETY - THE LEGAL FRAMEWORK

It is important that health and social care workers understand their own responsibilities and the responsibilities of others in relation to health and safety. Responsibilities in terms of health and safety are drawn from legislation and associated policies and procedures.

The main piece of legislation relating to health and safety is the Health and Safety at Work Act of 1974.

HEALTH AND SAFETY AT WORK ACT 1974

This Act outlines a number of responsibilities for employers, managers and employees.

Employers have a duty to:

- ensure the health and safety at work of all employees
- provide and maintain equipment and systems which are safe and not a risk to employees' health in terms of use, handling, storage and transport of articles and substances
- provide information, training and supervision relating to health and safety at work.

Managers have a duty to:

- maintain a safe working environment for all staff
- ensure that all staff adhere to policies, procedures and instructions
- provide training for staff practices and work methods
- explain **hazards** and safe working practices to new employees before they start work
- report/record all accidents.

Employees have a duty to:

- adhere to instructions relating to the operation of a site and equipment
- ensure that they use materials in line with recommended procedures
- utilise protective clothing and equipment as directed
- not misuse anything provided for health, safety and welfare.

Key term

Hazard is a possible source of harm.

THE 'UMBRELLA' EFFECT

The Health and Safety at Work Act 1974 is known as an umbrella piece of legislation. It covers a wide range of areas and a number of associated regulations are issued underneath the 'umbrella' of the original Act. Regulations are used in health and safety as they are more easily changed than an Act of Parliament, and health and safety issues need to be kept under constant review.

ASSOCIATED REGULATIONS

There are a range of regulations in the health and safety area, including:

- Management of Health and Safety at Work Regulations 1996
- Reporting of Injuries, Diseases and Dangerous Occurrences Regulations (RIDDOR) 2013
- Workplace (Health, Safety and Welfare) Regulations 1992
- Regulatory Reform (Fire Safety) Order 2005
- Control of Substances Hazardous to Health Regulations (COSHH) 2002
- Provision and Use of Equipment Regulations (PUWER) 1998
- Lifting Operations and Lifting Equipment Regulations (LOLER) 1998
- Safety Representatives and Safety Committees Regulations 1997
- Manual Handling Operations Regulations 1992
- Health and Safety (Display Screen Equipment) Regulations 1992
- Health and Safety (First Aid) Regulations 1981
- Food Hygiene Regulations 2006
- Health and Safety (Consultation with Employees) Regulations 1996

These are covered in more detail throughout this chapter.

To aid compliance, the Health and Safety Executive (HSE) implements new regulations on only two dates per year:

- 6 April
- 1 October.

The idea behind implementing new regulations only twice a year is to enable organisations to foresee change and plan for it. The HSE publishes an excellent (and brief) overview of current legislation – 'Health and Safety Regulation… a short guide HSC13'. This can be downloaded from the HSE website at www.hse.gov.uk.

The HSE is the national independent regulator for health and safety in the workplace, and as such it covers all workplaces. The HSE works in partnership with sector-specific regulators, so in relation to health and social care it works closely with the Care Quality Commission and Local Authorities to inspect, investigate and where necessary take enforcement action.

The HSE recognises that health and social care is a sector in which health and safety issues are vitally important. It therefore provides a range of information specifically for health and social care services on its website. This is worth reviewing as you work towards completing this unit.

Another Act which relates to health and safety at work and provides information on responsibilities is the Corporate Manslaughter and Corporate Homicide Act 2007.

This Act covers fatal accidents and redefines the offence of corporate manslaughter. In order for a case of corporate manslaughter to be brought:

- a death occurs – obvious really, but if someone is 'only' severely injured, standard health and safety legislation still applies
- the death does not have to be of an employee of the company concerned, but it does have to result from the way that company's activities were managed or organised
- also, the death must have arisen from a gross breach of the company's duty of care to the victim
- lastly, the organisational failings that led to the death must have been somehow authorised by senior management – that is to say, practices that were authored, or agreed to, or known about by senior management; senior management does not just include directors.

This Act demonstrates the vital importance of all health and social care staff being clear about policy and procedure and following this consistently. It also highlights how important it is for management to:

- ensure that policy, practice and risk assessments are fit for purpose
- keep policy and practice under review
- monitor whether staff follow policy and procedure.

HEALTH AND SAFETY REGULATION IN HEALTH AND SOCIAL CARE

You should have read your organisation's health and safety policies during your induction. It is worth revisiting these now to ensure that you are fully informed about the relevant policies and procedures.

RESEARCH

Make a list of all your organisation's policies and procedures that relate to health and safety in some way, and ensure that you have read them carefully. If you struggle to follow any of the policies for any reason make a note of this and ensure that you discuss this with your manager.

SAFETY REPRESENTATIVES AND SAFETY COMMITTEES REGULATIONS

If an employer recognises a trade union and that union has either appointed or is about to appoint safety representatives, then the employer must consult those representatives on matters which will affect the employees they represent.

The roles of trade union safety representatives appointed under these regulations are:

- to investigate possible dangers at work, the causes of accidents and general complaints by employees on health and safety and welfare issues and to take these matters up with the employer
- to carry out inspections of the workplace, particularly following accidents, outbreaks of disease or other events
- to represent employees in discussions with health and safety inspectors and to receive certain information from those inspectors
- to attend meetings of safety committees.

An employer must set up a safety committee if two or more trade union representatives ask for one.

WORKPLACE (HEALTH, SAFETY AND WELFARE) REGULATIONS

These regulations complement the Management of Health and Safety at Work Regulations, and cover the management of workplaces. Duties are placed on both employers and employees (in the sense that both have control over a workplace).

The main requirements created by these regulations are as follows:

- the workplace, equipment, systems, etc must be maintained in an efficient state and good repair
- enclosed workplaces must be ventilated by a sufficient quantity of fresh and purified air
- a reasonable temperature must be maintained inside buildings and a sufficient number of thermometers must be provided
- lighting must be suitable and sufficient
- workplaces must be kept sufficiently clean.

HEALTH AND SAFETY POLICIES AND PROCEDURES IN HEALTH AND SOCIAL CARE

Key terms

Policy in health and social care is a written statement explaining the service or agency's expected approach to an issue, area of practice or key aspect of people's work. Policies can be local and/or national.

Procedure is an agreed and understood way or order of doing something at work.

Policies and **procedures** go together.

WHAT ARE POLICIES AND PROCEDURES?

Policies are usually written and formal. Meanwhile, procedures may be:

- presented in writing, or in a flowchart or other formats
- formal, or
- informal – an informal procedure would be something that workers understand they follow in the work setting, but that is not necessarily written out, eg the way in which they are expected to greet and sign visitors in.

Policies and procedures will differ in every service setting. Health and social care workers need to have a working knowledge of their agency's policies and procedures in order to carry out their responsibilities in terms of health and safety. As a minimum, workers will need to be familiar with the policies and procedures covering the following:

- communicable diseases/infection control policy
- confidentiality and information disclosure
- control of exposure to hazardous waste (based on the COSHH regulations)

- fire safety
- hygiene and food safety
- record-keeping and access to files
- moving and handling
- dealing with accidents and emergencies
- responding to abuse.

It is important that all services have policies and procedures that reflect national legislation and good practice guidelines in this area. As an individual worker you may not have very much control over the nature of an organisation's policies, particularly if you work for a large organisation. However, you should:

- be aware of the legislative context in which you operate
- know about relevant policies and procedures and know how to access them if you need to
- understand policy and procedure
- keep up to date with necessary training to enable you to put policy safely into practice.

USING POLICY AND PROCEDURE – SMALL THINGS DO MATTER

In terms of health and safety, candidates may be unsure about the evidence they need to provide in this area. It is important to remember that a competent health and social care worker should generate the necessary evidence of health and safety as a matter of course, as it is central to all good practice in health and social care.

Workers who provide personal care will need to use gloves, aprons and so on in their work and are therefore likely to have evidence of their competence in terms of health and safety. However, all health and social care workers will work to health and safety requirements. For example, think about:

- using the kettle safely when making a cup of tea
- using the shredding machine
- moving a box to a different area in a store cupboard in an appropriate way
- supporting a service user to use a kettle, cooker or vacuum cleaner
- supporting a service user to cross a road
- using a computer safely or organising desk space.

The list goes on and on. These may seem incredibly obvious examples, but often health and social care workers miss them. Providing evidence of health and safety doesn't mean workers need to do anything new or different – it's about the detail of everyday health and social care practice.

WHY HAVE POLICIES AND PROCEDURES?

Policies and procedures are necessary in all sectors, but perhaps more so in health and social care for various reasons, to ensure:

- legal compliance – legislation (for example, National Minimum Standards) requires services to have policies and procedures in specific areas
- consistent practice – clear policies and procedures will ensure consistent practice in a staff team, and staff will be aware of minimum standards for their practice
- increasing confidence – having policies and procedures which are clearly stated can increase confidence in the service from the perspective of the service users, their families and carers.

BEING CLEAR ABOUT ROLES AND RESPONSIBILITIES

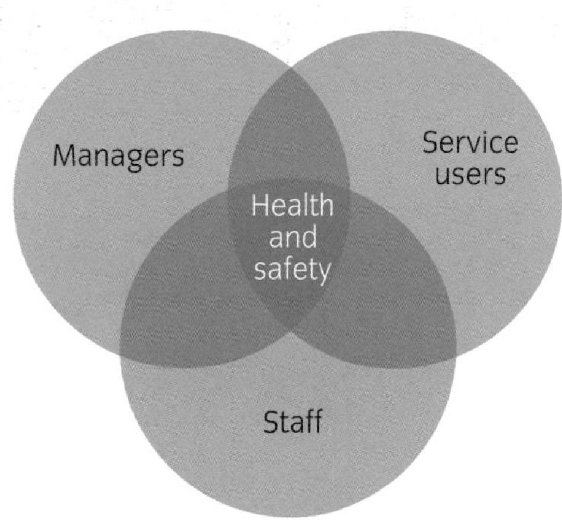

Health and safety in any workplace is a shared responsibility.

Under health and safety legislation managers have specific responsibilities. These include:

- ensuring that all equipment is properly maintained and safe to use
- explaining health and safety procedures to new staff
- providing training to enable staff to follow all necessary procedures and to use equipment safely
- assessing any risks of harm that could arise in work and taking steps to reduce risks of harm to a minimum
- providing protective clothing such as gloves and aprons.

Arguably the three key health and safety responsibilities that fall on management relate to:

- ensuring that all staff are familiar with health and safety practices
- monitoring staff compliance with procedures
- assessing new risks as they arise and either addressing these within the service or involving others to address and manage the risks.

Equally, under health and safety legislation all staff have a responsibility to:

- follow all instructions and procedures to ensure risks of harm are minimised
- use any protective clothing as expected (eg gloves, aprons)
- act responsibly
- report any dangerous occurrences, accidents, etc to the senior member of staff on duty; also to report any avoidable health and safety risks in the environment.

Service users also have a responsibility in terms of health and safety – but the extent of this will depend on their circumstances.

MAXIMISING SERVICE USER INVOLVEMENT

Values should always inform our practice. Involving service users in discussions about health and safety conveys respect and the fact that service users have a responsibility to maintain certain standards around health and safety if they are able to.

Discussions with service users could relate to what to do following an accident, supporting the service user to maintain their own personal hygiene or assisting them to follow accepted guidance on handling food safely.

Discussing matters with service users conveys to both the service user and colleagues that such involvement is a key aspect of good practice.

RESPONSIBILITIES TOWARDS NEW WORKERS

Health and social care workers are often involved in supporting new colleagues within a team. New workers need to have an induction plan, which should include:

- a tour of the service, highlighting health and safety and security matters
- shadowing a colleague as they carry out their ordinary responsibilities, and asking the colleague to talk through health, safety and security matters
- reading through policies, procedures and summaries of key regulations and legislation or having this talked through by a staff member
- watching health and safety training DVDs or related websites

KEY POINT

It is proposed that the Common Induction Standards will be replaced in England by a new Care Certificate in 2015.

- completing or meeting the Common induction standards for adult social care – it is expected that these will be replaced in 2015 by a new Care Certificate
- going to training events about health and safety matters
- reading through some care plans and discussing the risk assessments and management plans with other workers.

ONGOING RESPONSIBILITIES

Health and social care workers are likely to communicate regularly about health and safety issues within services. This communication is part of everyone taking an active responsibility for their own wellbeing and that of service users. Examples might include:

- at the beginning of a working day, discussing issues relevant to that day
- at team meetings, having a health and safety 'slot' on the agenda
- discussing 'buddying' arrangements each day in a service which involves lone working
- use of written forms of communication such as notebooks or memos
- discussions about changes to policies in supervision sessions.

The list could go on – the idea is that health and safety should not be seen as something extra to good practice, or a chore that is imposed by external forces, but as something integral to all good health and social care work.

HEALTH AND SAFETY (CONSULTATION WITH EMPLOYEES) REGULATIONS

Any employees not in groups covered by trade union safety representatives must be consulted by their employers under these regulations. An employer can choose to consult them directly or through elected representatives.

Elected representatives of employees have the following roles:

- to take up with employers concerns about possible risks and dangerous events in the workplace that may affect the employees they represent
- to take up with employers general matters affecting the health and safety of the employees they represent
- to represent the employees who elected them in consultations with health and safety inspectors.

Employers may choose to give elected representatives extra roles.

SPECIFIC TASKS THAT REQUIRE SPECIAL TRAINING

Some tasks cannot be carried out without specific training for the following reasons:

- because of your liability for and duty of care to the people you support
- because of your employer's duties and responsibilities to you and to the service users
- because it is not safe or appropriate for people with care needs to receive certain interventions if people have not had the right training.

These tasks include:

- moving and handling
- use of equipment
- first aid
- administering some types of medication
- clinical interventions
- preparing food.

RESEARCH

Talk to your manager about what tasks require special training with regard to health and safety. Are you up to date with this special training?

ACCESSING ADDITIONAL SUPPORT OR INFORMATION RELATING TO HEALTH AND SAFETY

Additional support and information about health and safety will be available from:

- your managers
- your colleagues
- training providers
- the internet (eg the HSE website)
- books and leaflets
- Local Authority and service health and safety advisors, trainers and experts.

It is part of your responsibility as a professional in the field of health and social care to know your duties, know your limitations and know your learning needs, and to access help, advice, training, information and support when you need this.

CARRYING OUT YOUR RESPONSIBILITIES FOR HEALTH AND SAFETY

Now that you understand the responsibilities that you and others have, you need to think about how you can carry out these responsibilities and how you can support others to carry out their role safely.

Using policies and procedures

You have explored policy and procedure in relation to health and safety and revisited them in relation to your work role. It is important now to think about the impact that they actually have on your work. Try developing a table which works through the following:

Policy/ Procedure	Impact this has on my work	What difficulties I encounter	What I can do to address these difficulties
Infection control	I wear gloves and an apron. I use cleansing gel on my hands between visits.	I do not always have a full supply of gloves. I feel uncomfortable putting on gloves – it feels very clinical.	Talk to my manager – to ensure that I have a sufficient supply of gloves.

The policies, procedures and agreed ways of working you cover in this table should be those that are most relevant to your role, and might include:

- fire safety procedures (drills, exit points, expectations in the event of a fire) – these are likely to be formal because of employers' legal duties regarding building and fire safety, but for social care workers who support people in their homes, these may not be quite so formal
- procedures for cleaning and storage of cleaning products (linked to COSHH)
- food preparation responsibilities and procedures
- procedures for access to buildings and information
- procedures for storage and administering medication to people

- procedures and expectations for storage of your own belongings and your own medication
- risk assessment policies, paperwork and procedures
- procedures to monitor safety warnings and equipment
- lone working systems and policies
- agreed ways of opening up and locking up a building safely
- expectations regarding training for and use of equipment (eg for moving and handling).

CASE STUDY

Lauren is completing her Level 2 Diploma in Health and Social Care. Lauren is particularly concerned about how she can provide evidence of health and safety. She therefore spends some time creating a table like the one shown on page 166. Lauren's assessor, Sarah, visits for an assessment discussion. Lauren and Sarah sit together at a desk – Lauren shows Sarah the table she has completed. During their discussion Lauren notices that Sarah's bag handles are trailing on the floor and she asks Sarah if she can move these. Sarah later explains to Lauren that the fact that she signed Sarah in to the building and the fact that she noticed her bag handles were creating a hazard provides evidence along with the notes she has completed. Lauren realises that providing evidence of her work in terms of health and safety might not be as difficult as she first thought.

- Why might Lauren have been concerned about providing evidence for the health and safety unit?

USING RISK ASSESSMENT IN RELATION TO HEALTH AND SAFETY

Following on from the responsibilities that health and social care workers have in terms of health and safety, it is vitally important that they are familiar with the importance of risk assessments. Some of the key concepts of risk assessments are covered in detail in Chapter 9.

MANAGEMENT OF HEALTH AND SAFETY AT WORK REGULATIONS

These regulations place on employers a duty to assess all health and safety risks associated with their work, and to introduce procedures and practices that minimise the likelihood of any identified risks occurring.

Additionally, employers have to provide training for staff:

- when they start work
- when their work or responsibilities change and there are new or greater risks
- periodically if needed – for instance, if the skills do not get used regularly.

The training must be during working hours and not at the expense of employees.

The Management of Health and Safety at Work Regulations place a legal responsibility on employers to carry out a risk assessment as the first step in ensuring a healthy and safe workplace. Risk assessments should identify possible hazards, assess the likelihood of harm resulting, and identify what measures could be taken to manage or minimise the risks.

HAZARDS AND RISKS

In understanding risk assessment it is important to be clear about the difference between a hazard and a risk. Essentially a hazard is something that has the potential to cause harm. For example, a sharp knife is a hazard.

Risk is about how likely the hazard is to actually cause harm. The hazard in itself does not necessarily represent a significant risk – the risk arising from a hazard will be different for different people and in different circumstances. For example, the sharp knife poses a significant risk to a child, who has little understanding of the hazard; however, the risk to a butcher who uses sharp knives on a daily basis would be very low.

To minimise risks you need to work through three steps:

1 Identify the hazard.
2 Identify the possible risks from the hazard.
3 Identify 'control measures' – what controls can be used to minimise the risk?

Some risks are easier to minimise than others, as the table on the next page demonstrates.

Hazard	Possible risks arising from the hazard	Control measures (ideas to minimise risk)
Trailing wires	• A person could trip and fall – this is a particular risk for someone who has mobility difficulties.	• Use a cable tidy, or move items around so they do not trail in people's way.
Wet floor	• A person could slip and fall – this is a particular risk for someone who has mobility difficulties.	• Put a barrier around the wet area of the floor to prevent people slipping. • Use a 'Wet Floor' sign to warn people. • Dry the floor.
Smoking	• Short term – risk of fire. • Long term – health risks.	• Education on the risks – not smoking indoors. • Education on the risks and support to stop smoking.
Medication	• Possible overdose or a person using medication which isn't theirs – particular risk if someone is confused.	• Secure storage of medication. • Training for people who administer medication. • Supporting people to self-medicate where appropriate.
Bleach on the table	• A person could drink the bleach – this is a particular risk if someone is confused.	• Ensure correct labelling, store safely.
Cars (when out in the community)	• A person could be involved in a road traffic accident – this is a particular risk if someone has poor pedestrian skills.	• Provide education and support in road safety and training in pedestrian skills.
Bodily fluids (when carrying out a personal care task)	• There is a risk of cross-infection.	• Wear personal protective clothing. • Dispose of any soiled items or bodily fluids following the agreed procedure.

If you identify a health and safety risk you must report this to your line manager as soon as possible. This is one of your legal responsibilities.

UNDERTAKING A RISK ASSESSMENT

The HSE (2006) has identified five steps in undertaking a risk assessment.

1 Identify and document possible hazards.
2 Identify who might be at risk of harm and what form the harm might take.
3 Evaluate risks arising from hazards and determine whether any existing precautionary measures are sufficient.
4 Complete a risk assessment.
5 Review the assessment periodically and update if necessary.

Aside from the legal requirement to produce and use risk assessments, there are further reasons to do so:

- They provide a measure of protection to the service user and to others who may be either directly or indirectly at risk. If specific risks such as those in relation to moving and handling or falls are completed for a service user, this can have a significant impact in preventing accidents or incidents.
- They provide protection to you, which may be by safeguarding you from a possible consequence of taking the risk, and by ensuring that you can justify any actions you take with respect to the risk.
- They can also help to protect other people, including the general public who may be exposed to risk.

USING RISK ASSESSMENT TO ADDRESS DILEMMAS

Chapter 4 covered the way that dilemmas and conflicts can occur between the duty of care and upholding rights and choices. Similar dilemmas can be caused where there is a delicate balance between a person's rights and health and safety concerns.

You will find reading pages 98–101 useful in helping you to recognise the way that risk assessment and adopting effective risk management strategies can be helpful in addressing such dilemmas.

Over-protection

It is widely recognised that services have in the past often been too protective of people. Services have always sought to minimise or eliminate any risk of harm, be it emotional, mental or physical. It is now accepted that the attempt to eliminate all risk undermines people's dignity and inhibits opportunities for personal development and growth. Often care environments that reduce risk as much as possible result in impoverished environments (ie a care environment which does not promote the person's rights, dignity and choices). Effective practice in risk assessment within care environments is about balance.

Risk taking is an integral part of daily life and is a significant way of supporting service users to maintain a sense of achievement and fulfilment. When risk is carefully assessed and handled in a planned and conscious way it can be a great springboard for promoting the rights and choices of all service users.

RESEARCH

Look into the risk assessments that exist in your service.

- Which issues and needs have been subject to a risk assessment?
- How often are these reviewed?
- Who is responsible for reviewing them?
- How could you have input into future reviews?

RESPONDING TO ACCIDENTS AND SUDDEN ILLNESS

In any work setting, a range of accidents or sudden illnesses could occur and create an emergency situation. In health and social care work, we are working with individuals who often need services because there are increased risks to their health and wellbeing.

The following accidents could occur:

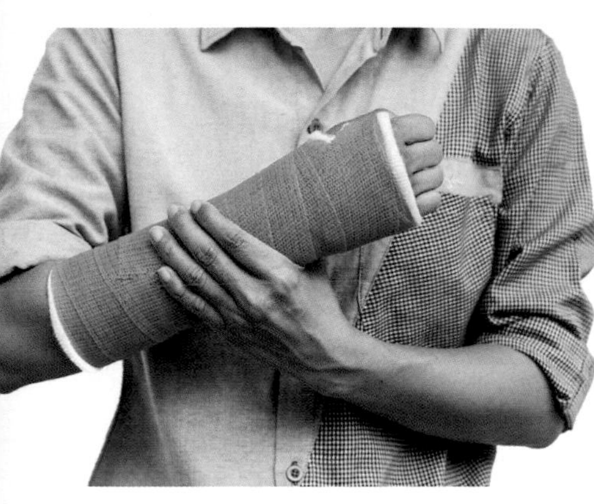

- fire
- falls
- trips
- spills
- road accidents (eg where a service user is accessing a resource in the community, or being transported as one of a group)
- scalds or burns
- fractures or broken bones
- cuts causing sudden or severe bleeding.

Sudden illnesses could also occur (either to you, colleagues or service users, although service users may be more vulnerable to certain conditions), such as:

- heart attack/cardiac arrest
- asthma and respiratory difficulties
- epileptic seizure
- losing consciousness
- choking.

PROCEDURES TO BE FOLLOWED IF AN ACCIDENT OR SUDDEN ILLNESS OCCURS

Every service or setting will have its own procedures for responding in the event of accidents or sudden illness. It is important that you are aware of these before an event occurs, as it is no use in an emergency if you have to go and find out what to do when you should be doing it.

One of the key skills of a competent worker is to remain calm and not to add to the sense of drama or crisis by panicking, or by getting angry or irritated.

If you are the first person at an emergency scene (or the first person who appears able to act), your response should include the following:

- assessing the emergency
- maintaining your own and others' safety
- summoning help
- supporting the casualty
- understanding your own limitations
- handing over the casualty to the emergency services and giving them relevant information
- seeking appropriate support for yourself and others, if required
- completing the appropriate paperwork.

Assessing the emergency

It is important that you remain calm and try to think rationally. Trying to gauge the casualty's condition is helpful.

There may be environmental clues as to why the emergency has occurred (eg a cord from a vacuum cleaner lying across the floor).

Maintaining your own safety

If there is anything you can do to make the area safe, then you should do it. It is often more important for you to make sure that you are safe first, so that you can respond better to the needs of others who require support in a crisis situation. There may be others who are more experienced or more able to deal with the person who needs immediate help.

Summoning help

If the emergency situation occurs in a care home or a day centre you will usually need to call for the manager on duty. It will usually be up to the senior staff member to either call the emergency services or delegate that task to another staff member.

If the incident occurs in a service user's own home, you may well be working alone. You may be able to contact the emergency services while remaining with the casualty.

Supporting the casualty

If the person is conscious, you should inform them of what has been done, and ask them what happened and how they feel.

Administer first aid if you are trained and authorised to do so.

Handing over the casualty to the emergency services

When the emergency services arrive, you should inform them about:

- what you know about the cause of the emergency and when it happened
- the casualty's name and relevant personal information
- what actions you have undertaken
- any changes in the casualty's condition that you have observed, eg when did they become unconscious?

HEALTH AND SAFETY (FIRST AID) REGULATIONS 1981

These regulations require employers to provide adequate equipment, facilities and personnel to enable first aid to be given to employees if they become ill or are injured at work. The regulations do not oblige employers to provide first aid for members of the public, although the HSE strongly recommends that employers make provision for them.

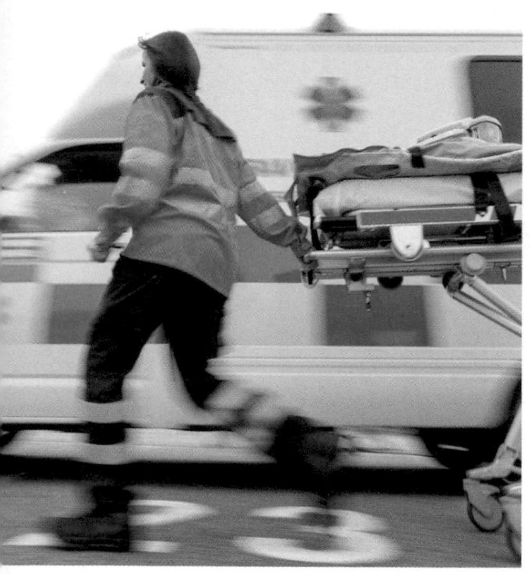

BEING CLEAR ABOUT YOUR ROLE

In all aspects of health and social care, you should be clear about your role and responsibilities, to work within this framework and not to exceed your role (or competence). This is never more important than when dealing with emergencies at work. If you exceed your role in an emergency, you may well put your own safety and perhaps even your life (and others' lives) at serious risk.

It is difficult to explore the whole range of potential emergencies in any detail. You will know what sort of emergencies may occur in your own work setting and should also be familiar with the policies and protocols that are in place to give guidance on the management of these emergencies.

REFLECT

- Have you ever been in a crisis situation in your work?
- What were the policies and procedures that you followed?
- How did you feel, and what support were you offered at the time and afterwards?

RESEARCH

- Find out who the trained first aiders are in your service. What training is available to you, and how would you access this?
- What procedures does your current employer have in place for dealing with accidents or sudden illness?
- Does your employer have regular test runs of these procedures to make sure everyone is confident about what they should do in an emergency?

CASE STUDY

Emily is a home care worker. She arrives at a visit to find that Mrs Hamilton is lying on the floor in the bathroom. She appears to have fallen during the night. Emily speaks to Mrs Hamilton to ask how she feels. Mrs Hamilton says her leg is very painful and she feels like 'such a fool'. Emily tells Mrs Hamilton that she will phone an ambulance. Emily then phones an ambulance and stays close to Mrs Hamilton, holding her hand to reassure her. Emily goes to the door to let the paramedics in and she explains what has happened and what Mrs Hamilton's general care needs are. She provides them with some basic information. The paramedics take Mrs Hamilton to hospital. Emily comes out of the house at the same time and ensures that the property is locked up. Emily then sits in her car and phones her manager to explain what has happened, and then phones Mrs Hamilton's daughter to advise her that her mother is on her way to the local hospital.

- Why does Emily leave the property at the same time as the paramedics left with Mrs Hamilton?
- How does what Emily does reflect the requirements for responding to accidents?

REDUCING THE SPREAD OF INFECTION

This subject is covered in detail in Chapter 14.

In relation to health and safety you need to know and be able to use the recommended procedure for handwashing covered on pages 420–1. You also need to know how to ensure that your own health and hygiene do not pose a risk to others.

MOVING AND HANDLING EQUIPMENT AND OTHER OBJECTS SAFELY

MANUAL HANDLING OPERATIONS REGULATIONS 1992

These regulations contain the following main requirements:

- Suitable and sufficient risk assessment of all moving and handling should be made, if the handling cannot be avoided.
- Risk reduction strategies must be considered by employers to reduce the risk of injury to the lowest level reasonably practicable.
- Employers must provide reasonable information about moving and handling.
- Employers must review assessments where there is reason to suspect that circumstances have changed, and then make any necessary changes.
- Employees must make full and proper use of any system of work provided by the employer.

PROVISION AND USE OF EQUIPMENT REGULATIONS (PUWER) 1998

These regulations impose a range of duties on employers (and to a limited extent to the employees who use the equipment). Aspects covered by them include:

- the initial state of the equipment
- use of equipment for the proper purpose
- suitability of equipment
- maintenance
- inspection
- training staff in its use.

The scope of these regulations has been interpreted very broadly so that it includes, for example, cupboards and curtain rails as well as equipment that is subject to heavy usage. The employer's liability is no longer strictly applied. However, employers must maintain all work equipment in a safe condition in line with the manufacturer's and regulatory guidelines, and employees must be suitably trained to operate work equipment.

LIFTING OPERATIONS AND LIFTING EQUIPMENT REGULATIONS (LOLER) 1998

These regulations apply to lifting equipment used at work. (Lifting equipment includes hoists, stairlifts and through-floor lifts.) The regulations impose a range of duties on employers and to a limited extent on staff who use or supervise the use of the equipment.

Duties include:

- ensuring adequate strength and stability of equipment
- safe positioning and installation
- marking of safe working loads
- organisation of lifting operations
- examination and inspection
- reporting defects, and acting on these reports.

All lifting equipment must be maintained and serviced in line with the manufacturer's guidelines. As well as being subjected to a regular maintenance programme, lifting equipment is required under LOLER to be 'fit for purpose, appropriate for the task, suitably marked and, in many cases, subject to statutory periodic "thorough examination"'. Where lifting equipment is used to carry people, as is often the case in health and social care, then a 'thorough examination' should be carried out by an appropriate person (often via an insurance company) at least every six months. The HSE has written an Approved Code of Practice called 'Safe use of lifting equipment (L113)' which clearly sets out the legal requirements for the use and maintenance of lifting equipment.

PRINCIPLES FOR SAFE MOVING AND HANDLING

Moving and handling includes:

- moving objects in the work setting (eg boxes, water cylinders, filing cabinets, bags of rubbish)
- supporting people to move.

The key principles when moving and handling items are as follows:

- *Avoid.* Do not undertake any moving or handling without having had the necessary training (eg to use specific equipment).
- Do not undertake moving and handling if you do not feel it is safe to do so.

- *Assess.* Ensure that moving and handling activities have been properly risk assessed.
- In risk assessing moving and handling, consider the following TILE model:
    - **T**ask (what is the precise task that is required; what factors make the task more or less difficult to achieve; what obstacles might there be, etc?)
    - **I**ndividual (what specific needs, capabilities or difficulties does the individual doing the moving or handling need to consider for themselves to be able to perform the task safely?)
    - **L**oad (consider the actual load which the task presents, and how this load can be moved most safely)
    - **E**quipment and **E**nvironment (consider the impact of temperature, space, flooring, hazards, posture, handles on equipment, wheels, training, and maintenance of equipment).
    - More information on the TILE model is available on the HSE website: http://www.hse.gov.uk/msd/pushpull/risks.htm.
- *Reduce risk.* Do not undertake any moving or handling without the right equipment.
- Do not undertake moving and handling by yourself if the task actually requires more than one person to do it safely.
- *Review.* Following any moving or handling activity, review how it went, and update risk assessments as required for future activities.

Remember: If in doubt, don't do it.

SUPPORTING A SERVICE USER TO MOVE

The first and most important principle links to the value base of social care – in order for practice to be person-centred, service users should be involved in planning any moving of themselves. They are not objects to be moved about without their full involvement and active participation in this form of personal support. Service users should be supported with the minimum of input from others – ie they should be supported where they need support, and enabled and empowered to do everything for themselves which they can do. This is an area where the principles of active support are at their most apparent and powerful.

Use of hoists should only be undertaken by workers who have been trained to use this equipment, and the safety of hoists, stairlifts and other equipment involved in moving service users should be regularly reviewed.

In terms of legislation (and your duty of care), it is your employer's responsibility to provide the necessary tools, equipment and training for moving and handling to be done safely, and it is your duty to use them safely and appropriately for individual service users.

CASE STUDY

Tara is a care assistant in a day service for older people. The service building is due to be decorated. The service manager tells staff that while the decorating is being done, the conservatory is going to be used as the seating area. The manager then asks Tara and one of her colleagues to move the furniture from the main room into the conservatory – he says that the service users will prefer their usual chairs rather than the ones in the conservatory. This will mean Tara and her colleague moving eight large chairs and the full-sized television into the conservatory. Tara is concerned that these chairs are extremely heavy.

- What could Tara do in this scenario?
- How can she ensure that proper moving and handling procedures are followed?

REFLECT

Have you been involved in a moving and handling activity (either at work or in your personal life, eg lifting items when moving house) that has caused you concern?

- What could you and others have done to make this activity safer?
- If your role involves moving people, how do you achieve the principles of active support?

RESEARCH

If your job role involves moving and handling, review the risk assessments on the equipment in your work setting. When were these last reviewed, and how do reviews take account of the need for any changes?

HANDLING HAZARDOUS SUBSTANCES AND MATERIALS

Substances can be hazardous in a range of ways:

- explosive
- flammable
- toxic
- irritant
- corrosive
- harmful to the environment.

HAZARDOUS SUBSTANCES THAT MAY BE FOUND AT WORK

In health and social care settings, hazardous substances can include:

- cleaning products and bleach
- office equipment (eg correction fluid and photocopier/printer cartridges)
- needles and sharps
- medical equipment (eg used dressings and linen)
- **medicines.**

Key term
Medicine is a drug that is used to diagnose, prevent or treat an illness.

All such items will need:

- clear labelling
- risk assessing
- controlled access
- safe storage
- a file to be kept with information on them for all team members to access.

CONTROL OF SUBSTANCES HAZARDOUS TO HEALTH REGULATIONS 2002

These regulations are often referred to as COSHH.

The regulations cover substances which can cause ill-health, such as cleaning materials, waste products, fumes and so on.

In order to comply with the regulations, employers must:

- assess the risks to health arising from work
- decide what precautions are needed
- prevent or control exposure to substances hazardous to health
- ensure that control measures are used and maintained
- monitor exposure of workers to hazardous substances and, where assessment shows that health surveillance may be needed, carry out such surveillance
- ensure that employees are properly informed, trained and supervised.

STORING, USING AND DISPOSING OF HAZARDOUS SUBSTANCES AND MATERIALS

As described, both you and your employer have specific responsibilities for ensuring safe practices with regard to COSHH. The table below details some of these responsibilities.

Responsibility of the employer	Responsibility of the employee
Ensure there is an assessment of the risks to health arising from work from COSHH.	Assess the risks to health arising from work.
Decide what specific precautions are needed.	Know about the precautions that have been identified, and follow them.
Prevent or control exposure to substances hazardous to health.	Prevent or control exposure to substances hazardous to health (for you, your colleagues and service users).
Ensure that control measures are used and maintained.	Ensure that control measures are used and maintained.
Monitor exposure of workers to hazardous substances and, where assessment shows that health surveillance may be needed, carry out such surveillance.	You may be involved in monitoring the exposure of others to hazardous substances, or in carrying out surveillance (recording/reporting) of the impact of COSHH on you or other people.
Ensure that employees are properly informed, trained and supervised.	Access the training which is made available, and put the learning from this training into practice.

Storing hazardous substances

You should follow agreed procedures for storing substances that are potentially harmful. These could involve:

- use of a lockable cabinet (eg for cleaning products)
- safe storage of sharps
- procedures to ensure that cabinets and storage facilities have limited access and that they are locked up at all times when they are not in use.

Using hazardous substances

This sounds self-explanatory, but your service is likely to have procedures and/or informal expectations in place in order to ensure that substances are used safely and appropriately. For example:

Key term

Personal protective equipment (PPE) most commonly includes gloves and aprons.

- ensuring that there is no cross-contamination, where two substances are mixed when they should not be
- making sure that substances are used in the right/safe quantities
- using the right containers to put products in
- using **personal protective equipment (PPE)** where required.

Disposing of hazardous substances

Disposal of hazardous substances is critical in order to ensure that there is no harm caused to people and the environment.

Some items must be disposed of in certain ways (eg sharps and dressings). Sometimes there will be best practices for disposal (eg of bodily fluids or human waste) which will include agreed expectations about how a work area is then cleared and made safe after the substance has been disposed of.

REFLECT

- In your work setting, how do you apply the above principles relating to COSHH?
- What training have you had on this, and how are you involved in reviewing and updating or amending risk assessments for COSHH?

RESEARCH

Look at the HSE website and the information on COSHH. How does your agency or service meet its duties with regard to hazardous substances?

PROMOTING FIRE SAFETY AT WORK

Employers have a set of responsibilities relating to fire safety.

REGULATORY REFORM (FIRE SAFETY) ORDER 2005

This statutory instrument reforms the fire safety regulations that apply to England and Wales.

In any workplace the employer has a responsibility to:

- take fire precautions to ensure, as far as possible, the safety of all employees
- ensure that there are general fire precautions to keep the property safe (and so protect the general public) (article 8).

The employer's duties include:

- carrying out a risk assessment to identify the general fire precautions that are needed (article 9)
- applying any fire prevention measures and having in place an evacuation procedure (articles 10 to 18)
- informing employees of the risks and the fire prevention measures (articles 19 to 21).

Employees have duties, which include (article 23):

- following all fire safety requirements as directed by their employer
- informing the employer of any risks not adequately addressed.

UNDERSTANDING FIRE PREVENTION

Prevention is better than cure, especially when it comes to fire. Employers and services must have specific measures in place to ensure that fire safety is considered, for example:

- electrical checks
- risk assessments
- regular fire drills
- fire exits with clear standard labelling
- signing in and out procedures (in a portable form which can be taken out of a premises for a register check in the event of a fire)
- fire alarms (regularly tested)
- fire wardens with specific responsibilities

- fire extinguishers in key places in the premises
- fire blankets
- training on fire safety (updated regularly)
- posters to show where the designated fire assembly point is (all service users, staff members, visitors and contractors should be made aware of this when they access the premises or service).

All fires involve:

- oxygen
- heat
- a fuel (something that burns).

Without any one of these factors in place, a fire cannot start.

In order for any fire to be put out safely, one or more of the contributing factors must to be tackled/removed.

FIRE EXTINGUISHERS

You need to have awareness of which colour fire extinguisher is used for which type of fire. Extinguishers should always be labelled, but it still is helpful for you to have basic knowledge of them. You should always read instructions before you activate any extinguisher, and if you are uncertain, it is better to evacuate everyone safely instead of tackling a fire and possibly causing greater harm.

For solid-fuelled fires, you usually need to point the extinguisher at the bottom of the flames and move it across the area of the fire. For all fires, make sure that all of the flames are out before you finish using the extinguisher.

Colour on extinguisher	Contents	Use on	Do not use on
Red 	Water	• Solids, eg paper, cloth, wood	• Electrical fires • Burning liquids

Colour on extinguisher	Contents	Use on	Do not use on
Black	Carbon dioxide (CO_2)	• Some liquids, eg paint, petrol, fats • Electrical fires	• Chip pan or fat fires • Do not use in areas without sufficient ventilation, as fumes can be harmful
Blue	Multi-purpose dry powder	• Solids, eg paper, cloth, wood • Some liquids, eg paint, petrol, fats • Electrical fires	• Chip pan or fat fires
Blue	Standard dry powder	• Some liquids, eg paint, petrol, fats	• Chip pan or fat fires
Cream	AFFF (Aqueous Film Forming Foam)	• Solids, eg paper, cloth, wood • Some liquids, eg paint, petrol, fats	• Chip pan or fat fires • Electrical fires
Fire blanket		• Can be used on both solids and liquids • Make sure the whole fire is completely covered in order to cut off the oxygen supply to the fire	

EMERGENCY FIRE PROCEDURES

The emergency procedures are likely to be slightly different in every work setting you access, and it is important that you familiarise yourself with the following in every setting that you work in:

- all procedures, including how to raise the alarm
- fire exits
- the responsible person for fire safety
- telephone points
- risk assessments relating to fire
- the fire assembly point.

Bear in mind that when you provide care in a service user's home, this is a very different setting from a day care centre or residential provision.

Standard procedures and expectations in the event of a fire

1. Sound the alarm.
2. Call the fire brigade.
3. Evacuate the premises – safely and without causing increased risk. In health and social care settings, the needs, mobility and vulnerability of service users should be considered and addressed at all times. Planning and identifying specific actions and necessary support is a critical element of good fire risk assessment in social care. You need to know about people's individual needs as part of your job role, and you need to enable people to move if they can do so themselves, or to be moved quickly and safely in the event of any emergency. As part of this, you also need to know what your service setting's expectations are about people who cannot be safely moved to a safe area in an emergency.
4. Do not stop for belongings.
5. Do not use lifts.
6. Do not try to be a hero – the fire service are the experts. If you feel it is safe to, attempt to use the correct extinguisher to attack the fire, but if it is not safe, it is better to evacuate the building and let the fire service do their job.
7. Consider your own safety – for example, do not take hold of a door handle which may be very hot and present a risk to you – test it with the back of your hand instead.
8. Go to the identified fire assembly point.
9. Take the register out so you know who is in the building and can check that everyone is out.
10. Do not go back to the service premises until it is safe to do so.

Ensuring that clear evacuation routes are maintained

Trailing wires, office equipment, clutter in people's homes or frayed carpets could all cause a hazard in the event of an emergency evacuation because of a fire, bomb threat, chemical spill or any other reason. Maintaining vigilance, updating risk assessments, monitoring and reporting any concerns and completing regular tests or practices of service procedures are all critical in order to ensure that, if an emergency does occur, evacuation is swift and safe.

It is essential to maintain clear routes for evacuation.

REFLECT

- What are the procedures for fire safety in your work setting?
- Have you signed anything to say that you have read and understood these?
- On a scale of 1 to 10, how confident do you feel in applying these procedures in an emergency?
- If you feel you have further training needs, or that you have identified issues with your work environment, this is a good opportunity to flag these up.

RESEARCH

What are the expectations in your service around the following:

- Fire training; risk assessment; emergency evacuation (especially of vulnerable people); fire extinguishers; fire notices; assembly points, etc?
- If you work in service users' own homes, how do you put all of the above into practice?

IMPLEMENTING SECURITY MEASURES AT WORK

Ensuring the security of information is covered in more detail in Chapter 7.

ENSURING THE SECURITY OF PREMISES AND INFORMATION

Ensuring the security of premises is important in order to keep service users, colleagues, yourself and information safe and secure. Each work setting is likely to have different procedures, and for health and social care workers who support people in their homes these procedures are likely to be very informal in their nature (but no less important for that).

Agreed procedures and systems may include:

- use of doors and locks where people's identity is checked before the door is released
- asking people for their identity badge (many have a number on the back for the person's employer which you can ring to verify the person's identity)
- ensuring people sign in and out of buildings (for fire purposes and for verifying who was in the building on any day)
- use of logbooks or day books
- verifying people's identity with their employer (especially where there may be concerns and double-checking is felt to be needed)
- calling people back on the telephone when they have rung in for information, so that you can check their identity
- using agreed policies for access to records and formal requests for information from other agencies
- ensuring that contractors sign a document to show that they understand local/service safety procedures – this also provides a record that their identity has been checked.

For your assessment for your qualification, you are likely to need to demonstrate your understanding of your service's procedures, and your application of these procedures in a consistent way in your practice.

PROTECTING YOUR OWN SECURITY AND THE SECURITY OF OTHERS AT WORK

Measures to protect your own security and those of colleagues and service users include:

- training in risk identification, assessment and minimisation
- gaining confidence in using procedures (eg emergency procedures, and procedures for locking up a building at the end of a day)
- tools and measures to secure people's personal belongings
- learning skills for de-escalating situations
- using tools that are within the work environment (eg limiting access to the building or areas of the facility).

In health and social care, workers need to be skilled in protecting themselves and those they work with. Organisations should provide workers with the information to enable them to work through the following steps:

1 Identify potential risks.
2 Avoid potentially dangerous situations.
3 De-escalate.
4 Disengage.
5 Call for help.
6 Use appropriate physical interventions.

Because staff work in a wide range of areas it is difficult to give examples that apply to all workers. Therefore, what follows is bound to be limited. Workers do need to develop their own sense of risk awareness and to plan what to do should a situation become dangerous.

Identify potential risks

In terms of identifying the behaviour an individual may engage in, the biggest single indicating factor is previous behaviour. If a service user has been violent in the recent past, there is a risk that they could be violent at some point in the future.

If a service user is on the whole reasonable, but once they drink alcohol they become aggressive, then the consumption of alcohol is a risk factor. If a service user is in group care (at a day centre or residential care home) and the presence of certain other service users triggers an aggressive cycle, then that would be a risk factor.

Avoid potentially dangerous situations

Having a sense of the potential risks should lead you to seek to minimise the likelihood of an aggressive incident occurring. Once a potential risk is identified, how to manage this should be included in a care plan. The service user should also have been consulted about what response you and other workers will be required to take.

De-escalate

It may be possible to calm a situation that has started to become of concern. Tactics for **de-escalation** include remaining calm, listening to the person and, wherever possible, acknowledging that the service user has a point. Emphasise that their concern can be pursued through 'normal' routes, eg following the complaints procedure.

Key term

De-escalation refers to techniques used to calm people down.

Disengage

You need to be aware that leaving a potentially dangerous situation is a legitimate and responsible action to take if you feel threatened.

You may enter a situation that you quickly perceive to be potentially dangerous. To keep open the option of leaving, you need to consider practical aspects such as remaining near the door.

Call for help

You should be aware of how to summon assistance. This is usually easiest when an incident occurs in a service or office. Home care staff working alone are the most vulnerable, and it is essential that they know how to call for help.

Use appropriate physical interventions

Any staff who are expected to use physical intervention will receive training as to what is expected and what physical interventions are acceptable. They will rehearse applying these in training.

One common feature of such training is to convey that using physical interventions should be the option of last resort.

If any staff member is in a situation that is so threatening that they are actively concerned for their own wellbeing, then there is a common law right to use reasonable and proportionate force for the purpose of self-defence. It is worth checking within your own service for any expectations which your employer may have in place around this. This may be expressed within a policy, or may be more informally understood.

LONE WORKING – ENSURING THAT OTHERS KNOW YOUR WHEREABOUTS

In health and social care, workers are frequently doing their jobs in situations where there may be risks:

- to people who are being supported
- to the worker themselves – these could be risks presented either from the person being supported, from relatives or others known to the person, or from others in the community.

You may well be working in very isolated settings, and it is important that someone knows of your whereabouts at all times. This should be done via the service or employer, as it is not appropriate in terms of confidentiality for your own family or friends to know the addresses of service users who you work with.

Most services have – or should have – agreed and understood procedures in place to ensure the safety of workers who provide services in people's homes and in the community. These procedures might involve the following:

- Signing in and out of the office – usually the administrator or manager should monitor the 'in and out' board and flag any concerns if people do not return at the time they have specified they are due back.

- A named buddy for out-of-office-hours work – so someone knows where you are, what time you are due out and what to do (ie call a manager or the police) if you do not buddy in at an agreed time or respond to their efforts to contact you.
- Most services that depend primarily on lone workers will consider in detail specific issues in the risk assessment for lone working. For example, if you are working in the community, you will need to consider such things as finding service users' homes, where you should park for a visit (ensuring that if you need to leave somewhere suddenly for your own safety, you can do so), what to do in extreme weather conditions and so on.
- Using a system which the service purchases from an independent agency (or call centre). In these systems, the worker texts or calls in to a central point of contact which coordinates the information on workers' visits, and knows when the worker has said they are due to be out of a visit. The coordinator also has a number of a named person to contact if the worker does not make contact at the designated time.

Of course, all of these systems are only effective in keeping workers safe if they are used regularly by everyone in the team, and if their effectiveness is tested and reviewed.

Even where all your work is within one building, it is still important that others know your whereabouts within that building, and know what to do if you are not where you should be.

REFLECT

- Have there ever been occasions when you have felt unsafe at work?
- What did you do, or what could you have done differently?
- If you work out of hours and in the community, how are buddying/lone working policies and procedures applied and implemented? Are there any gaps which you can identify in your local procedures?

MANAGING YOUR OWN STRESS

Stress can have positive as well as negative effects, but in the context of this chapter the word is used to refer to negative stress. For most of us, especially at work, a little pressure can be helpful as it enables us to feel motivated and able to respond. Stress is the result of pressure becoming too much, and therefore overwhelming.

Stress is a feature of everyday life, but is particularly relevant in health and social care, which is about working with people who need support, are often vulnerable and who can display behaviours that challenge.

There is no specific regulation that addresses stress at work, but under the Health and Safety at Work Act 1974 and Management of Health and Safety at Work Regulations 1999, employers must ensure the safety and welfare of their staff. This includes minimising the risk of stress-related illness.

The HSE has produced the Management Standards to support employers in managing and reducing and workplace stressors. The Management Standards identify headings as the main contributors to workplace stress:

- *Demands.* This includes issues such as workload, work patterns and the work environment.
- *Control.* How much say the person has in the way they do their work.
- *Support.* This includes the encouragement, sponsorship and resources provided by the organisation, line management and colleagues.
- *Relationships.* This includes promoting positive working to avoid conflict and dealing with unacceptable behaviour.
- *Role.* This is about whether people understand their roles within the organisation and whether the organisation ensures that they do not have conflicting roles.
- *Change.* This is about how organisational change (large or small) is managed and communicated in the organisation.

(Source: HSE)

As with other workplace hazards, your employer will have carried out a risk assessment for employee stress that will set out the measures to reduce the risks as far as practicable. The next section looks at how you can help to reduce stress.

WHAT ARE THE SIGNS AND INDICATORS OF STRESS?

Everyone reacts to stress in different ways. However, people generally react to stress in three dimensions – physical (sometimes referred to as physiological), emotional (psychological) and behavioural.

Behavioural responses involve significant changes in a person's behaviour

Physiological responses are based on a stimulation of the autonomic nervous system, and changes in bodily systems

Psychological responses include strong negative emotions, anger, anxiety, irritation, depression, etc. These are accompanied by changes in cognition, including decreased self-esteem

The signs and symptoms of stress are generally seen in all three dimensions.

Physical reactions to stress

Someone experiencing stress might experience the following:

- muscle tension
- aches and pains
- sweating
- twitches
- pins and needles
- nausea
- dry mouth
- tiredness
- headaches
- frequent urination
- dilated pupils
- rapid or uneven heartbeat
- sleep disturbance
- restlessness and fidgeting
- indigestion
- hair loss
- chest pain or tightening
- high blood pressure
- butterflies in the stomach
- rapid breathing
- constipation or diarrhoea
- palpitations
- changes in appetite
- lack of concentration.

Our bodies react to chronic stress in the same way as to an emergency situation. This is the 'fight or flight' response, where our bodies become prepared for reaction by stress hormones and surges of adrenaline. Our physical symptoms of stress are caused by these hormones. Usually the fight or flight response is self-limiting, and once danger has passed, we return to normal, but in chronic stress the reaction persists.

Emotional reactions to stress

Someone who is experiencing stress may have exaggerated emotional reactions. They may feel:

- anxious
- under pressure
- mentally drained
- fear
- frustration
- anger
- irritable
- tearful

- unable to relax
- conflicting emotions
- gloomy
- embarrassed
- agitated
- suspicious
- restless
- indecisive
- negative.

Behavioural reactions to stress

Someone experiencing stress might do the following:

- sleep much less than usual or much more than usual
- become irritable and snap at people
- smoke more than usual
- over- or under-eat
- become dependent on drink or drugs
- change their sexual behaviour (loss of interest, increase in casual sex)
- become withdrawn where they were once very sociable
- engage in behaviours to constantly seek reassurance
- make more mistakes
- engage in self-harming behaviours
- engage in obsessive-type behaviours (eg excessively checking that things are switched off).

STRESS IN HEALTH AND SOCIAL CARE WORK

Research indicates that health and social care is one of the occupations where work-related stress is most common. The research identifies that this is because of the following work characteristics:

- long hours
- poor work–life balance
- the speed of work expected
- lack of clarity about requirements
- overloaded work schedule
- lack of support
- significant consequences when things go wrong
- high emotional demands at work
- lack of recognition and value
- regular changes in the work environment
- conflicts of values
- risk of violence and harassment.

(Milczarek, Schneider and Gonzalez 2009)

UNDERSTANDING YOUR OWN STRESS

As everyone is different, what makes you feel stressed and the way in which you show your stress will be unique.

How to recognise the signs of stress

It is important to be fully aware of the signs and symptoms of stress, as covered on pages 193–4. However, when people are experiencing chronic stress they are often unable to recognise the signs of stress in themselves.

It is much more likely that those around you will recognise the signs of stress and the changes in your behaviour.

There are a range of warning signs that someone is experiencing 'dangerous levels' of stress:

- thinking you are indispensable
- negative thoughts
- extreme, exaggerated or misplaced emotional reactions
- getting away from the workplace physically, but not being able to properly 'switch off' mentally
- fatigue and lack of energy
- frequent illness
- poor relationships.

Is stress controlling you?

Remember, the aim is not to eradicate all stress – the aim is to use stress positively and to ensure that you are controlling stress, rather than the other way around. As part of keeping your stress diary regularly ask yourself the following questions:

- When I feel agitated, do I know how to quickly calm and soothe myself?
- Can I easily let go of my anger?
- Can I turn to others to help me calm down and feel better?
- When my energy is low, can I boost it easily?
- Do I often feel tense or tight somewhere in my body?
- Does conflict absorb my time and attention?

FACTORS THAT TRIGGER YOUR STRESS

Everyone is different, and we all have different resilience and triggers for stress. The following is a non-exhaustive list of possible factors which cause stress in health and social care practice:

- *A busy workload.* Most health and social care workers understand this stressor all too well. There are often not enough hours in the day to do all the things that need doing, and it is stressful for well-motivated and caring professionals to feel sometimes that they are not giving the best possible service to people because of their workload.
- Likewise, health and social care work frequently involves long hours and shift work, and you may feel tired and stressed at the end of a long and busy day or week.
- *Issues in your personal life.* You may work to the best of your ability, but sometimes when there are issues outside of work, this does impact on work itself. Modern life is busy and stressful, and it can be harder to be as focused and calm at work in difficult times as you may be when you are happy.
- *Working with individuals who challenge you.* Health and social care workers should be experienced in remaining calm, professional and respectful in work. We all know, though, that some service users respond better to different workers, and sometimes the work itself can be challenging. Service users who display behaviour that challenges can bring into question your sense of your own skills in your job role. We all need support at times to consider and address the impact that this can have at work.
- *Feeling unsupported by colleagues and/or managers.* This one is perhaps obvious, but maybe this is a greater cause of pressure in times of tight budgets and anxiety over the future of some services.
- As mentioned above, people often feel extremely stressed when their own job role may be at risk, and uncertainty about the future causes stress for most people.
- Working with other agencies and professionals who have a different view of an issue can be challenging and stressful.
- Not having the resources you may need or wish for to do your job is challenging and likely to create stress.
- Dealing with safeguarding issues or concerns is stressful, and you need to acknowledge the impact this has on you personally.
- You may have your own health issues to deal with.
- Many workers feel increasingly isolated in the role – perhaps more so when providing support in service users' own homes – you may feel less of a team and therefore less supported by colleagues.
- Keeping up with paperwork can be difficult for some people, or particularly difficult in some work settings. The paperwork never reduces, and certainly never goes away; this is harder for some workers than others to deal with.

REFLECT

- Which of the factors on the previous page cause you stress in your work?
- Consider that how you experience and handle stress is really about getting a balance between the demands that you face and the resources (strategies) that you can use to meet these demands.

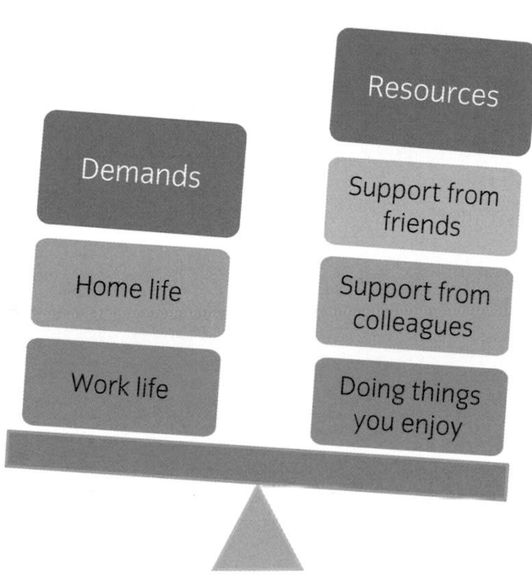

DEVELOPING A PERSONAL STRESS MANAGEMENT PLAN

Stress is a very personal experience, and what helps one person deal with stress won't necessarily work for another – so stress management plans need to be unique to every individual. In developing your own personal stress management plan you need to think about the following:

- *Recognise.* How do you know when you are stressed?
- *Reduce.* How can you reduce the stress in your life?
- *Reverse.* What helps you to de-stress?
- *Resilience.* How can you develop your **resilience** to stress?

The remainder of this chapter should help you to develop your personal stress management plan.

Key term

Resilience is best defined as a person's ability to 'bounce back'.

Strategies for managing personal stress

Again, everybody's strategies for managing stress are different, and ideas that work well for some people will not work for others. There are some strategies that people use which are not helpful in the long term (such as an alcoholic drink or a big bar of chocolate after a stressful day).

It is important for you to know what works best for you, and apply the principle of 'self-care' to your work and life. Caring for yourself enables you to care effectively for others, and not doing so makes you ineffective.

Here are some ideas for self-care:

- exercise – letting off steam through exercise is proven to help and improve mental wellbeing
- keeping a diary (bearing confidentiality in mind)
- keeping up with friends
- taking time to relax (music, TV, walks or whatever works for you)
- laughter (often the best tonic in the world)
- hobbies
- taking care of animals (again, proven to help reduce stress)
- trying relaxation techniques
- herbal teas and health foods
- doing something to make a clear distinction or break between work time and your own time, such as going for a walk, reading for half an hour or going to the gym.

Here are some other ideas that could help reduce stress at work:

- Talk to your manager. If you have not had supervision for a while, make sure you ask for this. There is nothing 'weak' or wrong in acknowledging that the work you do is stressful, and asking for the help that you need to do the job to the best of your ability. Doing this is actually part of the duty of care for those you work with.
- If paperwork is an issue, are there adaptations that can be made to help you get back on track and stay up to date with recording? Can time be set aside to help you get up to date? Can others help you with this? Often, spending time worrying about this is not productive, and sitting down and doing some helps to relieve the stress.
- Many employers provide confidential and free counselling or telephone support for staff.
- If a service user is causing you concern or causing you to feel stressed because of their behaviour or needs, it can be helpful to take advice from your manager, access training or talk to colleagues about what works for them in dealing with this person. Also, accessing specialist input from other agencies can help.

If the stress continues despite trying these strategies or other techniques that work for you, you should talk to your GP. Stress that endures will limit you both in and out of work.

Developing a 'stress aid kit'

First aid kits are an essential requirement in every workplace, and we all know how important they are in terms of health and safety. A 'stress aid kit' builds on the same idea. A personal stress aid kit should be made up of things you find helpful in combatting or addressing stress. So for example, a stress aid kit might include:

- a favourite music CD or DVD
- something that encourages you to take time out – this might be something as simple as some bubble bath
- a favourite book or magazine
- some special treats
- positive images and photographs that bring back happy memories.

REFLECT

What would you include in a personal stress aid kit?

TOP TIPS FOR STRESS MANAGEMENT

The International Stress Management Association (2009) recommends the following top ten tips for avoiding stress:

- Learn to manage your time more effectively.
- Adopt a healthy lifestyle.
- Know your limitations and don't take too much on.
- Find out what causes you stress.
- Avoid unnecessary conflict.
- Accept the things you cannot change.
- Take time out to relax and recharge your batteries.
- Find time to meet friends.
- Try to see things differently; develop a positive thinking style.
- Avoid using alcohol, nicotine and caffeine as coping mechanisms.

REFLECT

- What works for you in managing stress?
- Which strategies work less well for you?
- Is there a strategy you have not tried before, which you could make a deliberate effort to implement, and then reflect on whether this works for you?

CASE STUDY

Melanie has been a home care worker for 15 years. She has a regular group of people to support and works early mornings. Melanie has always enjoyed her job. However, Melanie's daughter Lily is 16 and she has recently been diagnosed with an eating disorder; Melanie has been taking her to lots of hospital appointments. Melanie's husband does not understand Lily's condition and thinks that Melanie should be telling Lily to 'pull herself together', and this is putting a strain on Melanie's relationships at home. Melanie is finding her work increasingly stressful and she finds she is often in tears in the car between visits. Melanie has never found her work stressful before, but she now finds herself dreading work. She realises that her home life is having an impact on her work, and feels totally unsupported. Melanie decides to talk to her manager about how she is feeling. Melanie's manager is very supportive and Melanie finds that talking to someone about how she is feeling really helps. Melanie's manager suggests that they have more regular meetings until Melanie feels better about work.

- Why might Melanie be finding her work more stressful than usual?
- Is it a good idea for Melanie to talk to her manager? Why?
- What else could Melanie do to reduce the stress she is experiencing?

Before going to the next chapter, take some time to consider:

- what you see as your responsibilities in terms of health and safety
- how clear you are about the purpose of risk assessments
- whether you feel confident that you would know what to do in the event of an accident or sudden illness
- whether you know how to identify when you are feeling stressed
- how you will take care of yourself to ensure that you are not adversely affected by stress.

CHAPTER 7

Handle information in health and social care settings

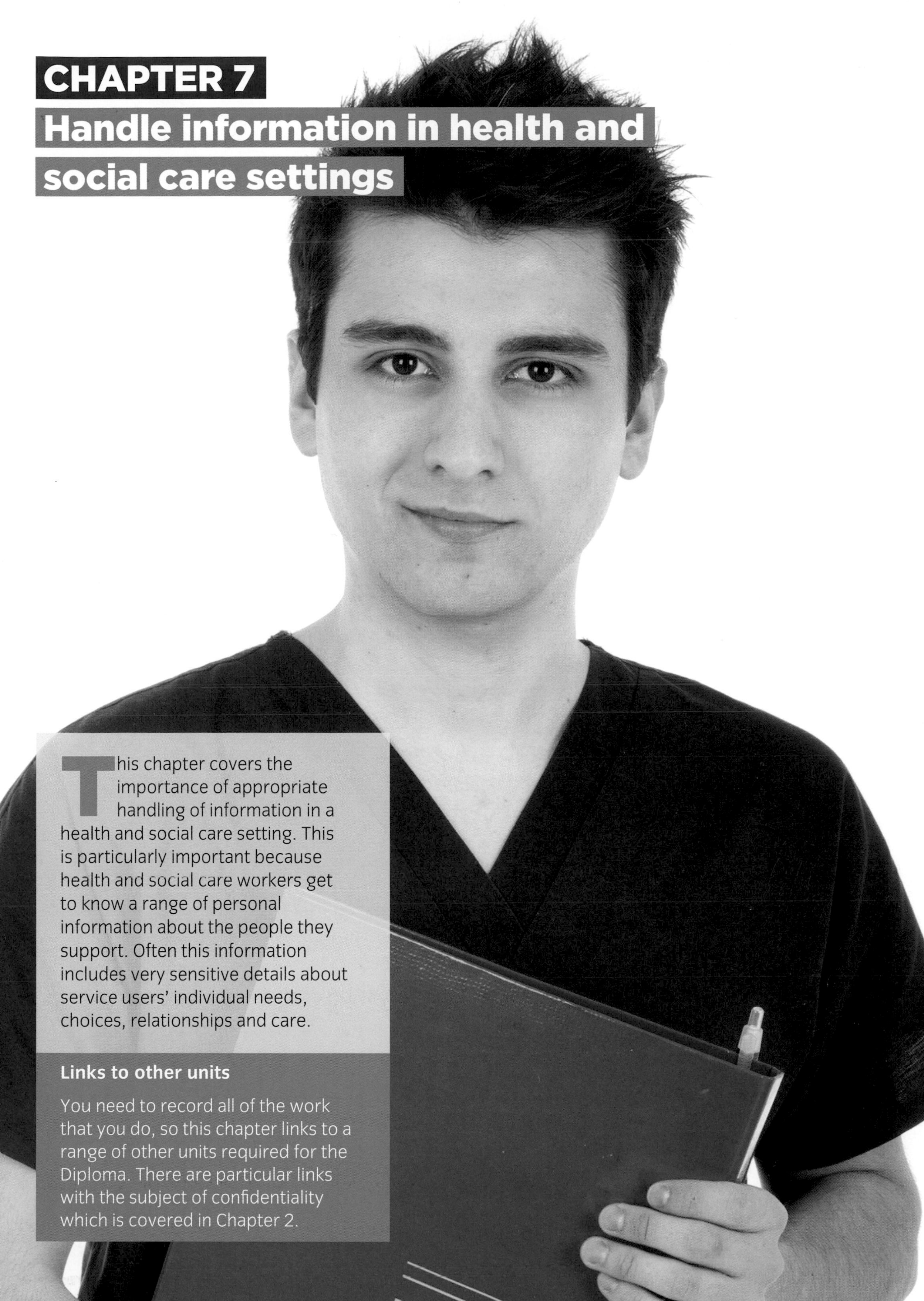

This chapter covers the importance of appropriate handling of information in a health and social care setting. This is particularly important because health and social care workers get to know a range of personal information about the people they support. Often this information includes very sensitive details about service users' individual needs, choices, relationships and care.

Links to other units

You need to record all of the work that you do, so this chapter links to a range of other units required for the Diploma. There are particular links with the subject of confidentiality which is covered in Chapter 2.

SECURE HANDLING OF INFORMATION

Handling information is an umbrella term which covers three areas:

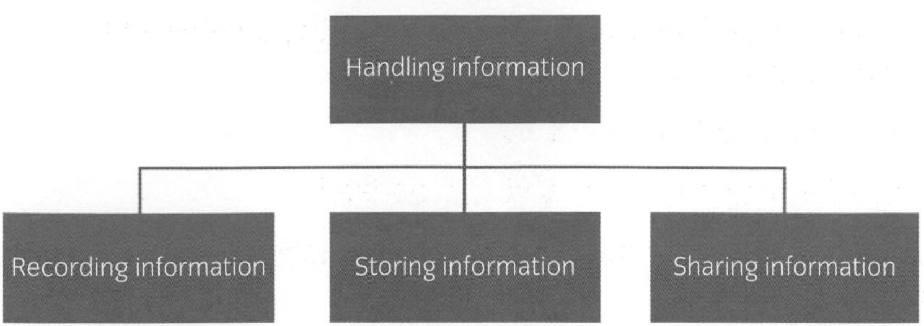

The way that information is recorded, stored and shared is vitally important in health and social care settings, not just because there are legal requirements about this, but because you are dealing with personal and sensitive information about people and their needs.

Personal information includes:

- a service user's name
- their address
- their date of birth
- their ethnicity
- the nature of any disability
- their phone number(s)
- their email address
- their family details.

Sensitive information includes:

- information about a service user's needs
- assessment information, which contains judgements about a service user's care or needs
- information relating to a health **diagnosis** or **prognosis**
- information about a service user's relationships and support networks
- financial information.

Key terms

Diagnosis is the identification of a medical condition.

Prognosis is the likely outcome of a medical condition.

YOUR RESPONSIBILITIES

Your duties and responsibilities in relation to handling information include:

- knowing the legal framework for handling both personal and sensitive information
- recording information effectively
- storing information securely and appropriately
- knowing about when, how and why to share (and not share) such information
- being open with people about what information is recorded and shared with others, and why.

THE LEGAL FRAMEWORK FOR HANDLING INFORMATION

Reflecting the fact that this is such an important area of practice, there is a clear legal framework around the handling of information in health and social care.

The following pieces of legislation are relevant to all workers in health and social care:

- Data Protection Act 1998
- Human Rights Act 1998
- Access to Medical Reports Act 1988
- Freedom of Information Act 2000.

DATA PROTECTION ACT 1998

The Data Protection Act 1998 concerns the recording of personal and sensitive information. It also covers requirements for confidentiality and access to records.

The Act sets out eight principles for the recording and use of information. The principles are that recording must be:

- used fairly and lawfully
- used only for a particular and lawful reason
- adequate, relevant and not excessive
- accurate and up to date

- kept for no longer than is necessary
- used in line with the right of individuals
- kept securely.
- Information must not be transferred between countries which do not have adequate protection for an individual's personal information.

The Data Protection Act is enforceable by law. It requires that organisations have appropriate measures in place to ensure that personal information is not unlawfully processed, lost or destroyed.

HUMAN RIGHTS ACT 1998

The Human Rights Act 1998 states in Article 8 that 'Everyone has the right to respect for his private and family life and his correspondence.'

ACCESS TO MEDICAL REPORTS ACT 1988

This Act gives individuals the right to see a medical report that is written by a doctor for employment or insurance purposes. The individual can comment on the report or ask for changes if they feel it is inaccurate.

FREEDOM OF INFORMATION ACT 2000

Direct care staff, support workers and professionals in regular contact with service users and family members should not get confused by this Act, which relates more to general rather than specific information.

The Freedom of Information Act 2000 gives people the right to request information from public authorities (Local Authorities, police, NHS organisations) about statistics and about decision making and policy making.

Information about specific individuals remains confidential and can only be accessed by the service user themselves in line with the Data Protection Act 1998.

REFLECT

In what ways does your practice meet the legal requirements for handling information? Try to give four or five specific examples.

RESEARCH

What are your service's policy and procedure in relation to:

- handling of information?
- confidentiality?
- access to recording systems?
- service user access to files?

HANDLING INFORMATION – WHAT DOES THE CODE OF CONDUCT SAY?

The importance of handling information effectively is recognised in the Code of Conduct for Healthcare Support Workers and Adult Social Care Workers in England 2013, which states that you must do the following:

- Maintain clear and accurate records of the care and support you provide. Immediately report to a senior member of staff any changes or concerns you have about a service user's condition.
- Treat all information about service users and their carers as confidential.
- Only discuss or disclose information about service users and their carers in accordance with legislation and agreed ways of working.
- Always seek guidance from a senior member of staff regarding any information or issues that you are concerned about.
- Always discuss issues of disclosure with a senior member of staff.

CALDICOTT GUIDANCE

Caldicott Guidelines govern the management of patient information in the health service, and it is essential for professionals working with health agencies to understand the key principles involved. The Guidelines are named after Dame Caldicott, who chaired a committee which looked at the flow of **patient-identifiable information** in the NHS.

Key term

Patient-identifiable information is any personal or sensitive information that can identify a patient.

The Caldicott Report

All organisations in the NHS and councils with Social Services responsibilities must have a senior manager with responsibility for ensuring that personal and sensitive information is safeguarded. The key principle of the Caldicott Report is that every use or flow of patient-identifiable information should be regularly justified and routinely tested against the principles on the next page.

Principles

- Justify the purpose(s) for using confidential information.
- Use it only when absolutely necessary.
- Share the minimum information required for the purpose.
- Access should be on a strictly need-to-know basis.
- Everyone must understand their responsibilities.
- Understand and comply with the law.

These principles are in accordance with those in the Data Protection Act, but have been developed into much more detailed procedures to uphold the security of information in health organisations, for example, the security of information sent by fax.

CASE STUDY

Sandra works for a domiciliary care agency. The agency has a system where care plan folders are kept in people's own homes. When Sandra visits a service user to provide care she makes a note in the folder about what she has done and any issues which need noting. Although Sandra always closes the folder when she has finished writing, one of the other care workers on her team always leaves the folder open – as she thinks it speeds things up if she doesn't have to look for the place to write. Sandra is concerned that this means very personal information about service users is open for everyone to see.

On one occasion Sandra notices that a neighbour has popped in to see one of the people she supports. Sandra sees that the neighbour is looking at the file which is open on a coffee table in front of her. Sandra feels that the system in place is not ensuring that personal information is handled securely. She can see the other worker's perspective about it taking time to find the right page to record but she feels that the system could be improved in some way and decides to take this to the next team meeting for discussion. At the next team meeting a decision is made to place the most recent records at the front of the folder so that it doesn't take long to find where to write, and to insist that the folders are always closed, so that no one else can see the sensitive and personal information which is recorded.

- What are your thoughts about this example?
- What practical methods do you use to maintain confidentiality in your own practice?

REFLECT

- Why is it important to have secure systems for the recording and storing of information in a health and social care setting?
- What challenges in maintaining the security of information are there in the setting you work in?

GOOD PRACTICE IN RECORDING INFORMATION

If you are registered with a doctor, a credit card company, or even if you have been to school, you have used a service and people have written things down about you. There are hard copy and electronic files about you 'out there'. If you were left alone in a room with these files, how long could you wait before wanting to take a look? What might *your* concerns be about the things that have been written about *you*?

Here are a few key issues to consider when recording information:

- *Accuracy*. Is it all correct?
- *Veracity*. Is the record true?
- *Timeliness*. Is the record up to date?
- *Completion*. Are there gaps in the record, and if so, why?
- *Judgement*. Are facts and opinions clearly differentiated, and are opinions backed up by evidence?
- *Power balance*. How would you feel if this record was about you?

As you think about these things, you will begin to get some idea of the power of information – or more particularly, the power of actually holding it. The point is that we all have a duty to record and handle information in a way that respects the truth and makes clear the difference between fact, opinion and hearsay. You should record information in a way that you would like information about you to be recorded. It's that simple – in theory. In practice though, it may not be so straightforward.

RECORDING AS A FORM OF COMMUNICATION

It is not unusual for people working in care services to complain that too much time is spent on paperwork – as though 'paperwork' is a pointless task, whereas it is actually a vitally important aspect of good-quality care. An essential part of a health and social care worker's role is recording information (for example, in a service user's care plan, in risk assessments and so on).

Recording information is a form of written communication. Written communication is of vital importance in care work – particularly in terms of completing care plans and contact sheets.

Perhaps the key difference between written communication and other methods of communication is that written communication is more permanent than any other form. While what someone has said may be forgotten or confused, what is written is permanent – it can be read time and time again, perhaps for years afterwards. Written records can therefore influence future actions. For this reason, it is vital that you recognise the importance of developing your skills in recording.

WHAT TO RECORD

One of the difficulties in record-keeping is that different people may choose to record different information – what one person sees as important, another may not. Some people may record too much information, and others too little. Because the recording of information is so vital to effective health and social care practice, it is important that there is consistency in *what* is recorded. This part of the chapter looks at the process of deciding *what* to record before looking at *how* to record the information.

Getting the balance

It is important to get the balance of information right.

Too much?

Some people tend to record too much information. In fact this is pointless, as no one will have the time to read through reams of information just to pull out one or two key points.

Too little?

On the other hand, it is important that sufficient information is recorded so that all relevant information is shared with the team responsible for providing a service user's care and support.

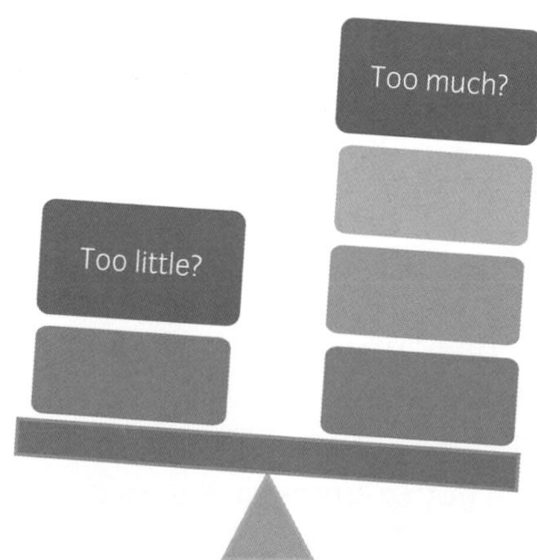

To get the balance of what to record right, try using the following pointers:

- Match what is recorded to the purpose of the record. Different records require different information – for example, a medication chart and an incident report form will require very different information to be recorded.

- Record what is important for other staff to know. In a contact sheet or a message book, health and social care workers will need to record what other staff will need to know to provide the care and support a service user requires. Workers should be aware in doing so that they should record positive as well as negative messages. For example, when a person displays aggressive behaviour, this is always recorded, but when that person displays respectful, thoughtful behaviour, this is rarely recorded. This can result in a person being labelled as aggressive as a result of behaviour which is actually infrequent.
- Record information that is not held anywhere else. A great deal of information is recorded in care plans and review notes. In your day-to-day recording, you do not need to repeat this information. You should record new information rather than repeating what is already known.
- Check with your line manager for guidance if you are unsure.

Remember – poor record-keeping:

- undermines good care practice
- leaves health and social care workers vulnerable to legal and professional problems
- increases workloads
- could put service users at risk.

HOW TO RECORD

Having considered *what* to record it is important to explore *how* information should be recorded. It can be helpful for new workers to ask for support from a more experienced colleague. You should make sure that your recording follows LACES. It should be:

- **L**egible
- **A**ccurate
- **C**oncise
- **E**quality based
- **S**hareable.

Legible

Some people's writing is very difficult to read. It doesn't matter how good the information is if it cannot be easily read by others in the care team. If your handwriting is poor, try slowing down when you write, as this may help.

Accurate

Accuracy includes aspects such as making sure you have recorded the information correctly, and keeping it factual. Recording should always be based solely on facts, without opinion. Where a particular record asks for opinion (which is rare) you should make clear that it is your opinion, for example, by writing 'In my opinion ...'.

When a worker has observed something, the record they make should include only what they have observed and not their interpretation of the information.

Keeping recording factual is vitally important, not least because one person's opinion might be wrong.

Opinion-based recording	Factual recording
Mary's flat is very dirty	There are a number of used pots and pans in Mary's kitchen, and the floor is sticky

Concise

While workers do need to record everything that is important, recording should also be as concise as possible. This means that less time will be taken in recording, and it makes it more likely that the information will be read and understood by others. Remember KISS:

- **K**eep
- **I**t
- **S**hort and
- **S**traightforward

(How many times have you heard the old saying 'keep it short and sweet'?)

Equality based

It is important that the health and social care value base underpins all record-keeping. You need to use positive language to reflect, respect and value diversity and equality, and should avoid recording in ways that:

- label people – eg 'Simon has challenging behaviour' or 'Mrs Khan is aggressive'
- refer to people in a childlike way – eg 'Mrs Scholes had a big tantrum' or 'Mr Jarman was really naughty'
- presents a 'diagnosis' – eg 'Muriel was very depressed today'.

If recording keeps to factual information, then it is more likely to promote equality and less likely to be disrespectful. It is worth considering whether statements like those expressed above need to be recorded at all, and if they do, whether more appropriate, positive and inclusive language can be adopted to express the same ideas.

Shareable

It is important to remember that service users have the right to access their records, and therefore the recording must be fit for sharing with service users. Recording may also be shared with colleagues and possibly other agencies – so it must be understandable and fit for purpose.

PRINCIPLES OF GOOD PRACTICE IN RECORDING INFORMATION

Different agencies will have different requirements about the recording of information. Even within agencies there will be different requirements relating to different forms of recording, but the following general rules for good practice in recording will always apply:

- Records should be made in black ink, as photocopies may need to be made at a later stage and this will make it easier.
- Records should centre on the facts rather than opinion.
- It should always be clear where any information came from: how do you know what you are saying? For example, if a service user's relative told you something, make this clear in the records – so 'Malcolm's wife said that Malcolm didn't sleep well last night', rather than 'Malcolm didn't sleep well last night'.
- Records should be signed, dated and timed.
- If any mistakes are made, a single line should be put through the error. Correction fluid must never be used. Whatever was originally written – even if it is a mistake – must still be visible.
- Any crossings out or changes made (for example, to spellings) must be initialled and dated to show who made the changes, and when.

USING RECORDING TO UPHOLD RIGHTS

Records can be used to uphold service users' rights:

- Records can assist in looking at a service user's progress, and can help to develop a picture over time of their needs.
- Records can inform decision making at reviews, etc. This can be particularly important if a service user is unable to express their views verbally – the records can inform professionals about a service user's behaviour and therefore what they are trying to express.
- Records can be used to support an application for additional support/services.
- Records can be reviewed to ensure that a service user's rights have been upheld.

APPLICATION OF SKILLS

Would you?

Read through the following extracts from recordings, and consider the questions that follow:

- Mrs Jones is attention-seeking.
- Mr Hamlin's daughter is manipulative.
- Mrs Beckford's son is very demanding.
- Jane has BO. She needs a bath urgently.
- Patrick was a real problem today.
- Mohammad is very easily offended by other service users.

What do you think of these extracts?

Do they follow the principles of good record-keeping?

(Think about KISS and LACES.)

RESEARCH

How would you summarise the key points of your service or agency's recording policy?

KEY PRINCIPLES WHEN COMPLETING DOCUMENTATION IN CARE SETTINGS

- The rules of confidentiality always apply to all records.
- All records could be read by the service user in question – you should bear this in mind when recording.
- All documentation should be objective. It should not contain information about the feelings, thoughts, instincts or assumptions of the carer.
- Documentation should be fact based.
- Judgemental language must be avoided.
- If there are particular concerns about a service user, committing those concerns to paper will ensure that other people are aware.
- Paperwork should be clear, concise and to the point.
- When completing paperwork, you must consider what it is important for someone else to know if you are absent.

USING JARGON IN RECORDING

Professional jargon can interfere with communication and understanding on many levels.

Abbreviations and acronyms are perhaps what most of us think of when we hear the word 'jargon'. Acronyms tend to be used as a form of shorthand, but they can be one of the most dangerous forms of jargon. What one person believes an acronym to stand for may not be the same as another person's understanding. Take the example of 'NFA', which can either mean 'no fixed abode' or 'no further action' – which could lead to a real problem when trying to communicate a service user's needs.

Abbreviations and acronyms often exclude and confuse people, so the best advice is to try not to use them – but this is easier said than done. Most of us will use some in our everyday work. However, it is vital that they are never used when communicating with service users. This can lead to real confusion and potentially dangerous situations.

- Abbreviations/Acronyms should never be used in case recording.
- Abbreviations/Acronyms should never be used in communicating with service users.
- Never make an assumption about what an abbreviation or acronym means – the person using it should always be asked to clarify what they are saying.

As a general guide, health and social care workers should try to avoid professional jargon as much as possible, because it is one of the most widely acknowledged barriers to effective communication at all levels.

For guidance on how to avoid jargon and make use of clearer, straightforward language, it is worth visiting the Plain English Campaign website at www.plainenglish.co.uk.

CASE STUDY

MOW

Mr Bateman is given a copy of his care plan. On it he notices that there is a reference to 'MOW' – he isn't aware that this is an acronym for 'meals on wheels'. When Mr Bateman's care plan is reviewed, he asks why no one has come to cut his grass when it clearly says this on the care plan.

DV

Jane, a social care worker, sends an email to her manager saying that she is concerned that Jeanette, a woman she is supporting, is 'experiencing DV'. Jane means that Jeanette is experiencing domestic violence, as her partner has been hitting her. However Jane's manager thinks Jeanette is experiencing diarrhoea and vomiting – so she sends a message back to Jane which reads, 'Don't worry. It is likely to go away in the next day or two – just advise Jeanette to drink lots of water and may be to contact the GP if it doesn't get any better.'

- How could these misunderstandings have been avoided?
- Have you ever been confused by abbreviations or acronyms? What did you do?

STORING AND ACCESSING INFORMATION

All agencies will have their own systems for handling information securely, whether this is using paper records, electronic recording or a combination of both. It is important that any records relating to service users, any documentation containing names and any other personal and/or sensitive information are kept securely in order to maintain confidentiality.

Some services use manual (paper-based) systems for recording and storing information, while others use electronic (computer-based) systems. Whichever system is used, the security of the systems should be upheld through the following practices.

Manual systems	Electronic systems
Lockable filing cabinets are always used.	Passwords are required to access the system.
People are well trained in the service not to leave files, letters or other paperwork lying around the office or in public view.	Workers understand the need to lock their computers if they leave their desks for a period of time (and the system also auto-locks after five or ten minutes of inactivity).
Policies and procedures are in place in the service (and understood by all workers) regarding access to records for service users, and when, how and why information can and should be shared with other agencies.	Policies and procedures are in place in the service (and understood by all workers) regarding access to records for service users, and when, how and why information can and should be shared with other agencies.

RESEARCH

Find out more about the information systems used in your organisation. What features of the systems uphold the security of information?

REFLECT

How do you use the information systems in your organisation to ensure that information is stored securely?

PRACTICES THAT ENSURE SECURITY WHEN STORING AND ACCESSING INFORMATION

As part of the requirements of the Diploma you will need to show that you use practices that ensure security when storing and accessing information. Using the systems in your workplace and being clear about how these improve the security of information are obviously vital for this.

In terms of your own assessment, you will probably need to show evidence to your assessor which contains personal and sensitive information about service users. This information should be located in confidential records. The way you share this information with your assessor will demonstrate whether you are employing practices to uphold the security of information. The only 'safe' method to use the recording you make as part of your work as evidence for the Diploma is for assessors to view the evidence in the place where the recording is held and then make a note about this evidence (and where it can be found – should there be any queries later). Service users also need to consent to assessors viewing their records for these purposes. This verification by the assessor that they have seen the original recording is what needs to go into your portfolio.

APPLICATION OF SKILLS

Secure or not?

Read through the following scenarios.

- Are you concerned about the security of information?
- Why?
- What should be done about these concerns?

1. A service manager takes home a memory stick which contains care plans to work on over the weekend. It slips out of her pocket while she is travelling home on the train. She doesn't realise until she gets home and so has no idea where it is.
2. Staff at a residential home always forget the password to the computer – so it is written on a sticky note which is attached to the screen.
3. Mary is a home care worker. She keeps notes about what she needs to remember – such as addresses and phone numbers of service users – in a notebook, and she jots down other notes about work in there too. This is also the notebook she uses to do her shopping lists and to jot down personal reminders – it is always in her handbag.

SHARING INFORMATION

As a health and social care professional you have a duty to maintain confidentiality, as explored in Chapter 1. However, this does not mean that you should keep things 'secret'. In your work it is important that all relevant information is shared so that everyone in the team can work in a consistent way to meet service users' needs. This means that potentially quite a few people know information about each service user. It is also crucial that you share information with your line manager.

However when information is shared within an organsation, or between agencies, the information remains confidential. The fact that it has been shared does not mean it can be shared further – the obligation to maintain confidentiality is shared just as much as the information itself.

When sharing information it should always be done on a 'need-to-know' basis, and with the understanding and consent of the service user.

When deciding what information should be shared and with whom, the following points should be considered:

- the nature of the information (ie is it essential information?)
- the wishes of the person giving the information
- the service user's person-centred plan, which may state who can receive information
- the organisation's policy on confidentiality
- any legal requirements.

It is also vital when sharing information that you check a person's identity. Are they who they say they are? Ask for identification to be sure. This can be more problematic if a person telephones and requests information – in this situation you should ask for some details, check with your manager, and phone back (or ask your manager to do so).

INFORMATION SHARING – GOVERNMENT GUIDELINES

As part of the Every Child Matters: Change for Children initiative, the government published *Information Sharing: Guidance for Practitioners and Managers* in 2004. Following a number of inquiries and investigations identifying social care staff uncertainty about the sharing of information, the government revised its guidance and extended it to cover professionals working with adult service users in 2008. The focus of *Information Sharing: Guidance for Practitioners and Managers* is on sharing information legally and appropriately. The guidance comes with a range of associated materials designed to support good practice in information sharing between professionals.

The guidance contains the following seven 'Golden Rules' for information sharing:

1 *Remember that the Data Protection Act is not a barrier to sharing information* but provides a framework to ensure that personal information about living persons is shared appropriately.
2 *Be open and honest* with the person (and/or their family where appropriate) from the outset about why, what, how and with whom information will, or could, be shared, and seek their agreement, unless it is unsafe or inappropriate to do so.

3 *Seek advice* if you are in any doubt, without disclosing the identity of the person where possible.

4 *Share with consent where appropriate* and, where possible-respect the wishes of those who do not consent to share confidential information. You may still share information without consent if, in your judgement, that lack of consent can be overridden in the public interest. You will need to base your judgement on the facts of the case.

5 *Consider safety and wellbeing.* Base your information-sharing decisions on considerations of the safety and wellbeing of the person and others who may be affected by their actions.

6 *Necessary, proportionate, relevant, accurate, timely and secure:* Ensure that the information you share is:

- necessary for the purpose for which you are sharing it
- shared only with those people who need to have it
- accurate and up to date
- shared in a timely fashion, and
- shared securely.

7 *Keep a record of your decision and the reasons for it* – whether it is to share information or not. If you decide to share, then record what you have shared, with whom and for what purpose.

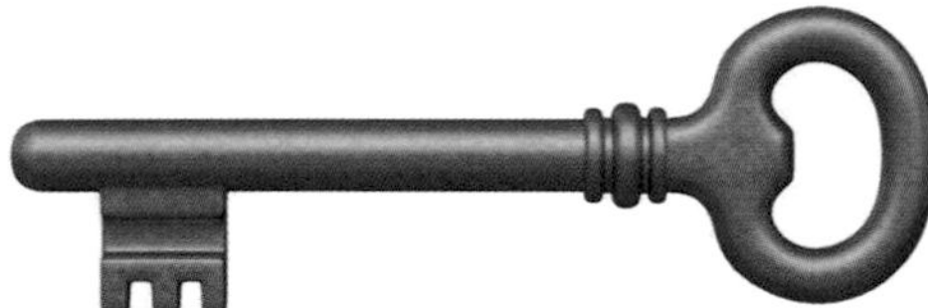

The guidance also contains a framework for decision making in relation to information sharing. It clearly identifies that practitioners should make decisions in conjunction with their manages about the sharing of information by working through seven key questions:

1 Is there a clear and legitimate purpose for you or your agency to share the information?

2 Does the information enable a living person to be identified?

3 Is the information confidential?

4 If the information is confidential, do you have consent to share?

5 If consent is refused, or there are good reasons not to seek consent to share confidential information, is there a sufficient public interest to share the information?

6 If the decision is to share, are you sharing information appropriately and securely?

7 Have you properly recorded your information-sharing decision?

CASE STUDY

Hakan has mental health problems. He has recently moved out of his family home and is supported in the community by a small team of mental health outreach workers. Hakan tells John, one of the support workers, that he was sexually abused by his older brother for a number of years and that he is feeling much safer since he moved out. Hakan says he doesn't want John to tell anyone about this. John talks to his colleagues. A number of them feel that since Hakan is now safe and no longer sees his brother, John should not pass this information on. John still isn't sure what to do, so he tells his manager about what Hakan said. John's manager contacts the local social work team and passes this information on, as she recognises that Hakan has a number of younger siblings still living at home who are potentially at risk.

- Is John right to share this information with his manager? Why?

RESEARCH

Read some information-sharing guides for practitioners'. *Information Sharing: Guidance for Practitioners and Managers* is very useful and contains a range of case studies and guidance. Don't worry – it is accessible and not written in highly legal language.

It can be downloaded from: https://www.gov.uk/government/uploads/system/uploads/attachment_data/file/277834/information_sharing_guidance_for_practitioners_and_managers.pdf

CASE STUDY

Cat works in a residential service. She receives a call from a social worker asking for some information about a service user. The social worker says she visited last week to do an assessment and there were a few things she forgot to ask – she is now completing the paperwork and just needs some basic information. Cat advises the social worker that she will speak to her manager about the request for information and then call her back. The social worker responds quite angrily, saying that she is not after any official secrets, just a bit of information, and that she needs to fill the document in now or else the service user might not get funding for her stay in the service. Cat wonders whether she should give the information over the phone – but recognises that this person may not be who they say they are and that she should check with a senior worker before sharing personal and sensitive information. Cat apologises to the social worker but insists that she will phone her back as soon as possible.

- Is Cat right?
- Why?
- What would you do in a similar situation?

APPLICATION OF SKILLS

Who needs to know?

Think through the following situations.

You are referring someone you work with to a college of further education. The admissions tutor asks you if the person has any personal care needs.

- What do you do?
- Why?

You are with a group of service users. A colleague comes and asks you about the financial situation of one of the service users. They need to know this so they can arrange a service that the service user needs.

- What do you do?
- Why?

You are one of a team of workers who supports Mrs Blake. On one of your visits the district nurse is present. She tells you that Mrs Blake has a urinary tract infection and that she needs to be encouraged to drink lots of water.

- Who do you need to share this information with?
- How do you do that?

ACCESSING SUPPORT FOR HANDLING INFORMATION

As a health and social care worker it is vital that you know where you can access guidance, information and advice about all aspects of your practice. This will help you to ensure that you are working in the way that is expected of you and to develop your practice. You will also know where to go and what to do if you have any concerns about your own or others' practice.

This chapter has provided information about the legislation and government guidance that you can look at for information. You should also discuss any concerns you have or any support you need with your managers or senior colleagues.

Chapters 3, 4 and 5 explored whistleblowing and the fact that your duty of care involves making your concerns clear and known. You should remember this concept when raising concerns about any aspect of practice. Where your concerns relate to the handling of information, the final layer of reporting will be to the Information Commissioner's Office, which is the UK's independent authority set up to uphold information rights in the public interest, promoting openness by public bodies and data privacy for individuals.

Stages for raising concerns about the recording, storage and sharing of information are therefore as follows:

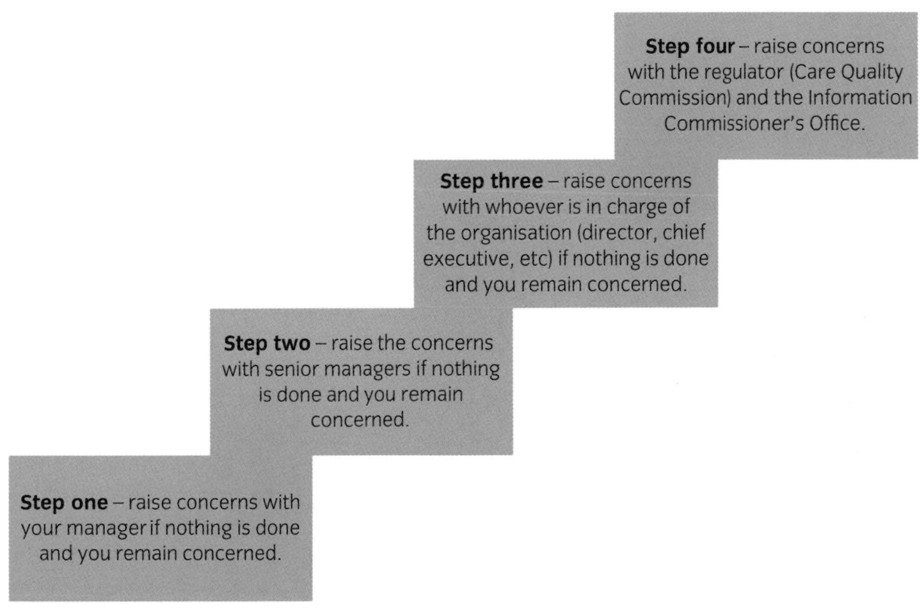

Keep a record of your concerns and the responses you have had at every stage of the process.

REFLECT

- How can you access support (guidance, information and advice) about handling information in your work?
- What would you do if you had any concerns about the recording, storing or sharing of information? Why?

Before going to the next chapter, take some time to consider:

- what you know about the legislation that relates to handling information
- what challenges you face in handling information
- what strategies you can use to overcome these challenges
- what skills you would like to develop further in terms of handling information
- how you will improve these skills.

CHAPTER 8

Introduction to personal development in health and social care

The concept of continuing personal and professional development is vital in health and social care. Health and social care is constantly changing, and workers in the sector therefore all have much to learn in order to provide the best-quality service to service users.

This chapter follows on from what you have learned about your role already, and helps you to consider how you can continually improve your professional practice as a health and social care worker.

Links to other chapters

When considering your practice and what you could improve, you will need to consider your work in relation to each unit of the Diploma. At the end of each chapter in this book you are invited to reflect on the content of the chapter – and you will find this reflection on each chapter useful when you are completing this unit.

UNDERSTANDING COMPETENCE IN YOUR OWN WORK ROLE

In order to understand what is required for you to demonstrate competence in your work role it is important to understand what is meant by competence. Competence is made up of three aspects: knowledge, skills and values:

Knowledge + skills + values = competence

To be competent in your role you must therefore understand what knowledge you need, what skills are important for you to have and what values should inform your practice.

Competence isn't simply about having the right knowledge, skills and values, though. It is also about:

- the way in which you use your knowledge in practice
- the way that you use your skills at work
- understanding the way that your values, beliefs and personal attitudes impact on your work, your skills and your knowledge.

The knowledge, skills and values required for effective practice in health and social care work are expressed in various standards, such as the standards on which the Diploma is based (National Occupational Standards). This is why working towards this qualification will significantly enhance your understanding of your role and help to improve your practice.

Key terms

Job description is a written outline of the role and responsibilities of a specific job.

Person specification is a written outline of the qualities a person needs to have for a particular job – this will include the experience they should have, the skills they should hold, the knowledge they need, the qualifications they need and so on.

You will have a **job description**, and this might have some associated documents such as a **person specification**. This will detail your role and responsibilities in your role and may also provide some specific information on what knowledge and skills are most important for your role. Quite often people don't look at their job description once they are employed in a particular role. However, it is worth re-looking at your job description as you work on this chapter.

REFLECT

How would you describe the duties and responsibilities of your role at work?

CASE STUDY

Wendy worked in a shop until she had children. She stayed at home for a number of years to care for her children. When her youngest son started preschool she started some voluntary work to build up her confidence in returning to work – she worked as a volunteer driver supporting people in attending hospital appointments and really enjoyed helping people. When her son went to school full-time Wendy secured a job as a home care worker.

When she started work, Wendy looked her job description and the associated person specification and made some notes about the skills and knowledge she would need. She then spent some time reflecting on the list, and scored each of the items a scale of one to five. She gave herself a score of five where she felt very confident. Where she felt less confident she gave herself a lower score. This enabled Wendy to work out where she might need to improve her practice in order to be the most effective care worker she could be.

Wendy found this preparation really useful when she was carrying out her induction, as she was able to focus on observing other workers in areas where she felt less confident about her own skills.

- What does your own job description say about the skills and knowledge that you need in your work?
- How could you measure your confidence against each statement in your job description?
- How else could Wendy measure her abilities to get evidence of her competence as well as looking at her confidence?

STANDARDS FOR THE HEALTH AND SOCIAL CARE WORKER'S ROLE

Standards	Status of the standards	Impact on your work role
National Occupational Standards	There are National Occupational Standards in many occupational areas. They are used to describe the standards that everyone working in that occupational area needs to meet. They are intended to be used in a variety of ways, including for the design of job roles, appraisal systems, procedures and in the development of qualifications in the area.	You need to meet the National Occupational Standards for health and social care in all of your work. They will be used to assess you when you are working towards a qualification. Your job role or job description could be based on them or they could be used in practical appraisals by your line manager.
National Minimum Standards	These are published by the government and cover a wide range of areas – for example, there are National Minimum Standards for domiciliary care. They cover expected standards of care.	These will cover what standards you and your service should meet. They describe the standards of care that people can expect to receive.
Care Quality Commission Essential Standards of Quality and Safety	These describe what health and social care workers and services should do in order to meet the requirements of Section 20 Regulations of the Health and Social Care Act 2008. The standards are written in the form of outcomes for service users, and provide detail on what health and social care professionals need to do in order to achieve these outcomes.	The Care Quality Commission is the current regulator of health and social care services. It makes use of the outcomes in these standards in order to inspect the quality of health and social care services.
Codes of practice and conduct	For details, see page 14.	These mostly describe the specific values and attitudes that health and social care workers need to have.
Legislation and government guidance	Various legislation and government directives set out standards for practice for both employers and practitioners in health and social care.	As a health and social care worker you need to understand the requirements of law and meet these in your practice.
Organisational requirements	Every organisation will have policies and procedures which need to be followed. They may also have specific standards of practice and mission statements.	As an employee you have specific contractual responsibilities to meet the standards of practice outlined in your job description.
Skills for Care Common Induction Standards (CIS)	The Care Quality Commission (CQC) states that all staff should receive a comprehensive induction that takes account of recognised standards within the sector and is relevant to their workplace and their role. The relevant induction for adult social care workers in England is currently the Common Induction Standards.	Social care workers should complete the CIS within 12 weeks of starting their job. Although it is expected these will be replaced by a new Care Certificate in 2015.

RESEARCH

- Locate at least three of the standards detailed in the table, and make some notes about the key implications these have for your practice.
- Based on what you have read, consider your role at work. Then detail what skills, knowledge and values you need to carry out your role effectively.

CODES OF PRACTICE

As professionals, health and social care workers need to follow the relevant code of practice. The Care Standards Act 2000 placed a responsibility on the relevant care councils to produce a code of practice for social care workers. However, the Health and Social Care Act 2012 revised the arrangements for the regulation of social care, and the General Social Care Council was abolished. This has led to a change in the responsibility for the code of practice for England, which currently sits with Skills for Care. You need to be familiar with the relevant code for your area of work:

- In England there is an additional Code of Conduct for Healthcare Support Workers and Adult Social Care Workers (Skills for Care and Skills for Health).
- In Wales the relevant code is the Code of Practice for Social Care Workers (Care Council for Wales).
- In Scotland this is the Code of Practice for Social Care Workers (Scottish Social Services Council).
- In Northern Ireland this is the Code of Practice for Social Care Workers (Northern Ireland Social Care Council).

Because best practice in health and social care is built on firm foundations, the codes of practice are very similar. Throughout this book reference is made to the Code of Conduct for England – if you work in a different nation you will need to ensure that you refer to the code that is relevant for your area of work.

PERSONAL DEVELOPMENT – WHAT DOES THE CODE OF CONDUCT SAY?

The Code of Conduct for Healthcare Support Workers and Adult Social Care Workers in England 2013 expects you to 'strive to improve quality through continuing professional development' and states that you must:

- ensure up-to-date compliance with all statutory and mandatory training, in agreement with your supervisor
- participate in continuing professional development to achieve the competence required for your role
- carry out competence-based training and education in line with your agreed ways of working
- improve the quality and safety of the care you provide with the help of your supervisor (and a mentor if available) and in line with your agreed ways of working
- maintain an up-to-date record of your training and development
- contribute to the learning and development of others as appropriate.

PERSONAL ATTITUDES AND BELIEFS

It is generally accepted that our attitudes and beliefs are influenced by a number of factors, which might include:

- our background and upbringing
- personal experiences
- education
- religious beliefs
- cultural background.

These factors will be different for every individual, so everyone will have a different set of attitudes and beliefs, or **values**. These are often referred to as **personal values**.

Key terms

Values are what is seen as important.

Personal values are what is important to an individual.

Professional values are what is important in a particular profession.

THE VALUES OF HEALTH AND SOCIAL CARE

Working in health and social care means that you need to adopt a set of **professional values** – the values of health and social care. While the professional value base does not replace each individual's personal value base, professional values should override personal values in terms of the way in which you work.

Organisations and services often develop their own internal codes of practice, codes of conduct or value statements.

Health and social care is about:

- people providing some form of support to other people
- getting the best for people who for some reason need to rely on others to meet some of their needs, whether these are basic care needs, or needs connected with being part of society or accessing services.

Key to this are the values of health and social care:

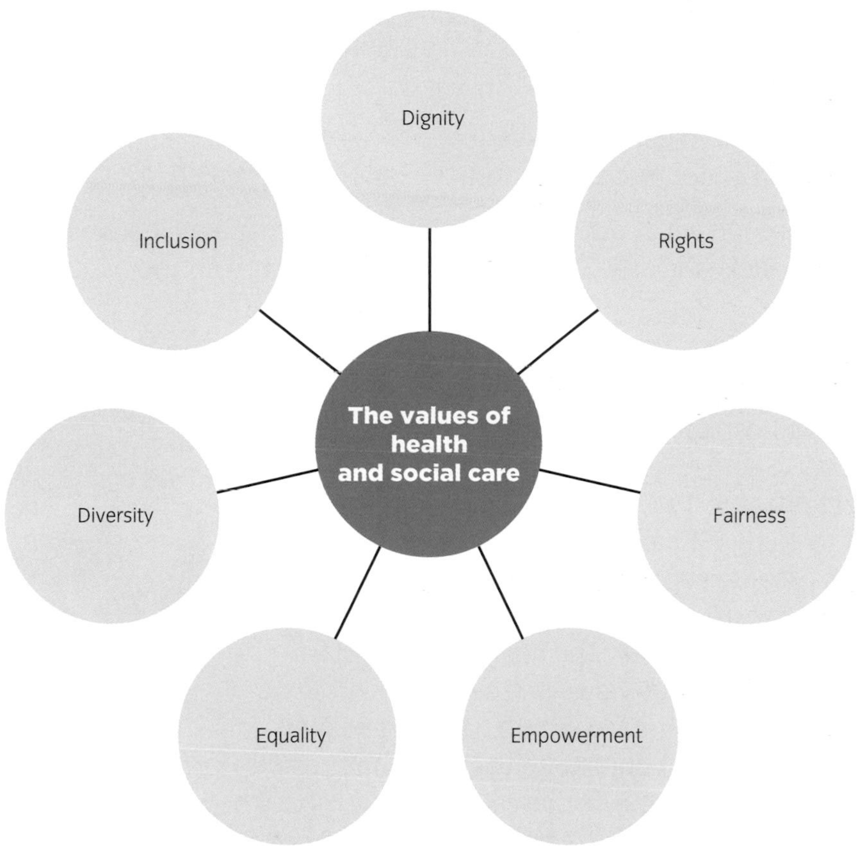

- *Dignity*. People must be treated with respect and as unique individuals with rights and choices.
- *Rights*. When people are vulnerable, their rights may be compromised. Health and social care involves upholding people's rights.
- *Fairness*. Society can be unfair in its treatment of individuals, and health and social care needs to model fairness in treating people in the best possible way.
- *Empowerment*. Health and social care should enable people to do everything they can for themselves, offering support when necessary.
- *Equality*. It is essential that health and social care workers recognise that every service user is equal.

KEY POINT

Many of these issues are covered in specific units of the Diploma – in recognition of their importance as the key values of health and social care.

- *Diversity*. Differences and uniqueness are things to be enjoyed and celebrated.
- *Inclusion*. Services and society should include everybody.

ENSURING THAT PERSONAL ATTITUDES AND BELIEFS DO NOT OBSTRUCT YOUR WORK

It is vital that your personal beliefs and attitudes do not impact on the quality of care you provide to people. To ensure that your attitudes and beliefs do not impact on your work, you need to:

- be aware of your own beliefs and attitudes – what are they? where do they come from?
- ensure that you are fully aware of the values of health and social care and adopt these at all times in your work practice
- talk through with your manager any conflicts that arise between your beliefs and attitudes and the values of health and social care.

CASE STUDY

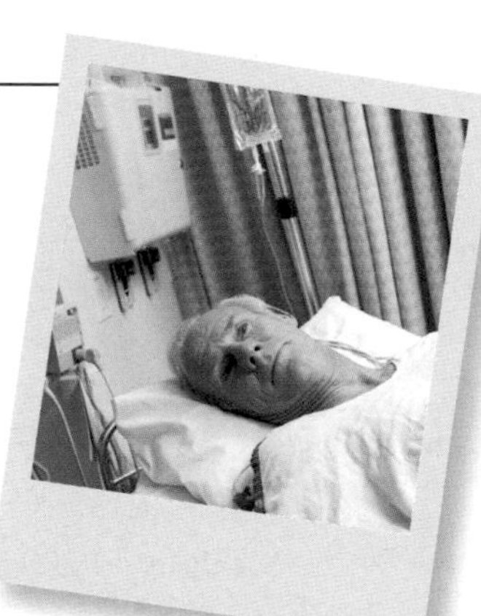

Ted is in hospital recovering from a stroke. His partner, George, visits daily and is openly affectionate to Ted, holding his hand, kissing him and stroking his hair. The man in the next bed takes great exception to this and demands that the healthcare assistant talk to Ted and George about their behaviour. The healthcare assistant has strong religious views and sees gay relationships as morally wrong. She agrees that Ted and George should not engage in public displays of affection. She talks to the nurse in charge of the ward about how she plans to raise this with Ted. The nurse advises that Ted and George have every right to kiss each other and asks the healthcare assistant to reflect on why she should not apply her personal beliefs and **morals** to her work.

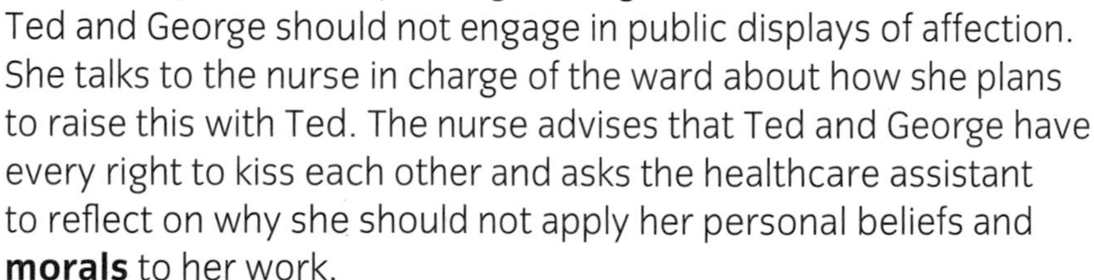

- How could the healthcare assistant reflect on this and reconcile this dilemma for herself?
- What consequences could there be for Ted and the worker if the healthcare assistant did raise her views with him?

Key term

Morals are about our belief in what is right and wrong, and are often associated with faith and our personal values.

APPLICATION OF SKILLS

Ensuring that personal attitudes and beliefs don't impact on the quality of your work

You are visiting Mr Hope to assist him with his personal care. When you are there his son comes out of the kitchen, and he is wearing women's clothes and make-up.

- How might you react?
- What should you do?

Mrs O'Callaghan lives in the residential service where you work. Her daughter Josie lives nearby but rarely visits. Today Josie visited for the first time in over a month. Josie said she is unhappy about the care Mrs O'Callaghan is receiving and wants to complain. Josie says she won't be able to sleep for worry if this is the way her mother is treated.

- How might you feel?
- What should you do?

Comment: In general we need to respect the lifestyles that people lead, and we need to recognise the importance and value of relationships that service users have, even if our own lifestyle or our own relationships are very different.

REFLECT

How might your own personal attitudes, values, belief systems and experiences impact on your working practice? Try to identify three or four specific issues which might affect your practice.

REFLECTING ON WORK ACTIVITIES

Reflecting on work activities is one of the most effective ways to develop knowledge and skills and improve practice.

Reflecting on work experiences is often referred to as reflective practice. **Reflective practice** improves health and social care practice in a range of ways. Perhaps most importantly, reflective practice opens up options – when we reflect on a situation it enables us to see more, and to see things differently. Effectively it illuminates our practice so that we can see things more clearly. This can lead to improved and more effective practice.

Key term

Reflective practice involves thinking about work experiences specifically on what went well and what could be done differently next time.

Reflective practice improves practice in a range of ways, as it:

- helps people identify gaps in their skills and knowledge – this helps them to identify their learning needs and improve their practice
- encourages people to consider communication and relationships – this means that working relationships can be improved
- supports people to examine the decision-making process – so that they are able to explain what they are doing and why they are doing it more clearly
- encourages a healthy questioning approach which can help people 'find their way'.

REFLECT

Why is reflective practice important in continuously improving the quality of service you provide?

WHAT IS REFLECTIVE PRACTICE?

To fully understand reflective practice it is important to recognise that there are three forms of reflection:

- reflection for practice
- reflection in practice
- reflection on practice.

Reflection for practice

Reflection for practice describes the stage of reflection where future actions are considered. As such, reflection for practice serves to guide future action. It is essentially reflection before an event – thinking through and planning what you are going to do.

EXAMPLE

Catherine is asked to provide personal care to Mrs Docherty. Mrs Docherty has dementia and is unable to communicate verbally. Catherine spends some time thinking through how she can communicate with Mrs Docherty about her personal care needs.

Reflection in practice

Reflection in practice is the process of reflection when you are working. Essentially it is working and being aware of what you are doing at the same time. Reflection in practice involves:

- thinking ahead ('right, if that's happened, then I need to ...')

- being critical ('this aspect of what I did worked well, but that didn't work quite so well because ...')
- storing up experiences for the future ('I could have dealt with that better; next time I will try ...')
- analysing what is happening ('she's saying that to test me – I think I should ...').

EXAMPLE

Emma is providing support to Mr Danks. She is helping him out of bed in the morning and notices that he looks sad. She asks Mr Danks if he is feeling OK, and he says he is worried that Emma hasn't given him a shave. Emma realises that the other worker who supports Mr Danks does things in a different order from her and that she hasn't asked Mr Danks which order he would like her to do things in. She apologises and asks Mr Danks what order he prefers – showing that she can improve her practice in action.

Reflection in practice is happening all the time – if your mind is on the job. While reflection in practice is good and can help workers to develop their practice, it does have drawbacks. The main problems with reflection in action are:

- You can only see things from your own perspective ('I think, I feel, I'm not sure ...').
- You will only have short-term reflection; if your mind is on the job, when the job changes so will your thoughts.

Reflection on practice

This is separate to, but linked with, reflection in practice. It is the reflection done later, after the event – talking things through informally or formally with colleagues, and maybe talking things through in supervision. Reflection on practice is free from urgency and any pressures of the actual event. As such it allows for longer-term reflection and addresses the drawbacks of reflection in practice. For example, reflection on practice allows for the opportunity to explore other people's views on the event. Feedback from others therefore adds an extra dimension to the reflection – allowing for more depth and analysis.

Reflection on practice requires space and time, and this is perhaps one of the most significant challenges for busy health and social care workers. One of the main drawbacks of reflection on practice is that because of time constraints, practitioners tend only to think in this way about more complex or critical work issues. In terms of more routine events and work practice there is a tendency for practitioners to only reflect *in practice*. This can mean that people do not make many changes to routine work practice. It is therefore important to plan reflection on practice to ensure that it covers every aspect of practice.

EXAMPLE

Jane attends a review of Mr Patterson's care plan as his primary carer. A number of people are present at the review. Jane doesn't say very much in the review as she feels uncomfortable and lacks confidence. After the review Jane reflects on what has happened. She concludes that some decisions have been made that she felt don't address Mr Patterson's concerns about his care. She decides that she will need to be more confident in future reviews – to make sure that the people she cares for have their concerns addressed.

If we apply the stages of reflection to a health and social care worker's role, it could look something like this:

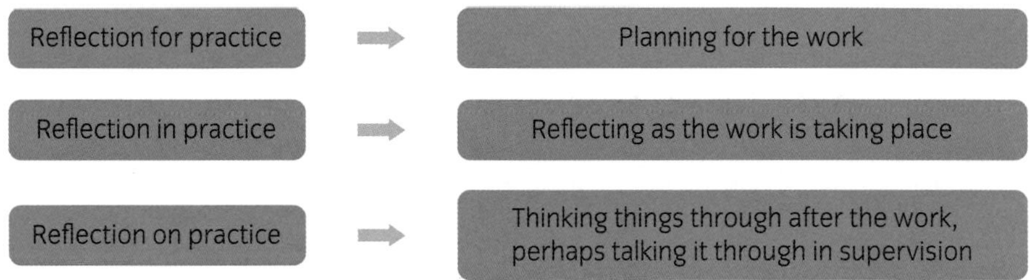

So the basic framework for reflection consists of three stages. This is often depicted as a cycle in the following way:

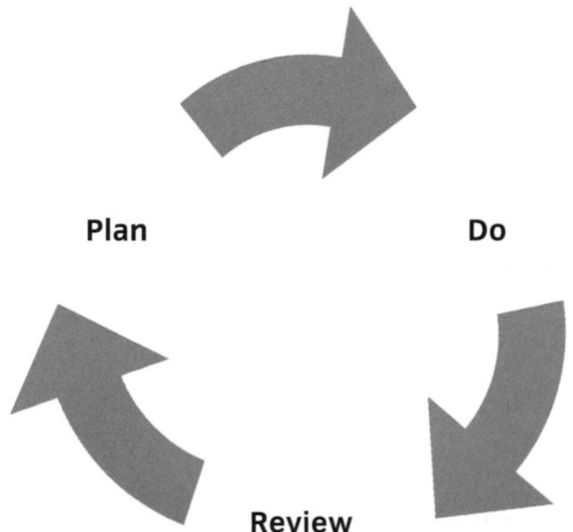

Reflection on practice should lead to further reflection for practice in terms of planning what to do next. Essentially, a reflective cycle is produced, in which a good health and social care practitioner will be reflecting all the time, at different stages.

HOW SHOULD I REFLECT?

The reflective stages show us how important it is to reflect all the time, but they don't really tell us how to reflect or what we should think about when we are reflecting. Reflection is often seen as considering the following issues.

The event

Think about what happened? Who did what? What were the results?

Feelings and thoughts

Think about questions such as:

- How were you feeling when the event began?
- How did your feelings change as the event unfolded?
- How did you feel about the outcomes?
- How do you feel about it now?

Evaluation

Think through what was good and what was bad about the experience. What went well? What didn't go so well?

Analysis

This develops from evaluation, but involves breaking the event down into component parts so that they can be explored separately. For example:

- What went well?

This could be followed up with:

- What did I do well?
- What did others do well?

And then:

- What didn't go so well?

This could be followed up with:

- What didn't turn out as it should have?
- In what way did I contribute to this?
- In what way did others contribute to this?

Conclusion

Now that the event has been explored from a range of perspectives, you should be able to draw some conclusions. This will involve asking yourself what you could have done differently and what impact this would have had on the outcome. If the previous stages have not been fully and honestly explored, the conclusions reached in this stage may well be flawed.

Action planning

During this stage, you should think about what you would do if you encountered the event again. Would you do anything differently, or take similar action?

THE REFLECTIVE RAINBOW

Another way to look at refection is to think about key issues in practice. Thinking about a rainbow can be a useful way of reminding yourself how to reflect on a piece of work.

RED = Relationships – Did you develop a good relationship with people involved in the activity? How do you know?

ORANGE = Obstacles – What obstacles did you face? How did you get around the difficulties?

YELLOW = Your feelings – How do you feel about what you did?

GREEN = Goals – What goals did you have for this work? Did you achieve them?

BLUE = Beliefs – What beliefs and attitudes had an impact on your work?

INDIGO = Identity – What is your identity? How is that different from the person you were working with? How did you ensure that their individuality was upheld?

VIOLET = Values – How did you put the values of health and social care into practice?

As you think through each of these issues you should think about what went well and what didn't go well – then consider how you could improve your practice in this area next time.

HOW GOOD AM I AT MY JOB?

Reflecting on your practice can help you to identify how well your own knowledge and skills meet the required standards. Obtaining feedback on your practice can also help you assess how good it is.

You need to plan how you can get feedback on your practice – think about the best way of doing this. You will probably need to seek feedback from different people in different ways. For example, asking for written feedback from your manager might be useful, but that won't work with a service user who has difficulties with writing. In addition to thinking about how you are going to get feedback, you need to put thought into what you want feedback about. If you want to get feedback on a specific area of your practice you need to be clear about this to get the most useful feedback.

SUPERVISION

Supervision is vital for all health and social care workers. Both the supervisor and the supervisee need to value the supervision process and be fully committed to it in order for it to be effective.

Supervision has a range of benefits for everyone involved in health and social care, including:

- allowing workers to share any concerns, dilemmas, etc
- providing opportunities for reflection, growth and professional development
- providing a safe forum for the provision of feedback
- providing a useful forum for reviewing actions and monitoring progress against plans
- providing a safety net for workers and organisations.

Ultimately, good-quality supervision leads to improved outcomes for service users. Good practice in supervision is a joint responsibility and involves the following aspects being in place:

- Supervision should be planned and thorough.
- The process of supervision needs to be explicit, and there should be a clearly agreed working definition of supervision.
- Past experiences of supervision should be acknowledged – in order to clarify current expectations.
- A written agreement (supervision contract) should be in place, and this should be regularly reviewed.
- Supervision should be accurately recorded and this should be shared – with both parties' signatures included.
- Power imbalances should be acknowledged and discussed. By virtue of the fact that one worker is accountable to the other in an arrangement formalised within the agency, the supervisor is in a more powerful position. However, it is important to remember that other general power imbalances (gender, race, disability, etc) may exist between the individual people in the supervision relationship.
- A safe environment should be fostered. This means that all of the above points need to be covered.

RECEIVING FEEDBACK

Receiving feedback is a fantastic learning opportunity, and the learning is maximised if the feedback is constructive. The feedback process will only be constructive if the person seeking the feedback has developed the necessary skills to receive it. When receiving feedback at any stage, health and social care professionals should work towards the following.

Maintain an open attitude

Don't be defensive or 'defend' yourself. This may sound easy, but it isn't easy to do. If you find yourself feeling defensive about a piece of feedback, you need to remind yourself that the reality is that a defensive reaction to feedback generally results from it being accurate.

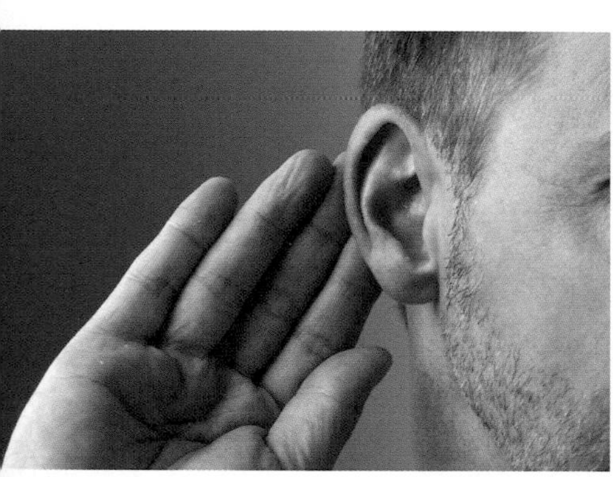

Use your active listening skills

Listen actively, look at the person providing feedback and maintain an open body language.

Clarify the feedback

Ask any questions you need to in order to make sure you understand the feedback.

Respect the person giving the feedback

Providing feedback is not an easy task. The person providing feedback is likely to have put a great deal of thought, time and effort into it. It is advisable to thank the person giving you feedback – just something like 'you've really given me something to think about there – thanks' not only demonstrates your commitment to learning but also helps you to maintain that vital positive and open attitude.

Write down the feedback

Try to write down what you can remember of what was said as soon as possible. You will find this assists with your reflection later.

Don't take criticism personally

Feedback is a professional process. Recognise that part of being a professional is learning from how others view your practice.

Recognise learning

Remember that simply because someone has picked up on an area of your practice which can be improved, this does not mean you are not a good health and social care practitioner. Even the very best worker can improve on some aspect of their practice.

Reflect

If some aspect of the feedback puzzles you, take some time to reflect. How might the person's perception have been formed?

Focus

Make sure that you are not distracted so that you can focus fully on the feedback. Stay 'in the moment' and try to truly understand the meaning behind the feedback. Try to avoid framing a response in your mind until you have heard all of the feedback.

Recognise your reactions

Notice your own reactions and how the feedback is making you feel. Sometimes it helps to partially dissociate yourself and imagine you are a 'fly on the wall' witnessing feedback being given to someone else. This can help you to think the feedback through objectively, rather than emotionally.

In receiving feedback, people tend to take either a negative (closed) style or a positive (open) style. The following table summarises these approaches.

Positive/Open reception of feedback	Negative/Closed reception of feedback
Open – listens without frequent interruption or objection	Defensive – defends actions, objects to feedback
Responsive – willing to truly hear what is being said	Attacking – turns the tables on the person providing feedback
Accepting – accepts the feedback without denial	Denies – refutes the accuracy or fairness of the feedback
Respectful – recognises the value of the feedback	Disrespectful – devalues the person giving the feedback
Engaged – interacts appropriately, seeking clarification where needed	Closed – ignores the feedback
Active listening – listens carefully and tries to understand the meaning of the feedback	Inactive listening – makes no attempt to understand the meaning of the feedback
Thoughtful – tries to understand the personal behaviour that has led to the feedback	Rationalising – finds explanations for the feedback that dissolve personal responsibility
Sincere – genuinely wants to make changes and learn	Superficial – listens and agrees but does not act on the feedback

REFLECT

- How do you make sure you get feedback on your practice?
- How do you use this to develop your practice?
- Think about a time when you received feedback on your practice – how did you use this feedback?

RESEARCH

Go back to the list of knowledge, skills and values you listed at the start of your work on this chapter (see page 227).

- How can you assess your own practice against this list?
- What might you use to inform your assessment?

CASE STUDY

Rhonda is completing the Diploma in Health and Social Care. She has been working as a home care worker for a number of years. She isn't very confident about herself, and although she feels she does her job fairly well she doesn't see herself as particularly skilled. As part of her work towards the Diploma she asks service users and their family members what they think of her work. She is delighted to receive some very positive feedback, which shows that she is very skilled in providing care with compassion. The feedback she receives helps her to have more confidence and pride in her work.

- How do you obtain feedback from those who you work with?
- How do you respond to less positive feedback when you receive it?
- How might the questions you ask and the way you ask them elicit different responses from people?

AGREEING A PERSONAL DEVELOPMENT PLAN (PDP)

To develop an effective development plan you need to understand the process of personal and professional development. This is often referred to as the continuing professional development (CPD) process.

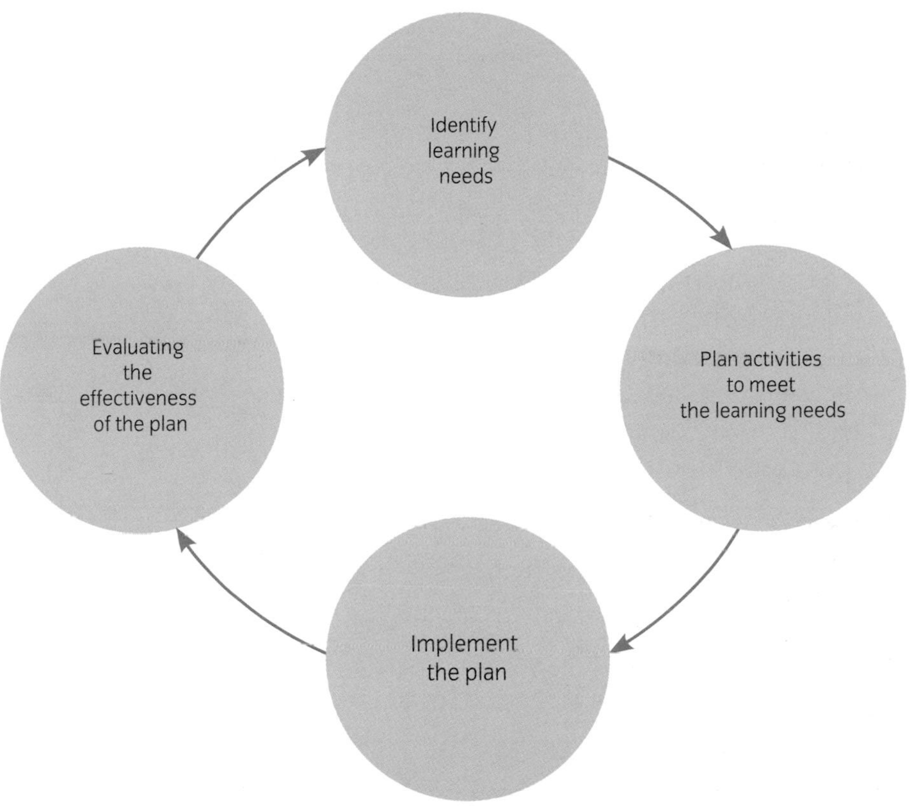

IDENTIFYING LEARNING NEEDS

In order to take a positive approach to your continuing professional development you need to begin by identifying your learning needs so that you can plan learning and development opportunities which will address them.

To identify your learning needs, you need to take account of:

- the standards you are expected to meet in your practice (these might include regulations, codes of practice, organisational policies and National Occupational Standards)
- any specific issues as a result of changes in your role and responsibilities
- any forthcoming changes in your workplace
- the needs of the service users you work with

- your aspirations for the future (perhaps in terms of improvements you want to make in your practice, or what you would like to do with your future career).

Identifying gaps in knowledge and weaknesses in practice can be particularly challenging, so it is important that you evaluate your practice effectively, drawing on feedback and reflection.

CASE STUDY

Andrew recently completed a health and social care course at college, and has just started working at Stoneleigh Nursing Home. Andrew feels that his knowledge about dementia is fairly good, as he did a presentation on dementia on his course. However, he has observed some of the other staff communicating with residents really effectively and he feels that he needs to develop his skills in this area much more. He starts to put some thought into how he can draw on the knowledge he has to develop his communication skills.

- How might Andrew put his ideas into a plan to improve his practice?
- What support might he need in order to check his plan out with others, and to make his plan happen?

PLANNING ACTIVITIES TO MEET LEARNING NEEDS

This will become the worker's professional development plan (sometimes referred to as a PDP). When planning learning activities you need to think about the whole range of activities available to you. These opportunities then need to be accurately matched to your learning needs. For example, if you want to develop a particular skill you may feel it would be useful to ask a colleague who is skilled in this area to assist you by talking you through the skill, observing you and providing feedback.

In devising learning plans, you will need to consider:

- any requirements for mandatory training (such as health and safety)
- any individual needs you have
- the views of service users
- any specific needs of service users and how you can learn about these.

Whenever you devise a development plan, you need to ensure that you keep the plan:

- ***S**pecific*. Your learning needs should be clearly defined.
- ***M**easurable*. You need to be able to measure your progress towards meeting the identified needs.
- ***A**chievable*. Make sure that you can meet the learning needs.
- ***R**elevant*. Learning needs should relate to the standards for your practice.
- ***T**ime-bound*. There should be a deadline for you to meet the learning needs.

EXAMPLE OF A PERSONAL DEVELOPMENT PLAN

Learning need	Learning activities	Support needed to achieve the objective	Link to standards for practice	Timescale
Improve recording practice by nsuring recording is brief, completed in a timely way and relevant	• Sample recording by colleagues • Look at Write Enough training (www.writeenough.org.uk) • Try bullet pointing more	• Manager to sample files every week • Access to training materials • Time to spend on recording – allocate one hour per day	• Data Protection Act	• Discuss progression at next supervision
Risk assessments – need to complete one for each service user who has not got one in place	• Discuss with Tsitsi as she has experience of completing risk assessments • Read risk assessment policy	• Time allocated for doing this	• National Occupational Standards on health and safety • Organisation's risk assessment policy	• 3 months
Look at communication aids and technology	• Research these on the internet • Attend a training day in April	• Training day • Time after this to make some recommendations for the service • Budget to buy any necessary items	• National Occupational Standards on communication and specific communication needs	• By May

DEVISING A DEVELOPMENT PLAN

You will need to prepare a professional development plan to meet the learning outcomes of the Diploma. If you are thoughtful about how you complete this, you will also be able to draw on it in relation to many of the units of the Diploma: for example, think about your learning needs in relation to each of the mandatory units – then use this as a basis for discussions about each unit with your assessor.

When you are agreeing your personal development plan you need to think about who you will involve and what sources of support you have.

Who should be involved?

You will need to involve a range of other people in planning your learning, and keep this under review.

Service users, carers and advocates

These people will have a fuller understanding of the needs of the people you support and they will therefore have ideas about how you should prioritise your learning needs. They will also be able to provide you with useful feedback about how effective your practice is, which will help you to reflect on it.

Supervisors, line managers and employers

These people will be clear about the standards you need to meet and can therefore provide valuable advice on what you need to develop by providing you with feedback and guidance.

Other professionals

These people will be able to identify what you need to do to provide a good service and will be able to provide you with feedback on your practice – helping you to identify your own needs.

All of these groups of people may also be able to support you in accessing learning activities that can meet your development needs.

Sources of support

It is important that you make use of a wide range of support in order to plan your own development, and keep this under review.

Informal feedback

You might get feedback informally in a range of ways – for example, through service users or through other individuals and their family members making comments about your practice, and so on. Draw on this feedback to help you evaluate your practice and plan your future development.

Formal feedback

You should receive feedback formally though supervision and appraisal. You can make use of this to evaluate the effectiveness of your practice and to plan how you need to develop your practice.

Learning activities

Page 248 provides information on the range of learning activities you can use to develop your practice. You can make use of these and reflect on your learning in order to evaluate your practice and to plan other learning activities.

Within the organisation

Your colleagues will be able to provide you with support to identify your development needs and improve your practice. For example, if you have a colleague who has a particular skill you could ask them for support if you want to develop your skills in that area.

Outside the organisation

A range of support might exist outside of your own organisation. For example, there may be careers advisors who can assist you with planning your career goals. There are also a number of national organisations that can support health and social care workers, which you can access via the internet.

IMPLEMENTING THE PLAN

You need to engage in the opportunities you have planned. In doing so you will find it helpful to consider the following questions:

- What do I want to learn?
- What are my expectations?
- How will I know when I have learned what I wanted to?
- How will I use what I learn?

Thinking through questions such as these will help you take an active and reflective approach to your learning. It might be useful to make some notes on your responses to the questions and on your experiences as you implement the professional development plan. This will help you with the next stage of the process.

EVALUATING THE EFFECTIVENESS OF THE PLAN

Once the plan has been actioned and you have effectively engaged with all the planned opportunities, it is vital that you evaluate what you have learned. A key aspect of the evaluation will be revisiting the originally identified learning needs and considering to what extent they have been met by the plan.

If the needs haven't been met, are there different opportunities that could be used? Would a different approach help? Where the learning needs have been met, this won't be the end of the process, as it is likely that the learning will have highlighted some further needs – and so the cycle continues (which is why this is called continuing professional development).

KEEPING A RECORD

It is good practice for all professionals to keep track of their professional development in a systematic way. The benefits of doing this include the following:

- the record can be used as evidence for a range of professional qualifications or recognition of prior learning against future qualifications
- the record can be used in appraisal systems
- continuing professional development records can be used to update CVs or provide useful information in job interviews
- reflection will be easier with a record to base thoughts on.

Some organisations provide a system for recording professional development – which makes it much easier for workers who then simply need to complete the documentation. Other workers can choose how to record their professional development. Whatever system you use, it should be easy to identify the following:

- your learning needs
- the activities you have undertaken to address these
- your progress towards meeting the learning needs.

CASE STUDY

Mary keeps a CPD portfolio. It is basically a folder where she keeps a range of material:

- certificates of training – she jots some notes down to go with these, outlining key learning and how she has used this in practice
- her supervision notes
- reflective notes about her practice experiences
- feedback she has received about her practice
- a copy of her job description.

Every six months Mary refers to her portfolio and makes some brief notes about her progress and her aims for the next six months. Mary has found the folder invaluable as evidence for her Diploma, to help her prepare for an interview for promotion and to help in her application for a college course.

RESEARCH

Put some thought into the formal and informal support networks you can use to plan and review your own development. Separate these into support within your own organisation and outside of your organisation.

- Are there any systems that you don't make use of?
- How could you draw on these support systems to plan and review your development more effectively?

DEVELOPING YOUR KNOWLEDGE, SKILLS AND UNDERSTANDING

Until quite recently, learning and development activities were viewed almost entirely in terms of training courses. Learning and development plans appeared to be little more than a 'shopping list' of training courses. However there is now an increasing level of understanding about the benefits of using a range of learning activities.

Some of the most widely used learning activities in health and social care include the following:

- supervision
- performance review or appraisal
- mentoring and coaching
- training
- e-learning
- assessment and feedback
- independent research and reading
- keeping up with the news and government policies
- team meetings.

LEARNING THE LESSONS FROM SERIOUS FAILURES IN HEALTH AND SOCIAL CARE

Where there are serious failures in care and support in health and social care settings, these tend to be widely reported in the press. Following such failures, inquiries are often set up to investigate the failings and to support people to 'learn the lessons' so that similar failings do not happen again. Keeping up to date with these inquiry reports can be very helpful to you in improving your practice. Issues of dignity, respect and poor practice in health and social care have been increasingly subject to attention in the media and by the general public.

Winterbourne View

In late 2012, six workers from Winterbourne View, a private care home near Bristol, were jailed for abusing residents, as exposed in a BBC documentary. The *Panorama* programme in 2011 showed people being slapped, pinned under chairs and subjected to cold showers as punishment (BBC 2012 online).

The people living in the home were subjected to appalling treatment and the exposure of this led to high-profile public debate about the placement and treatment of adults with learning disabilities. The BBC's article quoted Mark Goldring, the Chief Executive of Mencap, who described institutions like Winterbourne View being seen as a 'dumping ground' and 'warehousing' for people who display challenging behaviour.

Key learning from the Serious Case Review into this concerns the following:

- the perception of people with learning disabilities
- the inspection of institutional care, and the monitoring of safeguarding notifications by Local Authorities
- the need for better planning and commissioning of services
- the need for whistleblowing policies to be applied properly
- the need for the existence and use of other forms of alert and access to advocacy services.

(Flynn 2012 online)

Mid Staffordshire NHS Foundation Trust Hospital

The most in-depth inquiry in recent times into NHS failings concerned the Mid Staffordshire NHS Foundation Trust hospital in Stafford. A local pressure group of patients and relatives formed, calling itself 'Cure The NHS' after identifying common concerns about the standard of care and treatment at the hospital. A lengthy and detailed public inquiry was held involving ministers, the Department of Health, the Care Quality Commission, the local Primary Care Trust and the West Midlands Strategic Health Authority.

The conclusions reached included the following:

- The culture and systems at the hospital led to failures to diagnose people's conditions and neglectful treatment, which may have resulted in or hastened up to 1,200 people's deaths between 2005 and 2009.

- There were confusions over the number of agencies and bodies involved in monitoring the hospital, as listed above, and this is part of a bigger picture of systemic change in health which the current government is progressing.
- Whistleblowers were not listened to – one nurse submitted 50 reports and concerns which senior managers were seen not to take account of.
- There were serious concerns about 'the quality, competence and humanity' (Guardian online, 2012) of the nursing care and practices in the hospital, especially care for older patients.

Very often after reports on inquiries into serious failures the Government publishes a report in response. These reports often contain recommendations. Following the Francis Inquiry into Mid Staffordshire NHS Trust (which had responsibility for Stafford Hospital) the independent Cavendish Review recommended that the training and support of healthcare assistants and social care support workers should be strengthened. It suggested that all healthcare assistants and social care support workers should undergo the same basic training, based on the best practice that already exists in the system, and should get a standard Care Certificate before they provide care for people unsupervised. Further information on this should be available in 2015.

EVERYTHING IS A POTENTIAL LEARNING ACTIVITY

Anything that you do can be seen as a learning activity if you approach it in the right way.

Some opportunities to learn are formal and have formal access procedures – such as training. Other opportunities are informal, where everyday activities are undertaken in a reflective way in order to aid learning. Absolutely anything can be viewed as an opportunity to learn, and recognising this is, in many ways, what makes a worker a professional: what makes a job a career.

It's not what you do – it's the way that you do it.

Learning isn't automatic – it doesn't just 'happen' whatever the content and quality of the learning activity. It is important that before doing something you think about:

- what you want to learn
- why you need to learn it
- how you will use what you learn.

It will also involve reflecting on learning after the activity:

- What did you learn?
- How can you use this learning in your practice?

In fact, thinking about your learning is like following the three stages of reflection covered is more detial earlier in the chapter:

- *Reflect for learning*. Think about what you want to learn, why you want to learn it and what might be the best way to learn it.
- *Reflect in learning*. Reflect on the learning activity while you are doing it – think about what you are learning.
- *Reflect on learning*. Reflect on the activity and what you have learned after the event – how can you put what you have learned into practice?

CASE STUDY

Malcolm works as a care assistant in a residential service. He attends some training on person-centred practice. After the training he thinks about how he could apply what he has learned to his practice, and speaks to the home manager about developing a personal profile for each of the service users he is key worker to. He feels that these would be useful to have on file – so that casual staff can take a look at the profile and see at a glance the best way to support service users in a way that meets their personal preferences. In developing the personal profiles Malcolm learns more about the service users he supports, and this helps him to offer more personalised care.

REFLECT

Think about a learning activity you have undertaken (remember, this can be anything).

- How has that activity improved your knowledge, skills and understanding?

Before going to the next chapter, take some time to consider:

- how you would describe the duties and responsibilities of your role
- what you see as the most important knowledge and skills in your work role
- how you could develop your skills and knowledge further
- how you reflect on your practice
- how you get feedback from others, and how you use this feedback
- whether you have a personal development plan
- what would be on your personal development plan
- whether it is up to date
- when the last time you reviewed it was..

CHAPTER 9
Implement person-centred approaches

Health and social care is built on the foundations of person-centred approaches. The move towards person-centred practice has led to major changes in the way that health and social care services are delivered. We are moving from traditional service-led delivery of care and support towards care and support which is focused on the uniqueness of each individual.

Links to other units

The content in this chapter links closely to Chapters 10 and 11. In addition, it crosses over with many other chapters. Person-centred care is essential to all aspects of care delivery; therefore it is central to the whole Diploma.

PERSON-CENTRED APPROACHES IN HEALTH AND SOCIAL CARE

Person-centred approaches are based on a number of core values and principles which many people see as developing from the values of health and social care practice.

These values include the following:

- a commitment to promoting human rights
- upholding personal dignity
- seeing service users as unique individuals
- promoting choice and self-determination
- respecting service users
- listening to and empowering service users
- working in partnership with service users
- recognising and addressing potential conflict
- safeguarding service users
- recognising each service user's capacity to make their own decisions
- being sensitive to diversity
- putting service users in control.

The values of person-centred care can be summed up as follows:

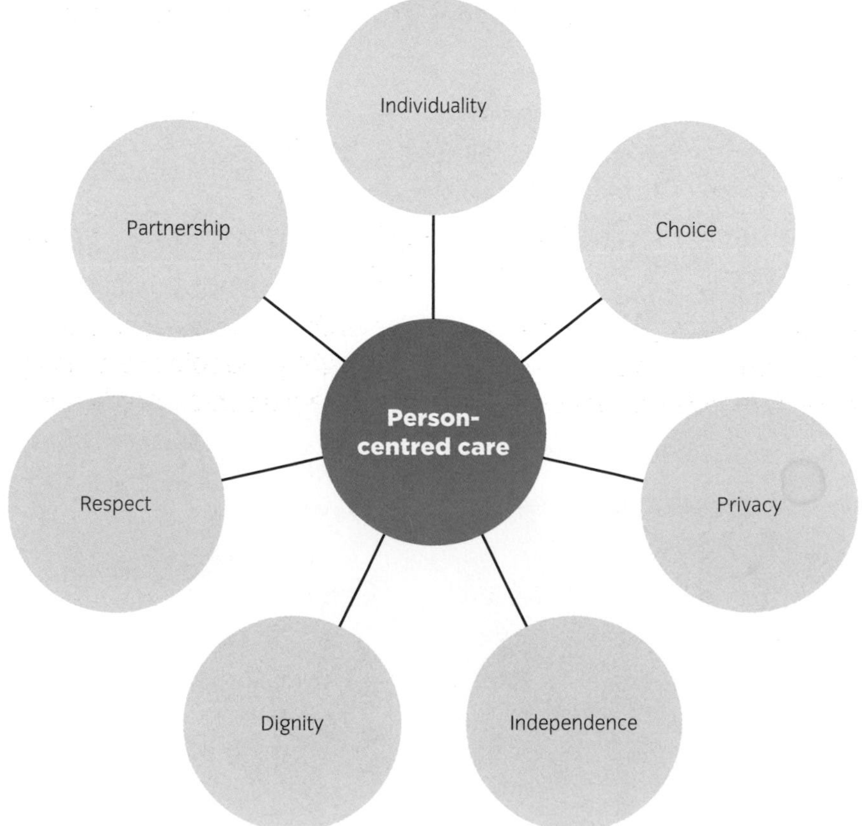

Ultimately these concepts all relate to individual rights. After all, the service users you work with have a basic right to be treated as unique individuals, with respect and dignity, and to be able to make their own choices.

WHY IS PERSON-CENTRED CARE SO IMPORTANT IN HEALTH AND SOCIAL CARE?

Person-centred approaches must influence every aspect of health and social care practice, as explained below. The approach should not simply be about the icing on the cake – person-centred approaches *are* the cake.

Person-centred approaches are important to all aspects of health and social care practice for the following reasons:

- Every service user is a unique individual with differing circumstances and needs. As such, their needs can only be met by support that focuses on them as a unique individual.
- Everyone has a unique history and 'life story'. This will impact on their needs, their life choices and their behaviour. Support and care will only be effective if they take this unique life history into account.
- Models of service delivery which are centred on the needs of the organisation or the service (and not the individuals who use the service) create climates in which power is easily abused and where service users are disempowered. This increases both dependence and vulnerability.
- Everyone wants to have control over their own life and has the right to make choices – only person-centred approaches to care promote choice and control.
- The population of the UK is becoming increasingly diverse. Person-centred approaches reflect this diversity.
- People have a legal right to make choices and to access services that promote dignity and respect. Quite rightly, people are making more demands on services to provide more person-centred care.

The number of unpaid carers (mostly family and friends of service users) in the UK is growing rapidly. Carers report increased satisfaction with person-centred care and they are more likely to accept support services that work on a person-centred basis (Carers UK 2012).

As such, all organisational policies, procedures and practices should reflect person-centred approaches to care.

REFLECT

How does your work with service users reflect the following person-centred values?

- Individuality
- Rights
- Choice
- Privacy
- Independence
- Dignity
- Respect
- Partnership

PERSON-CENTRED APPROACHES AND RISK TAKING

Taking some risks is a daily occurrence for everyone and is necessary if people are to take a full and active part in their communities.

Most people are able to balance risks against their potential benefits, and will take any necessary precautions to help minimise risk. It may not be quite so easy for vulnerable service users to achieve this balance for themselves. This is where support will be required.

Risk assessments are designed to ensure that those making decisions are aware of all the risk factors and have considered any precautionary measures which might help to reduce identified risks.

The purpose of a good risk assessment is not to prevent people from making choices that carry a degree of risk. The purpose is to raise awareness of risk with the individual and all those who work with them, so that decisions can be made with:

- the full knowledge of the range of possible consequences of each decision
- the ability to anticipate any measures which might be taken to reduce unnecessary levels of risk.

The result of a risk assessment can sometimes be that service users are prevented from undertaking activities that might bring them pleasure and satisfaction. However, the aim should be the opposite to take preventative measures to actively reduce the possibility of the person being at risk.

Working in a person-centred way is about wanting those we support to live as full a life as possible, whatever the nature of their needs. Living a full life is about making choices and feeling in control. All of us do things that may not be what others would see as 'best' for us, but the important thing is often that we make the choice to do or not do something. Being person-centred means that we involve service users in the same way in making informed decisions about their own lives and the risks they may wish to take. However, because of your duty of care in your work roles, you have to be able to demonstrate the way in which risk has been considered when providing the support that people need and deserve.

CASE STUDY

Andrea lives with her parents. Andrea has a learning disability, and since she left school she has stayed at home with her parents, although she does go out regularly. However, as Andrea's parents have got older they do not go out as often and they have given up their car. Andrea feels that she is 'trapped in the house' and she wants to go out alone. Andrea's parents are concerned that Andrea won't be able to keep herself safe when she is out. They are particularly concerned about her using public transport, as she has never done this before.

Andrea and her parents meet with a social worker, who arranges for Andrea to receive some input from a support worker. The aim is for Andrea to be supported in learning how to use the bus, and to help Andrea become involved in some local activities.

- Why might Andrea's parents be concerned?
- Why is it important for Andrea to be able to take some risks with support?

USING CARE PLANS TO PROMOTE PERSON-CENTRED PRACTICE

Key term

Task-centred care practice focusses on what tasks need to be done. This can mean that workers lose sight of the fact that they are assisting people.

In the past, health and social care services were generally delivered around **task-centred care practice**. For example, a care worker would have a list of tasks to complete during a shift.

In modern health and social care practice, the delivery of care and support is focused on individualised care plans. Every service user will have their own care plan which will detail their day-to-day needs and requirements, with reference to the outcomes that are expected (see Chapter 11). In some services, care plans may be known as support plans or individual plans, but the content will always relate to how the care worker can meet the service user's individual needs.

Sometimes practice in care planning is poor – and many service users receiving care from the same service have very similar care plans. Clearly, since everyone is a unique individual, every care plan should be different.

Individual care plans contribute to person-centred practice in the following ways:

- *Individuality.* The care plan should reflect the service user's individuality and support the worker to look at how they can uphold that person's individuality.
- *Choice.* The care plan should make the service user's preferences and choices clear.
- *Privacy.* The care plan should make clear how the service user's privacy will be respected, and it should be kept privately.
- *Independence.* The care plan should reflect the principles of active participation – showing how the service user should participate in their own care to maximise their independence.
- *Dignity and respect.* Dignity and respect should be addressed in the care plan, for example, by recognising the service user's right to make their own choices, by respecting their uniqueness, culture and rights, and so on.
- *Partnership.* Care plans should be drawn up in partnership between professionals and the service user being supported.

A number of organisations utilise the values of person-centred practice as the basic structure for a care plan – but even so, sometimes they can be very general and lack specific detail reflecting the service user's uniqueness. It is important that health and social care workers look at the service user's individual care plan and use this to provide person-centred care.

WORKING IN A PERSON-CENTRED WAY

Person-centred practice means:

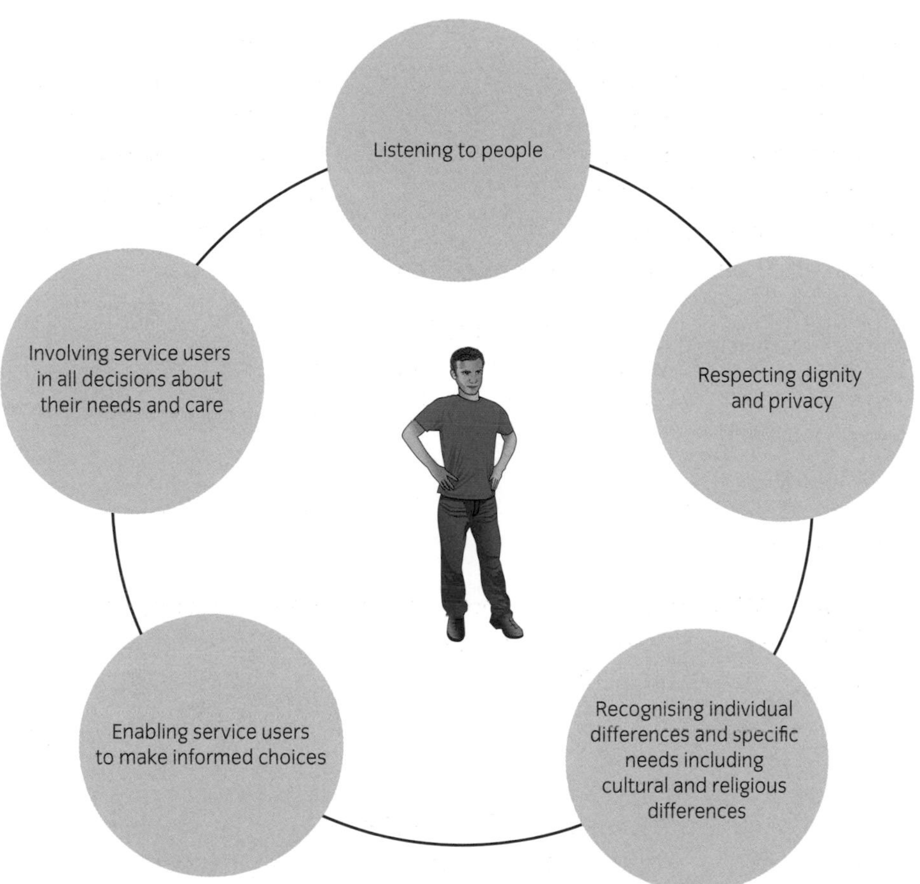

Working in a person-centred way essentially involves putting person-centred values into practice. Key to working in a person-centred way is to understand each service user as a unique person. One effective method for understanding individuals and for treating people in a person-centred way is to adopt what is known as the biographical approach.

BIOGRAPHICAL APPROACH

The biographical approach to health and social care is essentially about taking the service user's life story into account when working with them. As a theory it is fundamentally simple – think about how often we read the autobiography of a celebrity to understand 'where they are coming from' – or how interested people seem to be in the lives of celebrities (through various sources in the media). When we meet someone new we often ask them about their lives, as this shows interest and respect and gives us something to base a conversation on. The biographical approach recognises this – it reflects the influence of a person's life story on them and is a key part of person-centred care.

Health and social care workers need to find out about a service user's life story, and sometimes this involves detective work. How you do this will vary, depending on what the service user can tell you about themselves. The various methods that health and social care workers use when finding out a service user's life story include the following:

- talking to the service user themselves
- actively listening to *everything* the service user says (not just what they say verbally)
- asking family members about the service user's life
- looking through photographs with the service user
- reading past records and reports
- using a 'life story book' (sometimes prepared by family members or by staff who know the person well)
- using reminiscence group work (see page 277)
- playing music, films, etc that would have been popular when the service user was younger – and watching the person to see their responses.

LOOK CLOSER, SEE ME

This poem is said to have been found in the hospital locker of an older woman after her death. It shows in a very powerful way how it is vital to understand a person's unique life in order to work with them in a person-centred way.

What do you see, people, what do you see?
What are you thinking, when you look at me?
A crabby old woman, not very wise.
Uncertain of habit, with far-away eyes,
Who dribbles her food and makes no reply.
When you say in a loud voice 'I do wish you'd try!'
Who seems not to notice the things that you do.

LOOK CLOSER, SEE ME (CONTINUED)

And forever is losing a stocking or shoe.
Who, unresisting or not, lets you do as you will.
With bathing and feeding, the long day to fill.
Is that what you're thinking, is that what you see?
Then open your eyes, you're not looking at me.

I'll tell you who I am as I sit here so still!
As I rise at your bidding, as I eat at your will.
I'm a small child of 10 with a father and mother,
Brothers and sisters, who loved one another.
A young girl of 16 with wings on her feet,
Dreaming that soon now a lover she'll meet.
A bride soon at 20 – my heart gives a leap,
Remembering the vows that I promised to keep.

At 25 now I have young of my own
Who need me to build a secure happy home.
A woman of 30, my young now grow fast,
Bound to each other with ties that should last.
At 40, my young sons have grown and are gone,
But my man's beside me to see I don't mourn.
At 50 once more babies play around my knee,
Again we know children, my loved one and me.

Dark days are upon me, my husband is dead,
I look at the future, I shudder with dread.
For my young are all rearing young of their own.
And I think of the years and the love that I've known.
I'm an old woman now and nature is cruel,
'Tis her jest to make old age look like a fool.
The body is crumbled, grace and vigour depart,
There is now a stone where I once had a heart.

But inside this old carcass, a young girl still dwells,
And now and again my battered heart swells.
I remember the joy, I remember the pain,
And I'm loving and living life over again.
I think of the years all too few – gone too fast,
And accept the stark fact that nothing can last.
So open your eyes, people, open and see,
Not a crabby old woman, LOOK CLOSER, SEE ME.

(McCormack, 1966)

REFLECT

- How does this poem make you feel, and might it challenge you in any way towards how you and others see the people you work with?
- How do you find out about the history of the people you support?

ESTABLISHING CONSENT WHEN PROVIDING CARE AND SUPPORT

Key term

Consent is when a person consents to something when they are making an informed decision or giving informed permission.

Making sure that a person consents to the care you are to provide is very important in all health and social care activity. As part of this it is important to understand what is meant by **consent**. Consent is not simply about allowing something to happen. A person consents to something when they are making an informed decision or giving informed permission.

There are particular complexities around consent in health and social care as there may be questions about whether an individual has the capacity to consent. Concerns in this area generally relate to whether someone has the mental capacity to consent. Since this is such a significant issue in health and social care there is legislation that covers this area of work, explained below.

THE MENTAL CAPACITY ACT 2005

This Act represented a fundamental change for adult health and social care services, and is particularly relevant to this unit.

Where the Mental Capacity Act breaks new ground is that it departs from the idea that an assessment of capacity is made on a once-and-for-all basis and affects all other decisions that a person makes. It recognises that the ability to be able to make rational decisions may vary for a variety of reasons and according to the complexity of what is being asked of the person.

The Mental Capacity Act has five core principles:

- A person must be assumed to have capacity unless it is established that they lack capacity.
- A person must not be treated as unable to make a decision unless all practicable steps to help them to make the decision have been taken.
- A person must not be treated as unable to make a decision just because they make an unwise decision.
- Any decision made or act carried out on behalf of a person must be in their best interests.
- Before a decision is made or an act is carried out, consideration must be given about how this can be achieved in a way that is least restrictive of the person's rights and freedoms.

It is vital to recognise that a person's capacity to consent and to make decisions can change over time (even over a short period of time), and the Mental Capacity Act and the associated guidance makes this clear. For example, some people take medication with quite powerful side-effects which are often at their worst in the morning. The ability of people affected in this way to be able to make decisions and to give consent may be poor in the morning, but this may well improve as the day goes on.

ESTABLISHING CONSENT

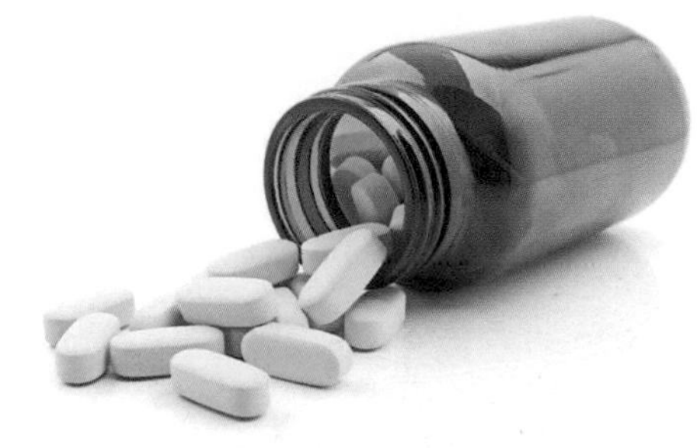

Consent should be:

- established formally in writing for some activities (eg consent to receive a service, and consent to keep a record according to the Data Protection Act 1998)
- established informally for each activity during the person's daily life where support is provided (eg asking people what they would like to eat, asking them if they want something to be done for or with them, or if they can do it for themselves, etc)
- established each time a personal care activity is started (eg 'Would you like me to …?', or 'Are you ready to …?')
- recorded – especially when someone does not consent to something, this should be recorded appropriately
- informed – people need to understand what they are consenting to, and often they also need to understand the potential consequences or risks if they do *not* consent to an activity or treatment.

RESEARCH

- What procedures are there in your organisation for establishing consent?
- Talk with colleagues about how they achieve this, especially when a service user's capacity to consent may be restricted. What strategies work for others, and can you adapt your own practices to test out another person's ideas?

REFLECT

- How do you establish and review consent with service users in your work setting?
- What approaches work for you in enabling people to express their consent, or to state when they do not consent?

CASE STUDY

Mrs Baju has a diagnosis of dementia, and her verbal communication is very limited. She has recently been admitted to hospital with a chest infection. She needs support with all her personal care needs, and the healthcare assistants who work on the ward spend quite some time talking to Mrs Baju's family about these needs.
Mrs Baju's daughter explains that Mrs Baju feels comfortable about care being provided while she is being sung to – but that she becomes very distressed without this.

The healthcare assistants talk to Mrs Baju about what they are doing when they assist her in the morning and then sing softly as they support her to wash. Mrs Baju seems to hum along. Later that day another healthcare assistant assists Mrs Baju – but she doesn't sing because she feels embarrassed about this. She also decides that there is little point telling Mrs Baju what she is doing, as she feels that Mrs Baju doesn't understand what is being said to her. Mrs Baju shouts loudly and demonstrates that she is distressed.

The nurse in charge of the ward hears what is happening and goes to intervene.

- What might the nurse in charge do?
- Why?

PERSON-CENTRED APPROACHES – WHAT DOES THE CODE OF CONDUCT SAY?

The Code of Conduct for Healthcare Support Workers and Adult Social Care Workers in England 2013 states that you must:

- be alert to any changes that could affect a service user's needs or progress and report your observations in line with your employer's agreed ways of working
- put the needs, goals and aspirations of service users first, helping them to be in control and choose the healthcare, care and support they receive
- always explain and discuss the care, support or procedure you intend to carry out with the service user, and continue only if they give valid consent
- know how to put person-centred values into practice in your day-to-day work
- know how to promote dignity in your day-to-day work with the service users you support
- understand why it is important to find out the individual histories, preferences, wishes and needs of service users.

ENCOURAGING ACTIVE PARTICIPATION

Active participation is closely linked to active support – you will therefore find reading Chapter 10 useful to help you fully understand active participation.

ACTIVE PARTICIPATION

Active participation is about service users being fully involved in their own care, as opposed to being a 'recipient' of that care (ie it is about something being *done with* someone rather than something being *done to* someone). Active participation also means that service users take part in the activities of daily and independent life as much as possible.

Promoting active participation in health and social care work is part of the duty of care, as this links with the key concepts of empowerment and enabling service users to do all that they can for themselves.

ACTIVE SUPPORT

Active support is a person-centred model for how to interact with service users combined with a daily planning system that promotes participation and enhances their quality of life.

Active support is about providing the right amount of support to service users, which recognises their rights while providing opportunities for growth and skill development.

ACTIVE PARTICIPATION IN HEALTH AND SOCIAL CARE

Regardless of whether a service adopts an active support model or not, all workers in health and social care will need to demonstrate their knowledge of and commitment to active participation. This is for the following reasons:

- Service users are not objects to be 'treated' or 'cared for', but are unique individuals who have rights, wishes and choices.
- The fact of needing care or support can mean that service users feel unable to do things for themselves – professionals intervening in their lives therefore need to optimise each individual's feelings of control and competence.
- Whatever service users' needs are, there are still things that they can do, and will want to do, for themselves.
- Without the opportunity to do these things for themselves, service users will feel more helpless and achieve poorer outcomes.

- Workers can sometimes think it is easier (or quicker) to do a task on behalf of a service user, or they can feel it is their role to do things. Considering how people can be more involved in their own care is about challenging these sorts of preconceptions.
- As well as being involved in their care, service users have the right to be involved in tasks around their homes and activities outside their homes. The lives of people in some care settings can be isolating, dull and lonely. Working in a person-centred way is about striving for the best and most active lives for them.

Chapter 10 explores these issues in more depth.

The benefits of active participation

Active participation benefits service users in a range of ways:

- They are able to maintain their skills and retain their independence for longer.
- They learn new skills and can adapt existing ways of doing things when they are fully involved in their own care.
- Their self-esteem is significantly improved where they are supported to participate as fully as possible.
- They feel that they are being treated with more dignity and respect when active participation is implemented.

Barriers to active participation

Despite all the benefits, there are a number of barriers to active participation. Understanding these barriers is important for health and social care workers – the first step in overcoming barriers is to understand them.

- *Lack of time.* Workers might find it quicker to do things *for* service users rather than do things *with* them. When time is short this can mean that encouraging active participation is challenging.
- *A wish to protect service users from harm.* The desire to help people and protect them from harm can lead to over-protection and the opposite of active participation.
- *Fear of being blamed if things go wrong.* Health and social care workers can feel that they will be blamed if something goes wrong – especially if they don't have good support from their managers.
- *Attitudes.* Attitudes can be a barrier to active participation in a range of ways. Some service users expect workers to do everything for them, which prevents active participation. On the other hand, some workers feel that service users can't do anything for themselves.

Encouraging active participation

Active participation in social care can be encouraged in a number of ways.

Care tasks

With any task that you as a worker could do for a service user, ask the service user if they would like support to do this, or do it for themselves *before* taking action. For example, it is important not to help someone get dressed, brush their teeth, get more comfortable and so on without asking first the key question 'Would you like ...?' Doing so enables people to say no as well as to say yes when they do want help.

Daily living

Consider ways in which service users can become more involved in the things we all do on a daily basis. We all need to keep our homes clean, wash clothes, shop for and cook food, and so on. However, service users often have a lot of these things done for them by others. The consequence can be that their days can be quite empty and dull. It is useful to consider what service users *can* do, as opposed to simply doing every task around the home for them because there are certain activities which they *cannot* do.

Social inclusion

Wanting the best for service users is about enabling them to participate in society as well as in daily living and their own care. We all benefit from contact with other people who have similar interests, beliefs or who simply acknowledge us as we go about our lives. Needing care can be isolating in itself, and working in a person-centred way is about enabling service users to be part of society, to enjoy activities, to meet other people and to feel valued and important.

Active participation is also encouraged through:

- praise, encouragement and recognition of achievements
- the involvement of carers and relatives – sometimes service users' carers can want to over-protect individuals, with the best of intentions, and active participation can need to be about ensuring that others recognise what the service user *can* do for themselves
- involving service users in discussions and assessments about choices and risk (see Chapter 4 for more detail on the dignity of risk taking)
- being sensitive to service users' individual needs and going at their pace – being asked to do too much too quickly can be as off-putting as being asked to do too little
- working as a team with your colleagues so that the care and level of support which service users receive is both consistent with their needs and consistent across a team
- focusing on service users' strengths and talents.

REFLECT

- How does your work setting enable active participation to be at the centre of work with service users?
- Can you suggest ideas, tools and methods to aid a greater level of active participation, either with a specific service user, or on a service basis?

RESEARCH

Even if you are not undertaking the unit on active support, read Chapter 10, and consider how the principles of active support and active participation overlap.

CASE STUDY

Mr Royale has recently been discharged from hospital. Andrew, a support worker, is visiting him at his home to help him get up and get dressed in the morning. Andrew gives Mr Royale his clothes and assists him to dress himself. He also passes Mr Royale a comb, and Mr Royale combs part of his hair, while Andrew finishes this off for him. Each day Mr Royale is managing to do more for himself. One morning Andrew is off sick and Mark is asked to support Mr Royale. Mark goes straight ahead and dresses Mr Royale and combs his hair. Mr Royale is very angry, and shouts at Mark.

- Why might Mr Royale be angry?
- What could Mark have done differently?

SUPPORTING SERVICE USERS' RIGHT TO MAKE CHOICES

Making choices is about being in control of your own life. Enabling people to make choices is therefore key to good person-centred practice.

The choices that service users make can either be simple and day-to-day (which drink to have, what to wear or where to go out), or they can be extremely significant (where to live, who to have a relationship with, what job to do).

INFORMED CHOICES

When people make choices they need to have information about the range of options they have and the implications of making a particular choice.

Making choices about your own life is a key right. However, people can make what we might consider 'bad' choices. For example, someone might choose to smoke, even though they are aware of all the hazards of this. If you think about your friends and family – they might make decisions which you think are wrong – but they are their decisions to make.

Your own thoughts and feelings should not influence the choices that other people make. People should be able to make their own choices as long as they have sufficient information to allow them to make that choice.

Actually doing this in practice can be hard to achieve, though. This is partly because we all bring our own values and thoughts to our work (as is discussed in Chapter 3), and partly because workers in health and social care have to consider their duty of care towards individuals at all times (see Chapter 4).

KEY QUESTIONS

When you are working with a service user to look at decisions they want or need to make, you need to ensure their choices are informed ones. Here are some key questions to ask of yourself.

Rights

Does the person have a right to make this decision? If they were prevented from doing this, would that deny them their rights? If they were to take a certain course of action, would it deny other people their rights (eg the right to be safe, the right to make their own choices, etc)?

Information

It sounds obvious, but in order for a choice to be an informed one, people need all the available information. How do you ensure that service users have all the information they need about the potential consequences of deciding to take a certain action? Equally, how do you make sure they have all the information about the potential consequences of *not* taking that action? When you provide information, this must be done in a way that meets individual service users' needs (eg access to information, language, communication needs).

Values

When you present and share the previous information, how do your own values influence the way in which you do this? What might you and others need to take account of in terms of a service user's own values, culture, beliefs and preferences, so that the choices they make are their own?

Checks and balances

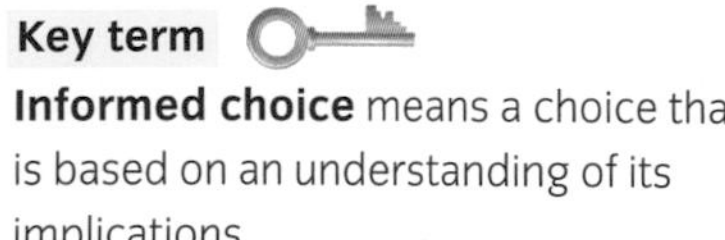

Key term

Informed choice means a choice that is based on an understanding of its implications.

- When a person makes a choice, how can you be really sure that this choice is their own, has not been unduly influenced by others and is an **informed choice**?
- How are the decisions that have been made recorded? Does your service have any specific policies, procedures or paperwork to do so?
- Are there risk assessments that need to be completed depending on the choices that the person wants to make?

USING RISK ASSESSMENTS TO SUPPORT CHOICES

Risk assessments are one of the main ways to support service users to make choices. Where the choice that a service user makes places them at risk, a risk assessment and a risk management plan can be developed to support them in making that decision. See Chapter 4 for more detail on risk assessments and risk management.

A risk assessment should be a tool that promotes decision making for individuals. Every day most of us do some activities that could be seen as presenting risks, such as:

- crossing the road
- driving a car
- getting money out of a cash point
- cooking food
- drinking alcohol
- climbing ladders or doing DIY at home.

Even if all risks could be eliminated from daily life (and they cannot be), this would make life extremely dull. Where services are 'risk averse', this means they do not enable service users to take part in activities that are seen as risky. This could be because an organisation is worried about potential legal action if things go wrong, because of a fear of being blamed, or because of issues connected with the cost of enabling people to do activities. Getting the balance right for service users is crucial so that they:

- can experience a full and dignified life
- can make their own choices about how to spend their own life
- can make decisions with all of the information they need to do so
- can receive the right level of support and protection for their individual needs.

Every service will have its own paperwork to use for risk assessments. All risk assessments will be:

- designed to make sure that everyone who is involved in making decisions has considered all of the risk factors
- designed to put in place any measures to mitigate the most serious risks
- completed in partnership with service users and their carers/family
- implemented in a way that promotes people's choices and which does not prevent them from making decisions and taking part in activities which enhance their quality of life.

Below is an example of a risk assessment.

Activity: swimming	Potential risks or hazards	Likelihood of the service user being harmed (1 is low risk and 5 a high risk)	Actions to reduce risk	Review
Going to the pool	• Vehicle safety (see transport risk assessment)	2	• See risk assessment for transporting people	
Getting changed	• Trips and falls	3	• Supporting the person appropriately • Ensuring there is enough time • 3:2 staffing ratio (consider gender of workers attending the activity)	
Swimming in the pool	• Trips and falls • Drowning	2	• 3:2 staffing ratio • Armbands and visible swimming caps • Using a reputable facility with a suitable number of lifeguards • Supporting the person to get in and out of the pool, and to and from the changing area	

Good practice in risk assessment involves:

- involving the service user in discussions about risk
- talking through the consequences of an action being taken (or not taken) so that decisions are informed ones
- involving the service user's carers and others who know them well
- reviewing the risk assessment and updating it as necessary
- following policy and procedure within your service and your job role
- taking account of a service user's individuality, culture, beliefs, wishes and preferences
- taking account of how a service user's needs, skills and wishes will change over time.

Working in a person-centred way is about wanting service users to live as full a life as possible, whatever the nature of their needs. Living a full life is about making choices and feeling in control. We all do things sometimes which others might think are not what is best for us, but the most important thing is that the choices we make are our own choices.

Being person-centred means that we involve service users in these discussions and decisions, because they are decisions about that person's own life and not our own. The main issue is that because you are a professional (ie you are paid money to do the work you do), you need to be able to demonstrate how risk has been considered as part of your duty of care in your job role.

CASE STUDY

Sarah is a young adult with a mild to moderate learning disability. She lives in a supported accommodation placement in the community. Recently, she has been spending a lot of time with an older adult male, who has taken her out for meals. Sarah confides in her keyworker, Pete, that she is falling in love with this man, and he has asked her to have sex with him. Sarah talks about her dreams of having her own family with this man, and being able to move out of her current accommodation to share his home with him.

Pete is concerned because of the age difference, and because Sarah is emotionally very vulnerable. He explains to Sarah that he will need to talk to his manager about what she has said, so that they can work together around her hopes and also around her safety. Sarah is annoyed about this, as she does not understand why Pete thinks she may be unsafe. She says that she and the man she is seeing are in love and it is nobody else's business.

- How might Pete, his manager and others begin to work on a risk assessment in partnership with Sarah?
- What might the risks to Sarah be, and how might she feel about this situation?
- How could some of the risks be managed proactively, safely and by working with Sarah?

REFLECT

Think about what choices you have made today and then reflect on whether the service users you support have been able to make as many choices as you.

- What limits the choices you can make?
- What limits the choices that the service users you work with can make?

CHALLENGES AND COMPLAINTS

The importance of complaints procedures is considered in Chapters 4 and 5. In relation to this, it is important to note that working in a person-centred way has to involve:

- informing service users of their rights to complain
- listening to service users' concerns, and acting on them
- enabling service users to make choices about whether to complain formally or make an informal challenge or request to a service
- promoting service users' rights to be listened to, respected and treated fairly at all times
- advocating on service users' behalf where requested to do so, necessary and/or appropriate.

Sometimes, service users are not able to make the choices they would like to make. This could be because of:

- changes in eligibility for a service
- cuts or closures to services
- the person's needs and circumstances, or changes to these
- a decision made by others about their capacity
- safeguarding issues or concerns about risk where the risk outweighs the service user's rights to make certain choices.

Even where any of these factors occur, service users still need to feel listened to, to be informed of their rights to challenge or complain, and to access the support they need to have their view heard. You may be in a good position to support a service user, or you may need to access an advocacy service on their behalf where the boundaries of your own role prevent you from doing so.

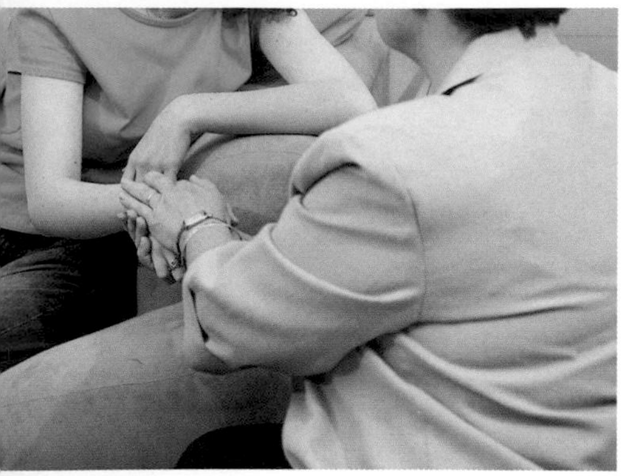

REFLECT

- How have you enabled a service user to make informed decisions in your work role?
- Can you think of an instance when you have had to champion this as somebody's right, or challenge others around their decision making? If so, how did you manage risk in a way that enabled the service user to make their own decision?

PROMOTING WELLBEING

It is vital that all health and social care workers recognise the importance of wellbeing. You will often hear the phrase 'health and wellbeing' – while health refers to someone's physical and mental health, the word wellbeing refers more to other aspects of a person's general happiness, which might include those shown in the diagram below.

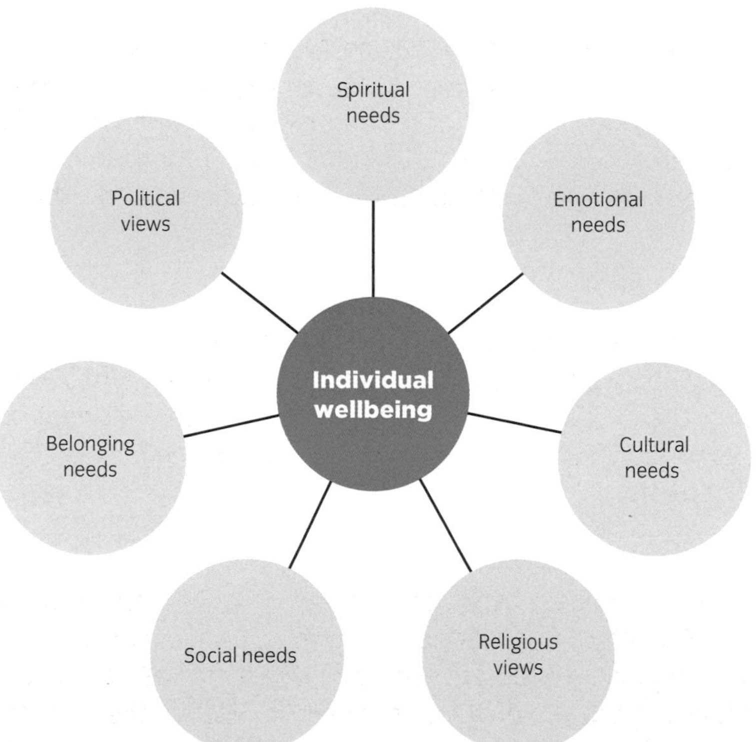

Key term

Holistic approach considers the service user as an individual, and all of the factors which make up their life, instead of focusing only on their support needs.

Addressing wellbeing is really about seeing someone as a whole person and taking a **holistic approach**. This is perhaps where health and social care workers have a specialist aspect to their practice. For example, while a nurse or doctor might prioritise someone's physical health, a health and social care worker will recognise that there are lots of other aspects to someone's wellbeing.

IDENTITY

Understanding identity issues is an important step in promoting wellbeing. Identity is partly an expression of two functions – self-image and self-esteem:

- self-image is essentially about how we see or describe ourselves
- self-esteem is about how we feel about or value ourselves.

Service users may have various threats to their positive sense of identity, self-image and self-esteem – many of which are covered in detail in other chapters.

Societal prejudice and discrimination

Chapter 3 discussed how there can be oppression at a societal level. Many adults in society are aware of the way they are discriminated against, and this can have an effect on self-confidence and generate a range of responses (including defensiveness and anger).

Institutional stigma

Being in contact with health and social care services can still carry a stigma. This is partly because in the past the quality of care services for adults was poor. Even today there are examples where service provision can be very poor (see Chapters 5 and 8 for examples, from Mid Staffordshire NHS Foundation Trust Hospital and Winterbourne View).

Individual attitudes

The attitudes and behaviour of staff can be a key element in supporting adult service users to maintain (or develop) their identity and self-esteem. Negative attitudes and a lack of commitment to person-centred values will negatively impact on a person's self-image and self-esteem.

Labelling and stereotyping

Labelling is the process by which a negative blanket term is applied to a person. The effect on other people, when they view that person, is to have a prejudiced and negative view, which can lead to the person being stereotyped. The effect on the person, both of the label and of other people's actions towards them, results in the person feeling judged and this undermines their self-esteem and confidence. The person who is labelled may then act in ways that are a distortion of their true identity. Issues of labelling and stereotyping are covered in more detail in Chapter 3.

PROMOTING IDENTITY, SELF-IMAGE, SELF-ESTEEM AND WELLBEING

Health and social care workers can adopt a range of methods to promote service users' identity, self-image and self-esteem, and many services have made progress in recognising and respecting the identity of service users.

Many of the methods that can be used to promote identity and wellbeing have been covered in this chapter, summarised as follows.

The development of person-centred plans and person-centred care

This is one way in that health and social care services are trying to promote wellbeing.

Meaningful activities

Where services work with adults of working age, many are seeking to give more relevant options. These options include further education, training for employment and support to get a job. Daytime occupation is a key aspect of identity. Often if you meet someone new the first question is 'What is your name?' and the second question is 'What do you do?'

Positive approaches to risk

Services are developing a more positive approach to risk assessment and risk management. Often the key decisions around risk management are made in multi-disciplinary meetings, but the view of the service user is now taken far more seriously as it is acknowledged that there is dignity within risk taking which people must not be denied. If services respect the service user's wishes, then often the service user can still live their life as they want to even if there is risk involved.

Environment

Some environments promote a feeling of wellbeing, while other environments might have a negative impact on people. For example, think about how you feel in a very busy, noisy environment. Different people like different kinds of environment, and finding out about this is a key part of person-centred care.

Addressing personal relationship needs

Personal relationships are a significant aspect of identity and wellbeing.

Life story work

In life story work, the aim is to generate a personal record of a service user's life. This record could be a book, a photobook, a memory box, a CD or DVD, and the record becomes the individual's property. Where a person has experienced many changes, life story work can result in them understanding more about their life and situation.

Reminiscence work

Reminiscence work is usually associated with older people, and is often done in groups. There are often props or prompts, which can consist of photographs or videos from the past, clothing or household articles (also from the past). The intention is to support the service user to talk about their past, both in terms of employment and personal life (right back to childhood).

Reminiscence work helps to confirm a person's identity and reinforces their individuality. It can also promote wellbeing very effectively.

Other aspects of person-centred practice that promote service users' identity and self-esteem include:

- enabling service users to make informed choices
- reviewing consent
- establishing and reviewing the service user's wishes, feelings and preferences
- involving a service user's family, carers and friends in an appropriate way in their care planning
- responding to a service user's unique communication needs and preferences
- using good listening skills
- avoiding making assumptions
- promoting active participation
- supporting the service user with the tasks they need support with, and avoiding over-supporting them
- spending time with service users
- promoting their unique talents
- praise, encouragement and recognition of achievements
- involving service users in society and their community
- encouraging service users to share time with other people who enjoy doing similar things.

CASE STUDY

Nav is having support from a reablement team following a serious car accident which has left him with a physical disability. Prior to his accident, Nav was a senior manager in a national company, and he has been experiencing feelings of depression and reduced self-worth as a direct result of the trauma he has been through. He is living with his parents again, and misses living in his own flat and having his space.

Sue is working with him to look at how he can live independently again in the future, and she understands that some work needs to be done around his identity and self-esteem in order to ensure that Nav feels able to continue to do all he can in his life.

- How can Sue and Nav agree a plan to address these issues together?
- What might Nav's biggest worries be, and how could Sue and others support him?
- How would Sue ensure that she provides Nav with the right amount of support (ie working in a person-centred way), but avoids over-supporting him?

Before going to the next chapter, take some time to consider:

- why you think person-centred practice is important in health and social care
- what main barriers you face in being person-centred in your practice
- how you can reduce these barriers.

CHAPTER 10
Provide active support

Active support is a person-centred model which is about providing the right amount of support to individual service users. Sometimes service users can be 'over-supported' and have things done for them which they could be enabled to do for themselves. Active support is about service users being supported in a way that recognises their rights and their needs, while also providing opportunities for them to develop new skills.

Whilst active support is mainly used when working with people with learning disabilities, this chapter will be useful to everyone working in health and social care, because aspects of active support can be useful in working with people with all kinds of different needs and from a wide range of backgrounds.

Links to other chapters

The content in this chapter links closely with Chapter 9, and there are also links to be made with promoting equality and the rights of people with specific needs (see Chapters 3 and 4).

WHAT IS ACTIVE SUPPORT?

Key terms 

Active support is a person-centred model of how to interact with service users, combined with a daily planning system that promotes participation and enhances quality of life.

Hotel model refers to institutional-style settings organised mainly around staffing needs. They are not person-centred and offer a poor quality of life to service users. For example, where health and social care workers undertake all the domestic tasks, and do not provide opportunities for service users to participate in constructive activities.

Active support was first established as a model of care for people in learning disability services. It was designed as a model of support to challenge what has become known as the 'gift model' of care provision.

- The gift model is where care is provided *for* or *to* people, eg tasks are done for or to people.
- Active support involves working *with* people to enable them to take part in all the activities of daily life.

Active support is now the preferred model for all health and social care services.

Historically, care services were delivered on the gift model basis. Care was seen as something to be 'given'. Often the care was provided in an institutional way – as in the **hotel model**.

THE HOTEL MODEL

Institutions following the hotel model are not person-centred and can offer a poor quality of life to service users. For example, this is apparent where health and social care workers undertake all the domestic tasks and do not provide opportunities for service users to participate in constructive activities. The ideas of the hotel and gift models overlap, but the concept of people being in a hotel links more with residential care provision.

Features of the gift/hotel models	Features of active support
Care or support is *given to* service users.	Service users are actively involved in as many aspects of their own care as possible.
Health and social care workers undertake most of the domestic or daily living tasks in the setting.	Service users are involved in tasks relating to daily living.
Service users are provided with a level of support which is perceived to be what is right for their needs, but which actually may be the same level of help for all service users.	The level of help provided is planned around the service user's own individual needs, and is provided in a way which maximises the person's own participation in their care.
The life of the service is centred around routines.	Service users are involved in planning their own care plan, and in the activities of the service.

Features of the gift/hotel models	Features of active support
Service users are more likely to be inactive for long periods during the day.	The day is planned to maximise the level of activity for each service user throughout each day.
Service users are more likely to experience feeling devalued and lack of purpose in their own life.	The balance of activity in each service user's daily life aims to match the level of activity which people have in the general population who do not have specific needs.

Active support has developed from the idea that many adults with social care needs, especially those with complex learning and/or physical disabilities, do not have the same quality of life as who do not have these needs. The lives of service users, particularly those in institutional care, can be dull, and their days can be unstructured, with lots of time where they do not have anything meaningful to do.

Adopting an active support approach within a service involves:

- training
- commitment
- reflection
- consistent application
- patience
- time
- seeking out opportunities for service users to participate in meaningful activities
- planning for service users to participate in their own care
- planning for service users to participate in domestic tasks and the daily life of the service
- planning for service users to interact as much as possible with each other.

BENEFITS OF ADOPTING AN ACTIVE SUPPORT APPROACH WITH SERVICE USERS

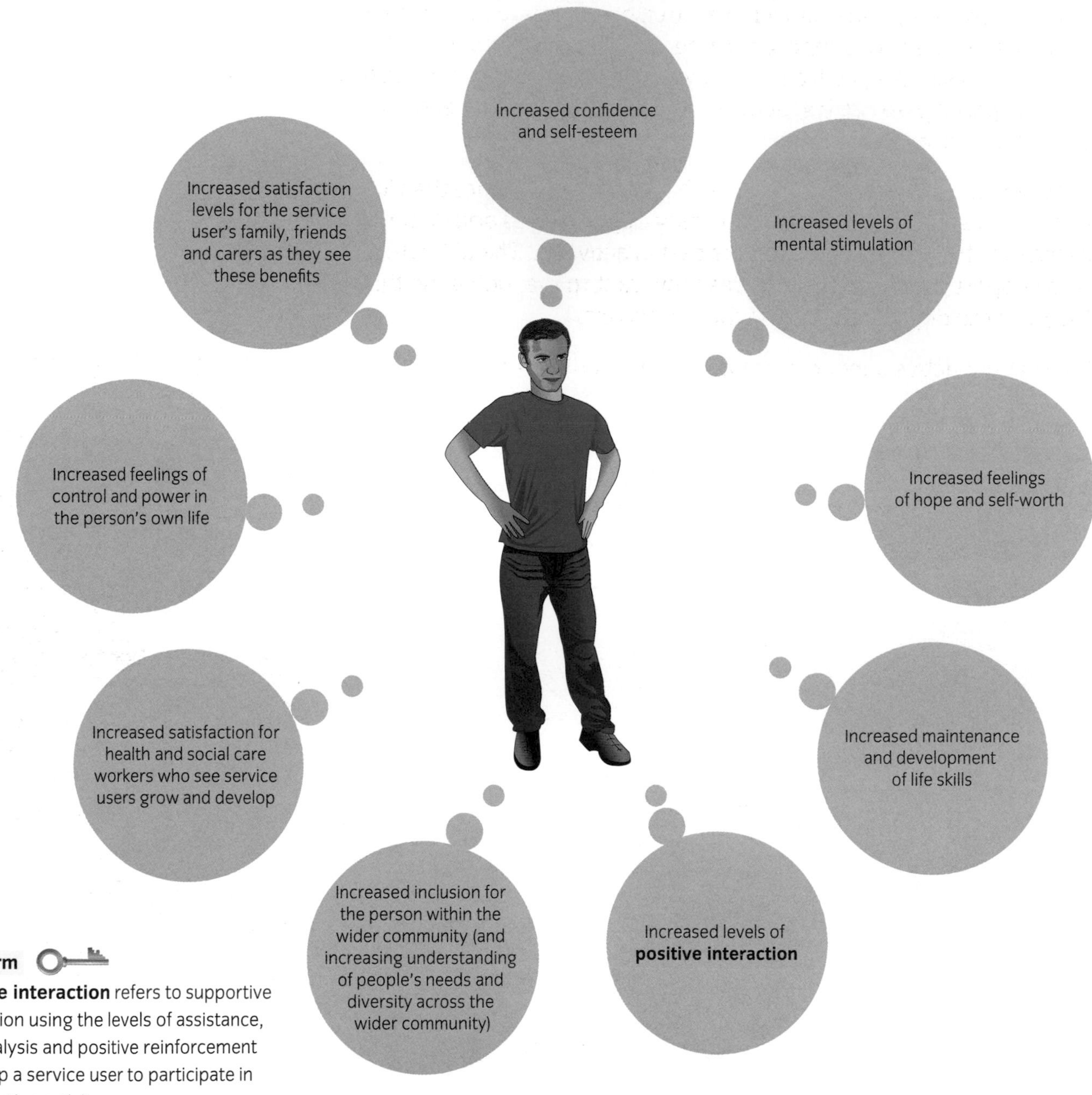

Key term

Positive interaction refers to supportive interaction using the levels of assistance, task analysis and positive reinforcement that help a service user to participate in constructive activity.

ACTIVE SUPPORT AND PERSON-CENTRED PRACTICE

Active support is often referred to as 'person-centred active support'. This is because active support must be delivered in a person-centred way. On a basic level, active support would be seen as enabling service users to participate more in activities, including those connected with their own care and daily living.

However, the active support approach involves much more than just health and social care workers providing opportunities and direct assistance to enable people to take part in activities. The ultimate aim is to support people to live the lives they want to live, doing the things they want to do, and respecting their decisions.

Think about active support as a journey or a continuum:

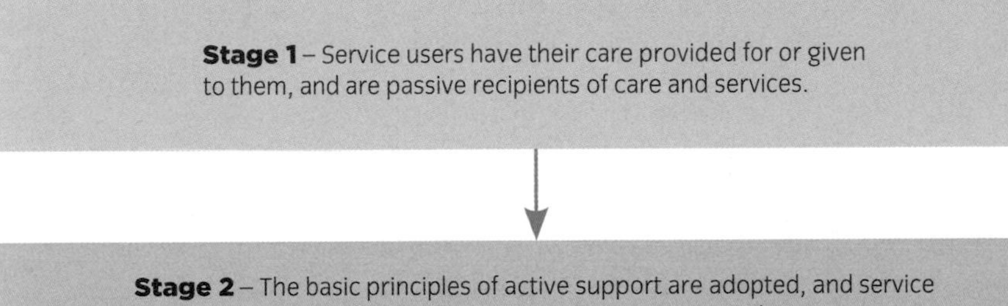

PROMOTING INDEPENDENCE, INFORMED CHOICE AND VALUED LIFE

These key terms and concepts all link together and are essential components of active support.

Promoting independence

Active support is about rights. All people, whether they have social care needs or not, have the right to as full and varied a life as anyone else. This is the starting point for active support. All have rights, including the rights to have meaningful relationships, choice and control, and access to activities. Focusing on these rights is critical in order for service users to enjoy the same quality of life as other people.

In order for independence to be promoted, service users' rights need to be understood and respected.

What does independence mean to you? Is it:

- being able to make your own decisions about how you spend your day?
- being able to decide who you spend your time with?
- being able to think about your own goals for the future, and how you plan to reach them?
- being able to enjoy your leisure time in the way you want to?
- being able to meet your own needs and live independently (ie without requiring the support of others to do so)?
- being able to avoid doing things you do not want to do?

Active support recognises that all service users need a sense of control and power in their own lives, and that this is vital in promoting their independence. However, when service users have care needs, and especially needs relating to their own personal care, they may require assistance from others in order to be as independent as possible.

Informed choices

In order for choices to be effective, we need information about the possible consequences of the choices we make. For example, if you decide not to brush your teeth, or eat healthily, there may be a negative consequence, and you are likely to have had information to help you understand this from a range of sources and throughout your life.

Active support enables service users to make informed choices by first respecting the fact that all service users have the right to make their own decisions, and that they need to do so to feel independent and in control of their own life. However, when services are involved in a person' s life, all professionals have a duty of care towards each individual service user.

Young people and vulnerable adults may need support to ensure that they are protected from abuse and harm, and to ensure that their basic needs are met and not ignored. However, this support must actively promote the service user's right to make their own decisions and choices, and to be fully involved in their own care.

Valued life

As outlined above, active support recognises that the quality of life for all service users (whether they require support from others or not) is about:

- being able to make their own decisions
- being in control over their own life and future
- having a balance between being as active as possible and being able to rest when needed
- being able to interact with others in a meaningful way.

By promoting the rights of service users and by focusing on promoting independence, active support aims to enable service users to live a full, varied and rewarding life of their own.

THE IMPACT OF ACTIVE SUPPORT ON A VALUED LIFESTYLE

Ashman and Beadle-Brown's 2006 research paper 'A Valued Life' showed that where active support was implemented:

- 50% of people showed an increase in engagement in activities
- 75% of people with severe disabilities showed an increase in their independence and skills.

The most significant factor in contributing towards these outcomes was health and social care workers' commitment to active support – providing an active lifestyle. They needed to show their commitment to changing the way they work with people, and to be given the time to implement strategies for active support to have the most impact.

A range of practical changes can be made within any setting to promote active support. The use of active support can promote independence, informed choices and a valued life for service users, and even services that are not adopting the full active support model can apply the key principles of it.

For this to be effective there needs to be a commitment to the philosophy of active support within a service. Managers need to enable health and social care workers to reflect on their practice, and how this promotes people's independence. Health and social care workers need ongoing training and opportunities to develop for the model to be implemented and sustained.

Some practical ways in which active support can achieve the above include the following.

Using everyday opportunities

Active support is not about putting on new or specific activities, but instead it is about using the opportunities that day-to-day life provides. Meaningful activity for most of us is not about the hobbies we have, but about how we conduct our lives. All services have things that need to be done in order for the service to function, just as all of us need to do certain things in our own lives to get to work, keep the house clean, make sure we and our families have food, etc. Active support involves service users in such tasks in the same way as they would be involved in managing their own lives independently.

Involving service users in their own care and support tasks

For example, every morning, most of us follow a set routine – get up, wash, get dressed, have breakfast, brush our teeth, etc. For some people with disabilities, all or most of these things could be done for them. Active support recognises that these sorts of daily living tasks provide opportunities to build people's skills, and thereby their confidence in their own abilities.

Promoting participation for service users within their community

Active support aims to avoid service users becoming isolated from their own networks and from their communities by promoting independence, and their inclusion within community networks and activities.

Doing all of this in a planned way

All of this should be done in a planned way for each service user, ensuring that each individual has the right level of help to achieve a specific task. These concepts are explored in more detail in the next section.

CASE STUDY

Markus works with older adults in a residential service. He has only just started this job, and has noticed that many of the residents spend a lot of their time inactive, watching television and looking bored. Markus is aware of the active support model from a training course he went on in a previous job, and he brings some literature in to show his manager, Lorraine. Lorraine asks Markus to share this information at the next team meeting.

Some of Markus's colleagues are excited about trying new ideas, and about improving the quality of life for the residents at the service. Others seem to find the information more challenging and are reluctant to take part in discussions about how the principles of active support could be developed in the service.

- Why might some workers find this model challenging? What might their worries or reluctance be based on?
- How could Markus and his managers support the whole team to see the benefits of active support?

REFLECT

You might work in a service setting where many of the principles and ideas of active support are useful to consider, even if the service does not adopt the full model of active support. If this is the case, how do you promote the key principles described above in your work with service users?

INTERACTING POSITIVELY TO PROMOTE PARTICIPATION

There are three key elements or concepts in active support that promote a service user's participation in activities:

- levels of assistance
- task analysis
- positive reinforcement.

LEVELS OF ASSISTANCE

Active support demands that health and social care workers step back from carrying out care tasks for people, and identify the minimum level of support in order for the service user to do that activity themselves. Active support matches the level of assistance to the service user, so that:

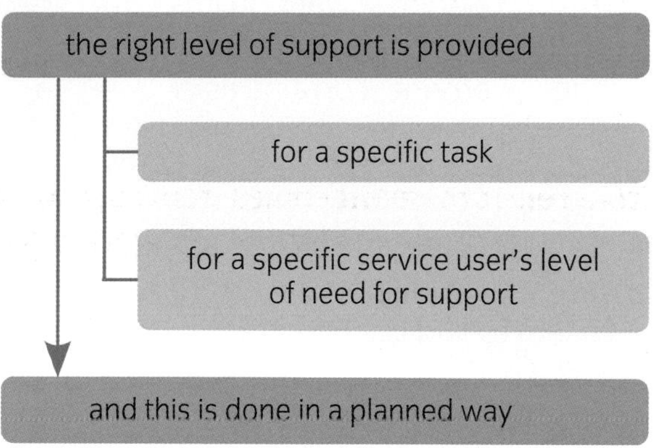

This principle can be applied in any service setting, and it can be valuable for all health and social care workers to reflect on the actual level of input that a service user needs to perform a task. This is because it is much more rewarding for people to experience the outcome of achieving something than to feel that others do everything for them.

REFLECT

Think about the people who you work with and the level of care and support that they actually require in order to ensure that their basic needs are met. Now think about you being in the position of a service user you work with. If you needed help or support to get dressed, to have a bath, to eat or to go out of the house, how would you feel? How would you want those supporting you to provide you with this help?

TASK ANALYSIS

Task analysis involves a health and social care worker understanding the specific detail of a task that a service user needs support with. By analysing the steps that the service user needs to take in order to achieve the outcome of a specific task, the health and social care worker can then match the right level of assistance for the person to be supported in the right way at every step. This is explored in more detail below.

POSITIVE REINFORCEMENT

Service users require different types of encouragement and rewards in order to feel motivated to:

- attempt a task which feels difficult or perhaps impossible to start with
- keep trying when things are tough
- feel a sense of achievement and recognition when they do achieve a step or a task.

The term **positive reinforcement** comes from psychology. It is a term used to describe how rewards can influence activity and behaviour.

Key term

Positive reinforcement refers to what a service user gains from undertaking a specific task. It can include naturally occurring rewards (eg drinking a cup of tea the service user has just made) or other things that the service user particularly likes (eg praise and attention or a preferred activity) as an encouragement or reward for participating in a specified activity.

The concepts of levels of assistance, task analysis and positive reinforcement link together, in that:

- You need to understand the detail of the tasks that a service user is working to achieve.
- This analysis of what the task is enables you and the service user to decide what level of help they need at each step.
- You must understand and respond to a service user's needs and preferences around encouragement, praise and reward in order to keep them focused, motivated and feeling that they are achieving what they want to.

BREAKING A ROUTINE TASK INTO MANAGEABLE STEPS

Task analysis refers to breaking down tasks into small, manageable steps, just as you would if you were following a recipe or a manual for using a new item of technology. Imagine if you were faced with cooking a complicated three-course meal or using a new gadget without any access to a manual or guide to support you.

The size of each step or the number of steps for a specific task should vary according to the service user's ability or need for support.

In planning for active support with service users, every task needs to be considered in detail. This means:

- looking at what the task involves (not taking for granted how you may do the task yourself)
- breaking this task into a number of small steps
- matching the level of assistance that the service user needs in order to achieve each step

- planning how to introduce the task to the service user
- planning for how you will encourage the service user, and how their achievements should be rewarded.

Consider a daily task in your own life, such as loading the washing machine. The steps involved could be:

- emptying the laundry basket onto the floor by the machine
- sorting out whites from colours
- putting the clothes you want to wash into the machine
- getting the detergent out of the cupboard
- measuring the right amount of detergent into the cup
- putting this detergent into the drawer in the machine
- pouring the fabric softener into the compartment (again, the right amount)
- selecting the programme you want and the right temperature
- switching the machine on.

Now consider this for a service user – a person who previously may not have had any involvement in the washing of their clothes, but may have had all of this done for them their whole life.

Using different levels of support to increase independence

The following model gives a structured way to increase a service user's participation in specific tasks:

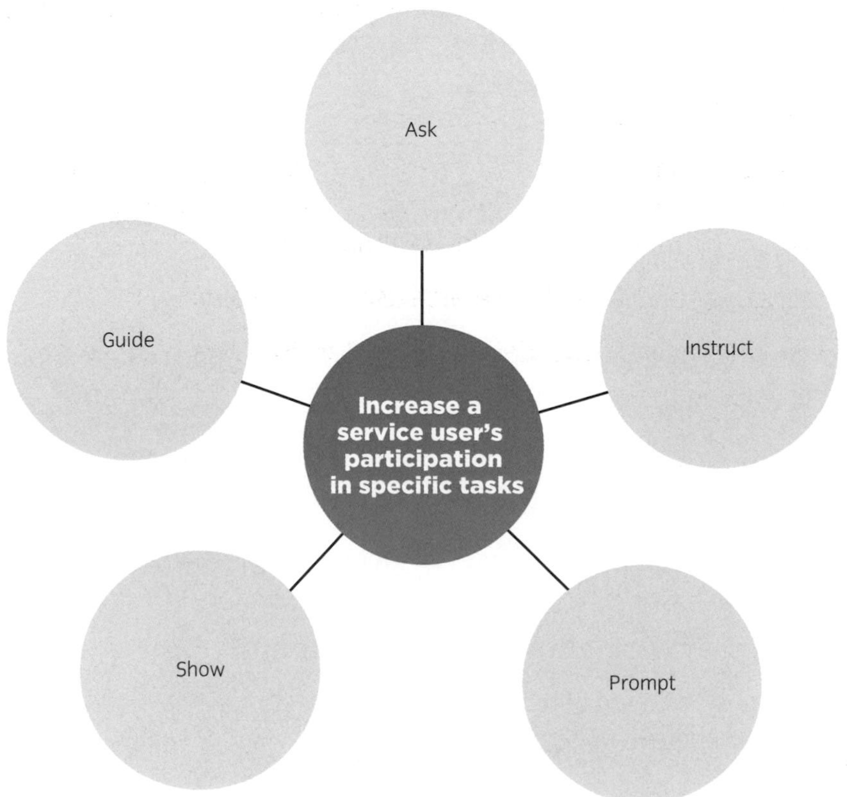

- *Ask*. The person should be given the opportunity to do something without any support if they want to and are able to.
- *Instruct*. Describe to the person (using appropriate communication) what steps to take to achieve the task, so they can then do this themselves – again, if they want to and are able to.
- *Prompt*. A person could be given a prompt or reminder if they are getting stuck. The principle of **minimal sufficiency** is critical to this, so if the individual is managing without a prompt, do not prompt them as this reduces their ownership of their activity.
- *Show*. If the person needs a demonstration of how to do something, show them, but do not then walk away. For example, if they need to be shown how to wash a plate, that is fine, but then let them wash the next one whilst you stay nearby to offer further prompts if necessary.
- *Guide*. Is about providing the minimal level of support that the person needs to be able to do the task. For example, if the person needs help in putting their socks on, the worker can guide them in this, but the key principles are around not doing this for them, but providing enough support so they can achieve it themselves, and then next time, letting them do this with slightly less support and input etc.

Key term

Minimal sufficiency refers to providing the minimal prompt (or support) to someone – just sufficient – not too much and not too little. It is all about getting the balance right between supporting someone but not doing too much for them. It is a key principle in active support and in promoting independence in support work.

Consider the above example in the context of using a washing machine. Some service users might only need to be asked, and they might then want to perform the task of putting the wash on themselves. Others might need a far greater level of instruction, prompting or actual guidance. Whatever level of support is provided, though, this needs to be:

- matched to the service user's needs
- considered in relation to each task and step along the way (eg guiding the service user in measuring out the detergent, and instructing them when sorting out the clothes)
- reduced gradually as the service user achieves the task
- encouraged and rewarded appropriately for that service user.

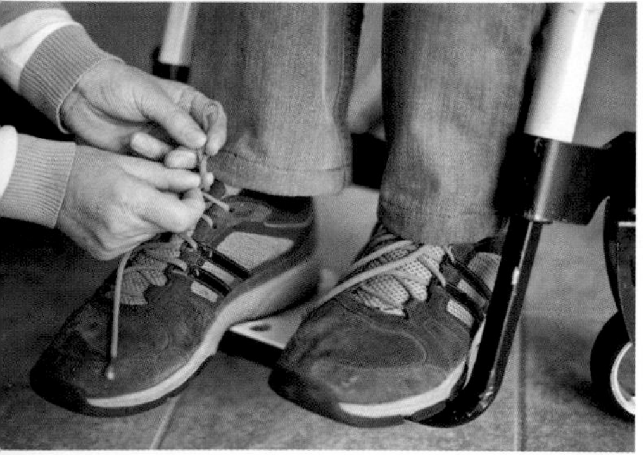

The key principles are to not do the task for the person, but to provide enough support so they can achieve it. Then next time, the idea is to let them do the task with slightly less support and input.

In terms of personal care or assistance, if a service user needs help in getting dressed, it may be most appropriate for the health and social care worker to guide them in this directly at first. Someone with complex physical needs and little verbal communication may need the health and social care worker's hand to guide their own hand when doing some of these activities. Another service user may simply need more instruction in the task and some prompting.

A service user with autism and challenging behaviours might need to take part in one of the steps (with the washing machine example, starting by emptying the basket), and to see this as enjoyable and rewarding before they will consent to moving forward with you for the rest of the steps. It is better that this service user sees the task as satisfying, rewarding and their own achievement than that they get demotivated or discouraged from trying the task again in future.

By following this process for daily tasks, and by building up service users' involvement gradually and in a way appropriate to their needs, they can:

- develop their skills
- build their confidence
- transfer these skills to other activities
- feel more valued and motivated
- experience greater independence and feelings of control and self-worth.

REFLECT

- Consider the task analysis above for using a washing machine.
- Can you do a similar task analysis for a daily activity in your work setting, and then apply the steps and the level of support needed to a service user you work with?

PROVIDING DIFFERENT LEVELS OF HELP

Service users all need different **levels of help**. Many health and social care workers are used to working with service users who require high levels of support in order to ensure their basic care needs are met. Undertaking work within an active support philosophy requires a shift in thinking towards *how* people can be enabled to do everything they can do, as opposed to focusing on what they *cannot* do without support.

The model described above of

- ASK
- INSTRUCT
- PROMPT
- SHOW
- GUIDE

gives a useful means for looking at what level of help or assistance a person may need to achieve a specific task or activity.

For some service users, the level of help or assistance they need to perform a task might be simple verbal reminders. These reminders would be about providing the lowest level of support for the person to do the task and achieve the outcome themselves. Other service users may need actual physical guidance, and therefore the highest level of support to achieve the same task. Help or assistance should be given flexibly according to the service user's need for that help, and should be focused on encouraging as much independence as possible.

The concept of matching the level of help to the person's need is about considering precisely what the service user needs in order for them to take part in a task, and avoiding assumptions about what they need to have done for them.

The key to this is:

- do not do the things for the person that they can do for themselves
- be very certain of what they can and cannot do before you assume they cannot do something, jump in and do it for them.

For example, look at your own morning routine, as follows:

Key term

Levels of help refers to graduated levels of assistance, from simple verbal reminders providing the lowest level of support to actual physical guidance providing the highest level. Assistance should be given flexibly according to the individual service user's need for help, and should be focused on encouraging as much independence as possible.

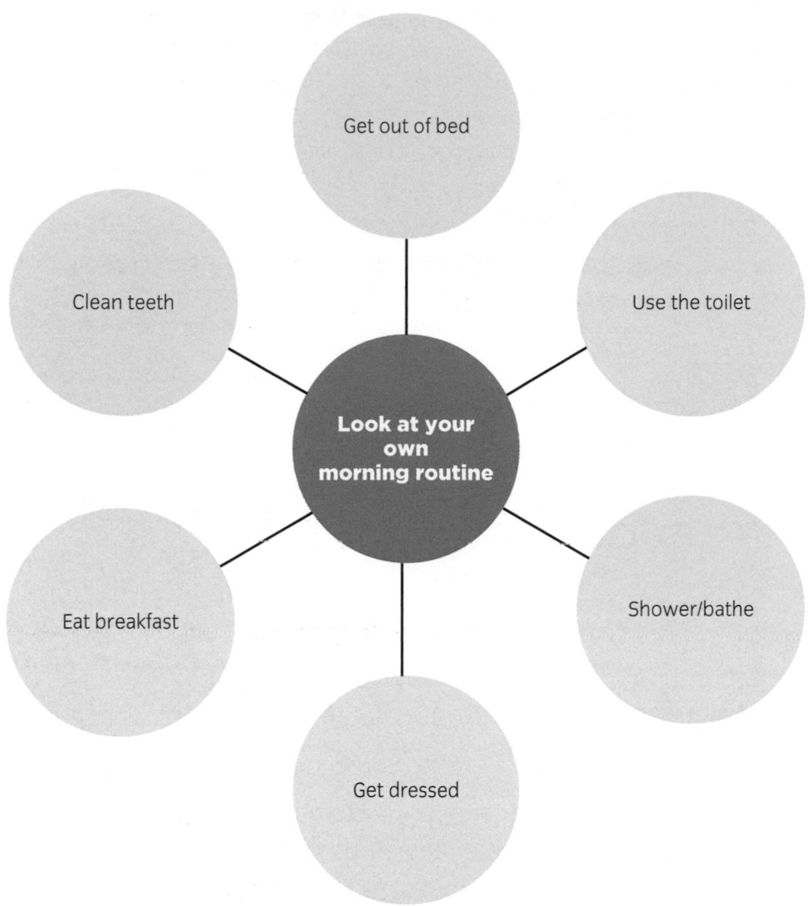

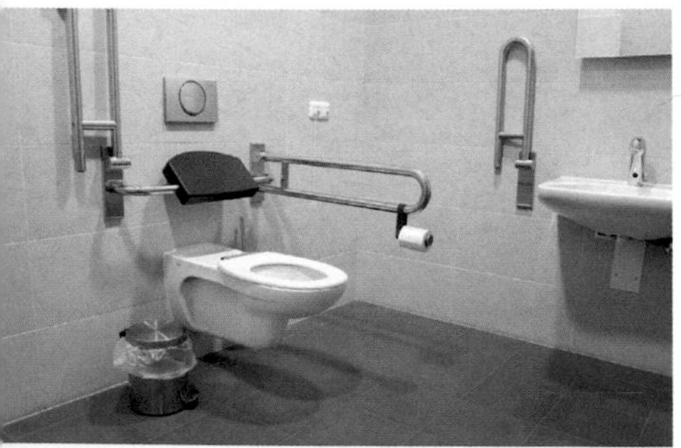

While most of us probably follow a set routine for the day, we still make a plan each morning of what we will do and in what order. This will include what to eat, how long to shower for, whether to reply to any messages we have, and so on. Some of the routine we perform on 'autopilot' as it is instinctive, but the activities are still our own choices and they are activities that we do by ourselves, and for ourselves.

For many of the service users we work with, all of the above are activities which they cannot (yet?) do fully on autopilot, or which they need some level of support or input from others to achieve. However, by matching different levels of support to different tasks, active support can be promoted.

For example, consider a service user with limited mobility and complex physical care needs:

- *Get out of bed*. Can the person be supported to move certain parts of their body themselves, as well as receiving support to move other parts, so that this is done *with* and not *to* them?
- *Use the toilet.* What tools and support are available to support the person to get on and off the toilet, and how are they involved in the moving and changing position?

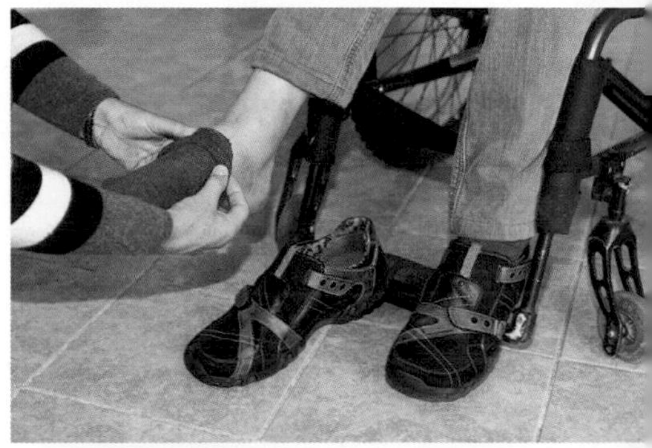

- *Shower/bathe.* Can the person hold the sponge and soap themselves, or can you provide them with a guide to use their own hands to wash themselves, instead of your washing and their sitting there still?
- *Get dressed.* To what extent can the person dress themselves (would some aids help with this)?
- *Eat breakfast.* Do you hold the cutlery and move it to their mouth, or can they do this with you?
- *Clean teeth.* As above.

In order for all of this to work, the service user needs to:

- receive the right amount of support – not too much so that the task is done for them, and not too little so that they fail and feel disempowered and demotivated to try again next time
- receive praise, encouragement and reinforcement (see below)
- feel that it is something that is enjoyable, that you do together, and that is valuable
- not become overwhelmed – in active support, it is better that someone undertakes a task actively for 10 seconds to start with, and that this success is then built up, than that the doing becomes a battle of wills, as the above three points would then become meaningless.

Active support involves applying these principles and ideas to the whole range of activities and tasks in people's daily lives. It is not just about involvement in formal 'activities', but is about the day-to-day things that keep most of us busy, take up our time, prevent us from sitting around bored all day, and that engage us with others in our environment.

Active support is about wanting all of this for the service users we work with, and promoting people's involvement in day-to-day living, for example, by:

- preparing meals
- laying the table
- cleaning up
- washing up
- caring for a pet
- walking the dog
- dusting
- doing the food shop
- packing and unpacking the shopping

- loading and unloading the washing machine
- watering plants and tending the garden
- using electronic equipment and choosing entertainment
- etc – the list goes on for all of us.

With each of these, the tasks need to be analysed in detail, the level of help should be matched as described above, and the opportunities that each day presents should be planned for in order to promote service users' active involvement in their own lives.

POSITIVELY REINFORCING PARTICIPATION IN AN ACTIVITY

We learn best when we receive positive reinforcement. The ideas of positive reinforcement and the importance of this come from psychology. Reinforcement is about:

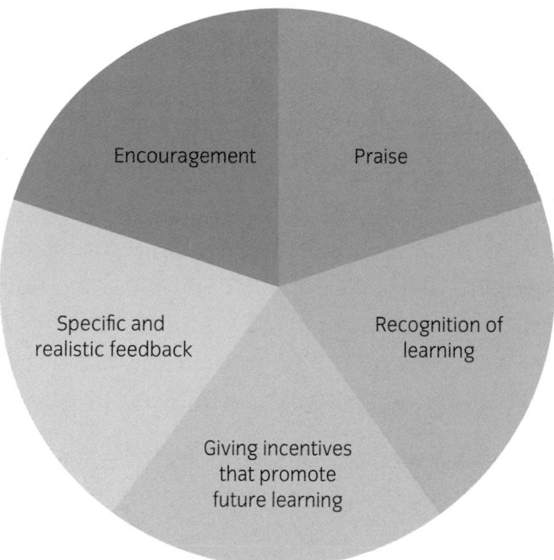

The term 'positive reinforcement' refers to what a service user gains from undertaking a specific task. These can include naturally occurring rewards (eg drinking a cup of tea the service user has just made) or other things that the service user particularly likes (eg praise and attention or a preferred activity) as an encouragement or reward.

Skinner's (1971) work into operant conditioning recognises that the environment around us has an effect on our behaviour. The idea of **operant conditioning** is that behaviours are influenced by a stimulus, and also by the responses that the behaviour provokes.

Key term

Operant conditioning is a term used to describe the way that behaviours are very often linked to some kind of stimulus or event. It also refers to the way that behaviours lead to a consequence which can reinforce the behaviour. This idea has been very influential in theories about behaviour.

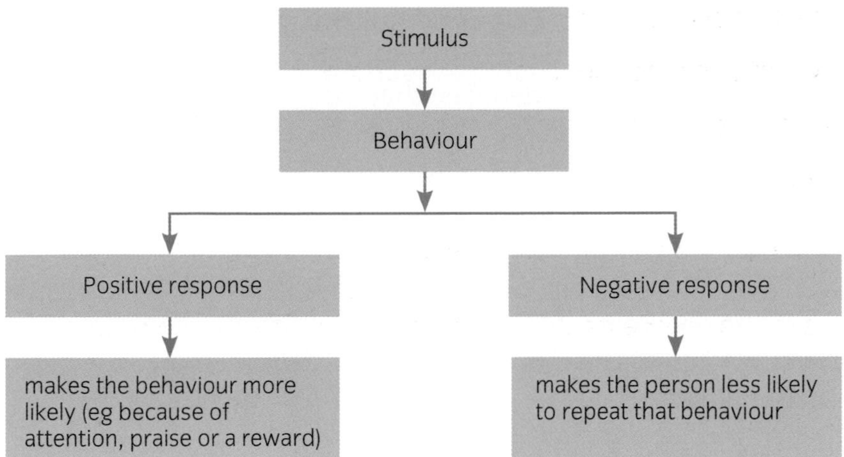

Operant conditioning shows some key insights which are relevant in health and social care work, including:

- The idea that most behaviours are responses which are caused by a stimulus or event.
- The idea that behaviours have a consequence, and service users learn from these consequences. Consequences can be positive (ie a reward for that behaviour) or negative.
- The idea that some behaviours do occur randomly, but whether we carry out this behaviour (or say a certain thing) will be strongly influenced by the response that we get. If we get little or no response, we may not do it again.

The ABC model was developed to show how most behaviours follow a certain chain or pattern:

'A' stands for 'antecedent' – an event happens, and as a result the person engages in a behaviour, 'B', as a response to 'A'. Immediately, or soon after the behaviour, the consequences, 'C', occur.

For example, a person might hear the doorbell (an antecedent), rush to see who is there (a behaviour) and be rewarded by seeing a friend or visitor arriving. The next time the doorbell goes, the person is likely to repeat that behaviour, as they are hopeful of the same reward or consequence.

ABC charts have commonly been used in health and social care services. Many services have developed ABC charts, so they try to understand the broader environment that influences how service users experience and respond to the world around them.

It is through this model of operant conditioning that knowledge of behaviour being shaped by rewards has been developed. Rewards (or reinforcers) should be identified that the person actually likes and values. In order to be effective, the reward should be:

- applied consistently
- given as soon as possible after the desired behaviour occurs.

If part of the reward is intrinsic to the person (internal sense of pride or achievement), this is helpful. Many rewards are external to the person and can include:

- activities that the person likes
- food, money or gifts
- social companionship or praise.

Some activities have rewards that automatically follow on, for example, preparing food or drink where the reward is the enjoyment of the food or drink.

Praise, recognition from others and social companionship are significant rewards and should not be underestimated.

Where a desired behaviour is complex or demanding, breaking it down into smaller tasks and having rewards that are provided for each step should result in the behaviour being achieved.

REFLECT

Consider an activity or task that you would find quite challenging. It could be a household task you find hard, like gardening or decorating, or it could be something extreme that you fear, like parachute jumping or white water rafting.

- If someone were trying to motivate you to do this task or activity, what reinforcers or rewards might you need them to consider offering you?
- How could they help you break the task into manageable chunks or steps?
- What could the person do to encourage you to give it a go, and are there things that they might do that would put you off having a go completely?

How this links to active support

In active support, understanding how a service user learns, and matching the type, level and frequency of reinforcement, is critical to the success of the work.

If a person responds well to verbal praise, active support requires lots of praise and encouragement to be:

- planned for
- given consistently
- given frequently.

Similarly, if a person enjoys a certain activity, this can act as a powerful reward and reinforcer when active support is used. For example, an adult with autism may initially not be keen on taking part in the morning routines described above. Using symbols and charts in a planned and consistent way can show the service user that by doing certain tasks, these then lead into the chosen activity as a result or reward.

The idea is that by applying all of the above in a planned way, the service user will gain an intrinsic sense of reward and pride through doing, learn independence skills, have less time being inactive and bored (and therefore sometimes displaying the behaviours associated with boredom), and they will build up gradually into learning new tasks and activities.

CASE STUDY

Sukbinder works in a day service for adults with learning disabilities, and she is using active support with one service user, Sharon, who has complex needs. Recently, they have been working together to promote Sharon's independence and daily living skills.

Sukbinder has been really pleased with how much Sharon has developed her cooking skills since they have been using active support together. However, over the past week, Sharon has started to show signs that she is getting bored with food preparation and she has begun to display this in her behaviour and by wandering off from Sukbinder.

- What might the reasons be for Sharon's boredom?
- How can Sukbinder re-engage Sharon with the cooking activities?

Key terms

Disengagement is where a service user is not doing any constructive or meaningful activity, and can include aimlessly wandering about, pacing, staring, sitting, lying down, purposelessly fiddling with items and so on, with no social contact.

IMPLEMENTING PERSON-CENTRED DAILY PLANS TO PROMOTE PARTICIPATION

It is important to provide opportunities for a service user to participate in activity throughout the day to avoid lengthy periods of **disengagement**.

Disengagement is where a service user is not doing any constructive or meaningful activity. As described previously, a gift or hotel model can lead to high levels of disengagement for service users. This could be shown in people's behaviours, such as aimlessly wandering about, pacing, staring, sitting, lying down, purposelessly fiddling with items and so on, with no social contact.

Research summarised by the Association for Real Change (ARC 2012 online) indicates that people with learning disabilities in care homes usually receive less than six minutes per hour of input from workers to engage in meaningful activities.

This research indicates that many adults who use health and social care services spend far more of their daily lives in periods of disengagement, without stimulation from other people, and without taking part in the activities that we all undertake as part of our daily lives.

Most of us cannot go out to work until we have gone through the morning routines discussed above, without shopping for the food for our breakfast, or without having clean clothes ready to wear for work. For many service users in health and social care settings, all of these tasks may be done for them by other people, which gives the service user less to do and more time to be disengaged.

With active support you will look at a service user's life day by day and week by week, and consider in depth how their life actually is experienced. By examining the level of activity the service user participates in, and looking at how much they are engaged in meaningful activity, you will be able to plan for this to be increased. In this way, lengthy periods of disengagement can be avoided.

REFLECT

- Consider the daily lives of service users in your service setting. What proportion of time do they spend being active and inactive?
- Can you suggest ways in which this balance can be improved?
- How can you incorporate this into individual daily plans, and into service development?

USING A STRUCTURED PERSON-CENTRED FORMAT TO ENSURE A VALUED RANGE OF ACTIVITIES

In order to ensure that people do not spend lengthy periods of time disengaged, it is important to develop plans in partnership with service users for a **valued range of activities**. If you do not take the time to understand how a service user's days and weeks actually look, you cannot plan effectively to address any imbalances in how much activity they are involved in.

Key term 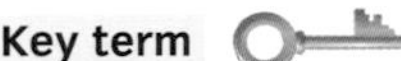

Valued range of activities refers to the balance of activities that contribute to a good quality of life for individual service users, and incorporates vocational, domestic, personal, leisure, educational and social activities.

Involving the service user, their carers and your colleagues in developing the daily plan is critical, in terms of:

- the plan being person centred
- the plan allowing the person's uniqueness, communication and cultural needs to be addressed
- the service user having an investment in their plan
- consistency in how the plan is applied in practice
- being able to measure the impact of the plan.

A weekly plan enables you to see:

- the service user's life across a full week, so that the level of variety in their week is visible and apparent
- the range of activities and opportunities that a service user is engaged in, and where the gaps are
- the amount of time where the service user is both engaged in activity and at risk of disengagement
- the level of social interaction a service user experiences
- the amount of choice and control which a service user has about how they spend their week
- whether this matches the level of variety and activity that is associated with a valued lifestyle (see below).

From the weekly plan, it is then possible to use daily plans to look at:

- every day having an appropriate amount of activity and reducing disengagement
- mapping out each day to increase variety
- the service user's self-care needs
- the domestic tasks that need to be undertaken, and where the service user can become more involved in these
- the service user's social, leisure and cultural time.

These two structured formats, weekly and daily plans, are looked at in turn below.

Weekly plan example

Day	Self-care activities	Domestic/ Household activities	Social/Leisure time
Monday	Does own personal care – needs prompts about remembering deodorant and needs significant support in brushing teeth	Vacuums lounge and cleans own room	Pottery class at college
Tuesday	As above	Personal laundry	
Wednesday	As above – and takes a shower after Zumba class		Zumba class at local community centre – early evening
Thursday	As above		
Friday	As above	Food shopping	
Saturday	Likes to take a long bath in the afternoon	Bakes cakes to take to church service tea	Watches *X Factor* on television
Sunday	As above		Attends church service – stays afterwards to socialise and help with the teas

REFLECT

- How does this compare with a weekly plan for service users in your service setting?
- How does this weekly plan compare with how you plan for and manage your own day-to-day living tasks, social and leisure time, and work and other commitments?
- What opportunities does this plan give for the service user to engage with others?
- What would you do to develop this plan further?

USING A STRUCTURED FORMAT TO PLAN SUPPORT FOR A SERVICE USER TO PARTICIPATE IN ACTIVITIES

Active support enables service users to work with health and social care workers to make structured plans, in order to increase the level of activity in the person's life. Using a structured format for these plans has the following benefits:

- plans can be agreed in partnership with service users, their families, carers and friends
- plans can be implemented consistently across a care team
- progress can be seen clearly, so that changes to plans can be implemented – this is especially important when looking at a service user learning new skills, and continuing to be challenged and developed once they have done so.

Daily plans

Detailed daily plans are important in active support to enable you to look at a service user's whole day in terms of the level of activity they are involved in. The length of time spent on certain tasks should also be considered. This is so you can then monitor the extent to which the person's participation changes over time.

For example, consider the Monday from the above weekly plan, and how this could be broken down into a more detailed daily plan.

Daily plan example

MONDAY	Self-care	Household	Leisure
7am	Get up Toilet Shower Wash hair Shave Brush teeth Get dressed		
8am	Take medication with breakfast	Breakfast – prepare together Wash up Put bins out	Radio
9am			Relax – free time
10am		Vacuum lounge Clean room	
11am			Cards Exercise
12pm		Lunch – prepare together Wash up	
1pm			Pottery class
2pm			As above
3pm			As above
4pm			As above
5pm		Prepare meal together Wash up	
6pm			Relax – free time
7pm		Local shop – bread and milk	Walk
8pm		Put shopping away Wipe surfaces down	
9pm			Free time
10pm	Bedtime – routine to include: Wash Brush teeth Get undressed and into nightwear		
11pm	Sleep		

Reviewing and revising daily plans

All plans need to be kept under review to ensure that they are working, and plans will need to be regularly amended to reflect changing needs and circumstances.

It is vital to ensure that daily plans are kept under review for the following reasons:

- The service user should have the right level of assistance to match their need in active support – for example, if they no longer need actual guidance to perform a task, will a prompt now be sufficient?
- Service users are likely to get bored and demotivated if the plan does not evolve as they learn new skills.
- Once a skill has been learned, it is important to stretch the service user and consider what is next for them.
- It is important to record progress and for this to be seen by everyone, celebrated, and for the service user to receive the acknowledgement and recognition they deserve.

CASE STUDY

Mark and his colleagues are planning how to implement their learning about active support within the residential home. The manager, Lorraine, has spent time analysing the proportion of the day that some residents have spent disengaged and inactive. The team are working on plans to increase the general level of activity for all of the residents, and also on specific plans for the service users that Lorraine has observed to be the most disengaged.

Mark is the key worker for one of these most disengaged residents, Bill. Bill enjoyed an active and busy life, working as a landscape gardener, and bringing up a large family. Bill now has dementia and spends a lot of his day looking out of the window and not engaging with workers or other residents.

- How can Mark develop a plan for Bill's days in partnership with Bill, which suits his needs and interests?
- How can Bill be supported to have a varied and valued lifestyle?

MAINTAINING PERSON-CENTRED RECORDS OF PARTICIPATION

Since active support is a person-centred approach, the recording of this work must be person-centred. This means that all records need to follow the key principles of person-centred practice, including the following:

- Records must be kept in partnership with service users.
- Records must be kept up to date and accurate.
- Records must be stored and accessed in appropriate ways.
- The balance between upholding the service user's rights and choices and their need for appropriate support and protection from harm must be considered.

Health and social care workers need to use good recording practices in active support plans, in order to:

- record and monitor the person's participation against these plans
- communicate any issues as part of handovers and recording so that changes to plans can be seen and necessary alterations made
- ensure that there is consistency in terms of the application of the plan across the team
- ensure that there is an appropriate level of input, support and activity for all of the different service users who access the service or setting.

The level of participation needs to be logged in an appropriate way for each service user. Doing this does not need to be time-consuming or a major chore though, as the example on the next page shows.

EXAMPLE

Person-centred daily record of self-care

	Mon	Tue	Wed	Thu	Fri	Sat	Sun	Amount of participation
Teeth	√	√	√	√	√	√	√	7 days
Shower self	√	√	√	√	√	√	√	7 days
Drying self	√	√	√		√	√	√	6 days
Dressing	√		√		√		√	4 days
Styling hair		√		√				2 days

From this it is clear that the person does not engage often in styling their hair – they may need extra prompts and support in this area.

Person-centred record of helping to make meals

	Mon	Tue	Wed	Thu	Fri	Sat	Sun	Amount of participation
Breakfast	√	√	√	√	√	√	√	7 days
Lunch	√		√		√	√		4 days
Dinner		√		√				2 days
Supper	√	√	√	√	√	√	√	7 days

From this it is clear that the person does not engage as much in making dinner as in making other meals – they may need extra prompts and support in this area.

Records such as this could be kept in every area of support. This can help in reviewing someone's participation in activities over a period of time.

DESCRIBING CHANGES IN A SERVICE USER'S PARTICIPATION OVER TIME

As service users gain in skills and confidence with tasks, the level of support they require will change. Active support is about changing service users' lives and enabling them to be more fulfilled. Therefore, this naturally involves an ongoing assessment of the progress the person makes.

As the evidence grows of the service user's abilities and preferences, the following should take place:

- The level of input should be gradually reduced.
- The type and nature of tasks should become more advanced.
- The time the service user spends inactive should be monitored and reduced.

For example, consider the scenario earlier in this chapter where active support is used to enable a service user to load the washing machine. Imagine the following:

- At first, the person is involved in emptying the laundry basket, but is reluctant to take part in the rest of the activity.
- They receive praise and reinforcement in a planned way for the achievements they make.
- They gradually increase their level of participation in other stages of the task, and receive further praise and encouragement.
- The plan then alters and grows accordingly to involve the person in unloading the machine.

The service user gradually becomes interested in putting the washing out to dry, or folding it and putting it away, for example – gaining pride in their appearance and an increasing interest in fashion along the way.

With an analysis of the person's daily activities and engagement in place, your role is then to address any imbalance.

For example, if there is a greater amount of independent activity by a service user than there is activity within a group, can the plan be altered to increase the level of group activity in the setting? Can more work be undertaken outside of the one room (we all get a little low when we feel confined to one place all day)? How can activities in the community be promoted in order to provide more stimulation, and opportunities for the service user to engage with others – including other people who can be involved in drawing service users into community life? How are the service user's cultural, faith and communication needs addressed by other people who engage with them who may not yet know them as well as your care team?

Considering all of the above will lead to staged, planned and achievable changes being made to the person-centred active support plan. Plans should not be static, and should allow for:

- reviews to be undertaken, both formally and informally
- information to be gathered from colleagues, the service user and their carers in order to inform reassessment and future planning
- the person's needs, wishes and preferences changing over time and as they gain in skills and confidence
- your own reflection and personal development informing new ideas and strategies.

REFLECT

Think about a service user you work with, and with whom you are working towards active support.

- How do you evaluate the service user's participation over time?
- What criteria do you (and the service user) use to judge whether their participation represents the balance of activity that is associated with a valued and active lifestyle?

REPORTING ON THE BALANCE OF ACTIVITY ASSOCIATED WITH A VALUED LIFESTYLE

Active support is all about wanting service users to have as active and fulfilled a life as possible. This includes them being involved in the day-to-day living tasks that we all need to participate in if we want to get through life, as well as engaging with others and enjoying stimulating and entertaining activities.

REFLECT

What do you consider to be a valued lifestyle? What does it mean for you personally? Is it more about social interaction, being able to make your own decisions, or feeling valued by others?

For what percentage of your day-to-day life would you say:

- you spend doing things you want to do?
- you spend doing things you might not want to do but have to do?
- you spend in the company of others?
- you spend active and busy, and inactive and resting?
- you feel in control of your own life and where it is going?

In order for active support to be effective, workers need to look closely at the balance of activity in service users' days. This links with the idea discussed earlier that people with learning disabilities usually receive six minutes of worker input associated with activities per hour. Active support aims to redress the imbalance between activity and inactivity in the lives of service users.

One way to do this is via planned observations. In your work setting, you could set up a chart which records, hour by hour during a service user's waking day, how much activity they are involved in. The chart could take the form of a graph, table or pie chart, depending on the tools available in your service and your technical skills.

Key term

Valued lifestyle refers to the balance of activities that contribute to a good quality of life for individual service users, and incorporates vocational, domestic, personal, leisure, educational and social activities.

In order for the balance to demonstrate whether the service user's level of activity is similar to that of other people with a **valued lifestyle**, the following questions need to be considered:

- How much of the activity that the service user is involved in is achieved independently, and how much with support or input?
- We do all need 'downtime', but what do you consider to be an effective and relevant amount of this for you and for those you work with?
- How much activity takes place within one room, and how can increased engagement in activity outside of the work setting be promoted?
- How much activity is undertaken by the person alone, and how much concerns engagement with other people?

EXAMPLE

Jenny's participation record

Week of	Self-care activities	Meals	Household activities	Shopping	Leisure activities	Engaging with family and friends	Total
Jan 4th	26	28	20	11	18	3	106
Jan 11th	27	30	20	11	20	3	111
Jan 18th	22	22	20	8	21	2	95
Jan 25th	30	25	19	8	11	1	94
Feb 1st	32	26	17	11	24	3	113

The numbers relate to the amount of times Jenny has participated in the planned activities outlined in the daily plan as shown above. The idea would be for the totals in the right-hand column to be shown to increase over time, and for any changes or gaps to be monitored, so that the plan can be adapted and developed for Jenny.

CASE STUDY

Denise works in a respite service for younger adults with complex needs, and she has been reviewing the progress that Chai has made while she has been working with him. She has been using active support with Chai on his weekly overnight stays to promote his involvement in his own care, and his confidence in his own abilities. She has worked closely with Chai's family so that everyone is using the same approach.

Denise feels that Chai has progressed a lot since she has been working with him. He is able to do most of his own self-care, has been developing an interest in preparing his own meals, and he has been happier in himself in her view. However, Denise feels that the plan for Chai needs to be developed so that the activities he is involved in represent more of what she considers to be a valued lifestyle. Denise also feels that Chai needs to be more involved in these discussions so that his hopes and ideas about how his own time should be spent are fully considered.

- Denise talks with Chai's family about this, and they agree to look at getting Chai involved in some activities where he can mix with people of his own age in the community.
- How can Chai, Denise and Chai's family find out what is available in the community?
- How can they find out what Chai might be most interested in from the range of available activities?
- What activities might represent a valued and balanced lifestyle for a teenager?

Before going to the next chapter, take some time to consider:

- what active support means to you
- what model of care you feel your practice reflects
- how you identify the level of support someone needs
- whether you record the activities someone has engaged in in a person-centred way, and what that means for you
- what the key challenges for you are when trying to follow a person-centred active support model.

CHAPTER 11
Support care plan activities

The care provided by health and social care workers should follow an individual care plan. This is developed to ensure that all relevant staff are fully aware of what support a service user requires, and the best way to provide this support. As a health and social care worker you will need to demonstrate and understand the agreed ways of working, by promoting a service user's preferences, wishes and needs in order to facilitate a person-centred approach to care planning and support. Accurate recording in care practice is vital in order to promote safe and effective care delivery. This chapter covers these issues to help you support care plan activities effectively.

Links to other units

The contents of this chapter link very closely to the earlier chapters which cover the *way* that work should be undertaken. So for example there are links with Chapters 3 and 4. Health and social care workers should always try to promote active support in the way they provide care and support – there are therefore clear links between the contents of this chapter and Chapter 10. The recording of care and support and the sharing of information about this are vitally important and so there are also links with Chapter 7.

WHAT IS A CARE PLAN?

A care plan may be referred to as a support plan, an individual plan or an individual support plan. In essence, a care plan is usually a written document that details:

- how identified needs are going to be met
- decisions that have been made by the individual in relation to their lifestyle choices.

A care plan may be a document that is specific to the workplace, or one developed by the worker and the service user which might be personalised. For example, it could include pictures of things that are important to the service user, such as a pet, football team or celebrity.

Diagrams can also be included if the service user prefers. For example, a care plan might include bubbles describing the following:

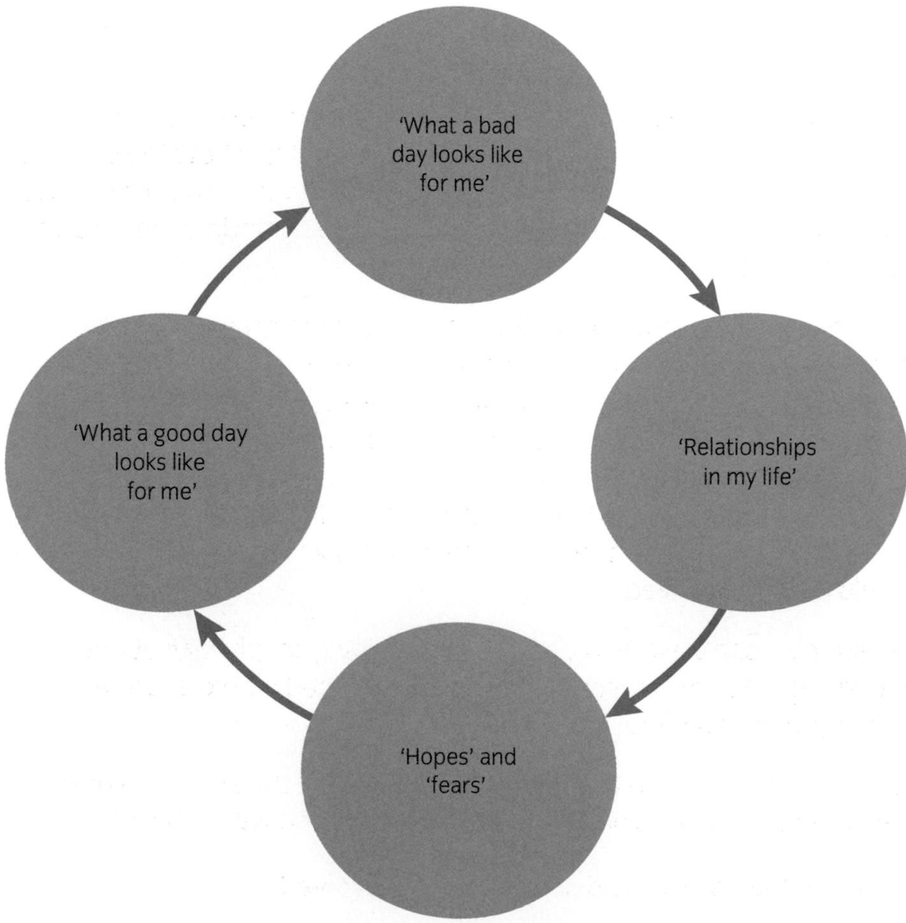

A care plan should help workers understand a service user better, especially if they do not know them well and need to provide care for them in a sensitive way that promotes independence and dignity.

A care plan should always be dated and signed, and should include basic information about the service user. Contact details of all the relevant professionals involved should be clearly recorded. The service user should give their consent to the plan and agree its content. If they are not able to do so then a family member may be able to advise and agree the care plan on their behalf.

The following diagram shows what to avoid when writing a care plan.

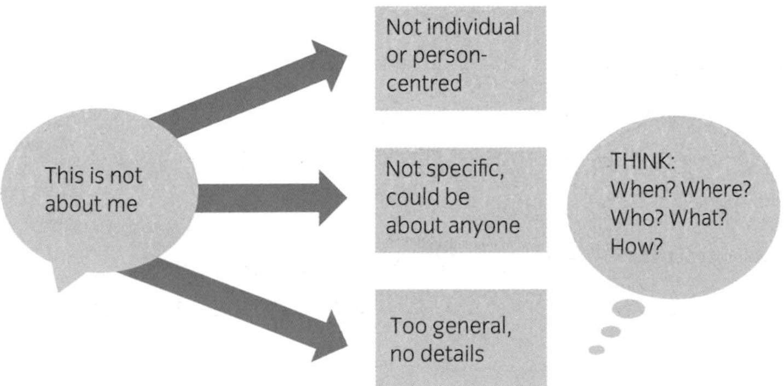

A person-centred approach uses an outcome-focused approach. This means that the care or support plan clearly identifies how the success of the support will be measured against the outcomes the service user hopes to gain from the support. Outcomes are sometimes referred to as goals or aspirations.

It is important to be aware that various people may contribute to the formulation and review of the plan. The service user is central to the process, with support from family or close friends, possibly an advocate, a social care worker and probably their line manager. Other professionals such as an occupational therapist, physiotherapist, social worker, district nurse, GP, specialist nurse (eg for Parkinson's, multiple sclerosis, diabetes) and representatives from voluntary organisations could also be involved.

A care plan can be drawn up in an informal way involving just one worker and a service user, or it can be developed within a formal setting such as a multi-disciplinary meeting.

If a care plan needs to be shared, the consent of the service user must be obtained. A care plan might need to be shared with others if:

- more than one provider of support is involved
- a referral is made to other agencies
- additional support is required.

When a care plan has been developed there is a clear process for health and social care workers to follow when using the plan.

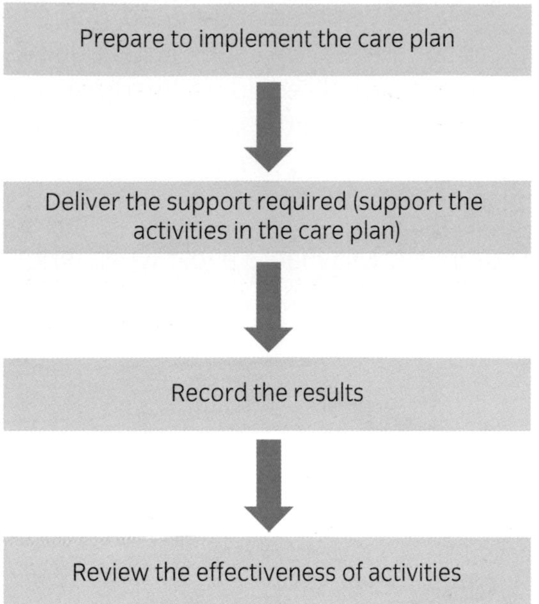

PREPARING TO IMPLEMENT CARE PLAN ACTIVITIES

The diagram below reflects the basic process of health and social care which is addressed throughout this book.

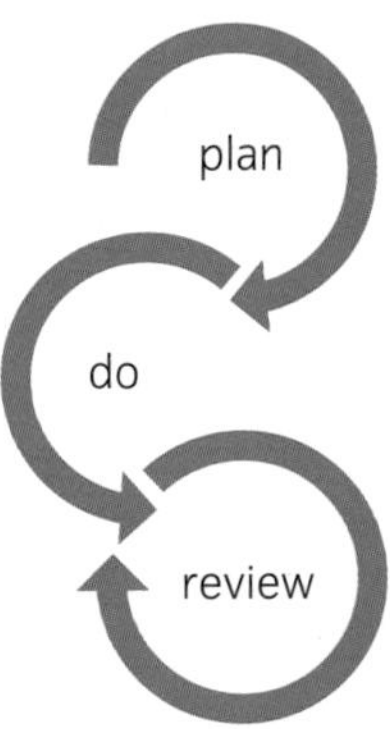

When preparing to implement care plan activities you need to think about who knows the service user best and what specific care plan activities you need to carry out.

For example if you are preparing to assist a service user to eat, you need to prepare by thinking about the following:

- If the person has short-term memory problems, it may be beneficial to ask a family member questions such as what food their relative likes or dislikes; the service user may be unable to provide this information as they cannot remember.
- Does the service user have special dietary or cultural needs, soft diet requirements, require the thickening of fluids, or require a specific diet (for example, for diabetes)?

- Is the service user able to eat unassisted, or do they need support such as having their food cut up, special cutlery or a different colour placemat in order to clearly see their plate if they have a visual impairment?

It is important not to underestimate such issues, as they could impact on health and wellbeing as well as the service user's independence.

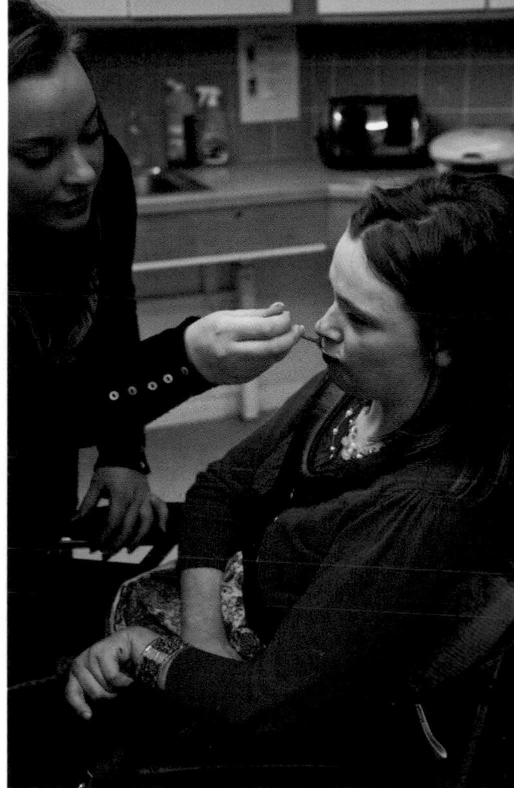

You can find out a service user's preference about how care plan activities are implemented in a number of ways. For example, in terms of meal provision, it is important to ask the service user:

- where they would like to eat their meal
- how they like their meal served
- if their preference is for a drink in a mug, a beaker or a cup and saucer.

All of these may seem very basic things that you take for granted. However, if an service user is reliant on others who do not take the time to ask questions or seek their preference, it may result in them having inadequate fluid intake merely because they don't like the way their meal or drink is presented.

If an individual is unable to provide the information you need to produce a care plan, you may consult others who know them better or look for other ways to establish their preferences. Consider the following.

- Do they finish all their meal, or is it pushed around the plate and little eaten; do they spit food out?
- Observing the facial expressions of an individual who cannot express their preference verbally may allow others to anticipate their needs to avoid undue distress.
- You could show a service user pictures or encourage simple gestures such as thumb up or down to express like or dislike, to encourage decision making.
- You could ask a person to write or type their preference if this is their preferred or only method of communication.
- Do they like sitting in a communal dining room or prefer a quiet space?
- Do they relate better to a particular worker? (This might be because of gender, ethnicity, age, heritage, etc.)

Others may be required to contribute to the care plan preparation, as there may be identified risk areas that need to be recorded in the plan. An example of this might be when a service user who has lived at home starts to attend a day care centre. The main carer knows that they have to watch the service user take their tablet, or they may spit it out or conceal it in their pocket or down the side of a chair. If this information isn't recorded in the care plan at the day centre, however, medication may be given to the service user without subsequent observation.

The risks of not fully preparing for care plan activities might include:

- risk to the health and wellbeing of the service user
- a decline in health or change in behaviour of the service user
- an adult protection referral may be raised if significant harm is caused to a service user due to possible neglect or omission by the service provider
- a complaint made by a service user's family/main carer.

CASE STUDY

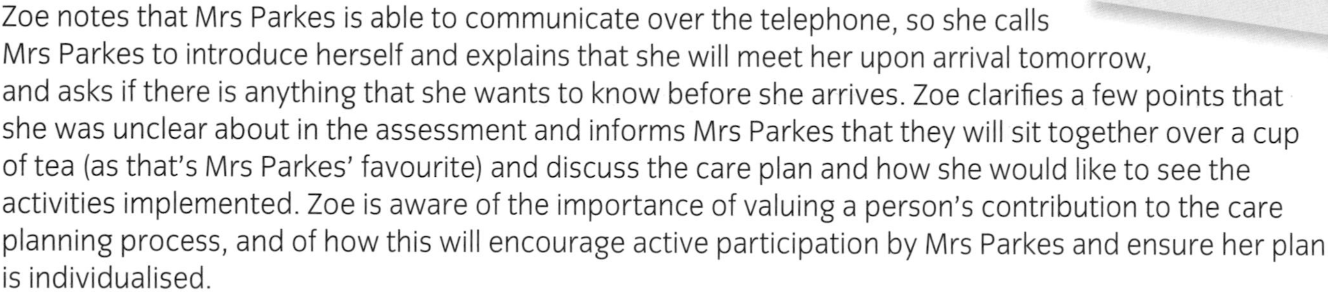

Zoe is a care assistant in a residential care home and is expecting an older adult, Mrs Parkes, to be admitted into the home the following afternoon. Zoe has been appointed as key worker and a part of her role is to prepare the care plan ready for implementation. She starts her preparation by looking at the assessment that was undertaken by the social worker, as she understands it is important to find out the past life history, preferences, wishes and needs of Mrs Parkes in order to reflect this in her care plan.

Zoe notes that Mrs Parkes is able to communicate over the telephone, so she calls Mrs Parkes to introduce herself and explains that she will meet her upon arrival tomorrow, and asks if there is anything that she wants to know before she arrives. Zoe clarifies a few points that she was unclear about in the assessment and informs Mrs Parkes that they will sit together over a cup of tea (as that's Mrs Parkes' favourite) and discuss the care plan and how she would like to see the activities implemented. Zoe is aware of the importance of valuing a person's contribution to the care planning process, and of how this will encourage active participation by Mrs Parkes and ensure her plan is individualised.

Zoe notes that Mrs Parkes has a daughter who supported her while she was at home, so she asks Mrs Parkes if she can ring her daughter, as she is aware that Mrs Parkes is a little forgetful and Zoe is mindful to ensure she has accurate and up-to-date information. Mrs Parkes' daughter is able to share information about her current daily routine which should help Mrs Parkes settle into her new environment. Zoe is keen to record this, as she is off-duty this weekend and she wants the other health and social care workers to be aware of Mrs Parkes' needs. Zoe is able to begin formulating the care plan, including a risk assessment, medication administration record and moving and assisting plan to prevent causing any undue stress for Mrs Parkes.

- How does Zoe prepare to support Mrs Parkes?
- What else could she do to prepare effectively?

Your preparation should help you to find out:

- a service user's likes and dislikes
- what outcome they most want to achieve
- what aspects of the service user's life are important to them
- what the service user would like to do or see done differently

- who to consult alongside the service user in order to support care plan activities
- if there is any equipment or assistive technology that could be utilised to meet outcomes.

CONFIRMING YOUR UNDERSTANDING OF A CARE PLAN

Care plans are often devised by social workers or service managers. They are rarely written by the people responsible for putting them into action. When you are preparing to implement a care plan it is vital that you understand what you are expected to do. In addition to talking to the person you are supporting about what you plan to do, it is a good idea to explain what you think the care plan says and what you plan to do with your manager or a senior worker to make sure that you have clearly understood the plan. Working in that way means there will be no misunderstandings.

REFLECT

What action would you take if there was something that you did not understand in a care plan?

SUPPORTING CARE PLAN ACTIVITIES

Care plan activities should be provided in accordance with the agreed ways of working. The agreed ways of working will relate to the preferences of the service user, as well as working practice and policy and procedure.

For example:

- Does the service user require one or two carers for personal care?
- Is equipment required for transfers? For example, a hoist, slide sheet, stand aid or bed lever?
- Were set times agreed during the planning stage for certain activities?
- Does the service user need prior notice of any changes to their plan, as they may get agitated or anxious if changes are unplanned?

A fundamental part of supporting care plan activities is promoting participation of the service user in the activity. If the person has been at the centre of the planning process their commitment, motivation and willingness to engage in the activity should increase. Individual ownership of the support plan is important so that each service user feels it is personal to them and not the same as those of all the other residents, patients, clients, customers or service users. It is essential that the plan records positives – it's not all about what a person is unable to do; it's what is meaningful to them rather than a focus on a lack of ability or capacity. It should promote independence and positive risk taking that enhances a person's quality of life. Small things can make a big difference in promoting dignity and participation.

Examples of good practice include:

- talking to the service user while doing the activity; this can reduce anxiety and make them feel a real part of the process
- sharing any important triggers or conversation starters within the staff group; this should reduce anxiety and encourage cooperation with other carers, and it's a good idea to record this for future use.

Actions may need to be adapted during a care plan activity for many reasons.

- Reframe the activity if it seems too long, for example, if the service user gets tired.
- Consider whether it was the wrong time of day; perhaps the service user is brighter in the morning but the activity took place in the afternoon.
- Think about whether it would it be better after medication, for example after pain relief.
- Remember that if a service user is highly agitated they may place themselves or others at risk, for example if they don't want to have a bath or shower.

Sometimes service users may display behaviours that challenge, and this may be as a result of unfamiliarity or a change in need, or for another reason. As a health and social care worker you may be able to address concerns simply by looking more closely at a situation, and taking time to reflect on what and how a person responds to in different situations.

REFLECT

Consider the following care plan activity dilemma.

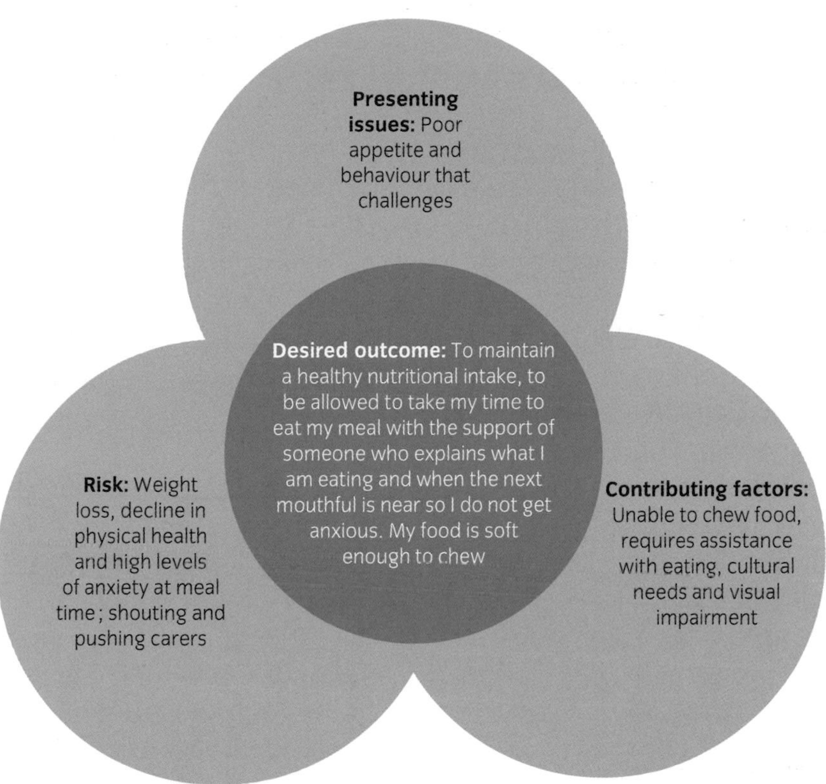

This diagram represents a service user who is struggling to eat the food that they are being given, but is unable to tell the workers who offer them support. If time is not given to looking more closely at the situation the service user might be labelled as having aggressive behaviour, being non-compliant or being uncooperative.

A lack of planning and preparation can result in presenting issues that could have been easily resolved by asking the right questions at the right time of the right people. Careful consideration needs to be given as to why a service user may be acting in a certain way. There may be a very simple answer which doesn't require a complicated response – just time to understand the person and their needs and make those important changes to their care plan.

In this instance weight loss could be attributed to the service user being unable to chew their food, so a simple change to a softer diet could resolve anxiety and improve appetite.

REFLECT

What action would you take if someone declined to have a shower and they had been incontinent? Are there aspects of a care plan that, taking into account this dilemma, you may consider changing?

CASE STUDY

Alex has recently started working as a personal assistant for Enid, who lives in her own home and requires support to maintain her personal hygiene needs due to poor short-term memory. Alex has been visiting Enid each morning at 9am. Frequently Enid states she has already had a wash and has her coat on ready to leave, stating that Alex can't stay as she wants to go shopping. Alex sees that Enid is still in the same clothes as the day before. Alex asks if she can use the toilet before leaving and, on checking Enid's soap, towel and wash hand basin sees they are dry. Her suspicions are confirmed – that Enid is unable to manage this task independently without support or prompting. Alex asks Enid if she can call earlier the following day, and Enid agrees. The following day, Alex finds Enid sitting eating her breakfast, again still in the same clothes, but she is not ready to go out. This change in time provides Alex with the opportunity to support Enid. She fills the sink as a reminder for Enid to have a wash and promotes independence by prompting her – talking about what Enid wants to wear (in order to promote choice and decision making), then laying her clean clothes out on the bed.

- What does Alex do well?

PROMOTING ACTIVE SUPPORT

Chapter 10 covers active support in detail, and you will find it useful to read this when thinking about implementing care plan activities.

Whenever you are implementing care plan activities you need to do so in a way that promotes active support. That is, the person should be encouraged to do as much for themselves as possible. You should do activities *with* the person rather than *for* the person.

By the end of this stage you should be clearly able to identify:

- when a care plan activity isn't working
- how the care plan activities can be adapted to meet needs and preferences
- whether the person is engaging in the activity
- what areas of independence can be promoted
- that the appropriate risk assessments have been undertaken in relation to the activity to ensure that agreed ways of working are followed.

MAINTAINING RECORDS OF CARE PLAN ACTIVITIES

It is important that a care plan record is kept up to date so that it shows a clear, concise and accurate reflection of the service user's needs and their desired outcomes, and how these outcomes will be achieved. A care plan record is an ongoing working document, and outcomes or goals may take time to achieve, especially if service users are in transition – perhaps recovering from trauma or illness. Therefore, an important aspect of a health and social care worker's role involves looking at service users' progression towards desired outcomes. Are they happy with their life choices at the moment? The document should also be accessible to the service user themselves in a suitable format.

Can you think of reasons why different formats may be required, and give examples?

Reasons for different formats might be as follows:

- English is the service user's second language.
- The service user requires large print or braille due to poor vision.
- The service user has a learning disability, and a simpler version would be more easily understood and therefore more meaningful to them.

Health and social care workers need to take responsibility for their actions, so all records should be dated, with clear details of activities and the amount of time taken, and signed by the worker(s) involved. The document should show a chronological record of what activities work well, levels of participation by the service user and how they are feeling, as well as recording any changes/amendments to the care plan in order to promote an outcome-focused approach to support activities. An out-of-date record could result in a service user being caused undue distress by someone repeating an activity that did not work, for example:

- assisting a service user to have a shower when they prefer a bath
- waking a service user up at 7am when they prefer to wake at 10am as they do not sleep well
- taking a service user out in a large group when they prefer to be with fewer people.

Maintaining the accuracy of care plans in a timely way will ensure that any signs of discomfort are recorded, so that preferences are taken into account and the relevant changes or revisions are made without delay. A care plan should always include a review date, as needs do not remain static. All involved professionals and family/friends should be included in the record, and any changes to contact details should be amended accordingly in case of emergency.

Below is an extract from a care plan entry about social interaction.

Date	Time	Activity	Outcome	Comments	Name of worker
12/06/2015	14:00	To encourage Fred to join in skittles or other similar activities in the communal lounge; one worker required.	To help Fred feel more at ease with other residents and make new friends.	Fred became agitated when he walked into lounge; he appeared frightened. Future action: Recommend sitting Fred near door in quieter area.	Sonia Field – Key Worker

CASE STUDY

Fred is 82 years old and has been discharged from hospital following a fall in which he fractured his hip. He has cerebral palsy and is slightly unsteady on his feet. Fred requires two carers to support with transfers, and he has been assessed as requiring a hoist.

Can you complete a care plan entry for Fred with respect to his mobility needs? Consider how many workers he may need, use of any equipment, whether he can carry out supervised or independent activities, and whether his ability is variable.

By the end of this stage you should be able to clearly identify:

- potential causes of discomfort or distress and how to avoid a reoccurrence
- clear agreed ways of working, and how and why changes may necessary
- what type of care plan format is required
- an out-of-date care plan record – and take corrective action.

IMPLEMENTING CARE PLAN ACTIVITIES – WHAT DOES THE CODE OF CONDUCT SAY?

The Code of Conduct for Healthcare Support Workers and Adult Social Care Workers in England 2013 states that you must:

- comply with your employer's way of working
- always ask your supervisor or employer for guidance if you do not feel adequately prepared to carry out any aspect of your work, or if you are unsure how to effectively deliver a task
- be alert to any changes that could affect a person's needs or progress and report your observations in line with your employer's agreed ways of working
- put the needs, goals and aspirations of service users first, helping them to be in control and choose the healthcare, care and support they receive
- always explain and discuss the care, support or procedure you intend to carry out with the service user, and only continue if they give valid consent
- improve the quality and safety of the care you provide with the help of your supervisor (and mentor if available), and in line with your agreed ways of working.

CONTRIBUTING TO REVIEWING ACTIVITIES IN THE CARE PLAN

A review is a process that evaluates how the support and the way it has been implemented have achieved the desired outcomes set out in the care plan. It provides an opportunity to reassess the service user's needs, ensure that they still meet the eligibility criteria for support and make any necessary amendments.

Reviews may be informal, or may be inter-agency appraisals or multi-agency/disciplinary if a person's situation is more complex and involves a variety of professionals (as described on pages 326–7).

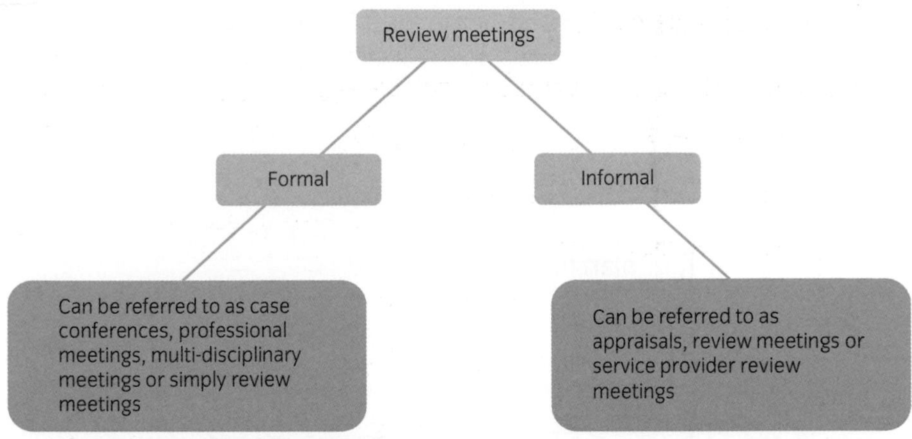

As a health and social care worker you may be asked to support a service user to attend and share their point of view at a meeting. At times you may sit with a service user before a meeting and obtain their thoughts so that you can represent them, acting as their advocate in order that their voice is heard. A multi-disciplinary meeting can be a daunting prospect for a service user, and the support that you provide as a health and social care worker could make all the difference to them; you will be a familiar face in a room full of strangers, and this is especially true if you have already built up trust with the service user.

Scheduled reviews take place on a regular basis as determined in the care plan, for example weekly, monthly, quarterly, biannually or annually. If a service user's condition suddenly changes, or the care plan activities no longer meet the identified needs and outcomes, an unscheduled review can take place in order to take account of the urgency of the situation.

In all instances there must be a clear purpose for the review. It should also take place in the appropriate venue, at an appropriate time and be free from distractions in order to maximise participation by the service user and any other relevant people who are present. If possible, consent should be obtained from the service user as to who they would like at the review, and you should discuss relevant options so that they can make an informed decision. Alternative options for contribution should be given to those unable to attend if a further date cannot be arranged, such as verbal or written contributions; sometimes a conference call may take place. Any contributions obtained prior to the meeting can also be shared at the care plan review meeting.

As a health and social care worker it is likely that you will be involved in both formal and informal review meetings. However, it is most likely that you will be more involved in informal meetings in which you discuss the effectiveness of a care plan with a service user and consult with a family member or carer as required.

The ultimate objective of a review is to:

- examine and evaluate the current care plan
- update the plan and set a new review date
- update the current needs assessment
- update risk assessments
- measure the success of outcome achievement
- ensure that feedback is obtained from the service user and carer if applicable
- discuss alternative options.

Some reviews can also involve eligibility criteria, which may also be referred to as fair access to care, prioritising need or access criteria. Many statutory agencies will only provide support if people meet the substantial or critical criteria, which basically means that without support the person would be at risk of significant harm, and deterioration of their situation would be very likely to occur.

Key areas to discuss include:

- communication
- mobility
- physical health
- mental health
- continence management
- social interaction
- access to community
- medication
- informal carers/family or social roles
- personal care
- nutrition.

Night-time needs may also require consideration, for example, if a person requires repositioning or medication, or safety aspects such as risk of falls or support to use the toilet.

To summarise, a review checklist may include the following:

- Who needs to be consulted or involved in the review process?
- Where is the most convenient venue?
- Are initial outcomes being met as set out in the current care plan?
- What worked well, and what didn't?

- Does the person require an advocate?
- Are all contact details up to date?
- Have there been any major life changes?
- What are the key areas to cover (see above examples)?
- Who supports the person with decision making (if required)?
- What is happening about safeguarding or associated risk identification?
- What happens in an emergency?
- Action plan and agree changes to be made to care plan?
- How you can support this process?

Importantly, make sure the care plan is personalised and individually tailored to the service user concerned. If they 'own it' they are more likely to engage in the activities.

CASE STUDY

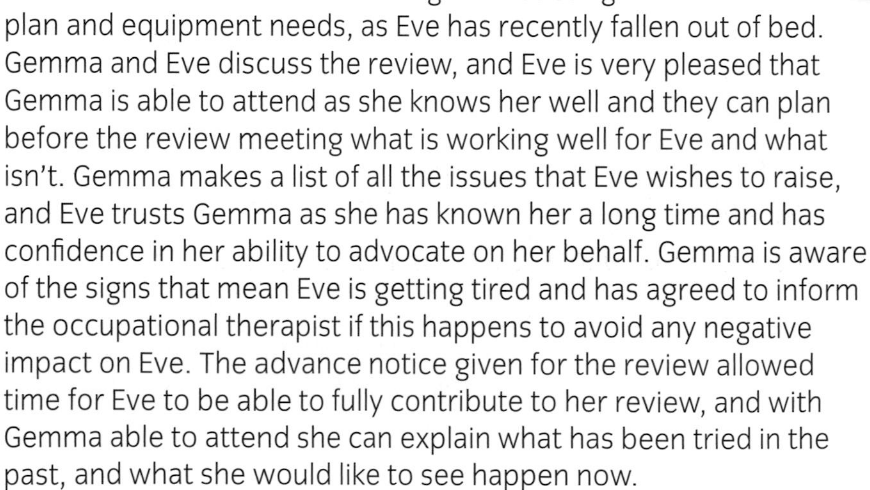

Gemma is a home care assistant who has been supporting Eve for the past three years. Eve has had a stroke and is unable to communicate verbally. She uses a lite writer which she can type into and is able to press a button so the words are read out loud, but she sometimes finds this very tiring. Gemma has been asked to attend a review by an occupational therapist who is due to review Eve's moving and assisting plan and equipment needs, as Eve has recently fallen out of bed. Gemma and Eve discuss the review, and Eve is very pleased that Gemma is able to attend as she knows her well and they can plan before the review meeting what is working well for Eve and what isn't. Gemma makes a list of all the issues that Eve wishes to raise, and Eve trusts Gemma as she has known her a long time and has confidence in her ability to advocate on her behalf. Gemma is aware of the signs that mean Eve is getting tired and has agreed to inform the occupational therapist if this happens to avoid any negative impact on Eve. The advance notice given for the review allowed time for Eve to be able to fully contribute to her review, and with Gemma able to attend she can explain what has been tried in the past, and what she would like to see happen now.

- If you were Gemma, what would your first course of action be?
- What potential outcomes would you hope to achieve?
- Remember that you may also ask Eve if there is anyone else she would like to attend.

CASE STUDY

Clive Petersham is a 78-year-old gentleman who has just moved into a residential care home. Previously, he has resisted interaction with professionals, as he feels that people in authority cannot be trusted, and so he has very reluctantly agreed to a trial stay in Rhianna Cottage Residential Care Home. Prior to his admission Clive was neglecting his personal care and had disengaged from the homecare support his family had arranged with the support of a social worker. He has been diagnosed with depression and anxiety, and does not like changes to his routine. Clive also has Parkinson's disease, and when he gets agitated or upset he loses his ability to communicate, becomes withdrawn and is unable to swallow. A specialist Parkinson's nurse has been to see Clive in the past to review his medication. Clive's Parkinson's is under control if he takes his medication regularly, but recently he has been feeling that he no longer needs to take his tablets, as they don't make him feel any better. On good days he is able to walk with a stick and loves the outdoors, and always wears his grey cap whether indoors or out. Clive, although a shy man, loves to chat about his former life as a farmer, especially about his chickens and pigs. He does get tearful, as he is no longer physically able to care for them, but he finds this aspect of his past life comforting.

- You have been asked to prepare and implement the care plan activities at Rhianna Cottage Residential Care Home. What do you consider to be the most important aspects for Clive?
- Think about what Clive would consider important, what his outcomes might be and who you would invite to plan and review his care plan.
- Are there any areas of the plan you might have to consider adapting due to a lack of engagement or possible distress?
- What timescale would you set for the next review?

REFLECTING ON YOUR LEARNING

By the end of this chapter you should be able to clearly identify:

- what currently does and doesn't work for a service user
- what the service user would like to do or see done differently
- what outcome they most want to achieve
- what aspects of the service user's life are important to them
- if any support can be provided in a less intrusive and restrictive way to ensure that independence is promoted
- the accuracy of an up-to-date record of needs and involvement
- how to evaluate and agree changes required to a plan
- how to assess if any further referrals need to be made outside of the agency for additional support
- how to schedule a date for the next review.

Before going to the next chapter, take some time to consider:

- What is important to you about maintaining your appearance and current image?
- Do you have any particular communication requirements?
- Whose company do you prefer?
- Can you clearly hear what is being said to you?
- Do you speak the same language as the other people around you?
- Can you see what is being written?
- Can you see someone when they are near?
- Can you move without the support of others?
- Can you eat and drink independently?
- Can you go to the toilet independently?
- Can you visit family and friends independently?
- How would you feel if you couldn't do any of these things, and what would you expect from those who support you?
- Do you have choice and control about the way you live your life?

CHAPTER 12
Support individuals to meet personal care needs

The care provided by health and social care workers should follow an individual care plan. This care plan is developed to ensure that all relevant staff are fully aware of what support a service user requires and the best way to provide this support. As a health and social care worker you will need to be able to work with service users to identify their needs and preferences in relation to the support they require for personal care. Dignity in care is vital at all times, and this becomes a particular issue when supporting people with intimate aspects of their daily living. This chapter will enable you to explore key issues in providing personal care and support.

Links to other units

The content of this chapter is closely linked to Chapters 9 and 10, because the care that you provide people should encourage them to be fully involved in their own care. There are also close links with the Chapters 3 and 4.

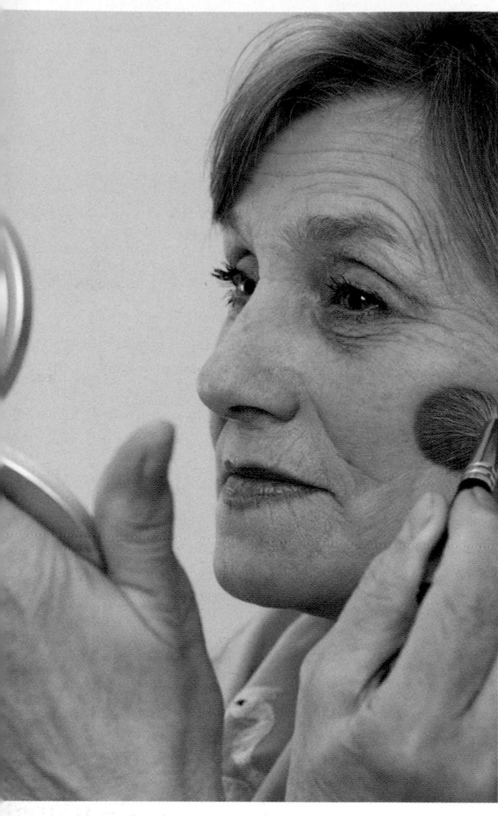

SETTING THE SCENE

Providing personal care has always been a key role for health and social care workers. However since the first report of the Francis Inquiry into care provided at Stafford Hospital (2010) there has been a renewed focus on the vital importance of personal care.

The latest report on the Public Inquiry into the Mid Staffordshire NHS Foundation Trust (2013) highlighted the following:

- There was a lack of even very basic care.
- There was an acceptance of poor practice.
- Patients were left in excrement-soiled bedclothes for lengthy periods.
- Patients were not assisted to use the toilet.
- Wards and bathrooms were left in a filthy condition.
- Privacy and dignity were denied.

The government has made a number of responses to the Francis Inquiry. In relation to the lack of basic care the Department of Health published its vision and strategy for *Compassion in Practice* (2012). This contains the 6Cs, as follows:

- *Care*. This is seen as 'core business'.
- *Compassion*. This is about how care is given – it involves developing relationships and promoting privacy and dignity.
- *Competence*. People providing care and support should have the ability to understand health and social care needs and should be competent in their role.
- *Communication*. This is central to good caring relationships.
- *Courage*. This enables care workers to do the right thing for the people they support.
- *Commitment*. A commitment to providing the best possible care is vital for everyone working in health and social care.

The 6Cs should be seen as underpinning everything contained in this chapter.

WHAT IS PERSONAL CARE?

Personal care is just what it says it is. It is the most intimate and sensitive care that is provided by health and social care workers.

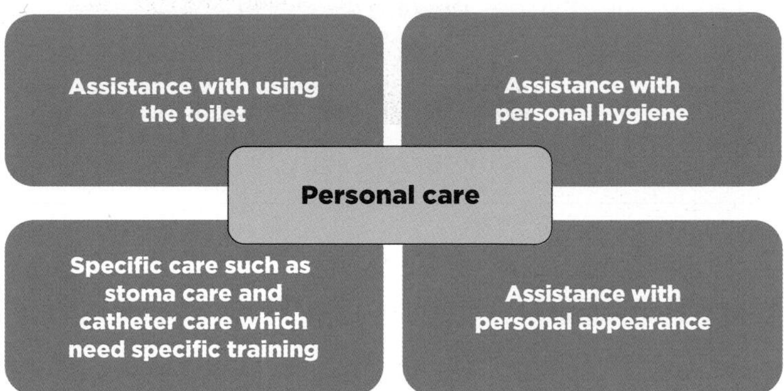

When personal care is provided it is important to remember that people may feel very uncomfortable about the fact that they need help with such sensitive matters.

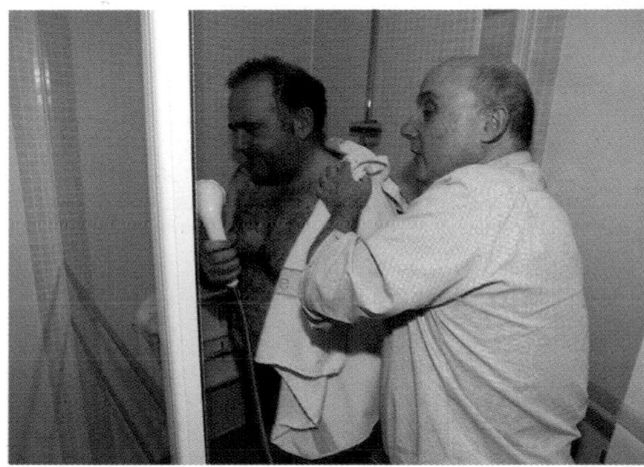

If you think about using the toilet yourself and maintaining your own personal hygiene you will realise how intimate this is. However, because some care staff provide intimate personal care every day they forget quite how personal a task this is. It is important that health and social care workers keep in mind how sensitive this aspect of their work is.

REFLECT

What would be important to you if you required assistance with personal care?

IDENTIFYING SERVICE USERS' NEEDS AND PREFERENCES IN RELATION TO PERSONAL CARE

It is important that health and social care workers take time to communicate sensitively with the service users they support to establish needs, preferences and personal beliefs that will affect personal care. The first thing that you need to consider is whether there are any barriers that might prevent service users communicating their needs (see Chapter 2 for more about communication). Remember too that needs may change over a period of time.

REFLECT

Can you think of reasons why a service user might:

- be embarrassed to share intimate details of the support they need?
- be unable to recognise that they require support to maintain their appearance and level of hygiene?
- be fiercely independent and unwilling to accept support?
- not like to ask for support with their personal care?

DIVERSITY IN PERSONAL CARE PREFERENCES

Everyone has very different preferences in terms of personal care – for example some people like to shower, some people like a full body wash, while others prefer to have a bath. There may be other differences in what people prefer, such as:

- an electric shaver or a wet shave
- to shave, use cream or wax to remove body hair
- to use a comb or brush
- to use an electric toothbrush or manual handheld brush
- what kind of skin products to use
- to wear deodorant in roll-on, stick or spray form
- to use a certain brand of shampoo, conditioner or soap
- what type of hair products – for oily, dry or colour-treated hair, or anti-dandruff, etc
- the use of talcum powder
- to use a flannel, sponge, brush or puffball
- to use a certain type of feminine hygiene product
- to use the toilet, commode, bedpan or urinal
- to use toilet paper or wipes.

When people require support with their personal care they will still have preferences (such as those listed above). A person's gender, age, religion or cultural heritage will also impact on the way support needs to be provided.

As a health and social care worker you should not make assumptions about how people may want to wash, what people might want to wear or how people wish to clean themselves after going to the toilet, for example.

An essential part of your role is to seek information about a service user's choices in order to ensure you are working in a person-centred way.

LEVEL AND TYPE OF SUPPORT

When working with service users to provide personal care you need to establish the level and type of support they require.

- The *level of support* refers to how much support a person needs.
- The *type of support* refers to what kind of support a person needs.

In all health and social care work the aim is to support service users to do as much for themselves as possible, since this can promote people's independence.

When establishing the type and level of support a service user needs in relation to personal care, a variety of creative methods to meet needs should be considered. A number of measures could be taken, as the following table shows.

Presenting need	Potential solution	Outcome
Unable to stand at wash basin to have a wash due to poor mobility/balance	Access to a perching stool	To have the support of a stool to enable them to take their time and wash themselves
Unable to turn tap on/off due to poor dexterity and grip as a result of arthritis or weakness following a stroke	Tap extensions to be fitted	To have a lever so that it is easier to grip or push and use taps independently
Unable to bend to wash feet	Long-handled sponge	To be able to maintain own personal hygiene without needing to bend so far

The best way to approach support with personal care is to avoid jumping straight to:

'I can do that for you'

And instead to think:

'How can I help you to do that for yourself?'

This can help you to establish both the level and type of support a service user needs.

Taking every opportunity to promote service users' independence in relation to personal care is probably even more important than promoting independence in other areas, because by its very nature personal care is very personal.

Aids and adaptations

Where service users have difficulties with their personal care a range of equipment, often referred to as aids, can help. Sometimes adaptations to a service user's home or environment can help too.

An assessment by an occupational therapist or rehabilitation officer will highlight what equipment might be useful in supporting individual service users.

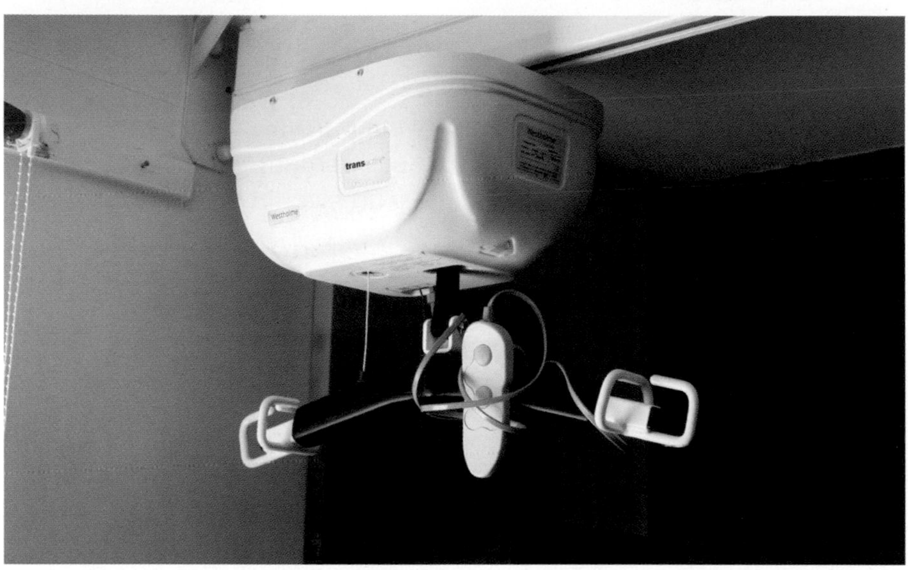

PROMOTING PRIVACY

Promoting privacy is a crucial aspect of your role and is central to person-centred practice. A few simple steps can make all the difference.

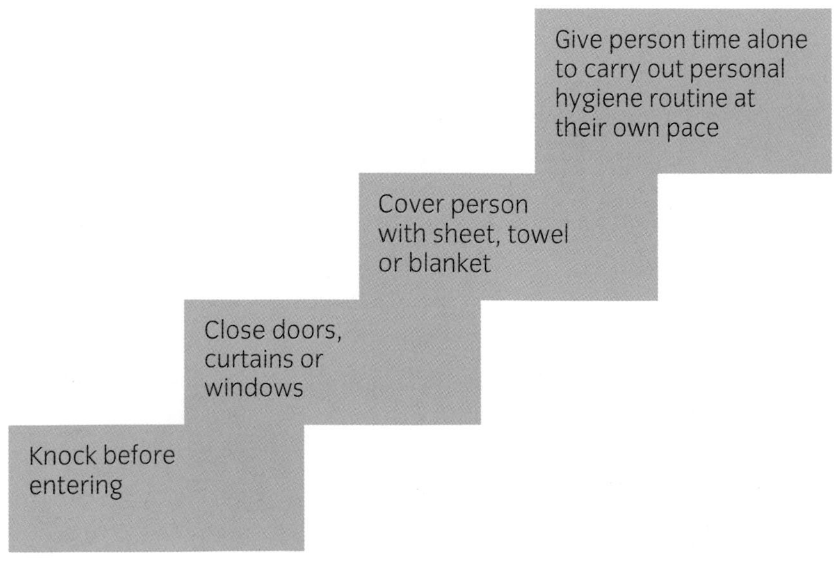

It is important that you ask the service user what steps they would prefer you to take in terms of privacy.

CASE STUDY

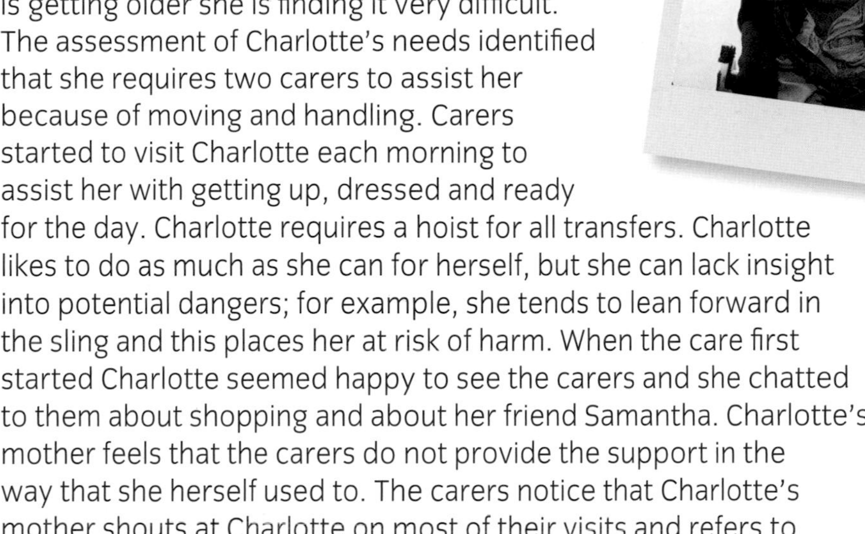

Charlotte is a 38-year-old woman. She lives with her parents in their home. Charlotte's mother used to provide all Charlotte's care, but as she is getting older she is finding it very difficult. The assessment of Charlotte's needs identified that she requires two carers to assist her because of moving and handling. Carers started to visit Charlotte each morning to assist her with getting up, dressed and ready for the day. Charlotte requires a hoist for all transfers. Charlotte likes to do as much as she can for herself, but she can lack insight into potential dangers; for example, she tends to lean forward in the sling and this places her at risk of harm. When the care first started Charlotte seemed happy to see the carers and she chatted to them about shopping and about her friend Samantha. Charlotte's mother feels that the carers do not provide the support in the way that she herself used to. The carers notice that Charlotte's mother shouts at Charlotte on most of their visits and refers to her incontinence pads as nappies. She also stands in the bedroom while the carers undress and dress Charlotte to 'keep an eye' on them.

- What could the carers do to promote Charlotte's privacy and dignity?

REFLECT

- Why are privacy and dignity important in providing personal care?
- What challenges do you face in promoting privacy and dignity?
- What could you do to overcome these barriers?

PROVIDING SUPPORT FOR PERSONAL CARE SAFELY

When providing personal care for service users, you need to think about any risks:

- to the person you are supporting
- to yourself.

Risks might include the following:

- risks to wellbeing and self-esteem – poor practice in personal care can leave people feeling very negative about themselves and their circumstances
- loss of independence – if personal care is *provided to a person* rather than the worker helping the person to be as fully involved as possible, then the person may lose skills and become more dependent on others
- risks of infection through cross-contamination
- risks of falls or injury if equipment (aids/adaptations) is used inappropriately or if it is faulty or has fallen into disrepair.

Best practice in personal care can minimise these risks:

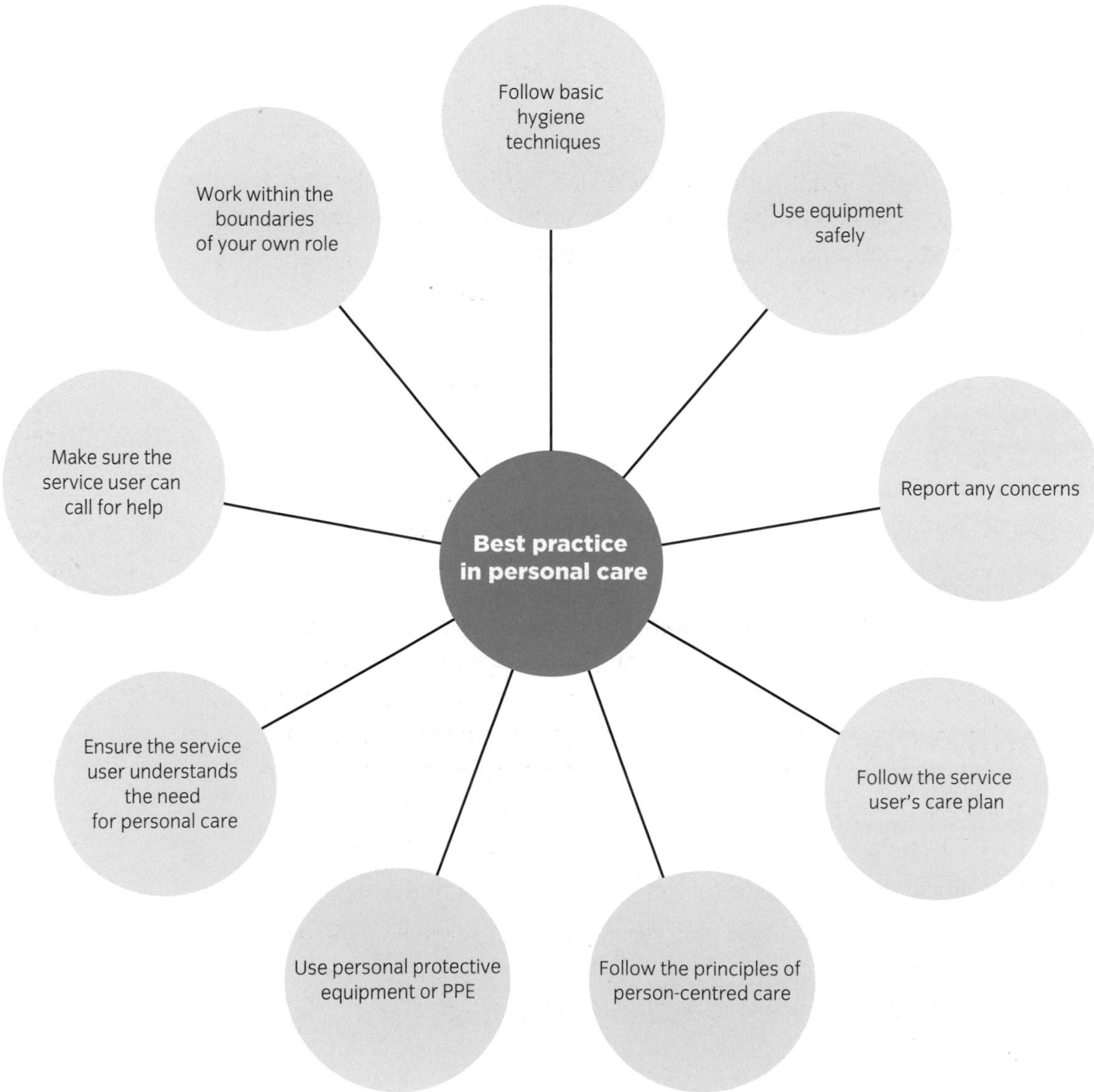

When considering how to provide personal care in a way that minimises any risks you will find it useful to re-read Chapter 6.

Chapters 14 and 15 provide information on how to prevent the spread of infection.

FOLLOW A SERVICE USER'S CARE PLAN

When assistance with personal care is required, the service user should have a care plan in place which should detail the support they need. It is important to follow individual care plans because everyone has different needs and preferences and you must take an individualised approach to providing personal care.

ENSURE THE SERVICE USER UNDERSTANDS THE NEED FOR PERSONAL CARE

It is important that you work with service users to ensure that they understand why there is a need for you to provide personal care – so that they can give informed consent to that care. Remember that washing and dressing are intimate and usually private activities and that the person may be embarrassed – they might therefore tell you that they don't want your support. You need to sensitively explain to the service user why it is important that they have help with their personal care.

If someone has, for example, been incontinent their skin may become sore if they are not supported in a timely way, and this needs to be shared with them in a way that encourages them to accept support. The service user will also need a wash, and support in ensuring their skin is dry, before helping them to replace their underwear and/or pad.

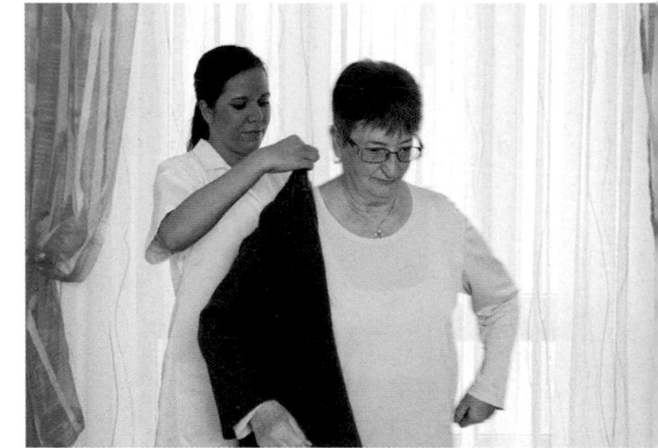

Sometimes service users may make choices about their personal care which can create risks. For example, they may wish to do things for themselves that others feel may not be appropriate (for example placing themselves at risk out of a wish to remain as independent as possible). In such situations it might be helpful to go through a risk assessment with the service user to ensure that they are fully aware of the risks they may be taking. Completing such a risk assessment means that hygiene needs and safety precautions can be discussed openly as part of the support process.

Supporting a service user to understand why they need personal care, and also praising the person when they have been assisted, can help them to accept personal care more readily when it is required again.

WORKING WITHIN THE PRINCIPLES OF PERSON-CENTRED CARE

The core values of person-centred care provide a constant theme in all the chapters of this book. Working within these values is vital when providing any aspect of personal care.

Individuality

When providing personal care it is vital to recognise every service user as a unique individual with differing needs and circumstances. Each will react differently to having support with their personal care. Sometimes one method of assistance works one day but not the next, dependent upon individual health needs and how the person is feeling on that particular day.

Choice

It is important to recognise that everyone will have different preferences in terms of their personal care needs. Therefore service users should be given a range of choices in relation to their own care.

Privacy

It is vital to recognise that personal care should be carried out in a way that promotes service users' right to privacy.

Independence

Service users should be encouraged to do as much for themselves as possible.

Dignity

Maintaining personal hygiene is important in promoting personal dignity, and the personal care provided to service users should promote dignity – for example, it is important to use dignified language when providing personal care. Dignity is closely linked to personal care in a range of ways – for example, people often report feeling better and feeling good about themselves if they have had their hair done, taken a shower or a bath, have new clothes or are wearing their favourite aftershave or perfume.

Respect

Care workers must respect individual service users and in particular their choices about personal care.

Partnership

Care workers should work in partnership with a range of other people to ensure that service users' rights are maintained.

USING PERSONAL PROTECTIVE EQUIPMENT

When providing personal care the risk of infection is increased given that one member of staff often supports more than one service user and that these individuals are potentially in a group at greater risk of developing infections (eg older adults or people who are already ill). It is therefore vitally important that health and social care staff wear gloves and aprons when carrying out personal care and that they remove these after the task and dispose of them safely. Using personal protective equipment (PPE) protects both the service user being supported and the worker providing the support.

FOLLOWING BASIC HYGIENE TECHNIQUES

Health and social care workers should employ basic hygiene techniques, such as:

- keeping nails short and clean
- removing any jewellery, to limit risk of injury to individuals and to prevent spread of infection
- washing hands after providing personal care or after dealing with bodily fluids, even when gloves are worn, as gloves do not provide 100% protection.

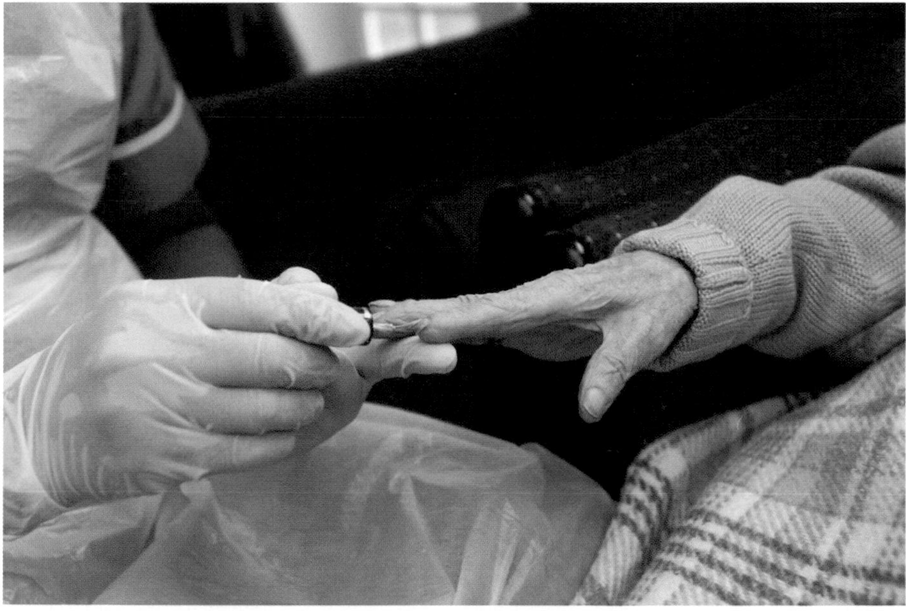

WORKING WITHIN THE BOUNDARIES OF YOUR OWN ROLE

Chapter 1 covers how important it is for health and social care workers to understand the scope of their role and to work within its boundaries. In relation to personal care service users may have specific needs that should only be met by staff with specific training. For example, only staff who have been trained in catheter care should be actively involved in assisting a service user with any aspect of care related to the person's catheter.

USING EQUIPMENT SAFELY

A range of equipment can assist in providing personal care. As a worker you need to be mindful that adult protection investigations can take place if equipment has not been used appropriately and as a consequence significant harm has been caused to an individual.

For example, consider the possible implications of the following.

Cause: A faulty call alarm buzzer/call system.
Effect: Service user unable to summon assistance.

Cause: A faulty sensor mat.
Effect: Service user has fallen but staff not alerted.

Cause: A door sensor not being activated.
Effect: A vulnerable adult service user is walking outside and is unable to find their way back in.

Cause: An ill-fitting bed rail.
Effect: Entrapment; a person could get a limb stuck between the bed and rail.

Cause: Inappropriate sling used on hoist.
Effect: The service user could tilt forwards or even fall out of the sling causing injury.

Cause: Service user left to sit in a sling for long periods of time.
Effect: The sling could dig into the skin causing reddening of the skin and this may have a significant impact on skin integrity.

Other simple things to look for are loose connections or wires, sharp edges, or broken equipment that could cause an injury to a young adult or skin tearing to a frail older person. Leaking items near electrical wires or sockets or splits in commode seats which may harbour infection are further potential – and common – risks.

ENSURING A SERVICE USER CAN SUMMON HELP IF NECESSARY

Service users may be left alone at some points while personal care is being provided. For example, a health and social care worker might help a service user into the bathroom and onto the toilet, and they may then leave to provide privacy. In order to prevent risks it is important that the service user knows how to summon assistance if they need it. There are several ways for someone to call for help:

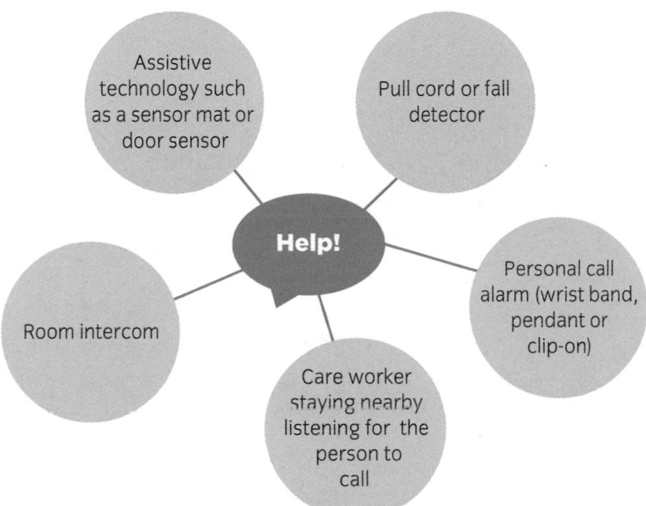

Before leaving a service user alone it is important that you always check that they can summon assistance if they need it. For example, equipment should be checked to ensure it is in working order and you must make sure the service user knows how to use it. Responses to a service user calling for help should be timely in order to prevent risk of fall or injury, as they may well try to do something that places them at risk of harm.

REPORT ANY CONCERNS

When following best practice in personal care, you may find you have some concerns. For example:

- You may feel that a service user's care plan is not sufficiently detailed.
- You may feel that a service user has developed more needs and that a new assessment is needed.
- Equipment may not be available.
- Equipment might be faulty.
- You might not have been trained to use the necessary equipment.
- There might be an insufficient amount of PPE (eg gloves and aprons) provided.

- You may notice changes in a service user's condition.
- You may notice changes in skin condition, bruising or other injuries.

If you have any concerns you should inform your supervisor or line manager as soon as possible.

CASE STUDY

Mrs Miller lives in a ground floor flat rented from the council. The flat is in a state of disrepair and the housing department is issuing notices to Mrs Miller ordering her to make improvements in order to avoid eviction. Until recently Mrs Miller was self-caring with the support of her daughter; however, her daughter was taken ill and has now passed away. Mrs Miller no longer goes out to do her shopping, she doesn't get washed or dressed, her skin has an unidentifiable rash and she has head lice. Her hair appears not to have been washed for a considerable length of time – it is long and matted. Her skin is quite dirty and there is a strong odour of urine, although she states she has a catheter. Her teeth are discoloured and her tongue is sore. Mrs Miller is wearing dirty clothes, her fingernails have faeces under them and her toenails are starting to curl into her skin.

- How could you support Mrs Miller to understand the reasons for hygiene and safety precautions?
- What personal care needs can you identify?
- What risks can you identify?
- What actions can be taken to provide personal care safely (in a way that addresses the risks)?

SUPPORTING INDIVIDUALS TO USE THE TOILET

A service user may need support to use the toilet as a result of:

- problems with remembering where the toilet is as the result of confusion or dementia
- loss of awareness and sensation of needing the toilet, for example following a stroke
- poor mobility and/or balance
- increased fluid intake to prevent urinary tract infections, leading to a need to use the toilet more often than usual.

Support could involve supporting a service user to use a bedpan, toilet, commode or urine bottle.

Using the toilet is very private and personal. It is vitally important to consider the feelings of service users who require support to use the toilet, and to follow best practice when assisting an individual. A number of risks and complications can arise where good practice is not followed. For example, there is the risk that a service user could cut down on their fluid intake so that they do not need to ask to use the toilet as much, and this can lead to the person becoming dehydrated. There is also the risk of infection if service users do not use the toilet as often as they need to.

When a service user needs support to use the toilet they may feel:

- a loss of dignity
- inadequacy
- discomfort
- embarrassment
- anxiety
- humiliation
- physical pain
- fear that they are a nuisance.

Health and social care workers must recognise this and work in a way that enables the person to feel as comfortable as possible. This includes:

- asking the person how they want to be supported
- using appropriate language that promotes dignity
- finding out what aids and adaptations might support the individual.

ASKING THE SERVICE USER HOW THEY WANT TO BE SUPPORTED

With this most sensitive of tasks it is vitally important that you show sensitivity and empathy when asking the service user about how they would like to be helped to use the toilet. Imagine if you were sitting in a room full of people and someone came and asked you very loudly if you wanted to use the toilet. Most people wouldn't like this to happen to them, and yet service users experience this every day in residential care homes, in day services and on hospital wards.

Some service users will not ask to use the toilet – they will wait to be asked by a support worker. It is therefore important to include this discussion when establishing how the individual service user would like to be supported.

USING LANGUAGE THAT PROMOTES DIGNITY

It is always vital to use language that promotes dignity for service users. It is important that you think about the language people themselves use and reflect this in your questions and discussions with them. There are probably more phrases used for going to the toilet than any other task, and some differences in language can be seen in terms of a service user's generation or depending on where they live. For example, people might talk about:

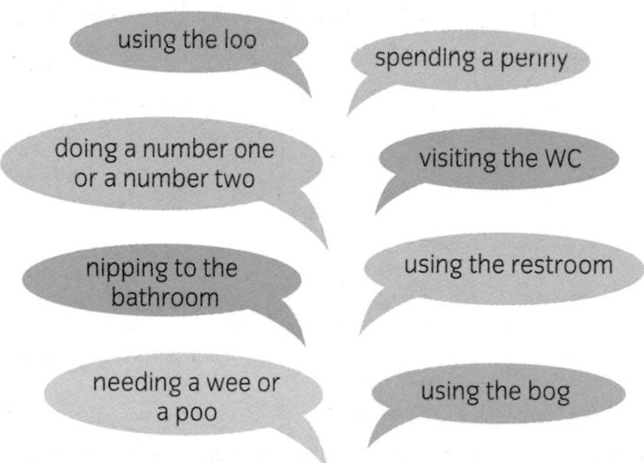

There are lots of ways to say the same thing. Other phrases are more clinical, for example:

- passing urine
- opening your bowels.

Because there are so many ways of referring to the use of the toilet there may be problems with some of the language used, as follows:

- Some service users might find some of these phrases (and others that may be used) offensive.
- Some service users might not understand what you are saying.
- Sometimes the language used by health and social care staff makes service users feel less than human – for example, when people refer to 'toileting' it sounds as though this is being 'done' to an object rather than a person being assisted to use the toilet.

Other language issues can occur around the use of childlike language – for example, the use of terms such as 'potty' and 'nappy' should be used only in relation to children and never in relation to adults.

Make sure that you use appropriate language that is understandable to the individual. Remember that the way health and care staff talk to service users is one of the most important ways of demonstrating dignity and supporting people in a compassionate way.

AIDS AND ADAPTATIONS

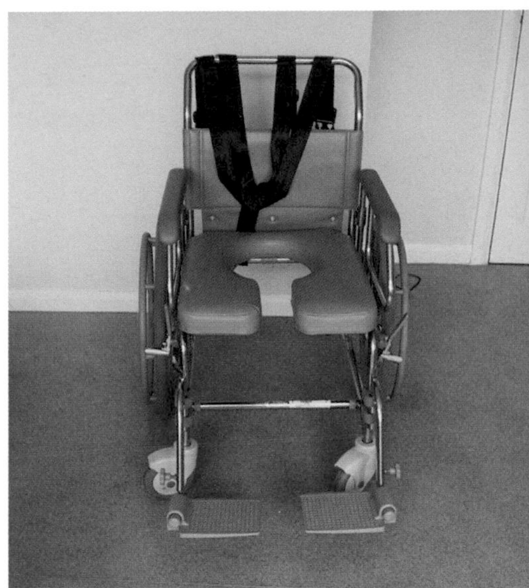

There are many aids and adaptions that can assist a service user to be more independent with using the toilet. Some commodes can be wheeled over a normal toilet, while others can be wheeled to the bed or chair to reduce the distance between the person and the toilet.

The correct positioning of equipment is also important. For example, when using a wheeled commode chair over a normal toilet, if it is not correctly aligned over the toilet, this could lead to accidents on the floor which in turn causes risks of slips and also leads to the service user feeling bad about their situation. Likewise, when using mobile equipment make sure the service user is not too close to a heat source such as a radiator, as this could lead to injury if the skin touches it and they are unable to communicate this.

Sometimes service users who require assistance to use the toilet will wear clothes that are easier and quicker to remove in order to reduce the risks of accidents, and these can include items with elasticated waists, skirts, no tights, jogging bottoms or slip-on or Velcro-fastening garments. However, it is important to remember that service users should select their own clothes. It is not appropriate for care staff to choose the individual's clothing with ease of care being the only consideration.

Incontinence wear

People may need support to put on incontinence wear after using the toilet, which may involve pads. This will be recorded in the service user's care plan.

Helping a service user to make themselves clean

It is very important to help the service user make themselves clean and tidy after they have used the toilet. A lack of care in cleansing after a person has used the toilet can result in soreness, reddening of the skin, odours, rashes or even skin breakdown. Service users should be encouraged to clean themselves, wiping from front to back to prevent risk of infection. Where service users are not assisted to tidy themselves – for example by closing trouser flies, or pulling clothing down to cover their bottom half – this can cause them great embarrassment.

PRACTICAL ISSUES TO CONSIDER WHEN HELPING A SERVICE USER USE THE TOILET

- Remember that when service users need support with using the toilet they may feel particularly vulnerable and powerless. They may also feel as though they are a burden or a nuisance. It is therefore vital to promote best practice when assisting people with using the toilet. Show empathy and understanding.
- Keep in mind that the aim of providing support is to ensure that the service user feels as comfortable as possible.
- Think about an appropriate use of language.
- Make sure that you observe service users' preferences. This should include meeting people's cultural needs.
- Encourage service users to do as much for themselves as they can.
- Where possible leave the service user alone once you have assisted them onto the toilet and make sure they know how to call you when they have finished. This promotes dignity and privacy.
- It is likely that there will be unpleasant smells when assisting a person – this can lead to service users feeling particularly embarrassed. It is vital that health and care staff manage their responses to this (for example it is really important not to react or make a comment).
- Make sure that you provide service users with sufficient time to use the toilet.
- Make sure that you are not interrupted when providing support to a service user using the toilet.
- Remember that younger women may be menstruating and may need to be assisted more frequently at these times.
- Discreetly monitor the service user and look for anything that is concerning – for example check on skin condition and, when helping a person to remove underwear, look for any evidence of offensive discharge.
- If a person uses a commode in the room in which they spend most of their time, ensure appropriate and timely cleansing of the commode, and use antibacterial disinfectants to ensure it is clean. This also freshens the equipment so it smells good, too. This is a simple yet effective way of promoting dignity.
- Be aware of any specific cultural needs.

Show empathy and understanding
Use language carefully
Allow time
Respect privacy and dignity
Avoid interruptions
Observe people's needs and preferences
Think about cultural requirements
Monitor health issues – particularly skin integrity
Promote hygiene, and ensure the person is clean and fresh

CASE STUDY

Neesha was admitted to hospital following a stroke, and is later moved from the admissions ward to a rehabilitation ward. Neesha needs some assistance to move from the bed to the commode. She presses a bell when she needs assistance – sometimes it takes quite some time for the nurses and healthcare assistants to come to Neesha, and they always apologise, explaining to her how busy they are. Neesha doesn't want to be a burden so she decides to restrict her drinks so that she doesn't need to bother the nurses so much. Neesha quickly becomes dehydrated and her dizzy spells increase – and she has to spend much longer in hospital as a result.

- How might Neesha be feeling about her need to use the toilet?
- How could the healthcare assistants and nursing staff support Neesha differently?

CULTURAL AWARENESS

To provide person-centred care you need to ensure that you are aware of any cultural requirements in relation to personal care. While some people may choose not to follow particular cultural practices at all, and others follow only certain ones, you may be interested in the following general principles:

- Sikhs do not cut their hair – leaving hair uncut applies to the whole body, not just the head and face.
- Rastafarians do not cut their hair or beards. They often style their hair into dreadlocks, which are difficult to cultivate. Once developed, dreadlocks should be groomed once a month.
- Cleanliness is very important in Muslim culture. Muslims cannot worship if they are unclean, so they wash before praying. Muslims should also wash their private parts after using the toilet. The left hand is used for washing after using the toilet.
- In Hindu culture washing hands and rinsing the mouth before and after eating is seen as essential. Hindus prefer to wash their hands in the same room as the toilet. Hindus prefer to wash in running water rather than sitting in a bath.

It is vital to remember that the extent to which people follow these cultural practices varies very considerably and you should never make assumptions and should check preferences and cultural needs with individual service users. Also be aware that the examples provided here are far from complete.

SUPPORTING SERVICE USERS TO MAINTAIN PERSONAL HYGIENE

'Personal hygiene' covers supporting service users with washing, showering and bathing, and oral and dental care. When supporting people with these personal hygiene activities health and social care workers need to take a range of factors into account:

- care plans
- active support
- person-centred approaches
- environmental issues
- use of equipment
- toiletries and materials.

DENTAL CARE

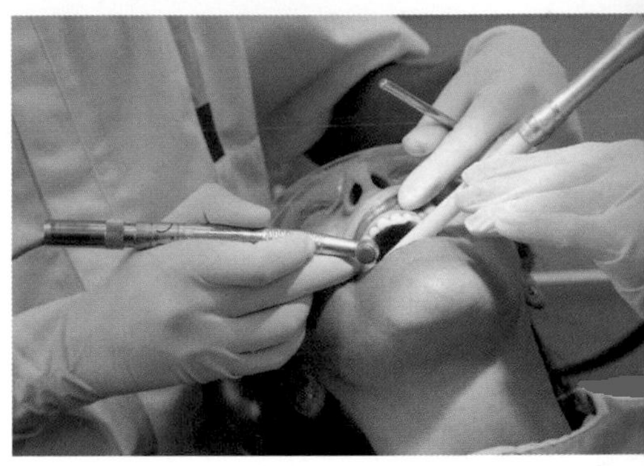

Many service users supported by health and social care workers will require assistance with oral and dental care. Some may have dentures that need to be removed at night and cleaned; others may wish for their dentures to be soaked overnight. Some service users will have separate toothbrushes for their dentures and their teeth. As with all areas of personal care, it is vital that you ask what support individual service users need – some may prefer an electric toothbrush, a particular toothpaste and use of mouthwash, for example. Others may be able to brush their own teeth but need someone to prepare the brush for them. Frail service users may require mouth care, including gentle cleaning and wetting of the lips with a sponge. The support that a service user requires should be detailed in their care plan.

HAIR CARE

Service users can have very different needs in relation to hair care. For example, some people need to wash their hair more frequently than others, and some need to use particular products to keep their hair and scalp healthy. If a service user has particular needs in relation to hair care this should be detailed in their care plan, and the health and social care worker caring for them should be provided with guidance on these specific needs.

NAIL CARE

As people get older their nail care needs may change quite significantly. Increased age means that nails can become more dry and brittle, and therefore the way people care for their nails may change. Nail growth slows down as people get older, and this can mean that fungal nail infections are more likely. It is therefore important to keep nails short. When providing personal care, health and social care workers need to monitor any changes to a service user's nails, as these might indicate an underlying medical condition.

FOOT CARE

Service users who require personal care may well need support with their foot care. Toenail cutting and dealing with dry skin are tasks that healthcare professionals should carry out – if you feel that a service user you support needs assistance with foot care you should raise this and get an appointment made. If you are providing foot care for a service user yourself you need to be clear about the advice that has been provided by professionals on the best way to provide this care.

SHAVING

Service users will have preferences about shaving and hair removal, and these should be addressed and adhered to wherever possible. It is important to seek advice if you are unsure about the provision of support for shaving and hair removal. Keep all equipment used for shaving clean and ensure that the equipment is in good working order.

SKIN CARE

Service users may have specific needs relating to skin care. For example, people may develop sores if they are not supported effectively. Requirements relating to skin care support must be included in a care plan, and these should be followed by all staff supporting the service user.

WASHING, SHOWERING AND BATHING

This is perhaps the area where there is the most diversity of preferences across the whole population. Some people like to shower, others prefer to use the bath, while others may prefer a strip wash. When assisting service users with their personal hygiene you must take account of the person's preferences and how you can assist them with these.

The way in which service users require support will also be diverse – for example if a person prefers a body wash they may like to be washed all over first and then dried, while others may prefer the top half of the body to be washed, then support to get dried before being assisted with the lower half. Likewise, some people may prefer to have support to wash individual body parts and dry them before moving on to the next part of the body.

ENVIRONMENTAL ISSUES

When assisting service users with their personal care, health and social care workers need to take into account a variety of environmental factors, such as whether the room and water temperatures meet the needs and preferences of the person being supported to get washed or bathed.

As a health and social care worker you will often care for people who are vulnerable to risks related to scalding or burning. The Health and Safety Executive states that bath water should be under 44°C in order to reduce the risk of scalding or injury.

You should assess potential scalding and burning risks in the context of the vulnerability of service users you are caring for.

It will be necessary to check the water temperature before you support a service user into the bath, in order to ensure it is safe to enter the water – use a thermometer to ensure accuracy. A further environmental factor includes making sure the room temperature is suitable, ie warm enough – ensure windows are closed and curtains drawn to ensure comfort and privacy. Similarly, some people may prefer their towel to be warm when they get dried in order to keep them warmer, especially if they are sensitive to changes in temperature.

USE OF EQUIPMENT

A range of aids and adaptations can be helpful in assisting service users to bathe or shower – for example people might have a bath chair, or use a side-opening bath.

It is vital that you know how to use the equipment safely and that you check it is working properly on a regular basis.

If a service user has a bath seat or chair, you will need to ensure that you regularly rinse the person with warm water to keep them warm, as they will not be fully submerged in the water.

TOWELS AND CLOTHS

There are a number of issues connected with cloths and towels. For example whether different cloths should be used for different parts of the body, and whether different towels should be used to dry different areas of the body, should be included in care plans. Whether a service user prefers to use a flannel or a sponge should be respected wherever possible. How you can ensure that there are sufficient cloths and towels in a person's own home should be taken into account, as should how these will be kept clean. Sometimes disposable washcloths are used to provide personal care and how these will be disposed of should be made clear.

TOILETRIES

A service user's choice of toiletries is a key aspect of their identity, and this should be respected. Examples include whether a person uses deodorant, and which brand they use – again such choices should be respected.

CARE PLANS

When service users need assistance with maintaining personal hygiene, an appropriate risk assessment should have been completed to see what controls and measures are in place to maintain safety. This risk assessment should be reflected in the individual care plan.

The care plan should also indicate the service user's preferences, such as whether they prefer a bath, shower or full body wash. Any specific needs in relation to personal hygiene should also be covered in the care plan.

Care plans should also contain information about any allergies a person has, and any medical conditions that might impact on the way the person should be supported.

It is therefore vital that you read and follow a service user's care plan when assisting them with their personal hygiene.

ACTIVE SUPPORT

It is vital to encourage the service user to do what they can for themselves – for example, you could provide a soapy flannel for the person to wash their own hands and face.

In order to promote as much involvement as possible it is important that toiletries and materials are easily reached by the service user.

PERSON-CENTRED APPROACHES

It is vital to apply the principles of person-centred practice as covered throughout this chapter.

HEALTH AND SAFETY

Chapter 3 covers how important health and safety is as a concept, particularly in relation to personal care. There may be particular issues connected with promoting privacy when assisting service users to bathe. For example, you should follow a service user's care plan, and not leave a vulnerable person unattended in a bathroom if they:

- may be likely to run their own bath, especially for those with poor memory, as they may forget to turn off taps or recognise if the water is too hot
- are unable to select the appropriate water temperature, as their sensitivity to temperature is impaired
- are unable to get safely in and out of shower or bath without support and/or equipment.

REFLECT

- When you have read a service user's care plan, how do you ensure you are meeting their individual needs and preferences?
- What special measures do you need when you are doubling up with another worker, in order to promote dignity?

CASE STUDY

Elsie lives downstairs in a large detached house. She is unable to access the upstairs of her property without the use of a stairlift. Elsie has a visit each morning from her carer, Kirsty, who gives her a full body wash – with the exception of Thursday, when she has a bath. Elsie finds bathing tiring due to her chronic obstructive airways disease, as she easily gets out of breath. However, she looks forward to having a bath once a week, as her daughter visits on Fridays and she always likes to look her best. Elsie's bathroom is upstairs. Her clothes, toiletries and towels are all stored downstairs.

Elsie is unable to use her stairlift without support, as she needs her oxygen removing and needs constant supervision at this time.

REFLECT

- What do you think are the key things that Kirsty needs to do to prepare to support Elsie to have a bath?
- How would Kirsty ensure that choice and control are promoted?

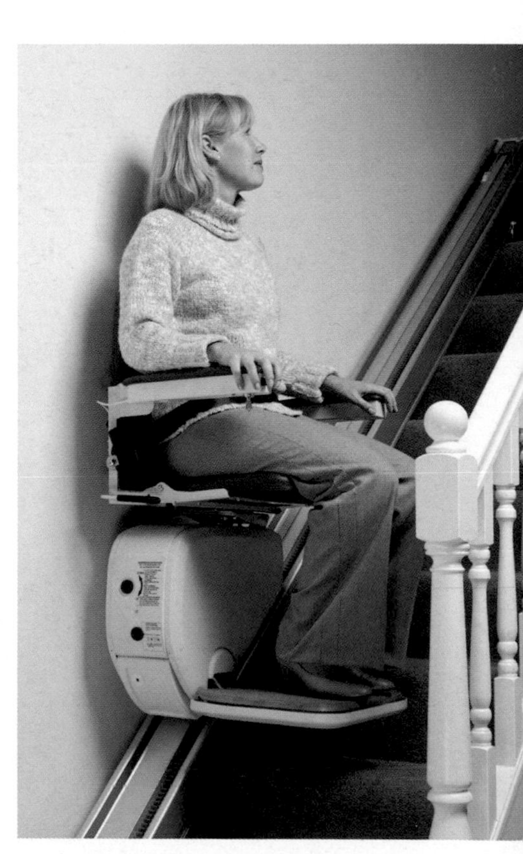

Notes on best practice

- As Elsie requires constant supervision when she is not on oxygen, it is important that Kirsty does not leave her unattended, and therefore everything must be taken upstairs before Elsie goes up.
- Any extreme change of temperature would impact on Elsie's breathing, so Kirsty needs to ensure that the house is warm and the bathroom is at a comfortable temperature in order to reduce the risk of Elsie becoming breathless.
- Kirsty still needs to ask each morning what Elsie's prefers that day, a body wash or a bath, so that Elsie remains in control of her own life choices.
- Kirsty also needs to check what Elsie prefers in her bath, and what body lotion, deodorant and clothes she wants to wear.

SUPPORTING SERVICE USERS TO MANAGE THEIR PERSONAL APPEARANCE

A key part of every person's uniqueness is the way they choose to present themselves. This includes the way they look, dress and smell, the way they choose to have their hairstyle or hairpiece, and whether they choose to wear make-up, aftershave/perfume or jewellery. Particularly in younger adults, a key aspect of a person's identity can be as specific as the brand of clothing or footwear they choose.

IDENTIFYING CHOICES AND PREFERENCES

As this chapter illustrates, it is vital to think about service users' choices and preferences in every aspect of their personal care. Making sure that you understand a person's preferences in relation to their appearance is vital, since this is such a key aspect of identity and how they feel about themselves.

Ask service users:

- how they like their hair styled (don't assume, for example, that older women like it permed and grey)
- about their choices in terms of make-up
- whether use of deodorant and aftershave or perfume is preferred
- what kind of support is needed in relation to the removal of unwanted hair – for example does a man want to shave, or grow his facial hair?
- what they would like to wear and how they choose to wear things.

If a service user is unable to tell you about their choices, look at photographs for clues or speak to family members about the person's appearance.

PROMOTING INDEPENDENCE

Take all practical steps to encourage independence, and to enable service users to do as much for themselves as possible:

- Help a service user to put on glasses if required, or provide a magnified mirror, brighter lighting or help to sit near a window to apply make-up, style hair, brush teeth or shave.
- Repositioning or using supportive equipment can encourage independence; for example, if a service user has arthritis they may find wearing wrist supports helpful.

- Show the service user a selection of clothing so that they can make their own choice when getting dressed.
- Seek professional advice and assistance if required – this is especially relevant in relation to dental and nail care.

KEEPING ITEMS CLEAN, SAFE AND SECURE

One key aspect of personal hygiene is keeping equipment clean and hygienic. This is vitally important as it impacts on services users' self-esteem and safety.

For example, if a service user is wearing dirty clothes this will have an impact on how they feel about themselves and on how others view them. If a shaver is not properly maintained this could cause an injury.

Service users should be encouraged to keep their own items in a clean and tidy manner. However, it is important to remember that everyone has different standards of hygiene and you should not impose your own standards on people.

Practical points:

- Monitor shaving equipment, as electric razors need to be in good working order and wet shavers need to have the blades replaced regularly to reduce the risk of skin damage.
- Ensure that items such as jewellery are put away securely.
- In residential care or sheltered housing where there are communal laundry facilities, it is worthwhile labelling clothes to reduce the risk of lost items.

MONITORING AND REPORTING ON THE PROVISION OF PERSONAL CARE

One of the main threads running through this chapter is the importance of following care plans. Service users' needs may change over time, and this will need to be reported so that the care plan can be amended in line with their current needs.

The best way of monitoring the provision of personal care is to ask service users if the care meets their needs and addresses their preferences. Feedback from individuals is very useful when monitoring care provision. Feedback could also be provided by a service user's family and friends or by other professionals involved in their care.

The service user's care plan should provide information on how their care provision and needs can be monitored, and what action should be taken if the care no longer meets their needs.

There will also be clear requirements about how the care support can be recorded, and it is vital that health and social care workers follow these arrangements.

ADDRESSING SELF-NEGLECT

Issues of self-neglect are covered in Chapter 5. Health and social care workers often encounter self-neglect issues when providing personal care support. The example of Mrs Miller on page 344 also explores a situation of self-neglect.

If service users refuse personal care support you should report this to your manager. For example, if a service user declines to change their clothes for a prolonged period of time, it is vitally important to record this and report it to your line manager.

DIGNITY IN SOCIAL CARE

- Treating service users with respect and promoting their dignity; treating them as a person, not an object, by offering person-centred support.
- Working towards the principle of active support by doing tasks *with* a service user and encouraging them to do as much as possible for themselves rather than doing tasks *for* a service user. This includes not doing something that a person can do for themselves.
- Challenging discrimination or prejudice on behalf of service users.
- Taking time and listening to service users during all support, particularly with personal care.
- Taking time to ask and find out about service users' needs and preferences.
- Respecting service users' rights – specifically their rights to privacy and to making choices.
- A positive attitude; calling service users by the name they choose to use, and seeing the individual as a person who really matters.
- Not grouping or labelling service users on the basis of their needs.
- Avoiding using dehumanising language, for example 'toileting' rather than 'going to the toilet'.
- Listening to service users' wishes and feelings with a non-judgemental attitude.
- Ensuring that service users are not unnecessarily exposed during support with personal care.
- Closing curtains and doors to maintain privacy.

SUPPORTING SERVICE USERS TO MEET PERSONAL CARE NEEDS – WHAT DOES THE CODE OF CONDUCT SAY?

The Code of Conduct for Healthcare Support Workers and Adult Social Care Workers in England 2013 states that you must:

- comply with your employer's way of working
- always ask your supervisor or employer for guidance if you do not feel adequately prepared to carry out any aspect of your work, or if you are unsure how to effectively deliver a task
- be alert to any changes that could affect a service user's needs or progress, and report your observations in line with your employer's agreed ways of working
- put the needs, goals and aspirations of service users first, helping them to be in control and choose the healthcare, care and support they receive
- always explain and discuss the care, support or procedure you intend to carry out with the service user, and only continue if they give valid consent
- know how to put person-centred values into practice in your day-to-day work
- know how to promote dignity in your day-to-day work with individuals you support
- understand why it is important to find out the history, preferences, wishes and needs of the individual
- improve the quality and safety of the care you provide with the help of your supervisor (and mentor if available), and in line with your agreed ways of working.

Before going to the next chapter, take some time to consider:

- whether you always provide personal care in a way that promotes privacy and dignity
- what you have learned from reading through this chapter
- what you might do differently as a result of your learning.

CHAPTER 13
Support individuals to eat and drink

An important aspect of your role as a health and social care worker is to support and enable service users to have adequate nutrition (food) and hydration (drink) in their daily lives.

In order to provide support for service users with eating and drinking you need to know what constitutes a healthy diet, and you need to support service users to make choices about their diet. To do this, you may also work alongside a speech and language therapist, dietician, occupational therapist or specialist nurse. An aspect of this may include monitoring the food and drink a service user consumes and any difficulties they may have in eating so that the appropriate support can be given.

Links to other units

The contents of this chapter links closely with Chapter 9, because all of the support you provide to service users should be person-centred. There are also links with Chapters 2 and 3, as the concepts of communication and equality and inclusion underpin all of your work with service users.

SUPPORTING SERVICE USERS TO MAKE CHOICES ABOUT FOOD AND DRINK

Everyone makes different choices about what to eat. These choices will be based on a variety of factors, including the following:

- knowledge and understanding about what makes a healthy diet
- cultural preferences
- habits and food choices over a period of time
- favourite foods
- preferences for how food is prepared and served
- food allergies, intolerances or dislikes
- following a vegetarian or vegan diet
- current eating and drinking routines – for example, eating fish on Friday, or fasting at certain times such as during Ramadan, or giving up certain foods for Lent
- any medical conditions which might restrict food choices
- any specialist support needs.

A HEALTHY DIET

To support service users to make choices about food and drink you need to have an awareness of what makes a healthy diet. Everyone needs to get a range of nutrients from their diet. The main nutrients are as follows.

Fibre

Fibre is an important part of a healthy diet. A diet high in fibre has many health benefits. It can help prevent heart disease, diabetes, weight gain and some cancers, and can also improve digestive health. Constipation can be a risk for certain groups of service users, including older service users and those with disabilities who have limited mobility. Constipation can be a side-effect of certain forms of medication, and not eating enough fibre or drinking sufficient fluids can also increase the risk.

Protein

Protein is essential for repairing the body, and it can also be a source of energy. Every cell in the body is partly made up of protein. People need a significant amount of protein in their diets, especially when recovering from illness or injury.

Vitamins

Vitamins are chemicals that are found in food and which are essential for maintaining good health. A balanced diet containing a variety of food types prepared correctly should provide all the necessary vitamins.

Some important sources of vitamins include the following:

- *Vitamin A (retinol)* – in cheese, eggs and yoghurt.
- *Thiamin (B1)* – in vegetables, fresh and dried fruit, wholegrain breads and liver.
- *Riboflavin (B2)* – in milk, eggs, fortified cereals and rice.
- *Vitamin B6* – in white meats, fish, oatmeal, peanuts and vegetables.
- *Folic acid* – in broccoli, liver, spinach, chickpeas and brown rice.
- *Vitamin B12* – in meat, salmon, cod, milk, cheese and eggs.
- *Vitamin C* – in oranges and orange juice, peppers, strawberries, potatoes, blackcurrants, brussels sprouts and broccoli.
- *Vitamin D* – in oily fish such as salmon, sardines and mackerel, eggs and dairy products.
- *Vitamin E* – in oils such as soya, corn and olive oil, nuts and seeds, and wheatgerm in cereals.
- *Vitamin K* – in green leafy vegetables, cereal and vegetable oils.

Minerals

Minerals can be found in all foods, but some foods are particularly rich sources. Important minerals include the following.

Calcium

Calcium is found in milk, cheese, white bread and hard water. Calcium gives strength to bones and teeth. Lack of calcium can cause osteoporosis, where bones become weaker, more prone to breakage and slower to mend.

Sodium chloride

Sodium chloride is the chemical name for salt, which is essential for maintaining the water content of the body – however, only a very tiny amount is needed each day to do this. Many foods contain small amounts of salt naturally, and salt is added to most processed foods to help to preserve them. You do not need to add salt to food for nutritional reasons, and it may be harmful to do this to any great extent. Some service users who have heart, blood pressure, kidney or liver problems may need a salt-free diet. Reducing the amount of salt in the diet is almost always a good thing, but for most people a little salt in moderation according to preference should cause few problems.

Iron

Iron helps to make up red blood cells, which transfer oxygen around the body. Red blood cells have only a short life and must therefore be replaced often. Iron is found naturally in liver, red meat, cocoa, bread and eggs. Vitamin C helps in the absorption of iron. Lack of iron causes anaemia, which in turn leads to a chronic loss of energy and often concentration. Anaemia can result from blood loss from menstruation in women or internal bleeding. Iron supplements should only be taken under the direction of a doctor.

A HEALTHY DIET – THE EATWELL PLATE

The 'eatwell plate', designed by the Food Standards Agency and Public Health England, shows the proportions of different types of foods people should eat in order to have a well-balanced and healthy diet which provides everything the body needs.

The eatwell plate divides foods into five groups. A healthy diet should contain a variety of different foods from the first four groups and only a small amount of foods from group five.

1 Fruit and vegetables
2 Starchy foods such as bread, rice, potatoes and pasta
3 Meat, fish, eggs and beans
4 Milk and dairy foods
5 Foods containing fat and sugar.

Fruit and vegetables

Fruit and vegetables contain fibre and many different types of vitamins and minerals which are essential for our bodies to keep healthy and to fight off infection.

The current recommendation is that people should eat five portions of fruit and vegetables every day.

This may sound like a lot, particularly if the service user you are working with is not keen on either fruit or vegetables, but it is surprisingly easy to achieve. The following can be regarded as single portions of fruit and vegetables:

- an apple, peach, banana or orange
- a slice of melon
- a glass of fruit or vegetable juice
- a small tin of fruit
- a handful of fresh or frozen vegetables
- a side salad
- a handful of strawberries or other summer fruit.

Starchy foods

Starchy foods include cereals, bread, rice, potatoes and pasta. These foods are the main source of carbohydrates in a diet. They also provide fibre. The eatwell plate suggests that about a third of our diet should be made up of this food group. The following points help when making choices about this food group:

- It is best to choose wholegrain varieties of starchy foods, as these have more fibre.
- Seeded, wholemeal and granary breads are the most healthy.
- Brown rice and pasta are good choices.
- If potatoes are eaten with the skins on, this provides even more fibre.

Meat, fish, eggs and beans

These are a good source of protein, vitamins and minerals. Choices in this food group should be balanced, and some of these foods should be kept to a minimum. For example, the Department of Health has advised that people who eat more than 90g (cooked weight) of red and processed meat a day should cut down to 70g.

Eggs contain cholesterol, and high cholesterol (a fatty substance) levels in a person's blood increases the risk of heart disease. However, the amount of fat that a person eats has much more effect on cholesterol levels than eggs – so there is no recommended limit on the number of eggs which can be eaten as part of a healthy diet.

Milk and dairy products

Dairy products such as cheese and yoghurt are great sources of protein and calcium. Lower-fat milk and dairy foods make healthier choices than full-fat versions, though. The total fat content of dairy products varies a great deal. Much of the fat in milk and dairy foods is saturated fat, and eating too much saturated fat can contribute to becoming overweight. It can also cause raised levels of cholesterol and can increase the risk of a heart attack or stroke.

Foods containing fat and sugar

Fat and sugar should be limited. Sugar should make up the smallest proportion of total foods eaten. Excess sugar can cause weight gain and tooth decay and can contribute to the development of diabetes. Fats should also be consumed in small proportions – too much fat can contribute to weight gain and a build-up of cholesterol which can cause heart and circulation problems. Examples of foods in this category can include butter, cooking oils, puddings and confectionery.

HOW MUCH SHOULD SERVICE USERS DRINK?

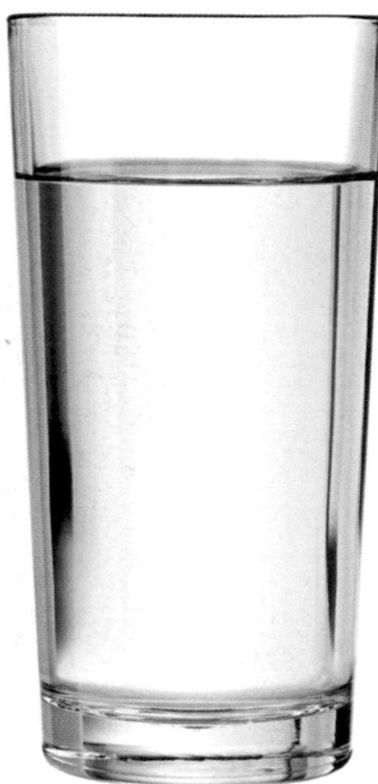

Water makes up over two-thirds of the healthy human body. It lubricates the joints and eyes, aids digestion, flushes out waste and toxins and keeps the skin healthy.

The European Food Safety Authority recommends that women should drink about 1.6 litres of fluid and men should drink about 2 litres of fluid per day. That's about eight 200ml glasses for a woman and ten 200ml glasses for a man.

However, the amount that a person needs to drink to avoid getting dehydrated will vary depending on a range of factors, including their size, the environmental temperature and how active they are. So, for example, if you are exercising hard in hot weather you will need to drink more.

All drinks count, including hot drinks such as tea and coffee, but water, milk and fruit juices are the healthiest. It is best to avoid alcoholic drinks.

Soft drinks (such as squash) and fizzy drinks can be high in added sugars.

DEHYDRATION

Dehydration occurs when the body loses more fluid than it takes in.

When the normal water content of the body is reduced, it upsets the balance of minerals in the body, which affects the way that it functions.

Common signs of dehydration include:

- dark urine and not passing much urine when you go to the toilet
- headaches
- lack of energy
- feeling light-headed
- feeling tired (lethargic) or confused
- dry mouth and eyes that don't produce tears
- dry skin that sags slowly into position when pinched up or damages easily
- rapid heartbeat
- blood in stools (faeces), or constipation
- vomiting or headaches
- a drop in blood pressure or feeling dizzy or faint
- change in behaviour, perhaps becoming agitated or aggressive.

Anyone can become dehydrated, but certain groups are particularly at risk:

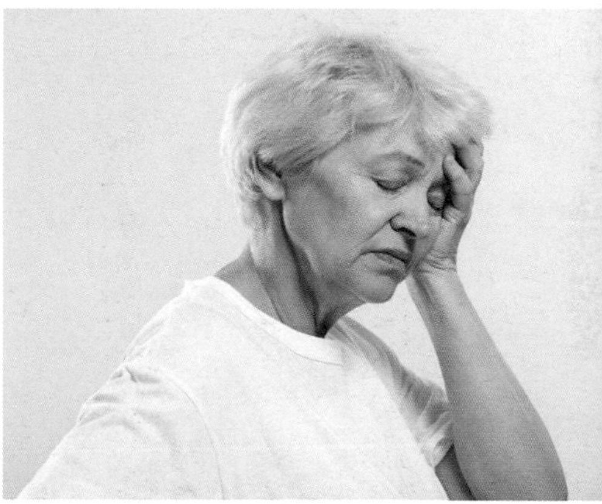

- *Babies and infants.* They have a low body weight and are sensitive to even small amounts of fluid loss.
- *Older service users.* They may be less aware that they are becoming dehydrated and need to keep drinking fluids.
- *Service users with a long-term health condition* such as diabetes.
- *Service users who are ill.* They can quickly become dehydrated as a result of vomiting and diarrhoea or sweating from a fever.

MALNUTRITION

Malnutrition is unplanned or unexplained weight loss. For example, if a person loses 5–10% of their body weight over the course of three to six months when they are not trying to lose weight.

Malnutrition develops when the body does not get the right amount of the vitamins, minerals and other nutrients it needs to maintain healthy tissues and organ function.

The following are signs that a service user may be malnourished:

- feeling tired and lacking energy
- taking a long time to recover from infections

- delays in the healing process in relation to wound care
- mood changes, perhaps being irritable or low in mood
- low levels of concentration
- extremities (hands and feet) feel cold; finding it hard to keep warm
- persistent diarrhoea
- weight loss.

THE IMPACT OF CULTURE ON FOOD CHOICES

Religion and culture can have a significant impact on food in a number of ways:

- the choices a service user makes about what and when they eat
- the way that food should be prepared and stored
- the way a service user chooses to eat – ie what utensils they use.

Consider the relationship with food and eating in the following cultures.

Chinese culture

- Rice or noodles are staple aspects of most, if not all, meals. A full range of meats and seafood may be eaten, but personal choices based on lifestyle or faith will mean that people may not eat certain meats. For example, some Buddhists and Taoists eat a vegetarian diet.
- Nearly all vegetables are cooked.
- May prefer boiled water that is left to cool rather than cold water.
- Chopsticks and a spoon (for soup) are most commonly used as eating utensils.

Hindu culture

- Most Hindus do not eat meat or animal by-products including gelatine (which is often found in sweets). Those that do eat meat may not eat beef, as the cow is regarded as a sacred animal.
- Food prepared outside of the home may be approached with extreme caution, as the true extent to which the food meets people's requirements may not be known. Vegetarian food will be seen as contaminated if it is kept or prepared near meat.

Islamic culture

- Muslims do not eat pork or pig products, and will only eat halal meat which has been killed in accordance to the Islamic law.
- Dairy products are acceptable provided they are halal.
- No alcohol is permitted.
- Fish and vegetables are permitted.
- Any food which contains animal by-products are only eaten if the meat involved is halal.

Jewish culture

- A Jewish diet has to be kosher (permitted). This refers to the fact that animals must be humanely slaughtered by a *shochet* (qualified slaughterer) and according to Jewish law. Kosher meats include those from animals with split hooves and those that chew the cud, kosher chicken and eggs from them, and fish which have both fins and scales, such as cod. *Treif* (forbidden) foods include horses, pigs, rabbits, birds of prey, and non-kosher fish, including all shellfish such as prawns, crabs and so on.
- Fruit and vegetables are kosher provided they are not cooked with non-kosher ingredients.
- Fish can be served with milk. Fish can also be served with meals that contain meat.
- Jewish law prohibits the mixing of milk foods with meat foods, and separate utensils and serving items should be used for these. A time lapse is observed between eating the two types of food.

Rastafarian culture

- Many Rastafarians are vegetarian, and avoid meat, fish and poultry. Others are vegan and will not consume any animal by-products, including fat, milk and gelatine.
- Some Rastafarians do choose to eat meat, although they may not eat pork, as it is regarded as unclean.

Sikh culture

- Many Sikhs refrain from alcohol, tobacco and other intoxicants.
- Meat should only be consumed if it is *jhatka*, where the animal has been instantaneously killed with one stroke. Those that eat meat must not eat halal or kosher meat.
- Many Sikhs are vegetarians.

Don't make assumptions

The extent to which service users from particular cultures will observe dietary requirements will differ depending on their background, their preferences and sometimes their generation. It is important never to make assumptions.

CASE STUDY

Maureen has just been admitted to hospital. When she was admitted her religion was recorded as Jewish. However, Maureen has not been Orthodox (practising) for many years, and she does not observe Jewish traditions.

On her second day in hospital Maureen marks her menu card requesting ham, potatoes, peas and parsley sauce. The healthcare assistant comes to collect the patients' menu cards, but as she is leaving the bay she realises that Maureen has requested ham.

The healthcare assistant, keen to be sensitive to service users' cultural needs, calls out to Maureen, 'You've asked for ham by mistake – shall I change it to chicken, with you being Jewish?'

- How might Maureen feel?
- What could the healthcare assistant do differently?

VEGETARIAN AND VEGAN DIETS

- Service users who have a vegetarian diet may not want to include meat in their diet for various reasons, including religious beliefs, on principle or from personal preference. Whatever the reason, the person's choices must be respected. Meat and dairy products can also be an important source of vitamins and minerals. For this reason vegetarians must take care to ensure that they eat a variety of foodstuffs to ensure that they receive all the vitamins and minerals they require.
- People who follow a vegan diet have decided to exclude all animal products from their diet. A surprising amount of processed foods include ingredients which are derived in some way from animals and it is important if you are supporting a service user who follows a vegetarian or vegan diet to look carefully at the list of ingredients of foods in order to help that person make an informed choice.

CHALLENGES IN SUPPORTING SERVICE USERS TO MAKE HEALTHY CHOICES

Health and social care workers can face a number of challenges in supporting service users to make choices about their food and drink. Consider the following examples. What would you do in each case?

- Mrs Barlow has always enjoyed having a cup of tea and a piece of cake mid-morning. She used to be very active, and this helped her to keep her weight down, but as Mrs Barlow has become older her arthritis has caused her more problems and she is struggling to get up and about. She is now putting on weight, which is adding complications to her limited mobility. A health and social care worker, Becky, is supporting Mrs Barlow. Becky has suggested that Mrs Barlow could eat more healthily, but Mrs Barlow is insistent that she still wants a slice of cake with her mid-morning cup of tea.
- Mr Fielding has been dependent on alcohol for a number of years. When he receives his pension he spends most of it on alcohol and doesn't think about what he will eat. Dam, who is supporting Mr Fielding, finds it difficult to support Mr Fielding to make healthier choices about his diet.
- Jason has a learning disability and is supported by Judy. Judy is finding it difficult to support Jason to make healthy choices about his diet. Jason is really keen on fast food and he is gaining weight quite quickly.
- Mrs Jones is not drinking very much. She has decided to limit her fluid intake because she is worried that she might have an 'accident' now that she can't get to the toilet very quickly.
- Mrs Parkes has advanced dementia. She is no longer able to communicate verbally. The health and social care workers at the residential home which she has just moved into are finding it difficult to establish what Mrs Parkes wants to eat.

When you face a challenge in relation to supporting service users to make choices about food and drink, it is useful to:

- make sure the service user understands what makes a healthy diet
- seek advice and support from others where necessary
- talk to the service user about the consequences of their choices
- ask family members about the choices a service user has made in the past, if you are finding it difficult to recognise what choices a service user is making (for example, if they are unable to tell you about what they would like)
- observe the service user when they are eating – their body language may help to clarify their choices.

SEEKING GUIDANCE ABOUT CHOICES OF FOOD AND DRINK

At times it will be necessary to seek additional guidance about a service user's choice of food and drink. For example, if you are working with a service user who has unstable diabetes or who is newly diagnosed with diabetes, a referral to a specialist diabetic nurse or dietician could be useful in providing information about what foods are suitable in order to better manage the service user's diet and maintain their good health.

A range of situations may mean that a referral is needed to one of the following:

- *Speech and language therapist.* Perhaps if a service user is at risk of aspirating or choking due to poor swallowing reflex. This could present as a service user coughing, spluttering or gagging at mealtimes, or general discomfort when swallowing while eating or drinking.
- *Occupational therapist.* For advice on specialist cutlery to encourage independence.
- *Dietician.* To seek guidance on foods that are safe to eat if a service user has allergies or intolerance to certain food groups.
- *Specialist meal provider.* To take account of cultural or dietary needs.

REFLECT

What action would you take if you were unable to resolve any difficulties or dilemmas in relation to the choice of food and drink for a service user?

PREPARING TO PROVIDE SUPPORT FOR EATING AND DRINKING

When preparing to support someone to eat and drink it is important to think about a range of issues, including:

- the level and type of support a service user needs
- issues around health and hygiene
- remaining person-centred
- providing any equipment/utensils necessary.

LEVEL AND TYPE OF SUPPORT

In understanding what level and type of support is required it is useful to start with thinking about *why* a service user needs support, as the following table illustrates.

Reason for support	Level and type of support
The service user has a physical impairment which means that they are unable to lift their hand to their mouth.	The service user may well be able to put food on to a fork or spoon, but will need support to bring this to their mouth.
The service user has advanced dementia and they forget to eat and drink.	The service user will need prompting to eat and drink.
The service user has an eating disorder.	Advice should be obtained from a medical professional about the level and type of support required. It is very likely that careful monitoring of food and drink will be required.
The service user has difficulty with chewing.	The service user will need food that is soft and moist and requires minimal chewing.
The service user has Parkinson's disease, which affects their coordination so they struggle to use a knife and fork.	The service user could be given finger foods some of the time and could be given a range of different knives and forks to try out; service users may find some cutlery easier to manage than others.

The level and type of support a service user needs with eating and drinking should be detailed in their care plan. Make sure that you read and understand the care plan before providing them with support.

It is vital to remember that a service user's support needs might fluctuate from day to day or might be different at different times of the day. Health and social care workers must be mindful of this and review the support provided regularly.

Eating disorders

Eating disorders are mental health conditions which involve an unhealthy relationship with food and eating, often coupled with a fear of being overweight. There are different types of eating disorders, with the most common being anorexia, bulimia and binge eating. Some service users may hide food or say they have eaten when they haven't, as they may feel guilty or upset when thinking about eating. Other behaviours can include making themselves sick, using medication called laxatives which make them open their bowels in order to lose weight, or over-exercising to promote weight loss.

HEALTH AND HYGIENE

To provide support with eating and drinking safely it is vital to take health and hygiene into account. The information provided in Chapters 14 and 15 will be useful in understanding the issues that can arise, and the actions that health and social care workers need to take when providing assistance with eating and drinking.

Handwashing

A key part of preparing to provide support for eating and drinking is to wash your hands effectively. Effective handwashing techniques are covered on page 421.

In particular, people who provide support with personal care duties must wash their hands if they are:

- helping service users to go to the toilet or emptying commodes
- cleaning up after an accident, such as sickness or diarrhoea
- touching dirty linen and clothing
- handling pets or their feeding bowls.

Hands also need to be washed between stages of food preparation, such as when touching uncooked and cooked items of food.

Using protective clothing

Protective clothing may be required for both the worker and the person they are assisting with eating. Health and social care workers should check specific requirements in their work setting.

Other issues

When proving support for eating and drinking, health and social care workers need to make sure that their hair is tied away from their face, take off any jewellery and keep nails short.

REMAINING PERSON-CENTRED

Perhaps the most important aspect of providing any kind of care and support is ensuring that it is person-centred. Different service users will have different preferences in terms of eating and drinking:

- how they like to eat (some people like to eat each type of food on their plate in order, while others like to have a little of each food in each mouthful)

- what they like to eat with (some people like bowls, other like plates, etc)
- some people like to eat at a table, while others prefer a tray on their lap
- some people like to eat with others and make a mealtime a social event, while others like to eat alone
- some people like to use a napkin over their clothes, while others don't.

In order to ensure that the support provided is person-centred, it is important to find out about a service user's likes and dislikes and to consider how these preferences can be met.

PROVIDING NECESSARY EQUIPMENT/ UTENSILS TO ASSIST A SERVICE USER TO EAT OR DRINK

A range of utensils and equipment can be used to assist a service user to eat and drink. These can promote a service user's independence and encourage active support in a range of ways.

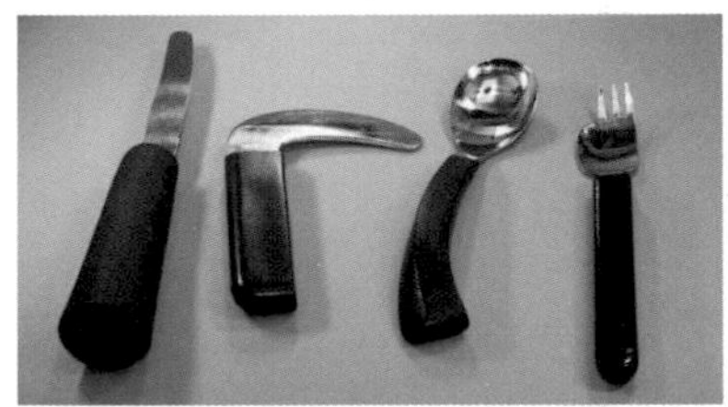

Cutlery can be angled, or larger than usual, and it can have contoured handles or may be weighted.

Plates and bowls can have high sides or partitions, and insulated plates and bowls and plates and bowls with slip-resistant features can also be useful. Plates and bowls that provide a colour contrast can also be useful for service users with a visual impairment.

Non-slip mats are useful if service users are shaky or have limited of use of their hands.

A liquid level indicator alerts a service user with a visual impairment when the liquid has reached the desired level.

Extra-long straws can assist with drinking without the need to use hands.

REFLECT

- What challenges do you face when preparing to provide support for eating and drinking?
- How could you improve your preparations?

CASE STUDY

Jackie is a support worker in a community setting. She arrives to make a meal for Mr Jones, but when he opens the door he is very upset as his cat is ill and has vomited on the floor in several rooms. He has tried to clean up but due to his general frailty he has had to leave much of it. Jackie sees that Mr Jones has used the dishcloth and left it on the work surface in the kitchen. Jackie puts on her disposable apron and gloves, gets a refuse sack and disposes of the cloth. She carefully cleans up all affected areas and starts to disinfect the floor and work surface, disposing of dirty cloths, apron and gloves in the refuse sack. Jackie reminds Mr Jones to wash his hands as she washes her own, and puts on another apron before preparing Mr Jones his favourite meal of fish, mashed potato and peas.

THE FRANCIS REPORT – EATING AND DRINKING

The Francis Report (2013) into the care provided at Stafford Hospital identified significant concerns about the support provided to patients with eating and drinking. The following recommendations were made about food provision and nutrition for patients (and these principles will mostly apply to service users in general):

- Food and drink that is as far as possible palatable must be made available and delivered at a time and in a form to enable patients to consume it.
- Food and drink should, where possible, be delivered to patients in containers and with utensils which enable them to eat by themselves, taking account of any physical incapacity.
- Time for meals should be protected in the daily schedule, but, if it is necessary for therapeutic reasons to interrupt mealtimes for a patient, alternatives should be made available when the patient is ready for them.
- If at all practicable, meals should be available to patients when they want them, rather than when it suits the catering service to offer them.
- It is essential that appropriate assistance is made available to patients who need it as and when necessary to consume food or drink.
- No meal or drink should ever be left out of reach of patients.
- Where patients have not eaten or drunk what is provided at mealtimes this must be noted and the reasons established. Steps should also be taken to remedy the deficit in nutrition and hydration.
- Systems, such as specially marked trays or jugs or other prompts, should be employed to remind staff of those patients who need assistance with eating and drinking.
- For patients capable of eating out of bed, where possible, facilities should be made available on the ward for them to eat at tables, together with other patients if they wish to do so.
- Mealtimes should be considered as an opportunity for non-intrusive forms of observation and interaction where this is desirable and appropriate.
- Patients' supporters should not be prevented from joining them at mealtimes, provided that this does not interfere with the preservation of appropriate levels of nutrition and hydration or with other patients on the ward. Supporters should be encouraged to provide assistance with eating and drinking where this is needed and should they wish to provide such help.

- For patients who have no willing supporters to assist, but who need help with eating and drinking, consideration should be given to engaging volunteers who have had the appropriate level of checks for this purpose.
- Feedback should be obtained regularly from patients, supporters and volunteer helpers on the quality of food and drink and about any necessary adjustments required for individual patients.
- Proper records should be kept of the food and drink supplied to and consumed by patients.

PROVIDING SUPPORT FOR EATING AND DRINKING

It is not enough to simply provide support to service users to eat and drink. It is vital to think about the way that you provide support. Person-centred support in helping service users to eat and drink involves:

- promoting dignity
- ensuring comfort
- making sure the service user is safe while eating and drinking
- promoting adequate nutrition
- meeting individual needs
- taking preferences into account and trying to reflect these in the support provided
- observing service users and their reactions while eating and drinking.

PROMOTING DIGNITY

Promoting dignity in all areas of health and social care is crucial. When assisting service users with eating and drinking there are some specific issues which should be taken into account in order to promote dignity.

In particular, language should be appropriate and should promote dignity. Language can label people negatively (see Chapter 3). Language can also impact on the way a service user feels about themselves. For example, use of the word 'feeding' should be avoided as this conjures up images of feeding animals or babies. Language should not be childlike (for example, you should not refer to a bib, but rather a serviette or napkin).

You should also ensure that:

- service users do not feel as though they are being ignored while being assisted to eat
- you do not talk to other staff while ignoring the service user you are assisting with eating
- service users are given sufficient time to eat
- you listen to what service users are saying about what food to eat next or whether they would like a drink with their meal
- you support service users to do as much for themselves as possible
- the food provided meets the service users' needs and preferences.

ENSURING COMFORT

What is comfortable for one service user will be different from what is comfortable for another – reinforcing the need for you to ensure that you respond to each service user's individual needs and preferences.

Aspects of comfort might include:

- where a service user sits
- what position they sit in
- the environment – well-lit, not too hot or too cold
- what the service user is eating with and where they are eating
- who they are eating with
- whether they have conversations while they are eating.

For some service users mealtimes can be a social event. It may not merely be about what food is put in front of them or what they are about to eat, it's about how support is provided, who else is sitting with them and what is happening around them.

Conversations at mealtimes are rarely about the food alone; taking time to share memories as well as everyday chatter often creates a sense of enjoyment. Two-way communication can create a pleasant, positive and personal experience for the service user being assisted to eat, and the support worker.

Service users who eat alone often also take part in other activities such as reading, watching TV or what's happening around them, or listening to music or the radio.

REFLECT

- What makes you comfortable when you are eating?
- How do you know what makes the service users you support comfortable when they are eating?

MAKING SURE A SERVICE USER IS SAFE WHEN EATING AND DRINKING

A health and social care worker could be at fault if the appropriate professional support had not been sought and a resident or service user became ill through aspiration (breathing or sucking in food which may cause choking), or worse. A referral can be made to a speech and language therapist (SALT) so that they can complete a specialist assessment to reduce risk of choking and recommend changes to dietary intake.

Within a residential or hospital setting a service user may be deemed to lack capacity in relation to their care needs. As a result of a service user's behaviour and consequent risk of choking, restrictions or restraint on access to communal areas within that setting or a requirement for intrusive support, such as a mouth sweep to check for any risk of choking, may be classed as a deprivation. In this instance an application should be considered by the care provider (Managing Authority), to the supervising body (Local Authority) under the Mental Capacity Act 2005 Deprivation of Liberty Safeguards to ensure that all actions are in the service user's best interests.

Alongside this, staff should also consider a referral to an advocacy organisation for an advocate to support the service user with decision making in relation to their eating and drinking care plans. All care plans should include the least restrictive options for those that lack capacity. As a care worker there is sometimes a need to be creative if a service user is unable to eat food as a solid; you could for example, make food into a softer alternative such as a mousse in order to address the risk with a proportionate response.

Care staff who work with service users at risk of choking should have mandatory training on the identification of choking and emergency treatment. Emergency first aid training highlights the increased need to be aware of the potential consequences if the service user chokes.

SUPPORT A SERVICE USER TO CONSUME MANAGEABLE AMOUNTS OF FOOD AND DRINK AT THEIR OWN PACE

Some people eat quite quickly, while others eat much more slowly. It is important that the service users you support are never rushed but that they are given enough time to eat sufficient food. It may be appropriate to consider how food can be kept warm if you are supporting someone who eats very slowly.

OBSERVING A SERVICE USER AND THEIR REACTIONS WHILE EATING AND DRINKING

Observations of a service user at mealtimes can highlight areas of difficulty, for example, with swallowing. Observations which may indicate a concern include:

- lengthy mealtimes (longer than 30 minutes) – this may mean that a service user is struggling to chew or swallow their food
- a refusal to eat or drink
- difficulties with biting, chewing and manipulating food in the mouth
- poor saliva control
- spitting, throwing or dropping food
- slow chewing or pocketing of food (holding food in the side of the mouth)
- difficulty coordinating breathing and swallowing, especially while eating and drinking
- vomiting at mealtimes
- adverse reaction to a certain type of food, noticeable swelling to the mouth and face or red blotching to the skin.

As a support worker it is important that you are well prepared when supporting service users to eat and drink, and that you are able to identify any safety concerns in order to take corrective action. Such actions may include mashing, liquidising or cutting up food.

If you observe anything that concerns you it is important to pass your observations to senior staff and discuss what actions might be useful.

CASE STUDY

Yvonne is an 80-year-old woman. She has dementia and is unable to communicate verbally, and lives in a residential care home. Yvonne is very independent and tries to do as much for herself as she can. However, she has poor vision and can often drop her food on to the table or her lap. Yvonne declines to wear her false teeth as she believes that they belong to someone else. A number of staff at the home think that Yvonne is 'very difficult'.

A new member of staff supports Yvonne to eat her meal one day. A number of other staff see Yvonne throwing her food on the floor. Yvonne starts to scream and hit out at the worker who is supporting her.

- What might be happening?
- If you observed this, what would you do?

REFLECT

If you needed support to eat and drink, how would you feel if:

- you were ignored while being assisted to eat?
- workers talked to each other over the top of you?
- you felt that you were being rushed because the worker assisting you needed to get on with another job?
- you were not given any choices?
- you didn't like the food on offer?

CLEARING AWAY AFTER FOOD AND DRINK

As a health and social care worker it is important to consider when and how you clear away after assisting a service user to eat. If you clear up too soon this could impact on a service user's health, as they may not eat and drink enough.

WHEN

You should be sure that the service user has finished eating and drinking before starting to clear away. The way that people eat differs greatly – for example, some people will choose to take their time, as they chat or need to chew slowly. If a service user has breathing difficulties they may need to take a break and may even put down their cutlery at this time, but it is important not to assume they have finished as they may be recovering from their breathlessness in order to resume their meal.

Make sure you:

- confirm that the service user has finished eating and drinking before clearing away
- tell service users that they can take as much time as they need
- ask if the service user would like any assistance if they haven't eaten very much, rather than simply clearing away – for example, with a different utensil they might eat more
- continue to assist the service user to eat for as long as they wish to
- ensure that your non-verbal cues do not indicate to the service user that you are busy and need to get on with something else.

HOW

It is important to try to clear away quietly. Residents of care homes have reported that the dining room is a noisy place, as care workers unconsciously bang plates together. This can disrupt social interaction between residents and staff alike. It is also important to ensure that service users' independence is promoted and that active support is encouraged in clearing away.

Active support is a person-centred approach, which is about helping service users to do things for themselves rather than having things done for them (see Chapter 10). Following the principles of active support means that service users should be supported to actively participate in all aspects of eating, drinking and tidying away.

Risk assessments may be required to ensure that this activity can be undertaken safely, and this will vary depending on the environment in which you are working and the restrictions that are in place there.

SUPPORTING SERVICE USERS TO MAKE THEMSELVES CLEAN AND TIDY AFTER EATING AND DRINKING

Helping service users to make themselves clean and tidy after they have eaten is very important in terms of promoting dignity and helping service users to feel good about themselves and their appearance. It is important to think about how service users can be best supported to make themselves clean and tidy at each stage of providing support. For example, it is useful to make sure that a napkin is available for the service user when they start to eat. In helping service users to make themselves clean it is vital not to use patronising language. For example, care workers should not make comments like 'you mucky pup', which is an example of something that might be said when assisting young children.

CASE STUDY

Mike is 80 years old and has problems with his breathing. He lives in a sheltered housing complex where he has the option of having a meal in the communal dining area with other residents, or eating on his own in his flat. Mike's key worker, Angela, has noticed over the past few months that Mike, who has always been keen to participate in activities, mealtimes and outings, has been declining to join other residents and has become quite withdrawn. Angela contacts Mike's daughter to discuss her concerns. Angela takes time to sit with Mike and express her concerns, and it transpires that Mike is embarrassed that, as he can not breathe properly, he is struggling to breathe and eat at the same time. He is worried that he is eating with his mouth open and that he is coughing during mealtimes. Mike says he is worried that this will upset other service users. Despite his reluctance, Angela requests a referral to a specialist respiratory nurse. The outcome results in Mike having treatment and oxygen. This gives him more confidence and he starts to eat with others again.

- What could have happened to Mike if Angela had not taken the time to follow up her concerns?

MONITORING EATING AND DRINKING AND THE SUPPORT PROVIDED

It is important to monitor the food and drink service users consume, and to keep any support offered under review, for many reasons. For example:

- a service user's needs may change
- a service user could become malnourished or dehydrated (see pages 366–7)
- a service user's preferences can change
- it may be unclear why a service user is losing or gaining weight
- there might be significant concerns about a service user's health
- there could be concerns about self-neglect.

A record should identify any needs that a service user may have, such as intolerance to certain food groups, special dietary requirements or any identified risks during eating and drinking. Some care environments adopt the Malnutrition Universal Screening Tool (MUST) recording system.

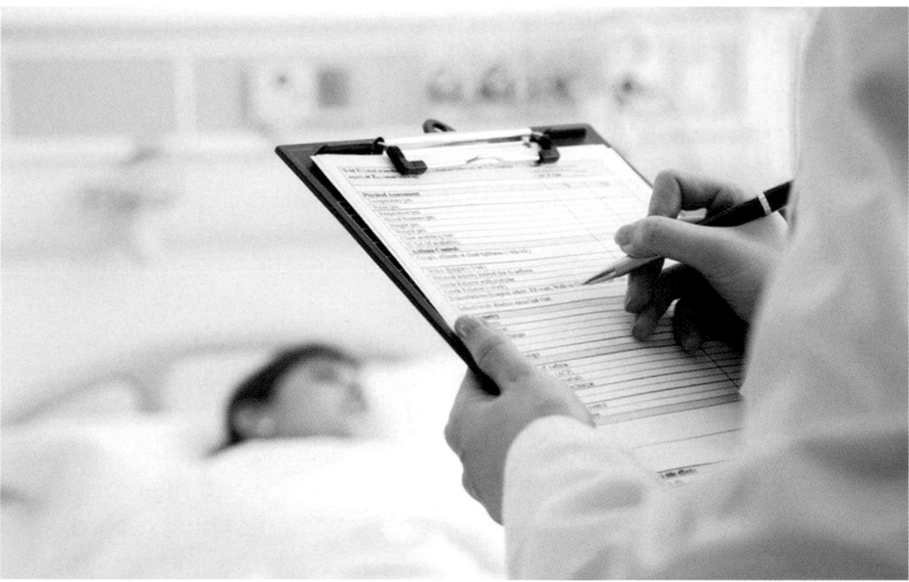

Separate charts are usually required in order to accurately record fluid and dietary intake.

Accurate fluid recording includes:

- the amount of fluid taken in millilitres
- frequency
- what drink was consumed.

Recording of fluids might be necessary at certain times. For example, if there are medical concerns then an input and output record may be needed. This records fluid intake and output. Such records can be helpful to ensure that a service user is passing adequate urine and that bowel movements are regular. Frequency of sleeping and activity may also be taken into account to ensure a holistic assessment of the service user.

Accurate dietary recording details:

- what was eaten
- what type of food was declined
- what was offered as a replacement
- how much was eaten.

A risk assessment will underpin both of these records, and will highlight any areas of risk so that a service user can be supported to eat and drink in a person-centred way that promotes independence and dignity. Any changes identified to the support required should be clearly recorded, and these records updated regularly to ensure accuracy.

Where there are any changes or any concerns, it is important to:

- ensure that all the workers involved in supporting a service user are aware of the changes
- make any necessary referrals
- seek feedback from the service user involved.

A health and social care worker must check whether a care plan is relevant and fit for purpose on a regular basis. It is important that any changes to support requirements are reviewed and communicated within the care team. Changes should be formally updated on written records and also exchanged as part of the handover process with colleagues. Any inaccurate and out-of-date information must be updated with immediate effect in order to promote and maintain a healthy nutritional intake. Likewise, risk assessments must record what actions are required to minimise the risk of harm and prevent any decline in a service user's condition, and these should also outline what to do if a service user becomes unwell.

EXTRACT OF FOOD INTAKE RECORD

Name: Carole Smith

Special dietary or cultural requirements: Carole needs a soft diet

Portion size preferred: Carole does not each very much and prefers smaller portion sizes

Date	Time started	Time finished	Details of food eaten	Amount/ weight of food eaten	How prepared	Where eaten	Type of assistance required	Any concerns	Sign
10.10.15	10.00	10.28	1x Weetabix with warm skimmed milk	About half	Organic milk used	Recliner chair near window in dining room	Chunky handle cutlery used by Carole	Carole is slipping to one side in the chair, will refer to OT for assessment	MB

CASE STUDY

Sally, a health and social care worker at Far Acres Care Home, has been called to cover an extra shift due to sickness. Sally is working in a part of the home she is not familiar with. Before lunch Sally takes time to read individual care plans to make sure she is aware of the support needed by each service user she will be assisting. Sally clarifies each service user's ability to communicate their needs and wishes and their capacity to make informed decisions. One resident called Fred does not eat much of his meal, which concerns Sally, as she has read that Fred usually has a good appetite. Sally records her observations in accordance with agreed ways of working and informs the senior care worker on the unit to ensure that Fred is monitored, as this is a change in his eating and drinking routine.

- Why is it important that records are kept up to date?
- Why is it important to record what you have observed and any actions you take?

Before going to the next chapter, take some time to consider:

- what is important to you about the food and fluid you eat and drink
- whether you have any particular dietary or cultural requirements
- whether you like to dine alone or with others
- if you eat slowly, what impact this may have at mealtimes when dining with others
- whether you can make menu choices independently.

CHAPTER 14

The principles of infection prevention and control

It is important to understand both employees' and employers' responsibilities in relation to infection control. This includes having insight into relevant legislation, understanding policies and recognising everyone's role in meeting these requirements.

The Health and Social Care Act 2008 Code of Practice on the prevention and control of infections states the following:

'Good infection prevention and control are essential to ensure that people who use health and social care services receive safe and effective care. Effective prevention and control of infection must be part of everyday practice and be applied consistently by everyone. Good management and organisational processes are crucial to make sure that high standards of infection prevention and control are developed and maintained.'

Links to other units

All activities undertaken in health and social care should be informed by health and safety requirements, and infection prevention and control is an aspect of health and safety. In this sense the information in this chapter links to many other activities and learning within the Diploma, in particular Chapter 6.

ROLES AND RESPONSIBILITIES IN THE PREVENTION AND CONTROL OF INFECTIONS

Everybody must contribute to the prevention and control of infection; employers and employees have specific roles and responsibilities.

BASIC RESPONSIBILITIES

The Health and Safety at Work Act 1974 states that:

- your health, safety and welfare at work are protected by law
- your employer has a duty to protect you and keep you informed about health and safety
- you have a responsibility to look after yourself and others.

Key terms 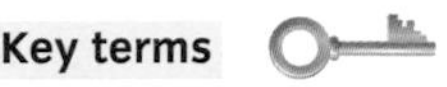

Micro-organisms are living organisms so small that they cannot be seen without the use of a very powerful microscope.

Hygiene is keeping yourself and your environment clean to maintain health.

Decontamination is removing contamination from somebody or something; to remove unwanted chemical, radioactive or biological impurities or toxins from a person, object or place.

EMPLOYERS' RESPONSIBILITIES

Employers should have Standard Infection Control Precautions (SICPs) in place. These standard precautions underpin safe practice, offering protection to both staff and users of the service from healthcare-related infections. SICPs, sometimes referred to as 'universal precautions', are laid down as safe working practices to be used by all workers for all service users, in order to reduce the transmission of **micro-organisms** from both recognised and unrecognised sources of infection. It is the employee's duty to follow such procedures.

SICPs might include instructions for:

- effective hand **hygiene**
- wearing appropriate personal protective equipment (PPE)
- safe disposal of sharps and waste
- safe management of spillages
- prevention and treatment of sharps injuries
- adequate and appropriate **decontamination** of the healthcare environment and service user-related equipment
- protecting cuts and abrasions on staff skin with an impermeable dressing, eg plaster
- ensuring that appropriate immunisations are up-to-date via routine employment screening
- maintaining the cleanliness of the environment
- risk assessment
- management of linen/laundry.

ESSENTIAL REGULATIONS

All health and social care providers must ensure that they meet the essential standards of quality and safety as laid down within the Health and Social Care Act 2008 (Regulated Activities) Regulations 2010 and the Care Quality Commission (Registration) Regulations 2009.

Regulation 12, Outcome 8 – Cleanliness and infection control states the following:

People experience care in a clean environment, and are protected from acquiring infections.

1 The registered person must, so far as reasonably practicable, ensure that:

   a service users;

   b persons employed for the purpose of the carrying on of the regulated activity; and

   c others who may be at risk of exposure to a healthcare-associated infection arising from the carrying on of the regulated activity

   are protected against identifiable risks of acquiring such an infection by the means specified in paragraph (2).

2 The means referred to in paragraph (1) are:

   a the effective operation of systems designed to assess the risk of and to prevent, detect and control the spread of a healthcare-associated infection;

   b where applicable, the provision of appropriate treatment for those who are affected by a healthcare associated infection; and

   c the maintenance of appropriate standards of cleanliness and hygiene in relation to:

      i premises occupied for the purpose of carrying on the regulated activity,

      ii equipment and reusable medical devices used for the purpose of carrying on the regulated activity, and

      iii materials to be used in the treatment of service users where such materials are at risk of being contaminated with a healthcare-associated infection.

ESSENTIAL REGULATIONS (CONTINUED)

Read the full document here: http://www.cqc.org.uk/sites/default/files/documents/guidance_about_compliance_summary.pdf.

To fully meet these requirements, service providers have to work to the Code of Practice for health and adult social care on the prevention and control of infection. This Code of Practice came into force on 1 April 2011 for existing registered providers and primary dental care and independent sector ambulance providers, and 1 April 2012 for primary medical care providers. It sets out the criteria against which a registered provider's compliance with the requirements relating to cleanliness and infection control will be assessed by the Care Quality Commission. It also provides guidance on how the provider can interpret and meet the registration requirement and comply with the law.

EMPLOYEES' ROLES AND RESPONSIBILITIES

Employees must take responsibility for their own actions and make sure that they comply with infection prevention and control policies and procedures. It is important that employees understand their legal duty to take reasonable care of their own health and safety and that of others; this includes following laid-down procedures and taking action if they are aware of other people who display poor work practices that could potentially lead to harm coming to others, for example, poor hand hygiene. If employees have any concerns about health and safety, including infection prevention and control, they have a responsibility to raise their concerns with the appropriate person.

REFLECT

- Do you know how to access a copy of The Health and Social Care Act 2008 Code of Practice on the prevention and control of infections and related guidance?
- Why it is important that staff at all levels are aware of this guidance?

RESEARCH

- What SICPs does your employer have in place connected with infection prevention and control?
- How are staff members kept up to date about SICPs?

CASE STUDY

The Care Quality Commission (CQC) is informed that a certain health and social care establishment is not meeting accepted levels of cleanliness. In light of the concerns raised, the CQC discusses the matter with the local community infection prevention team and agree on a joint inspection.

On the day of the inspection, the concerns raised are found to be justified. The communal areas are dusty, dirty and smelly. Armchairs and sofas are stained and dirty, with crumbs and debris under the cushions. Dining chairs are covered with stains and bits of food, carpets in both lounge and dining room are heavily stained, and there are crumbs and walked-in food on the dining room carpet. Bathrooms, toilets and the sluice room are very dirty and smelly. Pressure-relieving cushions, wheelchairs and hoists are dirty. Hoist slings are being shared by service users without being laundered between uses. Equipment – some of which is dirty and rusty – is stored in the bathrooms, including commodes, hoists and a bucket and mop. There are cracked and chipped tiles on both the walls and floor of the kitchen. Mattress protectors are stained with faecal matter, and some of them are cracked and split, compromising the integrity of the cover and risking the inner fabric of the mattress becoming contaminated and a reservoir for infection. Soap dispensers are empty; bars of soap are available on some sinks. A sharps container is overflowing. The refrigerator in the medicines room is dirty with a build-up of debris around the seals. Once-**sterile** dressings have been opened and kept past their use-by date.

Only 60% of the people employed by the home have attended training in infection control matters. Cleaning rotas are displayed on the notice board, clearly showing times and role responsibilities for carrying out cleaning duties.

Following the inspection it is decided that the home standards are not in accordance with the Health and Social Care Act 2008 Code of Practice, and a warning notice is issued.

- What responsibilities (if any) do you think the employees have for the unacceptable level of cleanliness and hygiene in this home?
- What responsibilities (if any) do you think the employer has for the unacceptable level of cleanliness and hygiene in this home?
- What do you think might be the knock-on effect of this inspection for all who live and work in this home?

Key term

Sterile means free from bacteria or other living organisms.

LEGISLATION

In the UK we have a wealth of health and safety legislation, the purpose of which is to protect individuals from harm. Some of this legislation applies to the prevention and control of infection. Below is a list of the legislation detailed elsewhere in this chapter.

- Health and Social Care Act 2008
- Essential Standards of Quality and Safety Regulation 12 of the Health and Social Care Act 2008
- Health and Safety at Work Act 1974
- Management of Health and Safety at Work Regulations 1999
- Control of Substances Hazardous to Health Regulations 2002
- Personal Protective Equipment at Work Regulations 1992
- Controlled Waste Regulations 1992
- Hazardous Waste Regulations 2005 (revised 2009)
- Environmental Protection Act 1990
- Waste and Contaminated Land (Northern Ireland) Order 1997
- Medicines Act 1968.

SYSTEMS AND PROCEDURES

The potential impact of poor infection control procedures on an organisation, its service users and workers cannot be stressed enough. Regulatory standards must be met for everyone's sake.

WHY GOOD INFECTION CONTROL PRACTICES ARE IMPORTANT

Poor procedures can lead to infections being passed from one service user to another. If the service users you support acquire infections, there is also the risk that you and other workers will too. This in turn leads to staff sickness levels rising, not to mention the risk of the infection being spread to the families of staff and the wider community, including visitors to the infected person. Many health and social care workers are not paid if they are off work due to illness, so there may also be financial hardships. If there is an outbreak of an infectious disease among care workers, staff shortages are likely, with all the knock-on effects that causes, such as staff working extra overtime and becoming exhausted, or the use of a temporary workforce not familiar with the service users or the workplace and its routines.

A serious outbreak of disease may even lead to the closure of the service provision, either temporarily or permanently. Some infectious diseases can make the infected person seriously ill, and in some instances can be fatal. It is no wonder that litigation can ensue. Even if legal action isn't taken, negative publicity often follows an incident of healthcare-acquired infection, leading to a lack of confidence in the organisation. Who is going to want to use a service provider that has not met regulatory standards, let alone one where service users have been put at risk due to poor infection control?

CLEANING/DECONTAMINATION

Keeping the environment clean/decontaminated is a priority measure in preventing the spread of infection. Care homes, hospitals and other establishments offering a personal service to individuals should be cleaned – and kept clean – to the highest possible standard. Service users and the public have a right to the highest standards of cleanliness. Service providers should be aware that standards of cleanliness are often seen as an outward visible sign of the overall quality of service provision. People are likely to have concerns about the quality of the service available in premises that are not kept clean.

Cleaning/decontamination must always be carried out using laid-down techniques, including the use of colour-coded equipment. The following equipment colour guidelines have been based on guidance from the National Patient Safety Agency.

- Bathrooms
- Washrooms
- Showers
- Toilets
- Basins
- Bathroom floors

- General areas
- Lounges
- Corridors
- Bedrooms
- Wards
- Departments
- Offices
- Basins in public areas

- Catering departments
- Kitchens

- Isolation areas
- Bedrooms, when someone has an infection and is cared for in their own room

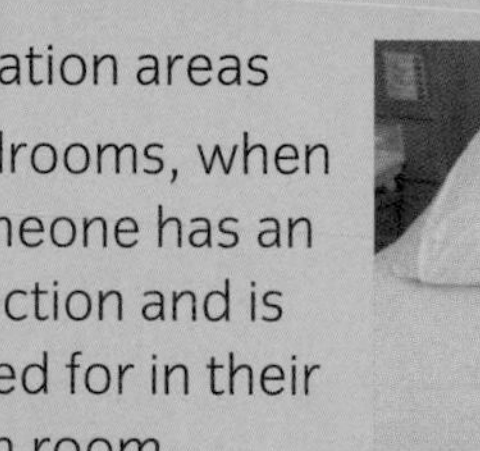

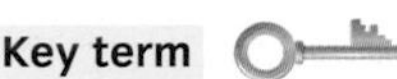

Key term

Cross-contamination means the process by which bacteria or other micro-organisms are unintentionally transferred from one substance or object to another, with harmful effect.

The aim of a colour-coding system is to prevent **cross-contamination**.

- It is vital that such a system forms part of any employee induction and continuous training programme.
- A minority of people are colour-blind to one or more colours. Employers should be aware of this and make additional arrangements for identification of equipment if required.
- The colour-coding system must relate to all cleaning equipment, cloths and gloves.

Note: Staff working in an infected area should follow the local procedure for their work area, such as using disposable gloves, which may not be of a specific colour.

Monitoring of the system and control of colour-coded disposable items against new stock release are extremely important.

A key part of providing consistently high-quality cleaning is the presence of a clear plan setting out all aspects of the cleaning service and defining clearly the roles and responsibilities of all those involved, including managers and their staff group of domestic/cleaning staff.

This plan or schedule of cleaning tasks lets people know how often to carry out cleaning tasks and what cleaning resources are required.

The schedule is likely to be a simple table, showing:

- items to be cleaned
- frequency of cleaning
- how the cleaning is to be done, including what materials are to be used – this may range from a cleaning product to equipment such as a steam cleaner
- the signature of the person who has carried out the cleaning
- the countersignature of the person who is responsible for checking the work.

If cleaning schedules are displayed, the service users as well as their visitors may be reassured that the cleanliness of the environment is seen as important by the establishment and the staff who work there.

Remember the following.

Always follow the correct colour-coding system

Colour-coding cleaning materials and equipment ensures that these items are not used in multiple areas, thereby reducing the risk of **cross-infection**.

Key term

Cross-infection is when an infection spreads from one person to another.

Always start by clearing dust and debris

Cleaning up dust and debris is required prior to any disinfection process because dirt, debris and other materials can decrease the effectiveness of many chemical disinfectants. Dry sweeping, mopping and dusting should be avoided to prevent dust, debris and micro-organisms from getting into the air and landing on clean surfaces, and dust cloths and mops should never be shaken.

Always use correct chemicals and equipment

Cleaning products and equipment should be chosen on the basis of their purpose, effectiveness and safety. Use the correct item for the task in hand. Mixing (dilution) instructions should be followed when using disinfectants – too much or too little water may reduce the effectiveness of disinfectants.

Always work from clean to dirty

Cleaning should always progress from the least soiled areas to the most soiled areas and from high to low areas, so that the dirtiest areas and debris that falls on the floor will be cleaned up last, and the cleanest areas will not be contaminated by dirt and debris from the most soiled areas.

Always leave the area in a safe and clean manner

Remove cleaning equipment from the cleaned area.

REFLECT

- What cleaning procedures are in place where you work?
- Who is responsible for ensuring that the correct procedures are carried out?

DECONTAMINATION METHODS

Decontamination can be achieved by a number of methods, which fall into the following three categories.

Cleaning

This means physically removing surface contaminants, usually with detergents or soap and water. Cleaning removes soil and bacteria but it does not kill bacteria or viruses. Even the most thorough cleaning leaves micro-organisms on the surface of the item being cleaned. It is difficult, although not impossible, to sterilise a surface that has not been properly cleaned in the first place. Effective cleaning is the most important step, because bacteria and viruses may survive beneath a layer of dirt, or beneath grease, dried blood, or in crevices or places that are difficult to reach by cleaning and that shield the organism from direct contact with the disinfectant. Disinfecting solutions require the object be effectively pre-cleaned first.

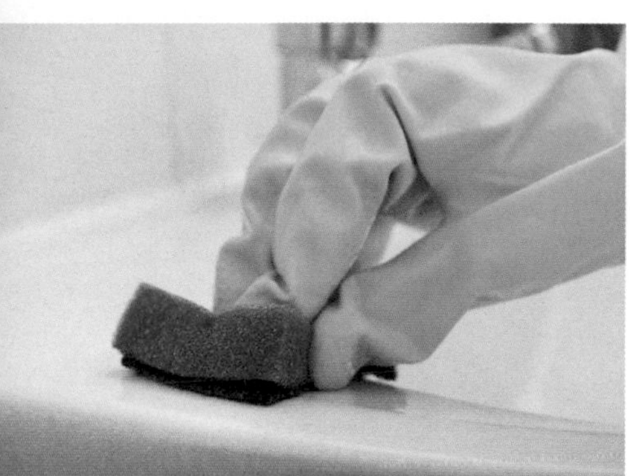

Disinfection

Disinfection is the destruction or removal of some of the harmful bacteria (but not spores) on the surface of an object, but disinfection cannot be expected to kill or inactivate all micro-organisms. Effective disinfection will remove or destroy bacteria to a level at which they are not harmful to health. Not all disinfectants destroy all types of micro-organisms, and some may leave harmful chemical residues which must be removed prior to sterilisation or use. These chemicals can be harmful to humans and animals. Disinfection may be carried out using chemicals, washer/disinfector, boiling water, and low-temperature steam.

Sterilisation

Sterilisation is a process intended to destroy or remove all living organisms, including spores – in other words, sterilisation renders an object free from viable micro-organisms including viruses and bacterial spores. Sterilisation can be achieved by a variety of means, including the use of:

- moist heat (autoclave)
- gamma radiation
- ethylene
- low-temperature steam with formaldehyde.

The difference between disinfection and sterilisation is that disinfection *reduces the number* of viable micro-organisms, while sterilisation *kills all types* of micro-organisms including bacterial spores.

The choice of decontamination method depends on the risk of infection to the person coming into contact with equipment or medical devices. Such items can be categorised into three risk groups:

- High-risk items are those used to penetrate skin or mucous membranes, or enter the vascular system or sterile spaces. They need to be sterilised if reusable, but single-use items are preferred.
- Medium-risk items are those that come into contact with intact mucous membranes or may be contaminated with particularly virulent or readily transmittable organisms. Such items require cleaning followed by disinfection or sterilisation, eg endoscopes or respiratory equipment.
- Low-risk items are those that come into contact with intact skin or do not contact the patient. They require cleaning but not necessarily sterilising, eg forehead thermometers.

SINGLE-USE INSTRUMENTS

Single-use disposable equipment is becoming increasing popular. The cheaper cost, good quality and availability of a wide range of disposable, single-use equipment and instruments such as gallipots and forceps has resulted in single-use devices being widely used. Any device designated as single-use must never be reused under any circumstances.

Suggested decontamination methods for commonly used equipment are shown in the table.

Bedding	• See section on laundering (pages 402–3). • Heat disinfection: 65°C for 10 minutes or 71°C for 3 minutes.
Bedpans and urinals	• Dispose of single-use items. • Store dry.
Bowls (washing)	• Each person should have their own washing bowl (if used). • Clean with detergent and water after use. • Rinse and dry. • Store separately and inverted to avoid contamination.
Combs	• Each person should have their own comb.
Commodes	• Wash with detergent, rinse and dry.
Curtains	• Should be laundered at least every six months.
Flower vases	• Change water regularly. • Wash vase in hot water and detergent after use and store dry.
Hoist (to assist with moving people)	• Surface clean the hoist frame. • Examine material and clips for wear or damage before each use. • Slings should be laundered in hottest wash cycle allowable, and not shared between service users.
Mattresses and covers	• Clean cover regularly as part of a routine and following use. Rinse thoroughly and dry. • Mattresses should be enclosed in a waterproof cover and routinely inspected for damage. • Discard if fluids have penetrated into the mattress fabric.

Nebulisers	• Clean all parts thoroughly with detergent and hot water between single use. Ensure all parts are thoroughly dried. Refill with sterile water only. • Do not share between people. Dispose of if service user leaves.
Scissors	• Follow your employer's instructions and clean according to the procedure they have been used for. This might include using any of the following – sanitizer gel, sterile wipes, Milton.
Crutches and walking frames	• Wash and clean with detergent.
Oral and rectal electronic thermometers	• Use a single-use sleeve each time.
Wheelchairs	• Clean, rinse and dry.

REFLECT

What procedures are in place where you work to ensure that the correct colour of equipment is used?

CLEANING AND DISINFECTING AGENTS

Your organisation will have policies and procedures that refer to the use of cleaning products. It is important that you know what these are and follow the laid-down procedures. Your employer must abide by the Control of Substances Hazardous to Health Regulations 2002 (COSHH). Cleaning agents are identified as hazardous substances.

To comply with COSHH, employers need to follow these eight steps:

1 Assess the risks to health from hazardous substances used in or created by workplace activities.

2 Decide what precautions are needed. Employers must not carry out work that could expose their employees to hazardous substances without first considering the risks and the necessary precautions, and what else they need to do to comply with COSHH.

3 Prevent or adequately control exposure. Prevent employees being exposed to hazardous substances. Where preventing exposure is not reasonably practicable, adequate control measures must be

put in place. An example of a hazardous substance is a chemical cleaning product used in the place of work. Safety data sheets provide information on chemical products that help users of those chemicals to make a risk assessment. They describe the hazards the chemical presents, and give information on handling, storage and emergency measures in case of accident. Such data sheets are not meant to replace risk assessments, but they can be used to help in risk assessment. Ensure that control measures are used and maintained properly and that safety procedures are followed.

4 Monitor the exposure of employees to hazardous substances, if necessary.

5 Carry out appropriate health surveillance where your assessment has shown this is necessary or where COSHH sets specific requirements.

6 Prepare plans and procedures to deal with accidents, incidents and emergencies involving hazardous substances, where necessary.

7 Ensure that employees are properly informed, trained and supervised. Provide employees with suitable and sufficient information, instruction and training.

8 All cleaning agents must be securely stored and used following the manufacturer's instructions. If products are to be diluted, it is very important that manufacturers' instructions are followed.

BLOOD AND BODY FLUID SPILLAGES

Spillages are highly unpredictable and occur in a wide variety of settings. All spillages of blood or body fluid should be considered as potentially infectious. Spillages should be dealt with as immediately as is possible to reduce the risk of exposure to infectious agents or further contamination. Infectious agents can survive for long periods of time in spillages.

See the following document for more detail: http://www.liverpoolcommunityhealth.nhs.uk/Downloads/SERVICES/ADULTS/Infection-Control/Spillage_Management.pdf.

It is essential, therefore, that all staff receive training in spillage management and, where possible, that appropriate equipment is readily available. The effective management of spillages in healthcare facilities tends to be less problematic than in people's own homes or in nursing and residential homes. This is because in hospitals surfaces such as walls, floors and upholstery are usually smooth, continuous and moisture repellent.

If a spillage occurs, assessment should be made of the:

- content of the spillage – blood, urine, other?
- size of the spillage
- material on which the spillage has occurred – fabric, vinyl, metal, other?

Appropriate protective clothing must be worn to prevent skin exposure, or contamination of clothing.

Blood spillages must be disinfected using a chlorine-releasing agent at a concentration of 10,000 parts per million, to render the area safe. (Again, see http://www.liverpoolcommunityhealth.nhs.uk/Downloads/SERVICES/ADULTS/Infection-Control/Spillage_Management.pdf.)

Where possible a spillage kit should be available to all staff, containing:

- plastic aprons
- gloves
- sanitiser granules
- clinical waste bags
- blue roll/paper towels or disposable cloths.

A number of companies now produce spillage kits. There are separate kits that can be used for either blood spillages or body fluid spillages containing blood. There are other kits for body fluids not containing blood, or for use on fragile material such as carpet. They also contain all the products necessary to undertake the procedure such as disposable gloves, aprons, scoops and so on. Staff should be trained how to use such kits in the event of spillages.

MANAGEMENT OF LINEN AND LAUNDERING REQUIREMENTS

The provision of clean linen is a fundamental requirement. Incorrect handling, laundering and storage of linen can pose an infection hazard.

Infection can be transferred between contaminated and uncontaminated items of clothing, laundry and the environments in which they are stored. Even during a normal washing cycle a number of micro-organisms can be passed between clothing and linen, and will only be partially removed during the rinse cycles. Thorough drying of the laundry can reduce the levels of contamination to a level that no longer poses a risk.

Within health and social care establishments, specific hygiene measures should be taken to reduce these risks, including:

- correct handling to prevent the spread of infection
- appropriate disinfection of the laundry
- a laundry area designated for that purpose only, with separate ventilation and a flow-through system, so that dirty laundry can arrive through one door and be quickly decontaminated, before drying and removal through a separate exit to a clean storage area
- provision of an industrial washing machine with sluice and hot wash cycles; it should be professionally installed and maintained with precautions to prevent contamination by creation of fine sprays of liquid (aerosols)
- provision of an industrial dryer that is regularly maintained to dry all clothing and linen
- a regular service and maintenance inspection schedule
- appropriate PPE and eye protection should be available for staff
- provision of hand decontamination facilities, including a hand hygiene basin with lever taps and no plug or overflow, liquid soap and disposable paper towels; hand decontamination solutions, eg alcoholic hand gel, should be available along with a pedal-operated clinical and domestic waste bin and first aid kit.

Under no circumstances should a manual sluice facility or sluicing basin be used or situated in the laundry.

As stated previously, it is the legal responsibility of your employer to ensure that risk assessments are carried out. The area of laundry management is one of the areas that requires a risk assessment under Regulation 3 of the Management of Health and Safety at Work Regulations 1999.

DISPOSAL OF WASTE

The handling of waste must be undertaken with care, and waste must be separated into different groups or categories in accordance with organisational policy and procedures.

There are two basic categories of waste:

- hazardous waste
- non-hazardous waste.

Any waste that is contaminated with blood or body fluids should be disposed of as 'clinical waste'. Examples of clinical waste include gloves, aprons, dressings, catheter bags or anything that has come into contact with blood or bodily fluids. All clinical waste must be disposed of in yellow clinical waste bags. Bags must be tied securely and not overfilled, and they should then be stored in the designated disposal area.

The following is taken from the Controlled Waste Regulations 1992 (issued under the Environmental Protection Act). Clinical waste is defined as:

a) '... any waste which consists wholly or partly of human or animal tissue, blood or other bodily fluids, excretions, drugs or other pharmaceutical products, swabs or dressings, syringes, needles or other sharp instruments, being waste which unless rendered safe may prove hazardous to any person coming into contact with it; and

b) any other waste arising from medical, nursing, dental, veterinary, pharmaceutical or similar practice, investigation, treatment, care, teaching or research, or the collection of blood for transfusion, being waste which may cause infection to any person coming into contact with it.'

You must take great care when disposing of waste, because inappropriate disposal of waste increases the risk of the spread of infection. Under the Hazardous Waste Regulations 2005 organisations can be fined for inappropriate disposal of waste. The organisation should have policies and procedures in place regarding the disposal and storage of waste for the worker to follow.

Healthcare waste definition

Healthcare waste is classified under the European Waste Catalogue code, (Chapter 18) as wastes from natal care, diagnosis, treatment or prevention of disease in humans or animals. Healthcare premises include hospitals, nursing homes, dental surgeries, GP surgeries and veterinary practices.

Examples of waste types include:

- infectious waste
- sharps waste
- medicinal waste
- laboratory cultures
- offensive waste.

Hazardous waste definition

Waste is deemed hazardous when it contains substances or has properties that might make it harmful to human health or the environment. The properties of waste that render it hazardous include being infectious, which is defined as 'substances containing viable micro-organisms or their toxins which are known or are reliably believed to cause disease in man or living things'.

Segregation of waste

A national colour-coded system is recommended for the segregation of healthcare waste into streams that are linked to appropriate disposal. All waste should be secured in an approved way and identified with a colour-coded tie or label. Areas where clinical/ hazardous waste is produced must have foot-operated bag holders. There should be a wall chart showing the correct containers to be used according to the type of waste, as shown in the table. (See also www.skillsforhealth.org.uk.)

Yellow stream	Infectious waste which requires disposal by incineration.
Orange stream	Infectious waste which may be treated to make it safe prior to disposal, or alternatively can be incinerated.
Purple stream	Cytotoxic and cytostatic waste which must be incinerated in a permitted or licensed facility.
Yellow/black stream	Offensive/hygiene waste which may be land-filled in a permitted or licensed site.
Black stream	Domestic waste which does not contain infectious materials, sharps or medicinal products and may be land-filled in a permitted or licensed site. Materials that can be recycled should be removed. Clear or opaque containers can be used for domestic waste.
Cardboard boxes	Marked GLASS AND BREAKAGES ONLY and lined with a heavy-duty clear plastic bag for bottles and breakages. Marked AEROSOLS ONLY and lined with a clear plastic bag for aerosols, which under the Control of Substances Hazardous to Health Act must be kept and disposed of separately. Aerosols must never be placed in black or yellow bags.
Sharps container	An appropriately sized, dedicated sharps container made and sealed according to the manufacturer's instructions and conforming to UN 3291 (United Nations) and BS 7320 standards (British Standards).

Categories of waste

Different categories of waste require different methods of disposal.

Clinical waste

The following must be disposed of in yellow bags:

- soiled surgical dressings, swabs and all other contaminated waste from treatment areas
- material other than linen from cases of infectious disease
- all human tissues (whether infected or not) and tissues from laboratories, and all related activities
- swabs and dressings
- tampons and used sanitary towels; where possible, these should be disposed of separately in dedicated sanibins.

Key term 

Macerator is a pump which reduces solids to small pieces.

The following should be disposed of in a **macerator**; if not, they must be disposed of in yellow/orange bags, whichever is appropriate to the work setting:

- incontinence pads, including those from non-infected residents
- used disposable bedpan liners, urine containers, incontinence aids and stoma bags, even from non-infected residents; water authorities are now expecting that healthcare providers seek authorisation before flushing away disposable bedpan liners, as they are known to block up pumps and drains.

Non-clinical waste or domestic waste

Other general waste (food waste, non-contaminated paper and household materials) should be disposed of in black bags.

The Hazardous Waste Regulations 2005 do not allow mixing; this includes mis-segregation of domestic-type waste into the clinical or hazardous waste disposal containers/bags.

Disposal of pharmaceutical products

Unused drugs and other pharmaceutical products should be returned to the pharmacist; they must not be administered to any person other than the individual for whom they were dispensed.

The legal framework that applies to these activities of waste disposal includes the Medicines Act 1968, Misuse of Drugs Act 1971, Health and Safety at Work Act 1974 and Management of Health and Safety at Work Regulations 1999, The Control of Substances Hazardous to Health Regulations 2002 and the National Minimum Care Standards 2002.

SHARPS

The following guidance is from the NHS Healthcare Cleaning Manual – Infection Control:

- Sharps such as small quantities of broken glass, drug vials, used needles, razors, blades, etc must be carefully disposed of into sharps containers using forceps or tweezers.
- If a sharp object is found, protect yourself, remove the item carefully and place into a sharps container.
- Wherever possible do not physically handle the sharp if a dustpan and piece of cardboard or plastic can be used to manipulate the sharp instead.
- Discard needles and syringes as one unit into the sharps container.
- Never attempt to re-sheath, bend or break needles or overfill the sharps container.
- Seal the container correctly and label when two-thirds full.
- Always use the handle when carrying a sharps container, holding it away from the body.
- Store in the designated disposal area.
- Never attempt to decant contents of small sharps containers into larger containers.

Remember that sharps should be disposed of by the person using them and never left for somebody else to dispose of.

ISOLATION

Even when all possible measures are taken to protect service users from infection, situations can arise in which a service user contracts a highly contagious infection. When this occurs the individual needs to be isolated in order to prevent the spread of the infection. The decision to isolate a person is never taken lightly. There is the potential for people in isolation to be forgotten – and neglected. It should also be remembered that people will feel cut off from everyone else, and lonely. However, it it is important to recognise that there are times when such isolation is necessary in order to stop the spread of infection. If isolation *is* necessary, it is very important that the need for it is explained to the service user concerned at a pace and level suited to their needs.

If isolation is required, you should refer to your employer's procedures. However, the following should be taken into consideration:

- consider whether people entering the room need to be **immune** to the patient's disease (important for rubella, chickenpox and tuberculosis)
- record in the care plan the reason for isolation, the date started and any special precautions necessary to prevent the spread of infection

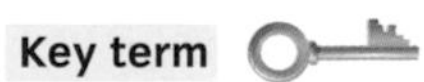

Key term

Immune means resistant to a particular infection or toxin.

- an isolation notice should be placed on the door of the room
- appropriate PPE should be available, as should the correct disposal facilities for refuse bins/bags
- the risks to visitors should be assessed (eg low risk for methicillin-resistant *Staphylococcus aureus* (MRSA), high risk for chickenpox); if in doubt, ask the Infection Control Team before allowing visits.

EXAMPLES OF COMMON INFECTIOUS DISEASES

The following are common infectious diseases that you may come across:

- *Clostridium difficile*
- gastroenteritis
- salmonella.

Clostridium difficile

Often called *C. difficile* or *C. diff*, this is a bacterium that can cause symptoms ranging from diarrhoea to life-threatening inflammation of the colon. Illness from *C. difficile* most commonly affects older adults in hospitals or in long-term care facilities, and typically occurs after use of **antibiotic** medications.

Key term 

Antibiotic is a substance produced by or derived from a micro-organism, that selectively destroys other micro-organisms or inhibits their growth.

Clostridium difficile bacterium is present naturally in the gut of around 3% of adults and 66% of children. *C. diff* does not cause any problems in healthy people. However, some antibiotics that are used to treat other health conditions can interfere with the balance of 'good' bacteria in the gut. When this happens, *C. diff* bacteria can multiply and cause symptoms such as diarrhoea and fever.

Infection with *Clostridium difficile* most commonly occurs in people who have recently had a course of antibiotics and are in hospital. Older people are most at risk from infection, with the majority of cases (80%) occurring in people over 65.

Most people with a *C. diff* infection make a full recovery. However, in rare cases, the infection can be fatal.

In recent years, the number of *Clostridium difficile* infections has fallen rapidly. There were 17,414 reported cases in England during 2011, compared with 52,988 in 2007.

Unfortunately a new strain of the *C. difficile* bacteria, called NAP1/027, has emerged in recent years. This new strain tends to cause more severe infection. There has also been an increase of *Clostridium difficile* cases occurring outside of a healthcare setting (known as community-acquired *Clostridium difficile* infection).

In most cases, *C. diff* infections can be prevented by following good hygiene practices in healthcare environments. However, it is extremely contagious and is spread very easily, particularly in healthcare environments, and it may not be possible to prevent the bacteria spreading altogether but a number of precautions can be taken to reduce the risk of infection.

Useful advice to give visitors to healthcare environments

- If you are visiting a person in a healthcare environment who has diarrhoea or a stomach upset, try to avoid taking any children under the age of 12.

Wash hands with soap and water when entering and leaving the healthcare environment. Alcohol hand gel is not effective against *C. difficile* spores, so the use of soap and water is essential.

- If you are feeling unwell or have recently had diarrhoea, avoid healthcare environments.
- Avoid sitting on beds.
- Observe visiting hours and all visiting guidelines in hospitals.

Healthcare environments

Healthcare workers should wear disposable gloves and aprons when caring for anyone who has a *C. difficile* infection, and the gloves and aprons should be disposed of prior to working with another service user. Whenever possible, people who are infected with *C. difficile* should have their own room and their own toilet facilities to avoid passing the infection on to others.

Staff, patients and visitors should be encouraged to wash their hands regularly and thoroughly. Thorough cleaning using water and detergent is an effective way of removing any spores that have transferred on to a person's skin or clothes.

Surfaces that may have come into contact with the bacteria or spores, such as toilets, the floor around toilets, bedpans, commodes and beds should also be cleaned thoroughly with water and a cleaning product containing bleach.

Gastroenteritis

Gastroenteritis is a non-specific term used to describe a condition in which there is a combination of symptoms – nausea, vomiting, diarrhoea and abdominal pain. The term is usually taken to mean a condition where there is an infection of the stomach and intestines. The most common symptoms are diarrhoea and vomiting. It's normally mild, and most symptoms will go within a few days without treatment.

However, if symptoms are severe, or the person is vulnerable, due to age or other illness, hospital treatment may be needed. This is because the diarrhoea can quickly make the person dehydrated, which in the most severe cases can be fatal. Gastroenteritis is very common. Every year, approximately one in five of people in the UK are affected. Deaths from it are common in the developing world and present a significant health problem; however, deaths are rare in the UK due to better levels of healthcare and nutrition and access to clean water.

Gastroenteritis can be caused by viral infections such as the norovirus or by a number of different bacteria. Typically, bacterial gastroenteritis develops as a result of food poisoning.

Treatment for gastroenteritis involves replacing the fluids lost by diarrhoea. In more serious cases, where a specific bacterial infection has been identified, antibiotics may be used.

Most forms of gastroenteritis are highly infectious. It is therefore essential to practise good hygiene, for example, by washing your hands after going to toilet and before preparing food.

People who have gastroenteritis or have children with gastroenteritis should not return to work, or let their children go to school or nursery, until 48 hours have passed since the last episode of diarrhoea or vomiting.

Salmonella

Salmonella bacteria cause food poisoning. Symptoms include diarrhoea, stomach cramps and sometimes vomiting and fever. On average, it takes from 12 to 72 hours for the symptoms to develop after swallowing an infectious dose of salmonella. Symptoms usually last for four to seven days and clear up without treatment, but if people become seriously ill they may need hospital care because the dehydration (fluid loss) caused by the illness can be life-threatening.

Anyone can get salmonella, but young children, the elderly and people who have immune systems that are not working properly (including people with cancer, AIDS or alcoholism) have a greater risk of becoming severely ill.

Most cases of salmonella are caused by contaminated food. Salmonella bacteria live in the gut of many farm animals and can affect meat, eggs, poultry and milk. Other foods such as green vegetables, fruit and shellfish can become contaminated through contact with manure in the soil or sewage in the water.

Contamination is also possible if raw and cooked foods are stored together. Tortoises and terrapins and other pet reptiles can also carry salmonella. Dogs, cats and rodents can occasionally become infected. It is impossible to tell from its appearance whether food is contaminated with salmonella – it will look, smell and taste normal.

Salmonella can be spread from person to person by poor hygiene, for example, by failing to wash hands properly after going to the toilet or after handling contaminated food.

Treatment

It is important to drink plenty of fluids, as diarrhoea or vomiting can lead to dehydration and the loss of important sugars and minerals from the body. A doctor may recommend a re-hydration solution, available from pharmacists.

In the case of nausea, small sips of fluid should be taken frequently. Tea, coffee, carbonated drinks and alcohol should be avoided. Sugary drinks should be diluted even if they would not normally be diluted.

A simple over-the-counter painkiller can help combat any pain, but if people are already taking prescribed medication it is important to check whether painkillers can be taken as well.

Sometimes, severe cases are treated with antibiotics. It is essential that the course is completed as prescribed.

People must keep away from work while they are ill and have symptoms, because they are infectious. Children and adults should stay away from nursery, school or work for 48 hours after the symptoms have stopped. They should tell their employer they have had salmonella if they work with vulnerable groups such as the elderly, the young and those in poor health, or if they handle food.

Measures to avoid salmonella infections

- Wash hands thoroughly with soap and warm water:
  - before preparing and eating food
  - after handling raw food
  - after going to the toilet, supporting another person to access a toilet or changing a baby's nappy
  - after contact with pets and other animals, especially reptiles and amphibians
  - after working in the garden.
- Keep cooked food away from raw food.
- Store raw foods below cooked or ready-to-eat foods in the fridge to prevent contamination.
- Cook food thoroughly, especially meat, so that it is piping hot – remember, in a commercial kitchen or care environment you must use probe thermometers.
- Wash raw fruits and vegetables thoroughly before eating. Keep all kitchen surfaces and equipment clean, including knives and chopping boards.
- Do not keep reptiles or amphibians in households where there is a child under a year old, or someone with poor immunity, eg being treated for cancer.

- If someone has salmonella, wash all dirty clothes, bedding and towels in the washing machine on the hottest cycle possible.
- Clean toilet seats, toilet bowls, flush handles, taps and wash hand basins after use with detergent and hot water, followed by a household disinfectant.

CASE STUDY

Sarah is a shift leader at the home where Tom lives. Tom has recently been diagnosed with *C. diff* following a stay in hospital. Sarah sees Joan, who is a new member of staff, coming out of Tom's room. Joan is wearing a disposal apron and gloves. Joan is about to knock on the door of the room next to Tom to gain permission to enter. Sarah stops Joan and asks her to remove the gloves and apron following the set procedure and wash her hands before working with another person. She explains to Joan that PPE is designed to protect both staff and service users. Sarah then adds to her own 'to-do list' to check which staff require training in infection control and prevention, and also to add it as an agenda item for the next staff meeting.

- Why does Joan need to change her gloves and wash her hands between working with different service users?
- How does a worker wearing gloves protect the service user they are supporting?
- How does correctly using PPE comply with the Health and Safety at Work Act 1974?

RISK ASSESSMENT IN RELATION TO THE PREVENTION AND CONTROL OF INFECTIONS

Risk assessments are carried out in all areas of work, and the prevention and control of infections is no different. We can deal with the risks from infection at work in the same way as any other health and safety issue. We need to:

- identify the hazards
- assess the risks
- control the risks.

Employers should have risk assessments in place to identify potential risks of infection. A risk assessment is simply a careful examination of what, in the place of work, could cause harm to people, to enable a judgement about whether enough precautions have been put in place or whether more should be done to prevent harm.

The Health and Safety Executive has produced a leaflet titled 'Five Steps to Risk Assessment' which offers the following process as a method for carrying out a risk assessment:

1 Identify the hazards (a hazard is anything with the potential to cause harm).
2 Decide who might be harmed and how.
3 Evaluate the risks and decide on precautions (the risk is the chance, high or low, that somebody could be harmed by these and other hazards, together with an indication of how serious the harm could be).
4 Record the findings and implement them.
5 Review the assessment and update if necessary.

In short, you can deal with the risks from infection at work in the same way as any other health and safety issue. You need to identify the hazards, assess the risks and then control the risks.

Hazard	Risk	Control measures or decontamination method (controlling the risk)
Anything that may cause harm, such as sharps, body fluids, soiled linen, working from ladders, an open drawer, etc.	The chance, high or low, that somebody could be harmed by these and other hazards, together with an indication of how serious the harm could be.	Will depend on what has caused the contamination, the micro-organisms involved, the type of material to be decontaminated and the risks to the people involved.

Anyone employing more than five people must write down the significant findings of their assessment and record hazards and the controls that are already in place or are to be implemented. Staff must make sure they know what is in the risk assessment and what actions they are supposed to take to minimise the spread of infection.

Risk assessments are living documents and should reflect changes in the work carried out, new equipment and new work activities that are added if they change the risk or lead to new hazards being introduced. Risk assessments should be reviewed regularly to make sure that the controls put in place are still appropriate and working.

CASE STUDY

John is a young man – full of curiosity – and he is using a local home for respite. On his first morning he notices a bright yellow box on the windowsill in the office. He picks the box up and shakes it and it rattles. With a little bit of effort he is able to poke his little finger into the slit at the top, but is unable to reach the contents at the bottom of the box; he is also unable to pull his finger back out. The sides of the slit in the box tighten and hurt his knuckle, so he lets out a howl of frustration and pain, which brings a support worker running to his aid. Luckily no damage is done to John's finger; however, things could have ended differently. While investigating this incident, the person in charge realises that no risk assessment had been carried out on the use and site of the sharps box.

- What might have been the outcome of this incident had the sharps box been more full?
- If you had to carry out a risk assessment of where to site a sharps box at your place of work, what factors would you take into consideration?

PERSONAL PROTECTIVE EQUIPMENT (PPE)

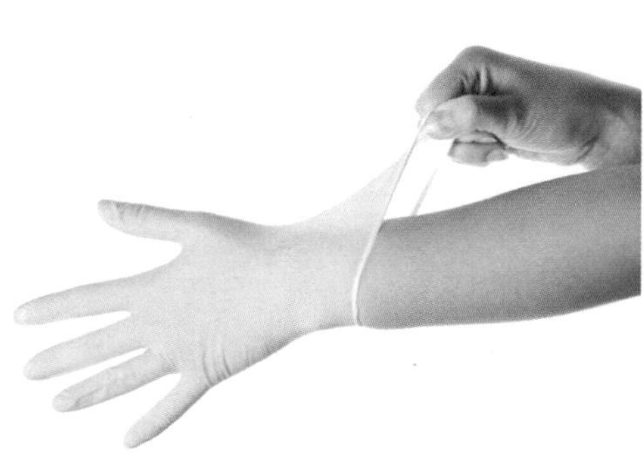

PPE is provided to prevent or control the spread of infection. This is for your protection and for the protection of everyone you work with. Without PPE, hands, clothing and so on can become contaminated. PPE should not replace other infection prevention and control practices such as hand hygiene.

The decision to use PPE should be made on the basis of an assessment of the risk of transmission of micro-organisms to the service user and the risk of contamination to the worker, in line with pre-assessed agreed ways of working outlined in local policies and procedures. A risk assessment should be applied to all situations and in all areas of service provision so that the appropriate PPE can be selected.

PPE should be stored in an appropriate container, which is normally the dispensing box/container in which the items were purchased. Ideally gloves should be available from a wall-mounted container.

EMPLOYERS' AND EMPLOYEES' RESPONSIBILITIES

Employers have basic duties concerning the provision and use of PPE at work. The main requirement of the PPE at Work Regulations 1992 is that personal protective equipment is to be supplied and used at work wherever there are risks to health and safety that cannot be adequately controlled in other ways. The regulations also require that PPE:

- is properly assessed before use to ensure it is suitable
- is maintained and stored properly
- is provided with instructions on how to use it safely
- is used correctly by employees.

Employers should ensure that all staff undertake appropriate training, including updating and refresher training. Training should be recorded.

An employer cannot ask for money from an employee for PPE, whether it is returnable or not. This rule also covers agency workers if they are legally regarded as employees. If employment has been terminated and the employee keeps the PPE without the employer's permission then, as long as it has been made clear in the contract of employment, the employer may be able to deduct the cost of the replacement from any wages owed.

Employees have a responsibility to use the appropriate PPE for tasks they carry out and to follow correct procedures in doing so.

TYPES OF PPE

The types of PPE you are most likely to use as a health or social care worker are:

- gloves
- aprons
- gowns
- masks
- goggles, face shields and visors.

Uniforms are not classed as PPE.

Aprons

The front of the body is the part most frequently contaminated by body fluids, and plastic disposable aprons provide adequate protection in most circumstances (such as when handling bedpans, dressing wounds or dealing with body fluid spills). In circumstances where considerable contamination by body fluids is predicted, for example, during surgical procedures, water-repellent gowns should be used.

Gloves

Gloves are to protect hands from contamination with organic matter and micro-organisms, and to reduce the risks of transmission of micro-organisms to both users of the service and staff. Gloves should not be worn unnecessarily, because prolonged and indiscriminate use may cause adverse reactions and skin sensitivity. Gloves are not a substitute for hand washing. As with all items of PPE the need for gloves must be subject to careful assessment of the task to be carried out and its related risks to service users and the worker. Gloves should never be carried in pockets. Remember to always wash your hands before putting on and after removing gloves.

Masks/Eye protection

Health and social care workers are vulnerable to infection if infected body fluid is splashed on to the mucous membranes of the eyes and mouth. Therefore, in some circumstances such as in operating theatres and when dealing with maternity cases, well-fitting masks and eye protection should be worn.

Respiratory protection

Occasionally, respiratory protection may be required when airborne transmission of micro-organisms is likely.

REMOVING AND DISPOSING OF PPE

PPE such as gloves, aprons and masks are single-use items and should be disposed of after each procedure or activity to prevent cross-transmission of micro-organisms. When these items are worn primarily to protect the wearer, the importance of their prompt removal between tasks on the same person or between service users can easily be overlooked and give rise to the possibility of contamination.

All PPE must be removed before leaving the area and disposed of correctly. Any body fluids that have inadvertently contaminated the skin must be washed off immediately.

It is important to remove protective equipment in the correct manner. There is no point in wearing aprons and gloves if you are going to touch the contaminated items with bare hands.

Always remove PPE in the following order:

1 Gloves

2 Apron

3 Eye protection (if worn).

Technique for removal of gloves

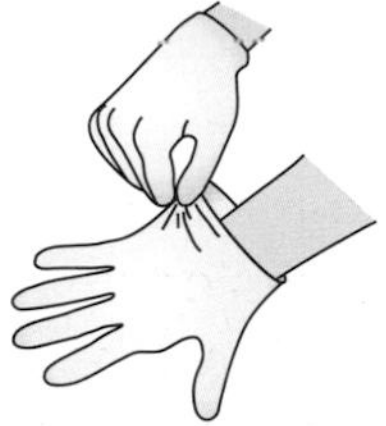

1 Using all four fingers grasp the outside of the first glove at the back of the hand close to the back of the wrist with the opposite gloved hand

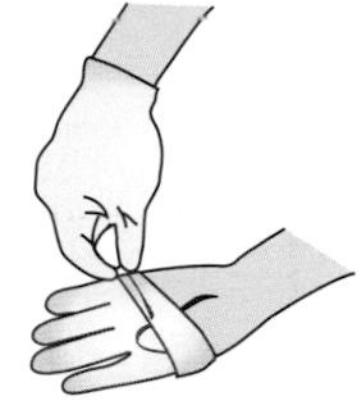

2 Peel off

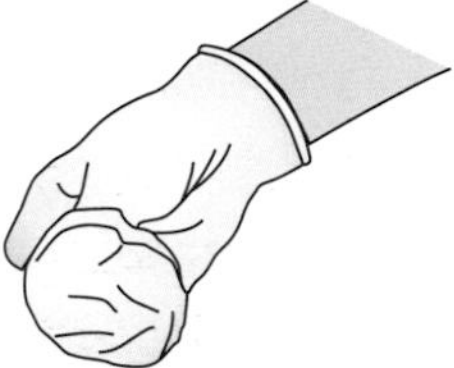

3 Hold the removed glove scrunched up in palm of still gloved hand

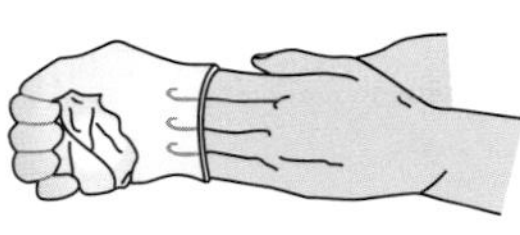

4 Slide fingers of ungloved hand under remaining glove at the wrist and peel the second glove off over the first glove

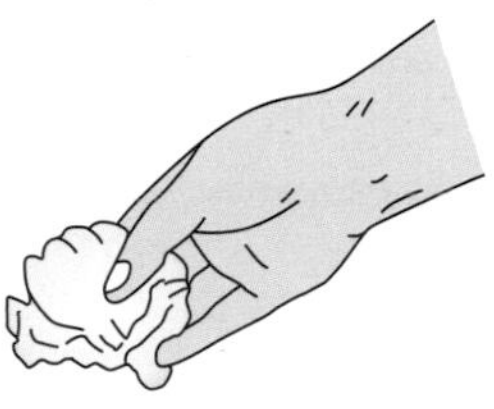

5 Dispose of in correct bin

6 Wash hands

Gloves must be discarded after each care activity for which they were worn in order to prevent the transmission of micro-organisms to other sites in that service user or to other service users. Washing gloves rather than changing them is *not* safe. Gloves are single-use and must be correctly disposed of once the task is completed.

Technique for removal of apron

1 Break the ties and neck loop.

2 Touching only the inside of the apron, roll it into a bundle.

3 Dispose of the apron in the correct bin.

4 Perform hand hygiene.

Technique for removal of goggles/visors

- Remove by only touching the headband or sides, preferably breaking the elastic to avoid pulling them back over your head.

REFLECT

- Who in your place of work has responsibility for ordering supplies of PPE?
- What are your responsibilities regarding PPE?
- Do you know what action you should take if you run out of PPE in your area of work?

THE IMPORTANCE OF PERSONAL HYGIENE IN THE PREVENTION AND CONTROL OF INFECTIONS

Poor hygiene practices can lead to the spread of infections.

HAND HYGIENE

The types of poor practice you must guard against include not washing hands or not using the correct procedure for washing hands.

Several studies have presented evidence that microbes have an ability to survive on the hands, sometimes for many hours. All of the studies clearly demonstrate that contaminated hands can be vehicles for the spread of microbes.

We all carry millions of microbes on our hands. Most are harmless, but some cause illnesses, such as colds, flu, diarrhoea, hepatitis and *Escherichia coli* (E. coli) infection. If you forget to wash your hands, or don't wash them properly, you can spread these germs to other people, or give them to yourself by touching your eyes, mouth, nose or cuts on your body. You can also pick up microbes from objects such as doorknobs, taps and wheelchair handles touched by other people who have not washed their hands.

Some bacteria can stay alive on your hands for up to three hours, and in that time they can be spread to all the things you touch, including food and other people. During the working day, health and social care workers touch many surfaces, including skin, and all of those surfaces will be covered with microbes. Washing hands reduces the amount of bacteria (germs) on them and helps prevent the spread of infection.

Key principles

Key term

Sanitise means to make clean or hygienic for example by using a preparatory hand sanitising gel.

- Wash/**sanitise** hands when appropriate, for example, between working with different service users.
- Keep nails short and clean.
- It is not advisable to wear nail varnish at work, as it can chip and harbour microbes.
- Ensure that you are fully conversant with your employer's policies and procedures regarding hand hygiene.

Always assess your hands for cuts, cracks and breaks in the skin. These are areas where bacteria can thrive, multiply and get into your system. Always cover open wounds, including cuts, chaps and abrasions, with a non-latex waterproof dressing and ensure that plasters are replaced immediately if they become loose due to wear and tear and frequent hand washing.

Catering staff and anyone else handling food should use either a blue or green plaster, and replace the dressing if it is lost or damaged. If you have eczema or similar skin lesions on your hands you will need to wear gloves for many procedures. If your skin condition is worsened by the use of gloves, consult your line manager and visit your GP and, if you have access to one, the Occupational Health Department. Do not scratch your skin, especially spots, as this will leave bacteria on your hands which can then be passed to another surface.

The following are examples of the types of microbes that can be spread on the hands of health and social care staff:

- *Staphylococcus aureus* (including MRSA)
- *Streptococcus pyogenes* (group A streptococcus (GAS))
- pseudomonas
- *Clostridium difficile*
- candida
- rotavirus
- adenovirus
- hepatitis A virus
- norovirus.

Hand washing must be carried out before, during and after many tasks.

Wash hands before:

- preparing food
- eating
- supporting others to eat
- changing dressings
- giving medicines
- starting work
- putting in contact lenses
- carrying out personal care
- every activity or procedure involving contact with a service user
- putting on protective clothing such as aprons and gloves
- handling equipment, eg wheelchairs, percutaneous endoscopic gastrostomy (PEG) feeding equipment, toileting equipment – and in these cases, afterwards as well.

Wash hands between:

- handling raw foods (meat, fish, poultry and eggs) and touching any other food or kitchen utensils
- working with different service users.

Wash hands after:

- going to the toilet
- supporting a service user to go to the toilet
- making a bed
- handling raw foods, particularly meat, fish and poultry
- blowing your nose
- smoking
- touching rubbish and waste bins
- carrying out personal care
- caring for the sick, especially those with gastro-intestinal disorders
- coughing or sneezing
- handling equipment
- carrying out cleaning duties
- eating finger food, including sweets (fingers touch lips)
- any activity that could have soiled your hands, even if they look clean
- handling refuse or contaminated items such as incontinence pads or catheters
- touching your hair or face, especially your mouth, ears, or nose.

The most effective method of hand washing is sometimes known as the Ayliffe technique, a step-by-step technique devised by Ayliffe et al. (1978) to ensure that all surfaces of the hands receive adequate contact with the decontaminating agent. This technique was developed for use in laboratory studies designed to compare the effectiveness of different skin antiseptics. In these experiments, the hands were artificially contaminated with a standard suspension of non-pathogenic bacteria, followed by a standard amount of the test product. Swabs were then taken at intervals to determine the number of bacteria remaining viable. The validity of the findings clearly depended on the hands of each volunteer being completely covered with the same amount of product every time, and the six-step technique was designed to ensure this. The same technique has been widely promoted in infection control manuals in the UK, because of its emphasis on the thoroughness of the hand decontaminating procedure.

Ayliffe technique for effective hand hygiene

Wet hands, apply liquid soap and carry out the hand washing procedure as follows.

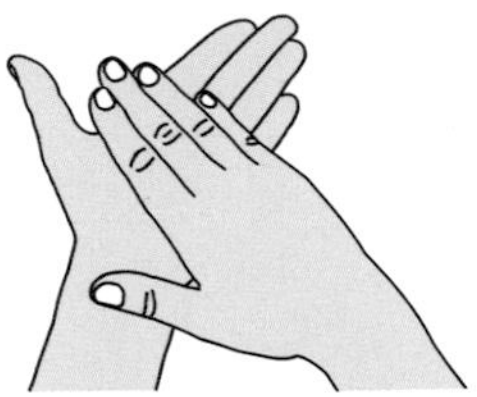

1 Palm to palm

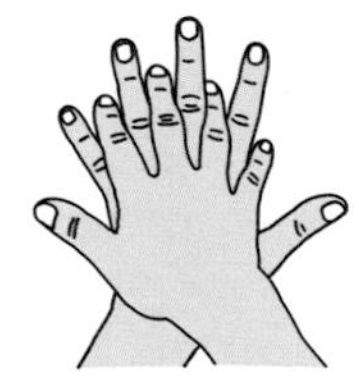

2 Right palm over back of left hand and left palm over back of right hand

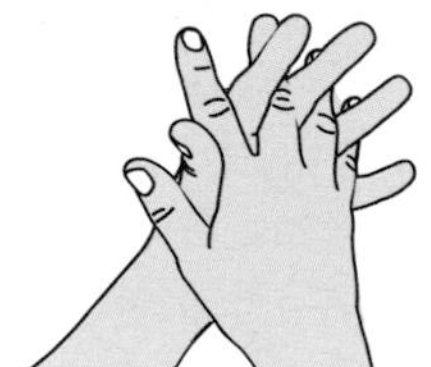

3 Palm to palm fingers interlaced

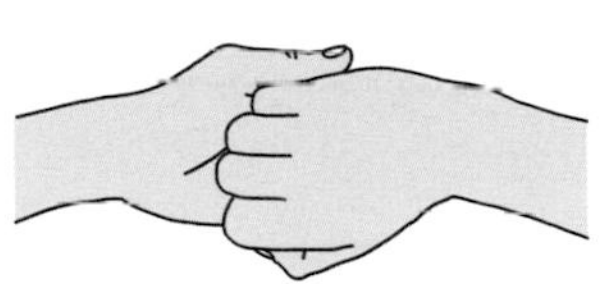

4 Back of fingers to opposing palms with fingers interlocked

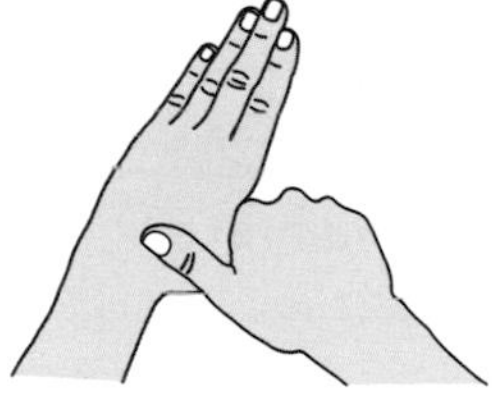

5 Rotational rubbing of right thumb clasped in left palm and vice versa

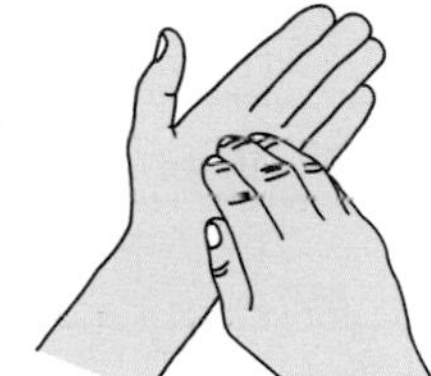

6 Rotational rubbing, backwards and forwards with clasped fingers of right hand in left palm and vice versa

- Rinse away soap under running water.
- After hand washing, dry your hands really thoroughly on a clean towel or paper towel, taking special care between the fingers.
- An alcoholic hand rub should only be used when there are no hand washing facilities available.
- Remember – alcohol rub will not be effective against spore-forming bacteria such as *Clostridium difficile*.

REFLECT

- Think about all the things you touch each day, and how many people may have touched them before you.
- How do you ensure that bad habits connected with hand hygiene do not creep in to your practice and that of others in your workplace?

CASE STUDY

Jeffrey lives with two other people in a house. He is always very willing to be helpful around the house, and one of the tasks he is particularly keen to undertake on a regular basis is laying the table for meals. He becomes agitated if anyone else carries out this task. However, Jeffrey's new key worker notices that his hand hygiene leaves a lot to be desired. She negotiates with Jeffrey that he agrees to her coaching him in basic hygiene practice, resulting in a framed certificate so that he can continue with the task of setting the table on a regular basis. Jeffrey is made aware that his willingness to carry out such tasks is greatly valued.

- In the context of infection prevention and control, why is it important that Jeffrey washes his hands before setting the table?
- What type of transmission is likely to occur due to poor hand hygiene – direct contamination or cross-contamination?

Before going to the next chapter, take some time to consider:

- how you can keep up to date with Standard Infection Control Precautions (SICPs) where you work
- what your role would be if a service user you supported contracted a contagious disease
- what responsibilities you have regarding risk assessment in the context of infection prevention and control
- what responsibilities you have to ensure that other people use good hand washing technique
- where you can obtain up-to-date information on good practice in preventing and controlling infections.

CHAPTER 15

Causes and spread of infection

You have a duty of care to protect the service users you work with, and other workers, from harm, including harm from infectious disease. To do this you need to understand the causes of infection and how infection is spread from one person to another. Once you have a clear understanding of where infections come from and how they are spread, you can take the necessary actions to reduce the likelihood of service users you support becoming infected.

Links to other units

Along with other health and safety issues, the information in this chapter should inform daily practice, so it links to many of the units that make up the Diploma.

In order to understand the causes and spread of infection you need to understand:

- what is meant by the term 'infection'
- how infection is spread from person to person
- the means (routes) by which the body becomes infected
- how the body can be affected by bacteria, viruses, pathogenic fungi and infectious parasites
- the chain of infection.

Key terms 

Microscopic means so small as to be visible only with a microscope.

Pathogen is a bacterium, virus, or other micro-organism that can cause disease. Not all bacteria, viruses or other micro-organisms are pathogenic; they will not all cause disease in humans.

Bacteria are microscopic organisms, some types of which are pathogenic. Bacteria are made up of just one cell and are capable of reproducing themselves.

Virus is a pathogenic microscopic organism. Viruses cannot multiply on their own, so they have to invade a 'host' cell.

Pathogenic fungi are yeasts and moulds which can infect humans.

Parasites are organisms that live on other organisms.

THE CAUSES OF INFECTION

Infection is harm caused by micro-organisms, which are often referred to as 'germs'. Micro-organisms (microbes) are living organisms so small that they cannot be seen without the use of a very powerful microscope – they are **microscopic**. Micro-organisms that cause infection are known as **pathogens**. **Bacteria**, **viruses**, **pathogenic fungi** and **parasites** are all examples of micro-organisms that can cause infection.

THE DIFFERENCES BETWEEN BACTERIA, VIRUSES, FUNGI AND PARASITES

The different kinds of micro-organisms have different characteristics.

BACTERIA

Bacteria are classified into different groups and can be pathogenic (capable of causing illness) or non-pathogenic (not likely to cause illness). Different types of bacteria are identified by their varying shapes.

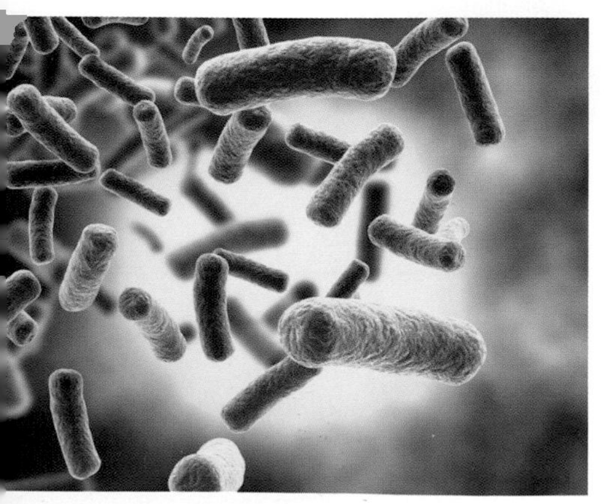

Bacteria are simple organisms, made up of just one cell, and are capable of reproducing by themselves. They do this through a process of growing to twice their original size and splitting into two; those two cells then split into two more, and so on. This may appear to be a very simple process; however, conditions have to be right for it to happen and for the bacteria to be viable. Under the right conditions they can divide and multiply rapidly. The term used for this process is binary fission.

Bacteria exist everywhere, including inside and on our bodies. Most of them are completely harmless and some of them are very useful. For example, most strains of *Escherichia coli* (E. coli) are required as part of the normal gut **flora**, as it has beneficial functions such as helping with the production of vitamin K2. Bacteria in the large intestine help with the final stages of digestion.

Key term 

Flora are microorganisms that normally inhabit the body without causing harm.

However, some bacteria are pathogenic and can cause diseases, either because they end up in the wrong place in the body, or simply because they are 'designed' to invade us. Some bacterial infections can make people very ill, while others have a fairly mild effect. Different streptococcal infections which are caused by strains (or varieties) of the bacterium *Streptococcus* can range from being mild, such as a sore throat, to life-threatening, as in necrotising fasciitis (in the latter they are often called 'flesh-eating' bacteria). Group A *Streptococcus* is commonly found on the skin and inside the throat, and in many people does not cause any symptoms at all. It is important to note that bacteria may have non-pathogenic and pathogenic strains. As mentioned above, most strains of *E. coli* do not cause us harm, but the strain known as *E. coli O157:H7* can cause food poisoning if ingested.

Bacteria tend to be vulnerable to an **antibiotic**, which is why people who have a bacterial infection are often prescribed antibiotics. It is important to understand that bacteria can become resistant to antibiotics as a result of several factors:

Key terms 

Antibiotic is a substance from a micro-organism that is used to destroy other micro-organisms or prevent their growth.

Resistance is the ability of a micro-organism to withstand an antimicrobial agent.

- Bacteria can mutate and eventually become resistant to specific antibiotics.
- If a person is treated with an antibiotic it is possible for that antibiotic to destroy harmless bacteria that live in and on the person, and this allows harmful bacteria to multiply and take their place.
- It is believed that the over-use of antibiotics in recent years has played a large part in antibiotic **resistance**, and the rise of what are often called 'superbugs', such as methicillin-resistant *Staphylococcus aureus* (MRSA).

Nowadays, doctors and GPs have to think carefully before prescribing antibiotics. Officials at Public Health England (PHE) remind GPs that many patients do not benefit from antibiotics even if the patients themselves think that they do. Health officials have acknowledged the pressure on GPs to prescribe, but have warned them that it adds to the cycle of antibiotic resistance.

PHE and the Royal College of General Practitioners have issued guidance to help GPs explain to patients when antibiotics are not needed. The TARGET antibiotics toolkit can be seen at http://www.rcgp.org.uk/TARGETantibiotics/.

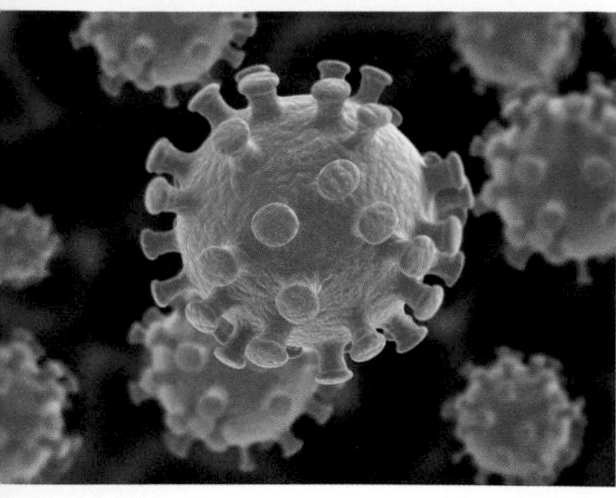

VIRUSES

Viruses are much smaller than bacteria, and more complex. They can survive out of the body for a time. Viruses are not affected by antibiotics, which is why antibiotics are not prescribed for viral infections. There are, however, antiviral drugs available to treat some infections. Viruses cannot multiply on their own, so they have to invade a 'host' cell and take over its machinery in order to be able to make more virus particles. They do this by latching on to human cells and getting inside them. Viruses consist of genetic materials (**DNA** or **RNA**) surrounded by a protective coat of protein.

The cells of the mucous membranes, such as those lining the respiratory passages we breathe through, are particularly open to virus attacks because they are not covered by protective skin. As well as all cold and flu infections and most coughs and sore throats, viruses are also the cause of many serious infectious diseases. In order to get rid of a virus, the cell which has been invaded by the virus must be killed, which results in damage to the cells themselves. For this reason doctors can only control the symptoms of a viral infection, but to date medical research has found no cures.

When a virus invades the body, the immune system releases white blood cells. These cells produce antibodies, which cover the virus's protein coat and prevent it from attaching itself to the cell. White blood cells also destroy infected cells and thus kill the virus before it can reproduce. Unfortunately, some viruses such as measles, influenza and mononucleosis (glandular fever) weaken the immune system for a period of time.

Key terms 

DNA (Deoxyribonucleic acid) is sometimes called 'the blueprint of life' because it contains the code for building organisms.

RNA (Ribonucleic acid) acts as a messenger of the above mentioned code when new cells are formed.

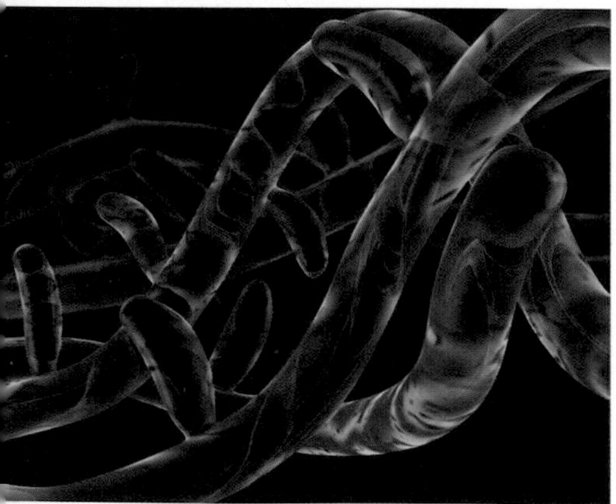

PATHOGENIC FUNGI

Pathogenic fungi can be either yeast or moulds, including yeasts (single-celled), and mushrooms and moulds (multi-celled). A fungus is a simple plant-like organism. Unlike plants, fungi do not make their own food. Some species of fungi get their nutrition by breaking down the remains of dead plants or animals. Others are parasites. Examples of fungal infections include athlete's foot, thrush and ringworm. Fungal infections are not often the cause of healthcare-acquired infections; however, it is possible for an individual to acquire an infection such as ringworm in a healthcare environment.

PARASITES

Some parasites are very complex; many are pathogenic and cause infection and can be spread from person to person. Parasites usually enter the body through the mouth or the skin. For example, threadworms, sometimes known as pinworms, are small, white, thread-like worms a few millimetres long that live in the human gut. The female worm lays eggs around the anus, which often leads to itching and scratching. Eggs can then become stuck to fingertips or under the fingernails and can be transferred to other people, food, children's toys, kitchen utensils or even toothbrushes. Other people then come into contact with the eggs, and if they touch their mouths and swallow the eggs they become infected with the threadworm.

Scabies is a contagious disease caused by tiny mites (*Sarcoptes scabiei*). The main symptom of scabies is itching caused by the mite burrowing under the skin. Scabies is spread by skin-to-skin contact with an infected person; this is the most common method. It can also be spread by sharing clothes, infected linen, towels and so on with an infected person.

COMMON ILLNESSES AND INFECTIONS CAUSED BY BACTERIA, VIRUSES, FUNGI AND PARASITES

The following table is not an exhaustive list, but is provided to further illustrate the types of illnesses that are caused by micro-organisms.

Condition	Type of micro-organism	Outlines of transmission
Acquired Immune Deficiency Syndrome (AIDS)	Virus	AIDS is the final stages of HIV (Human Immunodeficiency Virus). Most common modes of **transmission** are unprotected sex, sharing infected needles, HIV-positive mother to baby during pregnancy, birth or breastfeeding.
Bronchiolitis	Virus	Mostly common in babies and young children. Mode of infection is usually droplet infection from infected people sneezing and coughing.

Key term

Transmission means passing an infectious disease from one person to another.

Condition	Type of micro-organism	Outlines of transmission
Chickenpox	Virus	Common childhood illness. Mode of transmission is that it spreads through the air in tiny droplets – fifteen minutes in the same room as an infected person is likely to lead to infection; also spread through skin contact with the blisters.
Chlamydia	Bacteria	Mode of transmission is unprotected sex or from an infected mother to a baby during birth.
Cold and flu	Virus	Can be spread by droplet infection, or the unwashed hands of an infected person touching surfaces.
Cold sores	Virus	Modes of transmission include skin-to-skin, eg kissing, and sharing items such as cups, towels or any other item that has made contact with the cold sore.
Diphtheria	Bacteria	The most common mode of transmission is droplet infection; since the vaccination programme started in 1940 this once-common cause of death in the UK is now rare. Since 1896 there have been 15 cases reported in England and Wales. It is, however, still common in some other areas of the world.
Dysentery	Bacteria or parasite	There are two main types of dysentery; the most common type in the UK is caused by the *Shigella* bacteria. Amoebic dysentery is caused by an amoeba (single-celled parasite) called *Entamoeba histolytica*, which is mainly found in tropical areas. Both types of dysentery are commonly passed on through poor hygiene, and people often become infected by eating contaminated food.

Condition	Type of micro-organism	Outlines of transmission
Glandular fever	Virus	Mostly infects young adults. Common modes of transmission are kissing, droplet infection from infected people coughing and sneezing, and sharing eating and drinking utensils such as cups, glasses and unwashed forks and spoons.
Hepatitis A/B/C	Virus	Hepatitis A is caused by faecal contamination. Hepatitis B can be passed on through sexual contact, infected needles and from mother to baby. Hepatitis C is blood-borne so can be passed on by infected blood, contaminated needles, needle-stick injuries and from mother to unborn child.
Impetigo	Bacteria	This is an infection of the top layers of skin caused by bacteria getting into the skin when it is damaged, for example, by insect bites, tiny cuts and grazes. The mode of transmission is by contact with blister fluid either from direct skin contact or by cross-contamination from objects that have touched the blister fluid such as face cloths, towels, clothing or toys.
Measles	Virus	Modes of transmission are droplet infection, either by breathing in the droplets when an infected person has coughed or sneezed or by touching contaminated surfaces where droplets have fallen and then touching the mouth or nose area.
Mumps	Virus	Same as measles, above.
Norovirus (winter vomiting bug)	Virus	Caused by a group of viruses called noroviruses, this is the most common cause of stomach bugs in England and Wales. Modes of transmission are person-to-person, consuming contaminated food or water, and touching contaminated surfaces or objects.

Condition	Type of micro-organism	Outlines of transmission
Poliomyelitis (polio)	Virus	Poliomyelitis (polio) is a highly infectious vaccine-preventable disease. It invades the nervous system, and can cause total paralysis in a matter of hours. It can strike at any age, but mainly affects children under three.
Pneumonia	Virus or bacteria or fungus	Pneumonia means inflammation of the lungs usually caused by an infection.
Ringworm	Fungus	Can affect skin, nails and hair. The mode of transmission is by touching an infected person, animal or infected object or surface, eg shared towels or farm gates.
Rubella (German measles)	Virus	Direct contact and droplet infection breathed in when an infected person coughs or sneezes are the common modes of transmission.
Scabies	Parasite (scabies mite)	Contagious, very itchy skin disorder leading to a rash caused by the microscopic mite burrowing under the skin to lay eggs. The mode of transmission is skin-to-skin contact, eg prolonged hand-holding.
Scarlet fever	Bacteria	Caused by the same Streptococcus bacteria that causes impetigo. These bacteria are commonly found on the skin and in the throat, where they do not cause any problems. Unfortunately under certain circumstances they cause disease. Scarlet fever is highly contagious and is transmitted via airborne droplets from coughing and sneezing, and by direct contact with mucus or saliva from an infected person or items contaminated by droplets or saliva/mucus such as drinking vessels or eating utensils.

Condition	Type of micro-organism	Outlines of transmission
Tetanus	Bacteria	Tetanus occurs when a flesh wound becomes contaminated. The bacteria live in soil, house dust and animal and human waste.
Tinea pedis (athlete's foot)	Fungus	Spreads easily from person to person on towels, clothing and foot contact surfaces. The fungi survive and multiply in warm humid areas such as swimming pools, changing rooms and showers.
Tuberculosis	Bacteria	Spread by inhaling droplets from the coughs and sneezes of an infected person. Most commonly affects the lungs, but can affect any part of the body.
Warts and verrucas	Virus	Very contagious; modes of transmission are skin to skin and contact with infected objects or surfaces such as the areas around swimming pools.
Whooping cough	Bacteria	Spread by inhaling droplets from the coughs and sneezes of an infected person.

TYPES OF INFECTION

The following are terms commonly used to describe how and where microbes are affecting a person's body:

- *Systemic infection*. This is when the infection caused by a pathogen has spread through the body to several organs in different systems of the body, for example, the digestive, respiratory or circulatory systems.
- *Localised infection*. This is an infection that is confined or restricted to a specific location of the body, for example, an infected wound.

Colonisation versus infection

Infection means that the organism is present and is causing illness. Colonisation means that the organism is present in or on the body but is not causing illness. When someone is exposed to a micro-organism such as MRSA or *Clostridium difficile*, they can become colonised. This means that the organism takes up residence harmlessly (for example, on the skin, in the nose or in the bowel) but does not cause an infection. This colonisation may:

- continue harmlessly indefinitely
- clear spontaneously
- develop into an infection.

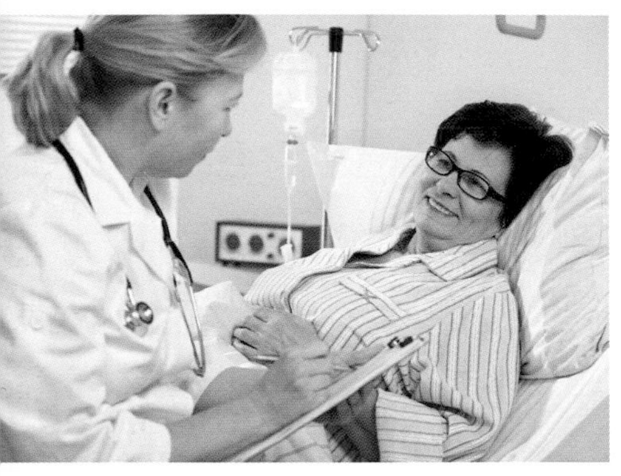

Sometimes it is possible and indeed necessary to use medical treatments to help the colonisation clear faster, for example, before an operation can take place. For this reason screening for MRSA often takes place prior to elective surgery, for example, in day cases having routine surgery.

THE TRANSMISSION OF INFECTION

Micro-organisms that cause infection may originate from:

- ourselves **(endogenous)** micro-organisms which transfer from one site on the body to another site where they invade and cause infection
- other people **(exogenous)** via hands, equipment, etc
- the environment, including contaminated food, contaminated equipment, contaminated surfaces, contaminated laundry, clinical waste and dust.

Key terms

Endogenous means originating from within.

Exogenous means originating from an external source.

The difference between infectious and non-infectious disease is that infectious disease can be spread from person to person. Infection can pass from person to person by cross-contamination (cross-infection, indirect contamination) or by direct contact (direct contamination).

Cross-contamination is where the pathogenic organisms are moved from their source to another location and then to a person. Sharing contaminated objects such as a bedpan or hairbrush can lead to cross-contamination, as can misusing cleaning equipment, for example, by using cleaning cloths in more than one location. Remember, hands are the most common vehicles of cross-infection.

It is very important to remember that some people are more susceptible to infection than others. For instance older people, babies and children are more susceptible, as are people with lowered immunity due to illness or existing health conditions.

One of the reasons that the organisms that cause infections spread so easily is because they cannot be seen by the naked eye. For that reason we need to be aware of how to minimise the conditions for their growth and how they get into our bodies. With this information we can start to minimise the chances of transmission of infections. Bacteria live on or in just about every material and environment on this planet: from soil, to water, to air; from inside home environments, to arctic ice. Every living creature, including humans, is covered with bacteria. Some microbes live on the skin and offer protection from harmful agents. The drier areas of the body, such as the back and forearm, have few microbes; moist areas, such as the armpit, have many more. Each square centimetre of skin averages about 100,000 bacteria. The forearms, which tend to be dry, average approximately 1,000 bacteria per square centimetre, while the armpits may have many millions per square centimetre.

CONDITIONS NEEDED FOR THE GROWTH OF MICRO-ORGANISMS

To multiply and reproduce, pathogenic micro-organisms require the following:

- moisture
- nutrients
- temperature
- time.

Moisture

Like most living things, bacteria must have moisture to stay alive. Bacteria will not multiply in dry areas, but as soon as liquid is added, for instance to dried food like powdered milk and dried eggs, the products will provide ideal conditions for bacteria to multiply. However, if enough salt or sugar have been added to foods such as bacon, savoury biscuits, jam and confectionery, this will absorb the available moisture in the food so the bacteria cannot multiply as easily. It is not only moist foods that provide the right environment for bacteria, though. Moist skin or damp areas of an environment will also provide the right atmosphere for bacterial growth.

Nutrients

Bacteria, like all living things, need nutrients to survive. Different types of food-poisoning bacteria can live on a range of foods, but most prefer food that is moist and high in protein such as meat, poultry, eggs, shellfish, milk and dairy products, cooked rice, pasta, or any product made from these foods.

All these foods are subject to bacterial growth even after they have been cooked and served cold later. This is why such ready-to-eat items are classified as high-risk foods.

KEY POINT

Photosynthesis is the process by which some organisms use sunlight to synthesize nutrients from carbon dioxide and water.

Bacteria will live on and in people, plants and soil, and they take nutrition from everything from sugar and starch to sunlight, sulphur and iron. Some bacteria are photosynthetic – they can make their own food from sunlight, just like plants. Also like plants, they give off oxygen. Other bacteria absorb food from the material they live on or in. Some of these bacteria can live off unusual substances such as the elements iron or sulphur. The microbes that live in your gut absorb nutrients from the food you've digested.

Temperature

Most food-poisoning bacteria multiply at temperatures between 5°C and 63°C, which is why this range of temperatures is often called the 'danger zone'. Ambient temperatures (room temperatures) are generally within the danger zone. The ideal temperature for bacteria to multiply is around 37°C, which is the average human body temperature. When food is kept at temperatures colder than 5°C and hotter than 63°C bacterial growth slows down or stops, but most bacteria can survive cold temperatures and resume multiplication when conditions are more suitable. Freezing will make most bacteria dormant, but it does not kill them, so when frozen food is thawed it is just as susceptible to risks as fresh food.

Time

When bacteria are left in warm conditions on the right type of nutrient with adequate moisture, they will reproduce quickly. For example, most types of food-poisoning bacteria take around 10 to 20 minutes to multiply.

VIRUSES

In order for a virus to multiply it needs to latch on and invade an appropriate host cell of an animal or plant. Once it is within the 'host' cell it takes over its machinery and makes more virus particles. The cells of the mucous membranes, such as those lining the respiratory passages that we breathe through, are particularly open to virus attacks because they are not covered by protective skin.

MAIN ROUTES OF INFECTION

There are four main routes of infection, or ways in which infections enter our bodies:

- *The respiratory tract (nose, windpipe, lungs)*. Airborne pathogens such as those causing coughs and colds can be inhaled.
- *Broken skin*. One of the functions of the skin is to provide protection against infection. This includes the mucous membrane of the nose and mouth. If skin is broken by bites, scratches,

puncture wounds or dry chapped skin that breaks down, this provides a route for infection to enter the body.

- *The digestive tract*. Infected products such as food and drink can be swallowed, often affecting the bowels or stomach.
- *The urinary tract and reproductive system*. Infections may remain localised or enter the bloodstream. One of the problems with catheterisation is the possibility of bacteria being carried into the urinary tract during the catheterisation procedure.

COMMON CAUSES OF THE SPREAD OF INFECTION

The most common causes of spread of infections in a health and social care environment are:

- lack of or poor hand hygiene
- lack of or poor cleaning procedures
- lack of, or incorrect use of, personal protective equipment (PPE) such as gloves and aprons
- contaminated bed linen or clothing
- infected food handlers – remember, this includes not only those who prepare food but also those who serve food or support people to eat and drink
- airborne infection (such as colds and flu).

Some of these are described in more detail below.

Lack of or poor hand hygiene

People carry millions of microbes on their hands. Most are harmless, but some can cause illnesses such as colds, flu, diarrhoea, hepatitis and E. coli infection when we forget to wash our hands, or don't wash them properly. We can spread these germs to other people, or give them to ourselves by touching our eyes, mouths, noses or cuts on our bodies. Microbes can also be picked up from objects such as doorknobs, taps, and wheelchair handles touched by other people who have not washed their hands. Think about all the things you touch each day and how many people may have touched them before you.

The Hand Hygiene Campaign – Give Soap a Chance states that some bacteria and viruses can stay alive on our hands for up to three hours. They can be spread to all the things touched during that time, including food and other people, so good hand hygiene is of the utmost importance. On its website, NHS Choices, the National Health Service gives a wealth of information about how long micro-organisms can live outside of the body. For instance, cold viruses can survive on indoor surfaces for more than seven days; however, their ability to cause an infection starts to decrease after 24 hours. Also, 40% of cold-causing viruses remain infectious on hands after one hour. Washing hands reduces the number of micro-organisms on our hands and helps prevent the spread of infection.

The following are examples of the types of microbes that can be spread on the hands of health and social care workers:

- *Staphylococcus aureus* (including MRSA)
- *Streptococcus pyogenes* (Group A Streptococci)
- Pseudomonas – a bacterium found in soil and water, likely to infect people with underlying health problems staying in hospital
- *Clostridium difficile* – a bacterial infection that affects the digestive system, most commonly affecting people staying in hospital
- Candida – fungi which live on all surfaces of our bodies; under certain conditions, they can cause infections such as vaginal thrush, oral thrush, skin and nappy rash
- rotavirus – a common cause of diarrhoea and sickness
- adenovirus – a common cause of respiratory tract infections and gastroenteritis, especially in young children; adenoviruses can also cause conjunctivitis and cystitis
- hepatitis A virus
- norovirus.

DID YOU KNOW?

- Around 20% of women and 40% of men don't wash their hands after using a public toilet.
- According to research carried out in the United States of America and presented to the International Association for Food Protection conference in San Diego in July 2002, 90% of germs on hands are found under the nails.
- A right-handed person tends to wash their left hand more thoroughly than their right hand, and vice versa.
- The number of bacteria can double in 20 minutes, and after one day without hand washing a single bacterium can multiply 2 billion, trillion times.
- There are between 2 million and 10 million bacteria between the fingertip and the elbow.
- The number of microbes on your fingertips doubles after you use the toilet.
- Pathogens can stay alive on hands for up to three hours.
- Millions of germs hide under watches and bracelets, and there could be as many germs under a ring as there are people in Europe.

(Foodink, Food and Drink Federation)

Hand hygiene is of utmost importance. It is important that you are fully aware of your employer's laid-down policies and procedures relating to hand hygiene, including which resources should be used for the various activities carried out during the course of your daily duties.

Generally, washing hands with liquid soap and water is sufficient as you go about your daily activities. Nowadays, hand rub containing alcohol is available at the entrance to hospital wards and residential support services. It is important that staff and visitors use it on entering and exiting such facilities. If you are supporting a service user from a social care environment into a clinical setting such as a hospital you must remember that your duty of care still applies, and that you have a responsibility to ensure that correct hand hygiene is adhered to by you, the person you are supporting and anyone else involved in the service user's support and health care.

The Code of Practice on prevention and control of infections published by the Department of Health within The Health and Social Care Act states that service providers must ensure that there is adequate provision of hand-washing facilities, and anti-microbial hand rubs where appropriate. This clearly indicates the importance of hand washing with soap and water. However, according to the National Institute for Health and Care Excellence (NICE) in its Clinical Guidelines, hand rubs containing 60% isopropyl alcohol and conforming to the current British Standard are the recommended products for ensuring effective hand hygiene, except when:

- hands are visibly soiled
- the patient is experiencing vomiting and/or diarrhoea
- there is direct hand contact with any body fluids, ie if gloves have not been worn
- there is an outbreak of norovirus, *Clostridium difficile* or other diarrhoeal illnesses.

In these instances hands should always be cleaned with liquid soap and warm running water.

Hand washing with soap and water

It takes at least 15 seconds to wash your hands thoroughly (about the same amount of time as it takes to sing 'Happy Birthday' through twice). The correct method for hand washing is covered in more detail in Chapter 14.

Damp hands spread 1,000 times more germs than dry hands. Clean towels should be available at all times – dirty towels mean exposing the skin to more dirt and the risk of infection. Ideally, 'single-use' disposable towels should be used, as the use of 'communal' towels can lead to contamination.

When using hand gel, apply gel to dry hands and follow steps 3–9 as shown above, ensuring that enough gel is applied. Refer to Chapter 14 for more information on how to wash your hands correctly.

REFLECT

What tasks do health and social care workers in your work environment carry out that require hand washing prior to starting the task and after completion of the task?

Lack of or poor cleaning procedures

If there is a lack of cleaning procedures in place, or they are poor, you and the service users you support can become infected. Pathogenic organisms can be moved from their source and into the environment, and cross-contamination can happen by people passing microbes from one area to another either by their hands or by cleaning equipment such as mops and cloths. For example, taps and door handles can harbour a multitude of micro-organisms, as can wheelchair handles and telephone receivers. In fact, any hand contact surface can be a breeding ground for pathogens.

If the correct methods are not used for cleaning the environment, be that in a hospital ward/department or residential/day services setting, micro-organisms may be transmitted from one site to another. For this reason it is important to follow laid-down processes and procedures using colour-coded cleaning equipment, which after use is decontaminated or disposed of in the correct manner.

REFLECT

- What surfaces are there in your work environment that could harbour harmful microbes? What measures are there in place to ensure that such risks are kept to a minimum?
- What antibacterial/viral cleaning materials do you have in your work environment, and what measures are there in place to ensure that everyone knows how to use them effectively?
- What measures are there in place where you work to ensure that no cross-contamination occurs due to inappropriate use of cleaning equipment?
- If you needed to clean up a spillage of urine from the floor of a toilet, what equipment (including PPE) would you use?
- Do you have a spillage kit at work to use in the case of blood spillage? If so, where is it kept – and could you explain to a new member of staff how and when to use it?

CASE STUDY

Silas is a home care worker. He recognises that service users have the right to live in a **non-clinical** environment, and he also knows about infection control. As he does not want to take away service users' dignity by refusing to use their soap and terry cotton towels, he always carries with him the bacterial hand gel provided by his employing agency. He uses the hand gel very discreetly before entering and after exiting people's homes in addition to using their own facilities.

- Name two infections that can be spread by sharing towels.
- What is the recommended percentage of isopropyl alcohol for hand gel to contain?

Contamination of food

Bacteria can cause food-borne illness. When food is kept warm, between the temperatures of 5°C and 63°C, these bacteria can grow rapidly and reach dangerous levels within hours.

The incubation period (the time that elapses between eating the food and feeling unwell) varies with each type of organism, and in some cases can be as much as 10 to 15 days. It is important to realise, therefore, that the last meal eaten may not be the cause of the symptoms. The government publishes a wealth of information about

KEY POINT

Incubation is the time from the moment of exposure to an infectious agent until signs and symptoms of the disease appear.

types of food-borne illnesses, symptoms and incubation times in their PHE guidance sheets, which can be found at www.hpa.org.uk.

The Food Standards Agency (FSA) identifies the following as the main causes of food poisoning and food-borne illness:

- not cooking food thoroughly (particularly poultry, pork, burgers, sausages and kebabs)
- not correctly storing food that needs to be chilled at below 5°C
- leaving cooked food for too long at warm temperatures
- someone who is ill or who has dirty hands touching food
- eating food that has passed its use-by date
- cross-contamination (the spread of bacteria, such as E. coli, from contaminated foods), for example, bacteria-harbouring juices of raw meat dripping on to foodstuffs that will be eaten without cooking or processing.

Anyone can become ill as a result of food poisoning or food-borne illness, but babies, young children and older people can quickly become very ill when infected. Pregnant women, people with a pre-existing illness and anyone whose immune system is weakened can also be especially vulnerable and seriously affected by food-borne illness.

CASE STUDY

Mary is supported in her own home by Georgie. Every Monday, food that Mary has ordered online is delivered by a local supermarket. Mary takes great pride in putting away her purchases herself. Georgie has coached Mary in the importance of ensuring that raw meat is stored at the bottom of the refrigerator, ensuring that no bacteria-laden juices can drop on to and contaminate food to be eaten raw, such as cheese.

- Why is cheese likely to be a high-risk food?
- Other than ensuring that the meat is stored at the bottom of the refrigerator, what other steps should be taken to ensure that no bacteria passes from raw meat to other foodstuffs?

Contaminated linen and clothing

Workers may become infected or cause cross-contamination if they do not use PPE such as gloves and aprons, for example, when dealing with soiled linen and clothing. Special care needs to be taken if there is any risk of splashing, spraying or splattering of faeces or vomit. Even when there is no visible sign of soiling of linen and clothing, microbiological pathogens may still be present. Putting soiled linen on chairs or floors instead of into laundry bags is especially bad practice and can lead to cross-infection.

CASE STUDY

Miriam is a new support worker at a residential establishment for older people. During her second week in her new job, Miriam is stripping a bed to change the linen when her supervisor comes looking for her to discuss her induction. The supervisor asks Miriam why, as a new member of staff, she is working alone and why she is stripping the bed without wearing gloves. The supervisor points out that the person whose bed is being stripped has urinary incontinence, and that by not wearing gloves Miriam is putting herself and others at risk of infection. Miriam explains that her colleague, who she was making the beds with, was called away to deal with something else, so she had agreed to strip the beds in readiness for the two of them to make them again later. The supervisor reminds Miriam of the care plans and risk assessments for all service users that she has been shown; she also makes a note to herself that new workers should have closer supervision until they are fully conversant with the care plans and risk assessments.

- In addition to wearing gloves, what steps should be taken when dealing with soiled linen?
- Would it be acceptable to wear the same pair of gloves to strip several beds of their linen? Why?

Infected food handlers

People suffering from certain infections (mainly from bacteria and viruses) can contaminate the food they handle or the surfaces food may come into contact with. This can spread infection to other people through the food. Food-borne infections from infected food handlers result primarily in gastrointestinal infections.

The FSA is an independent government department responsible for food safety and hygiene across the UK. It works with businesses to help them produce safe food, and with Local Authorities to enforce food safety regulations. The FSA states that *Campylobacter* is the most common cause of food poisoning in the UK. It is considered to be responsible for around 460,000 cases of food poisoning, 22,000 hospitalisations and 110 deaths each year, and most of these cases come from poultry. The FSA also tells us that norovirus, commonly known as the winter vomiting bug, is the most common cause of infectious intestinal disease resulting in diarrhoea and vomiting in the UK. The Second Study of Infectious Intestinal Disease in the Community (the IID2 Study) published in September 2011 suggested that there were approximately 3 million UK cases of norovirus annually. Norovirus poses additional problems in the management of outbreaks of infection, as even very low numbers of particles can lead to infection.

Although most cases are caused by contact with an infected person, a proportion of cases are due to contaminated food and drink. There are, of course, other infections with which food handlers can contaminate food and surfaces such as *salmonella* – and *E. coli*. *Salmonella* bacteria are often found in raw meat and poultry. They can also be passed to dairy products such as eggs and unpasteurised milk.

E. coli are bacteria found in the digestive systems of many animals, including humans. Most strains are harmless but some strains can cause serious illness.

In most cases, food handlers with diarrhoea or vomiting should refrain from work for 48 hours after symptoms subside. However, in some cases different action is required. Guidance is available from the Health Protection Agency.

Infected health and social care staff

Health and social care staff, in common with any other group of workers, can become infected themselves and, along with the rest of the population, carry bacteria within and on themselves. Because of the vulnerability of service users, workers must be extra-vigilant with their own health and consider how to best protect the people they support from infection by pathogens they might be carrying.

CASE STUDY

Carlos is a senior day services officer. One lunchtime he observes Raymond supporting a service user to eat his meal. Afterwards he gives Raymond some feedback. He tells Raymond how impressed he was with the way in which Raymond had treated the service user with dignity and respect, offered choices, supported them at their own pace and communicated well with them throughout the meal, using appropriate language to meet their needs. At one point during the meal Raymond had to cough, and Carlos had noted that Raymond had turned away from the service user and their food to cough, held his hand over his mouth while coughing and immediately apologised to the service user – all of this was, as Carlos said, very appropriate behaviour. Unfortunately, Raymond had not washed his hands immediately following the cough; instead he picked up a glass of water and handed it to the service user. It is almost certain that his hand was covered with bacteria, if not virus particles, from his respiratory tract.

On receiving the feedback Raymond understood his error and made a mental note never to repeat it.

- Name at least three infections that Raymond could pass to the service user by touching their glass with an unwashed hand after coughing into it.
- Name at least six daily situations at work in which you need to wash your hands.

HOW INFECTIONS ARE SPREAD FROM PERSON TO PERSON

The chain of infection shows how infection is spread from person to person.

The chain of infection

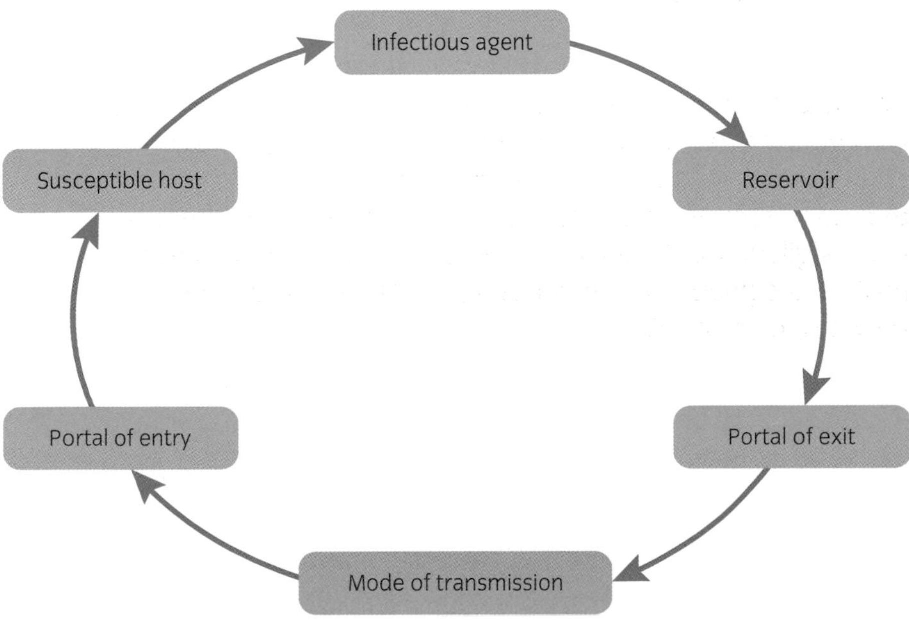

As stated previously, micro-organisms (eg bacteria and viruses) live in or on some parts of the body such as the skin, mouth and intestinal tract. This mixture of organisms normally found on or in the body that do not usually cause harm is referred to as the normal flora.

Some of these organisms may cause illness if they find their way into areas of the body where they don't belong. For example, if micro-organisms normally found in the bowel enter the bladder they may have the potential to cause infection. For this reason people are instructed to 'wipe towards the back' after using the toilet.

Normal skin flora which are there all the time are essential for good health and rarely causes infection. However, there are some procedures that can make people vulnerable to infection, because the micro-organisms can be carried from the surface of the skin – where they belong – into the flesh or blood vessels, where they do not belong. This may happen during surgery, insertion of catheters, or peripheral intravenous (IV) cannulation. Normal flora live naturally on the skin and are difficult to remove by routine hand hygiene techniques, although the numbers of micro-organisms will be reduced by this process.

Many other micro-organisms are acquired or deposited on the skin from other people or from the environment. These micro-organisms do not live permanently on the skin and are readily removed or destroyed by correct and frequent hand hygiene procedures.

The reservoirs of infection

The Health Protection Agency (HPA) describes a reservoir of infection as being where a micro-organism normally lives and reproduces, for example, in animals, water or food. The human body is the most common reservoir for micro-organisms. A person with an infectious disease such as salmonella, tuberculosis, polio, hepatitis A or hepatitis B may act as a source of infection to others because the micro-organisms are present in some of the body fluids and can be passed on to others.

There are two types of human reservoirs: clinical cases and carriers. Clinical cases are people who are infected with the disease agent and become ill. Because they are ill, their contacts and activities may be limited. They are also more likely to be diagnosed and treated than carriers. Carriers, on the other hand, are people who harbour infectious agents but are not ill. Carriers may present more risk for disease transmission than clinical cases, because their contacts are unaware of their infection, and their activities are not restricted by illness.

Depending on the disease, there may be different types of carriers:

- incubatory carriers
- inapparent infections

- convalescent carriers
- chronic carriers.

Incubatory carriers

These are people who are going to become ill, but begin transmitting their infection before their symptoms start. For example, in the case of measles, a person infected with measles can pass the virus to others via nasal and throat secretions a day or two before any symptoms are noticeable.

Inapparent carriers

Inapparent infections are where the individual is asymptomatic (has no symptoms of infection) but is carrying the infectious agent.

Convalescent carriers

These are people who continue to be infectious during and even after their recovery from illness. This happens with many diseases. For example, with salmonella, individuals may excrete the bacteria in faeces for several weeks and (rarely) even for a year or more. This is most common in infants and young children.

Chronic carriers

These are people who continue to harbour infections for a year or longer after their recovery. For example, the chronic carrier state is not uncommon following hepatitis B infection, whether or not the person became ill, and may be lifelong.

Contaminated food may also act as a reservoir of infection. A common example of this is the presence of salmonella. If food contaminated with salmonella is not thoroughly cooked, individuals who consume it can become infected.

The environment can also be reservoir of infection if it becomes contaminated by micro-organisms shed by people with an infection. This can then spread to others. Regular cleaning minimises this risk.

Poorly maintained or incorrectly decontaminated cleaning or medical equipment can also act as a reservoir of micro-organisms. For example, inadequately maintained and shared commodes can be contaminated with micro-organisms that cause diarrhoea.

Portal of exit

This refers to the way in which the pathogen escapes from the reservoir, such as via faeces, urine, wound discharge, mucus, blood, vomit, droplet transmission by sneezing, coughing or talking.

Mode of transmission

The mode of transmission is the method by which the pathogen gets from the reservoir to the new host. This can happen by one of the following means:

- Direct contact (actual contact with an infected person).
- Indirect contact (contact with contaminated surfaces touched by the infected person, or where droplets of body fluid have landed; spread on unwashed hands). Hands play a big part in spreading infection. Micro-organisms may be present in body excretions and secretions. If hands come into contact with these, the micro-organisms may be carried from one person to another unless the hands are properly decontaminated.
- Airborne – via 'aerosols', or tiny infected particles from an infected person released when they cough or sneeze, which can be breathed in. The viruses responsible for colds and influenza are found in nasal secretion, saliva and **sputum**. Coughing or sneezing near another person may pass on these viruses in the droplets or aerosol produced.
- Consumption of contaminated food/water or swallowing of micro-organisms carried on the hands.
- Exposure to blood.
- **Vector**-borne (parasite bites).
- Sexual contact.

Key terms

Sputum is mucus that is sometimes coughed up from the lower airways.

Vector is an organism, typically a biting insect or parasite, that transmits a disease.

Portal of entry

Every micro-organism needs to have an entry point into the human body. Different micro-organisms have different ways of achieving this.

Portal of entry	Example infection
Ingestion – eating contaminated food.	Salmonella, a group of bacteria that can cause food poisoning.
Inhalation – micro-organisms suspended in particles of liquid are exhaled by the infected person and inhaled (breathed in) through the nose or mouth by another person.	Influenza
Blood – this can occur through punctures to the skin by contaminated sharps.	Hepatitis B
Urinary tract – organisms causing urinary tract infections may enter during poor catheter care or poor personal care.	*Escherichia coli*

Portal of entry	Example infection
Skin – via breaks in the skin, which is normally a protective barrier, for example, during surgery or through punctures made by cannulation cuts, scratches or abrasions caused by injury.	*Enterobacteriaceae*, a group of bacteria including many of the more often heard-of pathogens such as *salmonella*, *E. coli*, *helicobacter*. *Staphylococcus*, a common type of bacterium often carried on the skin and inside the nostrils and throat, which can cause mild infections of the skin such as boils and impetigo. If *Staphylococcus* bacteria get into a break in the skin, they can cause life-threatening infections, such as blood poisoning or endocarditis (an infection of the inner lining of the heart). *Staphylococcus epidermidis*
Mucous membranes (in the mouth, eyes and nose) – having no protective skin, these can be very vulnerable to micro-organisms, for example, those that cause Streptococcal throat infections.	Streptococcus, a bacterium that is commonly found on the skin or in the nose and throat.

FACTORS THAT WILL MAKE IT MORE LIKELY THAT INFECTION WILL OCCUR

Susceptibility to infection varies from person to person. Risk factors for infection include:

- age (the very young and very old are more vulnerable to infections)
- physical wellbeing
- psychological wellbeing
- hygiene
- underlying or chronic diseases or medical conditions (eg diabetes, chronic chest and heart problems, or cancer)
- other existing infections
- medical interventions (eg an indwelling medical device)
- medical therapies (eg cancer chemotherapy or steroids)
- immune status.

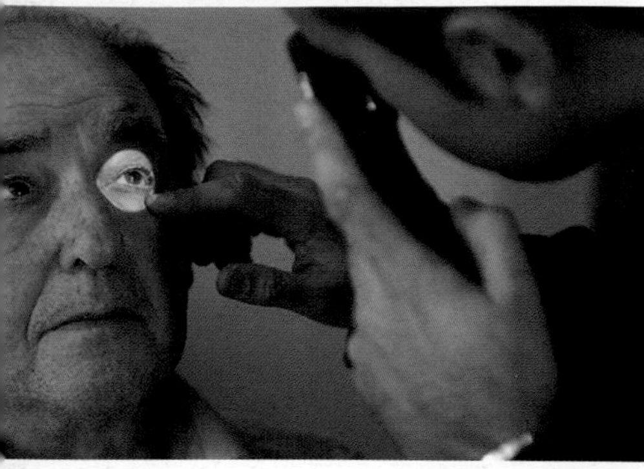

It is important that key factors that will make infection more likely are identified. These factors vary from one work setting to another, and according to the duties being carried out. Some activities – or lack of activities – put the worker at risk of becoming infected, others put the service user at risk, and some activities or the lack of them put both the worker and the service user at risk. The following are some examples of risk factors:

- dealing with personal care tasks
- a lack of personal hygiene
- wounds requiring treatment
- contact with body fluids
- long-term use of antibiotics
- close proximity to others, whether infected or uninfected
- age – very young or very elderly
- dirty and/or contaminated areas of the environment
- dirty and/or contaminated equipment
- dirty and/or contaminated laundry
- people who are ill
- people who are **immunocompromised**, ie where their immune system does not function properly.

Key term

Immunocompromised is where a person has impaired immunity due to disease (eg cancer) or treatment (eg corticosteroids or radiotherapy).

REFLECT

- Think about your work setting. What key factors can you identify that might make it more likely that infection will occur, and how are those factors managed?
- Can you identify any further steps that could be taken to reduce the risks?

Before going to the next chapter, take some time to consider:

- what policies and procedures you have in your work setting relating to the causes and spread of infection
- what your responsibilities are regarding stopping the spread of infection
- how you can help colleagues and others to understand the causes and spread of infection
- what you would do if you observed poor practice that might lead to the spread of infection
- if there is anything you can do to improve your own practice connected with stopping the potential spread of infection.

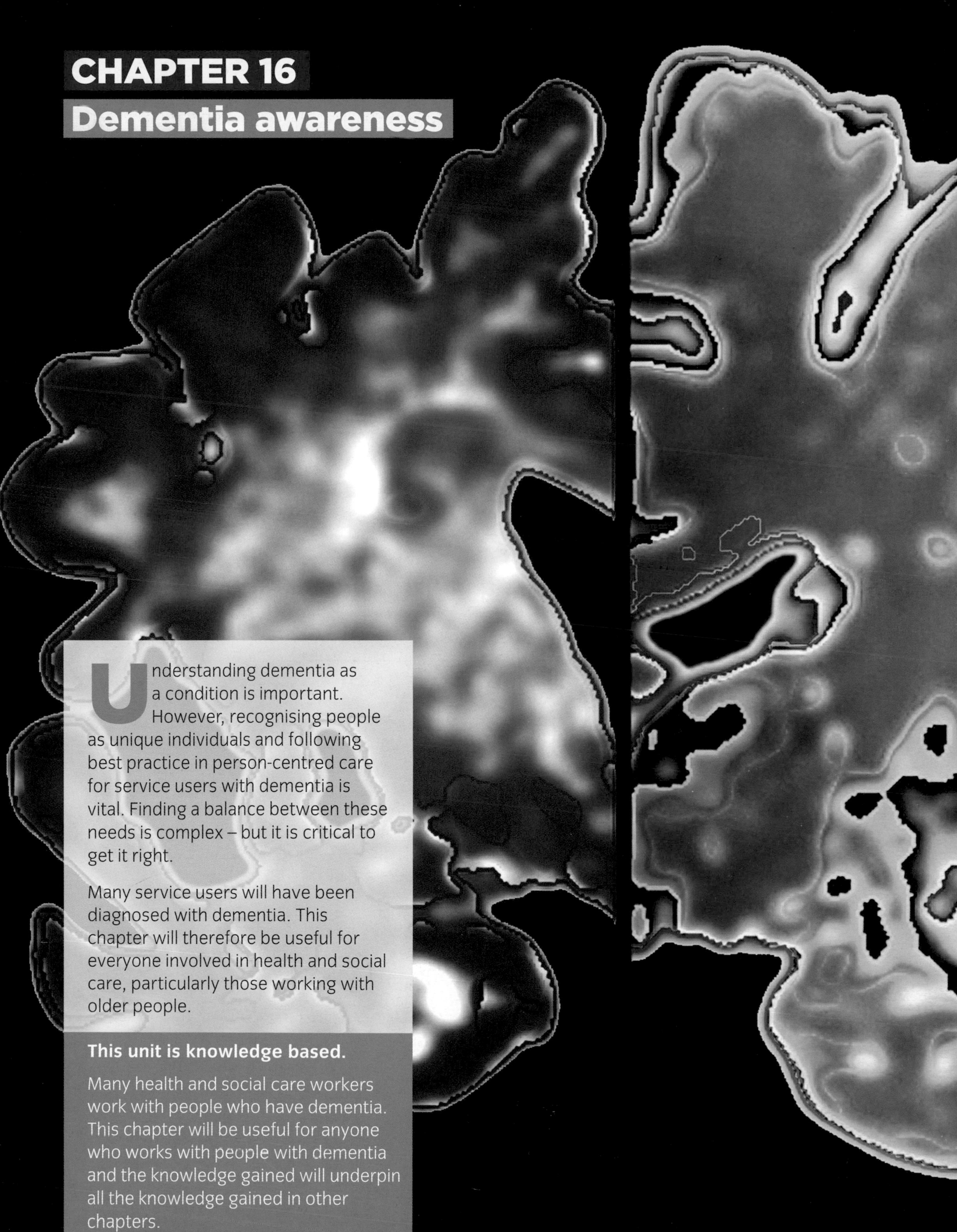

CHAPTER 16
Dementia awareness

Understanding dementia as a condition is important. However, recognising people as unique individuals and following best practice in person-centred care for service users with dementia is vital. Finding a balance between these needs is complex – but it is critical to get it right.

Many service users will have been diagnosed with dementia. This chapter will therefore be useful for everyone involved in health and social care, particularly those working with older people.

This unit is knowledge based.

Many health and social care workers work with people who have dementia. This chapter will be useful for anyone who works with people with dementia and the knowledge gained will underpin all the knowledge gained in other chapters.

UNDERSTANDING DEMENTIA

'Dementia syndrome' is an umbrella term which describes a range of symptoms such as memory loss, confusion, problems with communication and changes in mood. The rate at which the condition progresses varies for each individual, and according to the type of dementia they have. Types of dementia you may have heard of include Alzheimer's disease and vascular dementia. Dementia is a progressive condition and there is no known cure. Whatever type of dementia a person has, it is always important to treat them as an individual.

In understanding dementia it is important to know about the brain, and how dementia impairs this complex organ. The brain contains billions of cells, which are damaged by dementia, causing significant difficulties in brain functioning.

Alzheimer's Disease

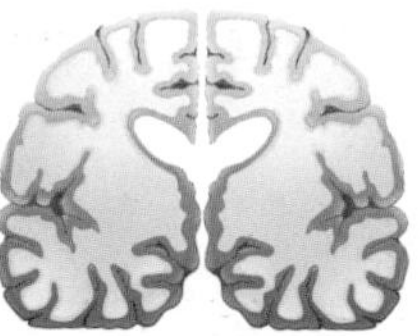

Healthy Brain

Mild Alzheimer's Disease

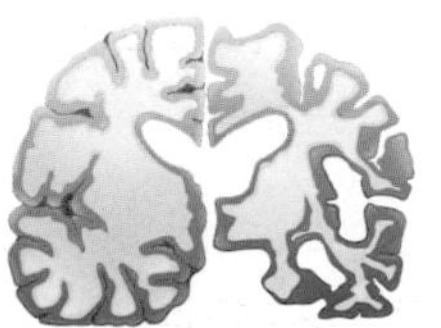

Severe Alzheimer's Disease

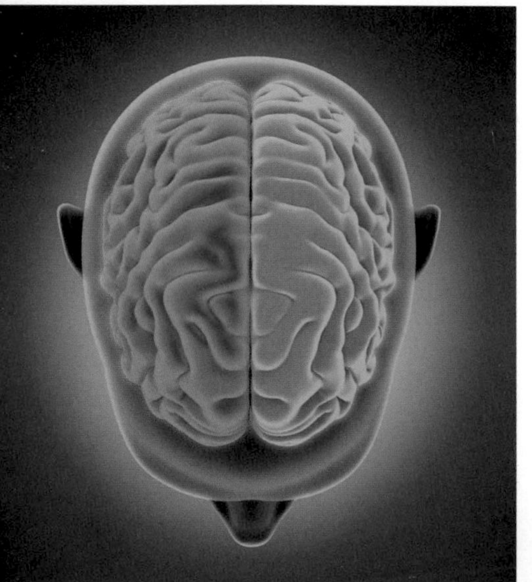

THE BRAIN AND ITS FUNCTIONS

The brain is split into two halves. Each half is responsible for different functions, which is why dementia that affects different parts of the brain may present with different symptoms.

- The right-hand side of the brain is responsible for gathering and collating the information received from the senses. Those with dementia that mostly affects the right-hand side of the brain can have more difficulty understanding the information their senses give them.
- The left-hand side of the brain is responsible for analysing this information. Those with dementia that mostly affects the left-hand side of the brain can have more difficulty with language, and they are more likely to experience depression.

POTENTIAL SIGNS AND SYMPTOMS OF DEMENTIA

The most common early signs of dementia include:

- memory problems
- decline in communication skills

- recognition difficulties
- co-ordination difficulties, which can affect mobility
- disorientation
- changes in behaviour, judgement and mood
- loss of daily life skills.

MEMORY IMPAIRMENT

Our brains are remarkable in their ability to store millions of memories, so that we can retrieve them when we need or want to. However, as they get older many people find remembering some people, phone numbers or events harder. Sometimes this is just because the more experiences we have, the more our brains have to discard other items stored in order to 'make way' for new events. Most people also find (at any age) that if they do not use a piece of information regularly, or practise a skill frequently, these become harder to remember.

However, as we age, the brain ages and may change. For example, the hippocampus (the part of the brain that stores our long-term memories) shrinks as a natural and normal part of ageing. The hippocampus is usually the first part of the brain to be affected by Alzheimer's disease, which is the most common form of dementia.

Memory problems can be caused by other factors apart from dementia, such as stress, mental health difficulties, being tired, physical ill-health, anxiety or the side-effects of some medicines. Some people also just have better (or more trained) memories than others.

The difference between having memory difficulties as a result of one or more of these factors or through the usual effects of ageing, and having them because of dementia can be difficult for untrained people to observe and diagnose. Sometimes the worry people have about being diagnosed with dementia can put them off asking for an assessment or help. This anxiety can also be made worse by others commenting on them becoming more forgetful.

It is important to recognise that the symptoms of dementia are unique to different people, and to the type of dementia. However, the symptoms are most likely to be shown by changes to the person's short-term memory.

Other changes can include:

- being able to remember things from much longer ago, but not from the recent past
- finding it hard to follow conversations, stories or television programmes

- feelings of confusion – even when they are in a familiar place
- losing track of what they are saying, or repeating themselves (eg asking the same question repeatedly)
- forgetting the names of people they know well, or of objects around them
- losing or misplacing items
- forgetting to take medicines
- forgetting that they have a disability – some people experience falls and so on as a consequence of this
- struggling to manage appointments and routines
- loss of self-care skills
- changes to their personality and lack of social etiquette.

Experiencing any of these changes is obviously distressing for a person, and they can feel that they are losing control of their own lives very quickly. The support and reassurance that you and others provide can be critical to their continued wellbeing.

PROCESSING INFORMATION

While most people know that dementia often affects people's memory, it is less widely understood that dementia can also affect the way that people process information. It is therefore useful to understand *how* people process information.

Key terms 

Neuron is a nerve cell. Most of the cells in the human brain are neurons.

Axon is the main body of the neuron cell.

Synapse is the space between the neuron cells.

Neurotransmitters are the chemicals that carry information in the brain.

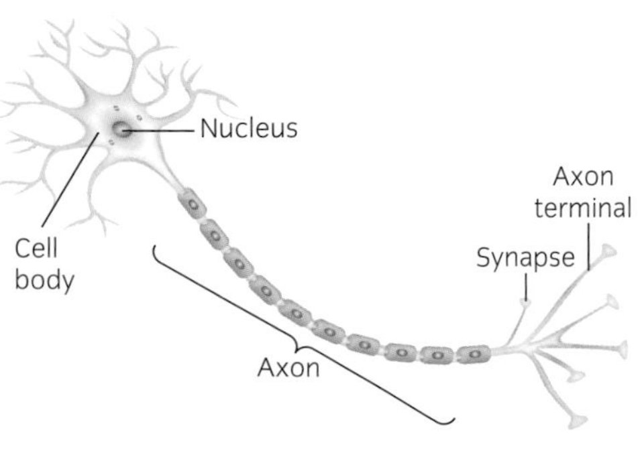

How the brain transmits information

Most of the 100 billion cells in our brains are **neurons**, and neurons communicate information with each other by transmitting chemicals. A neuron's 'body' is called its **axon**, and at the end of the axon, the neuron is able to fire information to the next neuron along. Think of this as like a row of people doing a Mexican wave, or transmitting a pulse by squeezing the hand of the next person in the row. The neurons are not connected to each other, but the chemical is fired across the tiny space between the neurons, which is called the **synapse**.

The chemicals that carry the information are called **neurotransmitters**. Over 60 of these have currently been identified, but you do not need to know about all of them. The main neurotransmitters are described in the table on the next page.

Chemical	What you need to know
Dopamine	• Controls the body's movements. • Controls the movement of information in the brain, so dopamine is associated with memory, attention and reasoning skills.
Serotonin	• Affects people's mood, anxiety levels, and thereby their behaviour. • Serotonin levels are enhanced by many anti-depressant medications, such as Prozac.
Acetylcholine	• Low levels of this neurotransmitter are associated with memory loss.
Glutamate	• Enables neurons to link up.

The way that dementia affects memory and the ability to process information is what creates the majority of the other symptoms of dementia.

HOW COMMON IS DEMENTIA?

Here are some key facts:

- Dementia affects both men and women.
- Over 820,000 people in the UK live with dementia (and this is predicted to rise as the population continues to age).
- A new case of dementia is diagnosed every 3.2 minutes in England and Wales.
- The cost of dementia to the UK economy is £23 billion per year, which is more than the total combined cost of heart disease and cancer.
- Research into dementia receives 12 times less funding than cancer research.
- 3.56 million people worldwide are living with dementia. The number is increasing all the time.
- Although the majority of people with dementia are over 65, younger people can have dementia, and over 17,000 people under 65 in the UK have dementia.
- One in three people over 65 years old will develop dementia.
- Research into dementia is complex and ever-evolving. There are key updates to research all the time, and research looks at causal factors and the impact of different treatments. Current research suggests that there could be some greater risks for individuals with a certain genetic make-up, but there are no proven links between dementia and inherited factors.

(Luengo-Fernandez, Leal and Gray 2010, Alzheimer's Research UK 2013, World Health Organization 2013)

TYPES OF DEMENTIA

Key term

Cognitive means relating to thinking and understanding.

The main forms of dementia that we currently know about are identified in the table below.

Type of dementia	What is known about it
Alzheimer's disease *According to the World Health Organisation (2013 online), Alzheimer's disease accounts for 60% of all dementia.*	• The most common type of dementia. • Cells in the brain die and the neurological processing of the brain changes. • Usually short-term memory problems are the first sign of Alzheimer's disease. • It is progressive. • There is no known cure.
Vascular dementia	• Occurs where there is a reduction in oxygen reaching the brain, caused by issues with circulation of blood within the brain which leads to the death of brain cells. • Often associated with the effects of a stroke, or many small strokes over a period of time. • A family history of heart disease, high cholesterol, diabetes and inactivity increases the risk of this condition.
Dementia with Lewy bodies	• Lewy bodies are abnormal structures which form inside brain cells – these then cause damage to the tissue of the person's brain. • Symptoms include the person feeling disoriented, or hallucinating. • The signs of this condition can be similar to those of Parkinson's disease, and individuals with this condition are more likely to struggle with problem solving and reasoning as well as loss of their memory.
Fronto-temperal dementia	• As the name suggests, this is associated with damage to the front part of the brain. • People are more likely to demonstrate changes in their personality or their behaviour in the first instance.
Prion diseases, eg Creutzfeltd–Jakob disease	• A rarer type of dementia. • Associated with the beef crisis from the 1980s. • Also referred to as 'mad cow disease'.
Dementia associated with HIV/AIDS	• In the later stages of AIDS, individuals develop **cognitive** impairment.
Other types, eg: • Dementia associated with the progression of multiple sclerosis, Huntington's disease, motor neurone disease or Parkinson's disease • Korsakoff's syndrome • Binswanger's disease • Progressive supernuclear palsy	• People who have certain other conditions have a higher risk of developing dementia. • Binswanger's disease affects some people aged over 60, and is a condition associated with the brain's 'white matter'. • Korsakoff's syndrome is associated with people who drink alcohol heavily over a long period of time. This leads to the loss of short-term memory.

CONDITIONS THAT MAY BE MISTAKEN FOR DEMENTIA

A range of other conditions can cause symptoms which might be mistaken for dementia:

- brain haemorrhage
- brain injury
- brain tumour
- issues with drugs or alcohol, or the side-effects of some medicines
- myalgic encephalomyelitis (ME), a condition which causes persistent fatigue
- hydrocephalus (a build-up of fluid on the brain)
- encephalitis (the brain becoming inflamed, usually because of a viral infection)
- multiple sclerosis (a neurological condition which affects the brain and spinal cord)
- tiredness or stress
- confusional states caused by infections
- depression or other mental health problems.

AGE-RELATED MEMORY IMPAIRMENT

As people get older they often find it harder to remember things. This is called age-related or age-associated memory impairment. Many people over the age of 60 have this problem, which can be mistaken for early signs of dementia.

DELIRIUM

Delirium is a state of confusion caused by rapid changes to brain function. It is often mistaken for dementia. However delirium is temporary and can be treated. It can be caused by infections, or liver or kidney failure, and might even be a side-effect of medication – particularly of anti-depressants.

DEPRESSION

If someone is clinically depressed they may experience slowed thinking, lowness in mood and lack of interest in life; their memory may be impaired and they might exhibit signs of confusion. According to the World Health Organization (2013 online), depression is more common than dementia in older adults. Because depression in older people leads to symptoms which are similar to dementia, people may well confuse the two conditions.

IMPORTANT NOTE

While this section has focused on the neurology of dementia and medical issues, it is vital to remember to adopt a social model of health and social care practice. This means recognising the person behind the diagnosis as a unique individual. It is also about the use of language – for example, it is important not to refer to a person as *suffering from* dementia, as this has negative and hopeless connotations. Rather you should talk about people *living with* dementia.

KEY THEORETICAL MODELS OF DEMENTIA

A theoretical model can be seen as a set of ideas – or a particular way of understanding something. So, the theoretical models of dementia are different ways of understanding dementia.

THE MEDICAL MODEL

The medical model focuses on dementia as a disease to be diagnosed and treated. It concentrates on people's needs and what is 'wrong with them'. The medical model sees the person with dementia as a problem that needs to be cured or corrected.

Within the medical model knowledge and expertise are seen as being located within the medical profession (doctors). Doctors are viewed as knowing what is best for the person. This knowledge is often made inaccessible by the use of language that is confusing. Words or phrases used within the medical model include:

- *diagnosis* – what is wrong with the person
- *prognosis* – likely outcome, eg cure or learn to live with the condition
- *aetiology* – cause or origin of illness
- *pathology* – change occurring due to illness or disease.

THE SOCIAL MODEL

The social model draws a distinction between impairments (a recognition that a part of the body is not functioning) and disability. A person with an impairment is disabled (prevented from doing things) by society. So the social model sees a person with dementia as being 'disabled' by society.

The social model has championed the expertise of the person: only the person themselves knows what is best for them. Just because a person has a diagnosis of dementia it should not mean that they are viewed as lacking in expertise about their own situation.

The social model often refers to the way that people are devalued by society, and oppressed once they have a label or a diagnosis.

In dementia care the social model covers key aspects of best practice in health and social care, outlining how people can be supported to live well with dementia. These aspects of health and social care include:

- communicating with people in ways that meet their needs
- seeing people as unique individuals
- treating people with respect and dignity
- care with compassion
- person-centred care
- supporting people in ways that promote active support.

These aspects of best practice are covered throughout this publication.

KEY POINTS

- Medical models emphasise people's needs, deficits and 'treatments'.
- Social models are about access to resources and people's rights.

INDIVIDUAL EXPERIENCES OF DEMENTIA

Everyone is an individual, and therefore everyone will have a different experience of dementia. The way that people experience dementia will depend on a range of factors, including the type of dementia they have, their age, the support they have from others, their level of ability, whether they have any other conditions and their physical health.

THE STAGES OF DEMENTIA

While everyone will experience dementia differently, it is commonly accepted that there are three stages to dementia.

Early stage

In the early stages of dementia, people may:

- forget about recent conversations or events
- repeat themselves
- struggle to take on new ideas
- lose the thread of what is being said
- become confused
- find it harder to make decisions
- lose interest in other people or activities
- mislay items and blame others.

Often, because these symptoms appear gradually, the early stage may not be recognised until the person moves into the middle stage. Those around the person may put the changes down to 'getting older', or to a stressful event such as a bereavement.

The early stages of dementia may be concerning to a person, but they do not generally have a very significant impact on that person's independence.

DISCUSSING NEEDS AND PREFERENCES

During the early and middle stages of dementia the person's impairment – particularly the memory loss they are experiencing – can be transient. This means that they may be more able to engage in detailed discussions at some times than others (there may be times when they are more 'lucid'). Therefore it is important to take the opportunity to talk to the person about their needs and preferences during these times.

Middle stage

At this stage the symptoms progress to the point where they begin to have a significant impact on people's lives:

- As they become more forgetful and confused they may need to be reminded and assisted to eat, to wash, to use the toilet, to get dressed, etc.
- As they become more confused they may get lost when they are out.
- People may become confused between day and night, which means they may go out at night.
- People might put themselves or others at risk as a result of increasing forgetfulness; for example, they may leave the gas turned on on the cooker without lighting it.
- People might begin to have hallucinations.

The way that people react to this stage is very individual, but they may also become angry and aggressive, or they may become withdrawn and clingy towards those they love.

While this stage of dementia is very concerning to the person and their family, they may still be able to maintain their independence by receiving help and support in specific areas and by changes being made to their environment. For example, a gas cooker may be replaced with an electric cooker.

Late stage

At this stage people generally become much more dependent on others. Their memory loss will become more profound and they will become unable to recognise familiar surroundings or even close loved ones. They may also become increasingly frail, and start to shuffle or walk unsteadily. They may also experience:

- difficulty in eating and, sometimes, swallowing
- incontinence – losing control of their bladder and sometimes their bowels as well
- gradual loss of speech, though they may repeat a few words or cry out from time to time.

People may become angry and aggressive, particularly at times when they are being given support with personal care. It is vital that those caring for them do not take this personally and that they do not consider actions to be deliberately aggressive.

The speed of these stages is very individual and is also related to the type of dementia a person has. As a general guide, people with Alzheimer's disease, for example, will probably live for eight to ten years after the onset of symptoms, while those with other forms of dementia will generally live about seven years. Life expectancy does depend on the age of the person (those diagnosed in their sixties and seventies will generally live longer than people diagnosed in their eighties and nineties) and their general health prior to the onset of symptoms.

MAKING EXPERIENCES MORE POSITIVE

The experiences of people with dementia can be made more positive through the use of positive care techniques, such as:

- person-centred care
- active support
- empowerment.

It is beneficial too when care workers adopt the values of person-centred care practice, including:

- individuality
- choice
- privacy
- independence
- dignity
- respect
- partnership.

CASE STUDY

Mr Kyle is a widower. He has a daughter and a son, but they live some distance away and he doesn't see them as often as he would like. Mr Kyle has had an allotment for a number of years and enjoys growing his own vegetables. Mr Kyle has regularly shared the vegetables he has grown with his neighbours, and he is well known in his local community.

Mr Kyle has been forgetting things for a while – he can't remember his neighbours' names now – but he still pops round with vegetables. Mr Kyle has put his memory loss down to getting older and he hasn't been too worried about it.

However, Mr Kyle's friends and neighbours have become increasingingly concerned about him. He has been seen walking down the road in his pyjamas, and the local shopkeeper has noticed that Mr Kyle is coming into the shop several times a day without buying anything. One morning Mr Kyle is seen at the allotments still wearing his pyjamas. When Mr Lanthus (one of the other allotment holders) approaches Mr Kyle, he becomes quite aggressive. Concerned for Mr Kyle's wellbeing, Mr Lanthus telephones the police.

- What might be happening to Mr Kyle?
- What risks might there be?
- What could be done to support Mr Kyle to remain as independent as possible?

MYTHS AND STEREOTYPES OF DEMENTIA

The impact of stereotyping, prejudice and discrimination is explored in detail in Chapter 3. In terms of dementia, some myths and stereotypes can have a negative impact on people and their family, as described in the table below.

Myth	Impact of the myth	Truth
People with dementia are like children (they are in their 'second childhood').	Adults are treated as children and will feel patronised. Services may '**infantilise**' people (which means treating people as though they are children) leading to a lack of rights, choices and freedom.	Adults with dementia are adults. They have a wealth of life experiences.
People with dementia are dangerous.	People may have their freedom restricted. Health and social care workers might approach people with dementia as though they expect them to be violent.	People with dementia are not dangerous. At times people may engage in behaviours which can be interpreted as aggressive but this is usually because of a misunderstanding in communication.
People with dementia don't know what is happening to them.	Health and social care workers might provide care without explaining this to the person. This can lead to further confusion and frustration.	Even in the very late stages of dementia people are aware of their surroundings, whether they are being treated with dignity and whether those caring for them are doing so with compassion.
People with dementia can't make any decisions.	Others may make decisions for the person – denying the person's rights.	A person's capacity to make a decision will fluctuate. People may be able to make some decisions but not others, or people may be able to make decisions at certain times of the day and not others, for example.
People with dementia need 24-hour care.	People may be moved away from their own home into unfamiliar surroundings – which can increase their confusion.	Many people with dementia live at home with various levels of support – even in the late stages of the condition.

Key term

Infantilise relates to the way in which adults who have disabilities can be treated as though they were a children.

All of these stereotypes can affect people (service users and their carers) in different ways:

- People may be reluctant to access assessments, a diagnosis, and service provision.
- People may not disclose their diagnosis (either to close family members, or to others in their wider network).
- Stereotypes and stigma increase anxiety and fear, which can in turn have a negative impact on the person's symptoms.
- Carers may be more reluctant to come forward and access their entitlements; they can also feel disloyal to the person and guilty about wanting or needing extra support in their caring role.

ATTITUDES AND BEHAVIOURS

What we think has an impact on how we feel and on what we do. Therefore, if people hold a negative view of dementia and believe some of the myths covered earlier, then this will have a negative impact on people with dementia.

If people hold more positive views about dementia and behave in a way that promotes dignity, recognising the person with dementia as a unique individual, this will have a positive impact on the way that people behave. This may enable people to discuss their experiences of living with dementia more openly.

REFLECT

Can you think of times when you have noticed people having negative attitudes towards dementia? How might you challenge these attitudes?

HOW TO SUPPORT PEOPLE WITH DEMENTIA AND THEIR FAMILIES

Health and social care workers should follow the principles of good person-centred practice when working with all individuals. It is following these principles that will best support people with dementia and their family members.

Remember the key aspects of person-centred care and the values of health and social care. These values include:

- a commitment to promoting human rights
- upholding personal dignity
- seeing people as unique individuals
- promoting choice and self-determination
- respecting individuals
- listening and empowering
- working in partnership with people
- recognising and addressing potential conflict
- safeguarding needs and the capacity of individuals
- being sensitive to diversity and putting people in control.

Ultimately, these all relate to individual rights. After all, the people you work with have a basic right to be treated as unique individuals, with respect and dignity, and to be able to make choices.

Before you conclude this chapter take some time to think about the following:

- What have you learnt about dementia?
- How might what you have learnt assist you in your work?
- How might you challenge some of the myths and assumptions about dementia?
- Why is it important to challenge these myths and assumptions?

Understanding the neurology and process of dementia is important in understanding dementia as a condition. However, recognising people as unique individuals and following best practice in person centred care for individuals with dementia is vital. People with dementia have unique experiences of the condition. Getting the balance is between understanding the condition but seeing people as unique individuals is complex but it is critical matter to get right.

CHAPTER 17
Understanding the context of supporting individuals with learning disabilities

This unit is generally completed by health and social care workers who specifically support adults with a learning disability. It covers the background context of learning disability support through exploring the meaning of learning disability, and some of the common experiences of people with learning disabilities particularly in relation to oppression and exclusion. Increasingly, as the support provided for adults with learning disabilities has become less segregated, health and social care workers working in a range of areas may become involved in supporting a person with a learning disability. This chapter will therefore be helpful to you even if you are not completing this particular unit.

This unit is knowledge based.

Many health and social care workers work with people who have learning disabilities. This chapter will be useful for anyone who works with people with learning disabilities and the knowledge gained will underpin all the knowledge gained in other chapters.

THE NATURE AND CHARACTERISTICS OF LEARNING DISABILITY

The terms 'learning disability' and 'learning difficulty' are often used interchangeably in health and social care services – that is, they are seen to mean the same or a similar thing. However, there are differences.

LEARNING DISABILITY OR LEARNING DIFFICULTY?

In education services the term learning difficulty may be used to describe a range of specific difficulties that people have with learning – for example, it may be used to describe a person who has dyslexia. This is very different from a learning disability.

Common terminology

In the UK it is most common to refer to learning disabilities; in other countries the most common terms are intellectual disabilities or developmental disabilities.

The professional definition of learning disability

The term learning disability involves three aspects:

- intellectual impairment (which is generally understood in relation to the intelligence quotient, or IQ)
- an impairment of social functioning
- onset at an early age (generally seen as onset before the age of 18).

In the general population, intelligence and social skills vary from person to person. Just as a person may go to university but have poor social functioning skills, so a person with a learning disability may not be academic but they could have the ability to learn a wide range of social functioning skills.

Key term

IQ means intelligence quota.

In relation to intellectual impairment, **IQ** tests are generally still used as the measure. While these tests have been criticised, they are still used. The continuum shown in the table is often used by professionals to explain learning disabilities.

Level of learning disability	Likely support needs
Borderline (IQ 70–80)	Formally a person labelled as borderline does not have a learning disability. They may have gone to special school but after that tend to integrate into society. People can still have difficulties with literacy, especially with official forms (eg for accessing benefits).
Mild learning disability (IQ 50–70)	People at this level may well be able to read and write and can learn many social and independence skills such that they are able to live independently with no formal support, or very low-level support. People with a mild learning disability are often able to engage in paid work if they are adequately supported.
Moderate learning disability (IQ 35–50)	People with a moderate learning disability may well have good social and independence skills. They are likely to require support in skills that are less well developed. If living away from a family home, people with a moderate learning disability will probably need staff support.
Severe learning disability (IQ 20–35)	People with a severe learning disability will have a range of skills and interests that can be further developed. It is likely that people will have significant support needs in relation to basic skills such as personal care. There are likely to be communication aspects to consider. People may also have physical disabilities, eg sensory impairments or cerebral palsy.
Profound learning disability (IQ below 20)	Sometimes this is termed 'profound and multiple learning disabilities' (PMLD). A person with profound learning disabilities is likely to have very significant support needs. Often there can be health issues as well.

LEARNING DISABILITIES FACTS AND FIGURES

In 2011 the British Institute of Learning Disabilities (BILD) reviewed a range of research, and estimated that:

- about 2% of the general population have a learning disability
- just under 0.5% of the adult population are known to use learning disability services
- just over 6% of people with moderate to severe learning disabilities known to adult social care services are in paid employment.

(Holland 2011)

Calderstones Partnership NHS Trust states that:

- males are more likely than females to have both severe learning disabilities (average ratio 1.2 males: 1 female) and mild learning disabilities (average ratio 1.6 males: 1 female);
- mild learning disabilities are more common among boys/men, young people, people who are poorer and people from disadvantaged family backgrounds.

(Calderstones Partnership NHS Trust 2013)

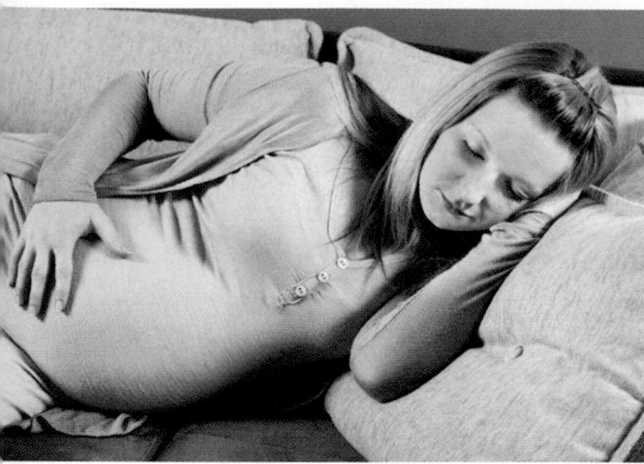

POSSIBLE CAUSES OF LEARNING DISABILITY

Learning disability can be caused before birth, during birth or after birth:

- **Before birth (prenatal):** Learning disability can occur before birth due to chromosomal or genetic factors. Examples of this include Down's syndrome and Fragile X syndrome.
- **During birth (perinatal):** Learning disability can also be caused during birth, for example, as a result of the baby suffering a shortage of oxygen.
- **After birth (postnatal):** For most people with a learning disability, the disability is present from birth or during very early development. However, learning disabilities can be caused by a range of things in early life. Metabolic disorders such as Phenylketonuria (PKU) or Reyes syndrome can cause severe learning disabilities. Illnesses such as meningitis and the onset of severe epilepsy can also cause learning disability. It is also clear that some learning disabilities can be caused by neglect and a lack of stimulation in early life.

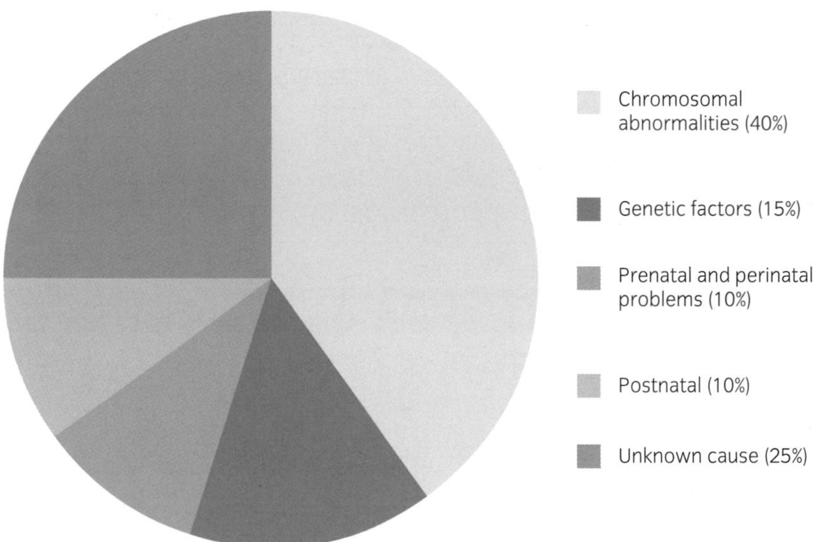

Unknown causes

In a significant number of cases the cause of a person's learning disability will always remain unknown.

The NHS Knowledge Network (2013a) identifies that about 50% of mild learning disabilities have no known cause. In people with severe or profound learning disabilities, chromosomal abnormalities cause about 40% of cases. Genetic factors account for 15%, prenatal and perinatal problems 10%, and postnatal issues a further 10%. Cases which are of unknown cause are fewer, but still high at around 25%.

THE MEDICAL AND SOCIAL MODELS OF DISABILITY

Historically there have been a number of ways of understanding disabilities. These are referred to as models of disability. The two most commonly used models to understand disability are the social model and the medical model.

The medical model

The medical model is based on understanding the reasons for a disability and seeing the 'problem' as lying with the individual. The medical model sees the impairment as the problem and thinks that the problem needs to be cured or corrected. The ideas promoted by the medical model are as follows:

- The learning disability is viewed as bad or undesirable. Having a disability is seen as suffering a personal tragedy.
- Knowledge and expertise are seen as located within the medical profession (doctors). They know what is best for the person. This knowledge is made inaccessible to others by a language that is confusing. Associated words and phrases include:
- *diagnosis* – what is wrong with the person.
- *prognosis* – likely outcome, eg cure or learn to live with the condition.
- *aetiology* – cause or origin of illness.
- *pathology* – change occurring due to illness or disease.
- The disability, impairment or mental health problem has to be diagnosed. This is a form of labelling. The label is viewed very negatively in society.
- The person with the learning disability has to fit into society as it is and if they can't, then they are excluded or removed.

FOCUS

Focusing on the causes of a person's learning disability can lead towards the medical model of disability. Focusing on each person as a unique individual is much more important.

The social model

The social model of disability was generated in the 1970s and has progressively evolved. The ideas behind the social model include the following:

- The concept of 'normal' is misleading and unhelpful. Instead there should be recognition that diversity is part of our human condition.

- The social model draws a distinction between impairment (a recognition that a part of the body is not functioning) and disability. A person with an impairment is disabled (prevented from doing things) by society.
- Society disables people due to viewing their impairment negatively and then comprehensively discriminates against people with an impairment.
- The social model has made clear that society can make itself accessible to all people and disabled people have a right to equal opportunities.
- The social model has worked to counter the negative stigma associated with the labels applied to people.
- Within learning disability services the stigma of the label has been so difficult to shake off that a mantra has evolved to counteract it: 'label jars, not people'.
- The social model has championed the expertise of the person. Only the person themselves knows what is best for them.

KEY POINTS

- The medical model emphasises people's needs, deficits and 'treatments'.
- The social model is about access to resources and people's rights.

The medical model of disability views disability as a 'problem' that belongs to the disabled person, while the social model draws on the idea that it is society that disables people. For example, if a person who uses a wheelchair is unable to get into a building because of some steps, the medical model would suggest that this is because of the wheelchair, rather than the steps. By contrast, the social model would see the steps as the disabling barrier.

THE IMPACT OF LEARNING DISABILITIES

Having a learning disability has a significant impact on both individuals and those around them – their family and friends, for example. The main impact of learning disabilities that people report is discrimination. It is important to note that in many ways it is not the learning disability itself that impacts on the individual, but the attitudes and assumptions of other people.

DISCRIMINATION AND LEARNING DISABILITIES

It would be useful for you to reconsider the issues surrounding discrimination covered in Chapter 3 at this point.

People with learning disabilities experience discrimination in society. This can take a number of forms:

- *Overt discrimination*. For example, where a person is treated less favourably than others because of their learning disability.

- *Discrimination in employment*. Many people with a learning disability want to work. However, the employment rate of people with a learning disability is much lower than the rate of employment among people with a physical disability, and even lower in comparison with the employment rate of the general population.
- *Being called names*. Even where this is not through negative intentions, there is still a lot of outdated and oppressive terminology in use connected with learning disabilities.
- *Covert discrimination*. For example, where perceptions and ideas about learning disability influence how the person feels they are being treated; how others approach the person (even where they do not intend to be discriminatory towards them); and how the person is able to access opportunities and resources.

THE SOCIAL IMPACTS OF HAVING A LEARNING DISABILITY

Regrettably, when a person has learning disabilities they are at risk of negative social experiences. Examples include:

- *Financial issues*. These come from having to live on state welfare benefits which are means tested and at a subsistence level, and do not readily allow for a comfortable lifestyle. Payment is often made to another party to manage on the person's behalf.
- *Transition to adult life*. Young people with learning disabilities often leave school without a clear route towards a fulfilling and productive adult life.
- *Choice and control*. Many people with a learning disability have little or no choice or control in their lives. Advocacy services are patchy. Direct payments have been slow to take off for people with learning disability. See pages 484-6 for more information on this.
- *Healthcare*. The substantial healthcare needs of people with learning disabilities often go unmet. This can mean that people either become unwell unnecessarily, or that they do not get well as quickly as they should.
- *Housing*. This is felt to be the key to achieving social inclusion. The numbers of people with learning disabilities being supported to live independently in the community remains small. There is often no real choice, and people receive little advice about possible housing options.
- *Social isolation*. This remains a problem for many people.
- *Employment*. This is just as much an aspiration for people who have a learning difficulty as it is for others. However, currently fewer than 10% are in any form of work, so most people spend a lifetime on state welfare benefits.

SERVICE DELIVERY

Generally the way a service operates is the most significant factor in the impact that a person's learning disability has on them, as can be seen from the following diagrams.

Negative service delivery

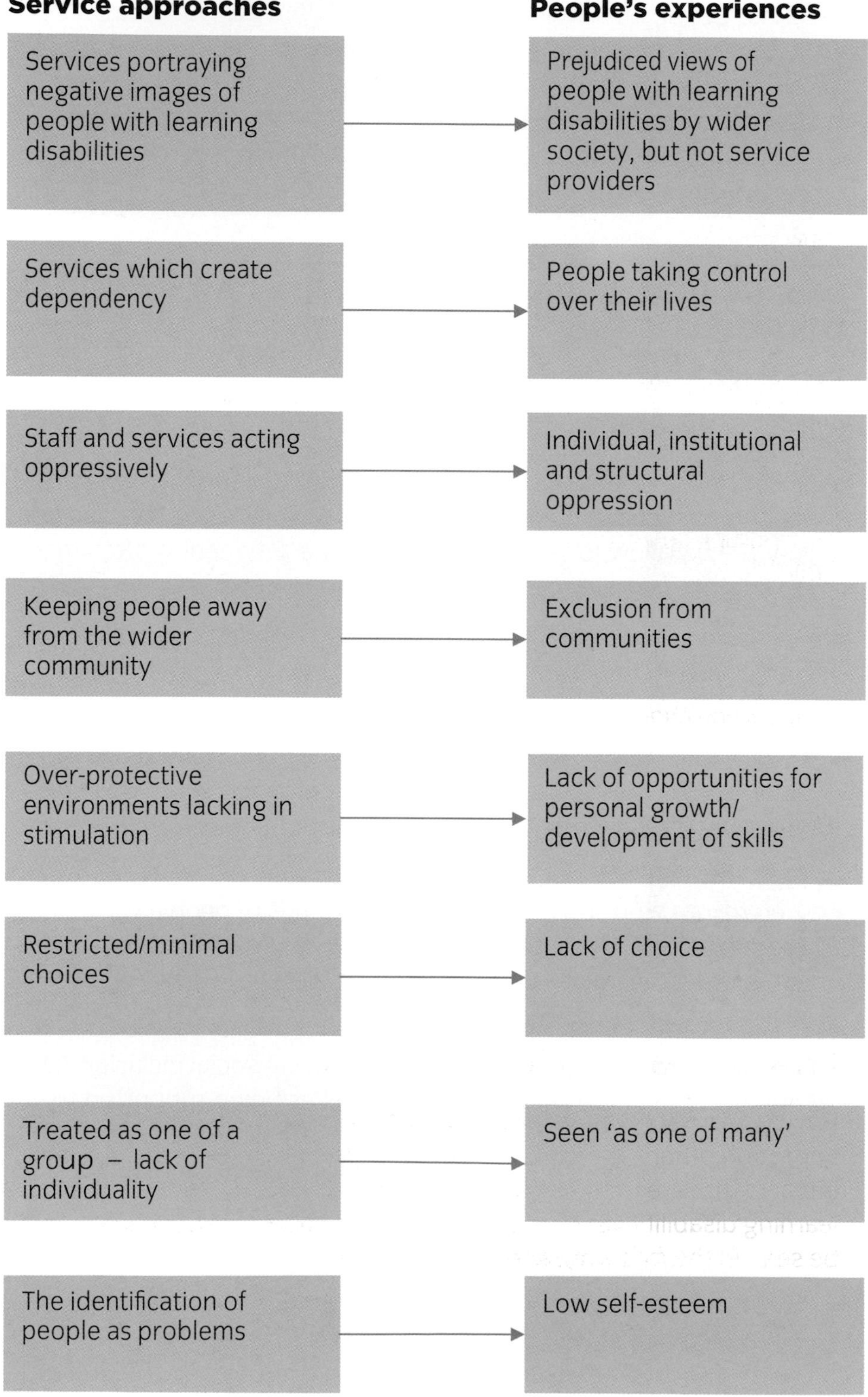

Positive service delivery

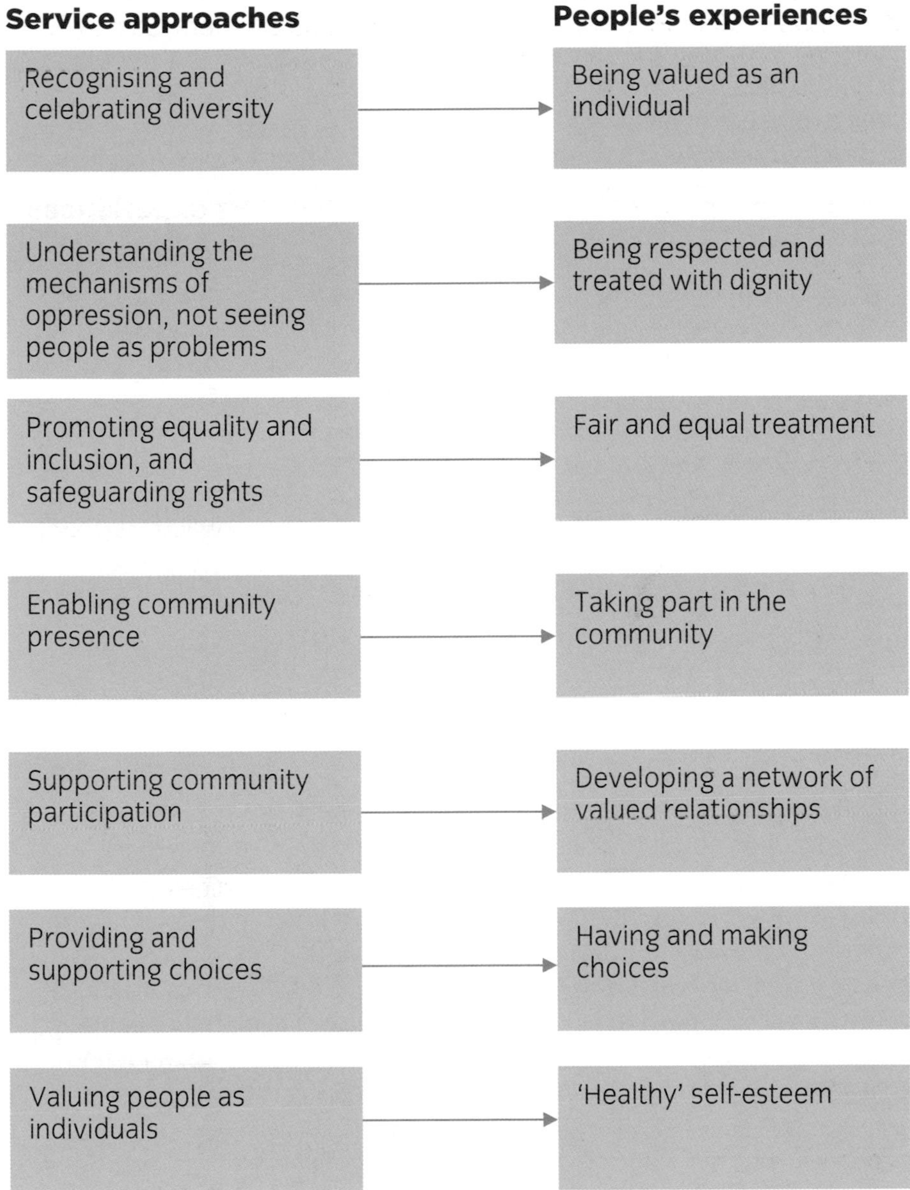

IMPACT ON A FAMILY OF A MEMBER HAVING A LEARNING DISABILITY

Having a family member who has a learning disability has a significant impact on other family members in a range of ways. Many of the impacts that are covered above in relation to the person with the learning disability also affect their family members. Other impacts can be seen in the following areas.

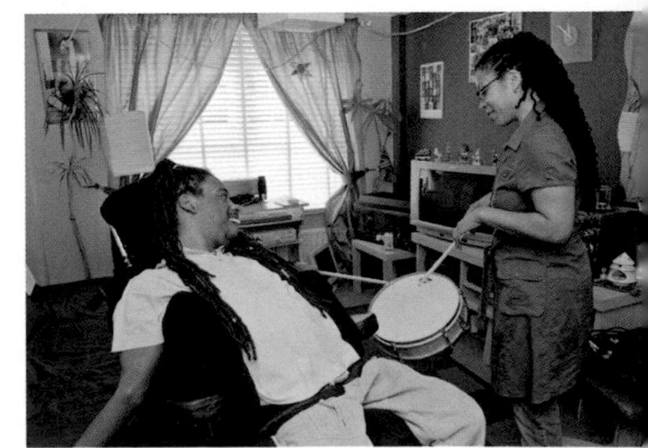

Psychological and emotional impact	People can experience a range of feelings about having a family member with a learning disability: • They may be embarrassed about their family member's disability – often siblings are embarrassed during their teenage years. • Often parents of a child with a learning disability report feeling guilty – that they are in some way to blame for the person's disability. They also report feeling a sense of loss for the 'normal' child they expected to have. • Family members can develop mental health difficulties because of the pressures of a caring role. • Family members – particularly parents of adults with learning disabilities – may well have fears for the future. 'What will happen after I'm gone?' is a concern for many parents, for example.
Practical impact	• Family members who need to provide care for their loved one may need to reduce their hours of employment, or stop working altogether in order to care for someone full-time. • There can be issues around getting everything done, especially if the person cared for has lots of appointments to juggle. In turn this can create additional stress for carers. • Family members and carers report that as they take on the caring role they have much less time available to themselves, and even where they can maintain their employment they will not be able to take part in leisure activities which they previously enjoyed.
Financial impact	• If a family member's employment situation changes, clearly this will have a financial impact on them. • Accessing carer's benefits and benefits for the person with the learning disability may be difficult. • A family with a member who has a learning disability may have higher costs and diminished employment prospects.
The impact of using services	• Family members are often confused by the number of professionals and services involved, and may need some clarification about the different services and their various roles. • Family members who are carers can feel undervalued by public services and lack the right information and enough support to meet their caring responsibilities. • Carers for those with learning disabilities may not always see themselves as a carer, but identify themselves as a father, mother, sibling, etc. Carers can also be focused on their family member's needs, and find it hard to talk about or recognise the impact of caring on themselves. This can also be exacerbated by feelings of stress, embarrassment and sometimes guilt (eg if someone is stating for the first time that caring is becoming too much for them).
Social exclusion	• Whole families can feel socially excluded because of the impact of discrimination. • Where people have to leave employment or stop being involved in leisure activities, this is likely to leave them more socially isolated.
Positive impacts	• Health and social care can concentrate too much on the negative impacts of having a person with a learning disability in the family. However, it is important to recognise the strengths of people with learning disabilities, and part of this is about recognising that there can be positive impacts on family members. • Also, many people with a learning disability are not fooled like so many of us. Someone's wealth, title, accent or dress may be of no consequence to a person with a learning disability. They will judge someone on how they act towards them. • Many people would say that when they are with a person with a learning disability they can be themselves more, and they can feel that all the barriers and defensiveness that they maintain against the world slowly recede.

CASE STUDY

Jude is a 32-year-old nursery nurse. She really enjoys her job and gets a lot of satisfaction from supporting children to develop new skills. Jude is single and recently joined a dating agency, as she is keen to have a relationship – she would like to get married and have children one day. Jude lives in her own flat. Her mother died recently and she spends quite a lot of time supporting her dad. Jude's sister is married and has children – she also regularly visits her dad to help out. Jude has Down's syndrome.

Jude would describe herself in many different ways – for example, she is a sister, a daughter, a nursery nurse and a single woman looking for love. Very often when health and social care workers become involved with a person their diagnosis or label becomes the first thing that is said about the individual. So a health and social care worker might describe Jude as a person with a learning disability before referring to any of the other aspects of Jude's life.

- How might Jude's father describe Jude?
- How might Jude's sister describe her?
- How might the children at the nursery where Jude works describe her?
- What might the dating agency profile say about Jude?
- What might a health and social care worker say about Jude?

THE HISTORICAL CONTEXT OF LEARNING DISABILITY

As described, stereotypes of people with learning disabilities may have a significant impact on the services that are provided and the experiences that people have. It is easy to see that the stereotyped views of people with learning disabilities have had a major impact on the provision of services historically. This is shown in the chart. (The modern views appear in the bottom row.)

The cause of the learning disability was seen as:	The individual was seen as:	The goal of society was:	The service model was:
God's will	Holy innocent	Mercy, pity	Charity/religious
Sin	Sinful (by choice)	Punish individual, protect society	Workhouse
Fate	Hopeless victim	Protect individual	Asylum

The cause of the learning disability was seen as:	The individual was seen as:	The goal of society was:	The service model was:
Single physical factor	Sick	Diagnosis and cure	Hospital
Contagious or hereditary	Dangerous menace	Protect society	Detain, imprison
Without rationale	Burden	Institutional, economic independence	Farm, colony
Individual needs	Person with rights	Ordinary life	Inclusion

In the past, the way that people with a learning disability were viewed directly affected the type of care they received.

Seeing the person as a child

Adults with learning disabilities were often viewed as perpetual children. This resulted in decisions being made for them, and people with a learning disability would be talked about but not talked to directly, even when they were present. Also many activities people engaged in were directly drawn from children's activities; children's jigsaws, children's colouring books, etc. Adults with learning disabilities tended to be over-protected.

Seeing the person as a dangerous menace

Adults with learning disabilities were often seen as a social and sexual menace – the worry was that they would have lots of children, most of whom would also have learning disabilities, and society would be swamped. This negative attitude resulted in the sexuality of people with learning disabilities being controlled. In the past, sterilisation without medical justification was conducted; more recently long-term use of the pill has been used. People were kept segregated so that men and women rarely mixed. When they did it was closely supervised.

Seeing the person as ill

People with learning disabilities were often viewed as sick or ill. This resulted in people being diagnosed and kept in institutions that were termed hospitals. They were cared for by nurses and doctors.

Difference being negatively viewed

Generally, since people with learning disabilities were seen as different and that difference was viewed as bad, undesirable and so on, they were kept in institutions (eg hospitals, asylums or workhouses) or were hidden by families and hardly went out of the family home. The intention was to keep people away from mainstream society – effectively segregating them.

Institutions, such as the old long-stay hospitals, gathered large numbers of people together and these hospitals were managed with the minimum of resources possible. This resulted in large dormitory wards with the most simple furnishings, minimum numbers of staff and basic meals. Too often there was not enough food.

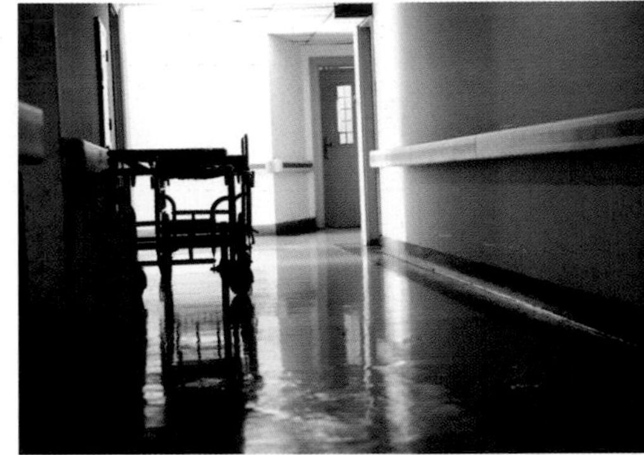

The process of institutionalisation resulted in controlling people being more important than providing care and support, and the smooth running of the hospital more important than meeting individual needs. As a result, people developed an adherence to rigid routines, agreeing with those in authority (they would never or rarely complain) and people would not have the opportunity to develop their own identities. The institution had an impact on all aspects of people's lives. The regimes were brutal and brutalising. In the hospitals, residents would steal clothes and food from each other because they lacked the basic necessities.

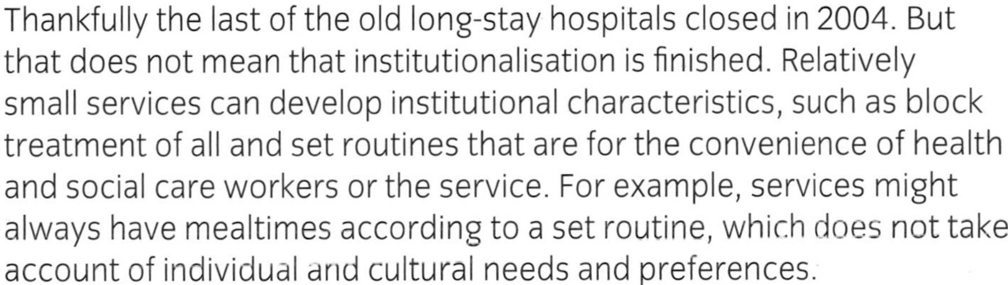

Thankfully the last of the old long-stay hospitals closed in 2004. But that does not mean that institutionalisation is finished. Relatively small services can develop institutional characteristics, such as block treatment of all and set routines that are for the convenience of health and social care workers or the service. For example, services might always have mealtimes according to a set routine, which does not take account of individual and cultural needs and preferences.

KEY CHANGES IN LEARNING DISABILITY SERVICES

As described, there have been significant changes in the way services for people with learning disabilities have been provided, and clearly this has had an impact on the experiences of people with learning disabilities. The key changes can be summarised as shown in the table.

	Historically	Key changes
Where people live	People lived in large 'hospitals' or segregated services.	People choose where to live. They may live in small supported-living environments or may be supported to live independently.
Daytime activities	People engaged in childlike activities, often in large group settings.	People choose activities based on their interests and skills. They engage in a wide range of activities which the general population enjoy.

	Historically	Key changes
Employment	People did not generally have access to paid employment.	A range of supported employment services exist which support people with learning disabilities to find employment and to learn the skills of the job with graduated support.
Sexual relationships and parenthood	People with learning disabilities were not seen as sexual. People were denied opportunities to engage in sexual relationships and were not able to become parents.	The right of people to have intimate and sexual relationships is recognised. 'Dating agencies' operate to support people with learning disabilities to meet a partner.
Provision of healthcare	People with learning disabilities received poor healthcare services. They were denied some medical procedures which could be lifesaving.	People should have access to healthcare services which recognise them as unique individuals. People should not be discriminated against in terms of healthcare procedures.

It is important to recognise that while significant changes have occurred in relation to the life opportunities of people with learning disabilities, there are still major problems in connection with equality of opportunity.

'INSTITUTIONALISATION WITHOUT WALLS'

Institutionalisation was an expression of negative attitudes towards people with learning disabilities. Unfortunately, as some negative societal attitudes persist, there is still a risk that people with learning disabilities could be subject to what has become referred to as 'institutionalisation without walls'. People may be denied or discouraged from taking opportunities to integrate into society, discouraged or not supported to develop friendships or personal relationships, and denied opportunities to become parents.

The nature and extent of social exclusion experienced by people with learning disabilities are of continuing concern.

The current government still believes that despite much committed work by health and social care workers, public services have failed to make consistent progress in helping people with learning disabilities overcome social exclusion (Department of Health 2009b). There are still key areas to be addressed:

- *Expense.* Families with learning-disabled members have higher costs and diminished employment prospects.
- *Transition to adult life.* Young learning-disabled people often leave school without a clear route towards a fulfilling and productive adult life.
- *Carers.* They can feel undervalued by public services, and lack the right information and enough support to meet their caring responsibilities.
- *Choice and control.* Many people with learning disabilities have little or no choice or control in their lives.
- *Healthcare.* The substantial healthcare needs of people with learning disabilities often go unmet. The poor quality of healthcare for adults with learning disabilities is evidenced in the *Six Lives* report (see the following page).
- *Housing.* This is felt the key to achieving social inclusion. The numbers being supported to live independently in the community remain small. There is often no real choice and people receive little advice about possible housing options.
- *Day services.* These frequently fail to provide flexible and individual support. Some centres remain large, and it appears that they offer just a daytime caring service rather than undertaking a wider range of individually tailored activities.
- *Social isolation.* This remains a problem for many people. A recent study showed that only 30% had a friend who was not either learning disabled, part of their family or paid to care for them.
- *Employment.* This is just as much an aspiration for people who have learning difficulties as it is for others. However, currently less than 10% are in any form of work, so most people spend a lifetime on social security benefits.
- *Minority ethnic communities.* People from these communities and their needs are too often overlooked. People with learning disabilities and their families encounter language barriers and a lack of understanding regarding cultural traditions and beliefs.

Six Lives: the provision of public services to people with learning disabilities (2009)

Key term

Local Government Ombudsman is an official who has been appointed to look into complaints about councils and other organisations.

Following a request from Mencap, the **Local Government Ombudsman** looked into complaints from family members of six adults with learning disabilities who died while in health and social care services between 2003 and 2005. The investigation 'illustrated some significant and distressing failures in service across both health and social care'. A range of recommendations were made as a result:

- People must be treated as individuals.
- Basic care must be well provided.
- Leadership needs to be improved.
- Policy, standards and guidance must be followed.
- Workers should demonstrate empathy for service users.
- Communication at all levels needs improvement.
- There needs to be improvement in partnership working and multi-agency cooperation.
- Services need to find constructive and positive ways to work with families and informal carers.
- advocacy may provide additional support for service users and families and opportunities to work with advocates should be available.

THE IMPACT OF VIEWS AND ATTITUDES ON LEARNING DISABILITY SERVICES

As this chapter has demonstrated, views and attitudes towards people with learning disabilities have a significant impact on services and societal responses – and this is true just as much now as in the past. Thankfully attitudes towards people with a learning disabilities are changing, but there is still some way to go.

There are a number of campaign groups working to promote change for people with learning disabilities on an international, national and local basis.

Mencap

Mencap is a national charity. It describes itself as campaigning to ensure that people with learning disabilities are valued equally, listened to and included. It describes how it works with people with learning disabilities to change laws and services and challenge prejudice.

For more information, see www.mencap.org.uk/campaigns.

Change

Change is a national organisation which works to promote the human rights and inclusion of people with learning disabilities. The main areas that Change focuses on are health inequality, hate crime and ensuring that all information is provided in an accessible way. Change employs people with learning disabilities who work alongside people without learning disabilities to campaign on key issues.

For more information see www.changepeople.org.

People First

People First is a national advocacy organisation, with branches across the UK. People First is run by and for people with learning disabilities. It campaigns to ensure that people have access to advocacy services and actively enables people with learning disabilities to contribute to national and local policy development.

For more information see peoplefirstltd.com.

While groups such as these and local-based user-led groups have had a significant impact on changing attitudes towards people with learning disabilities, it is important to recognise that promoting positive attitudes towards people with learning disabilities is not something that should be left to others. Everyone involved in health and social care services can promote positive attitudes and should work towards changing attitudes.

CHANGING ATTITUDES TOWARDS PEOPLE WITH LEARNING DISABILITIES

'Public Perceptions of Disabled People: Evidence from the British Social Attitudes Survey' was published by the Office for Disability Issues in 2010. This measured how much prejudice there is in the UK towards disabled people. It specifically examined how attitudes have changed between 2005 and 2009. The report suggests that people are more comfortable interacting with people with physical or sensory impairments in social situations than they are interacting with individuals with learning disabilities or mental health conditions. The conclusion was that attitudes towards people with physical disabilities had changed much more significantly than those towards people with learning disabilities.

THE CURRENT LEGAL FRAMEWORK OF LEARNING DISABILITY SERVICES

A range of legislation relates to all people in terms of promoting rights, inclusion, citizenship and equality. These are covered in various chapters of this book. Those that are most relevant include:

- the Equality Act 2010 – see Chapter 3
- the Human Rights Act 1998 – see Chapter 3
- the Mental Capacity Act 2005 – see Chapters 4, 5 and 9.

In terms of learning disability services specifically, the most important of the legislative frameworks is *Valuing People*.

VALUING PEOPLE

The government white paper *Valuing People: A New Strategy for Learning Disability for the 21st century* (Department of Health 2001) stated some key issues for learning disability services at the turn of the century. This was the first white paper on learning disabilities in 30 years, since the command paper 'Better Services for the Mentally Handicapped' in 1971.

Valuing People highlighted major problems in learning disability provision, including:

- poor coordination of services around transition to adulthood
- lack of support for carers, and poor support for families of disabled children in particular
- lack of choice and control in the lives of people with learning disabilities
- specific issues over people's housing, unmet health needs, opportunities for employment and access to day services which provide individualised care
- lack of provision for people with learning disabilities who are from minority communities
- lack of emphasis between agencies around partnership working.

Valuing People listed four key principles that should be at the heart of all service delivery:

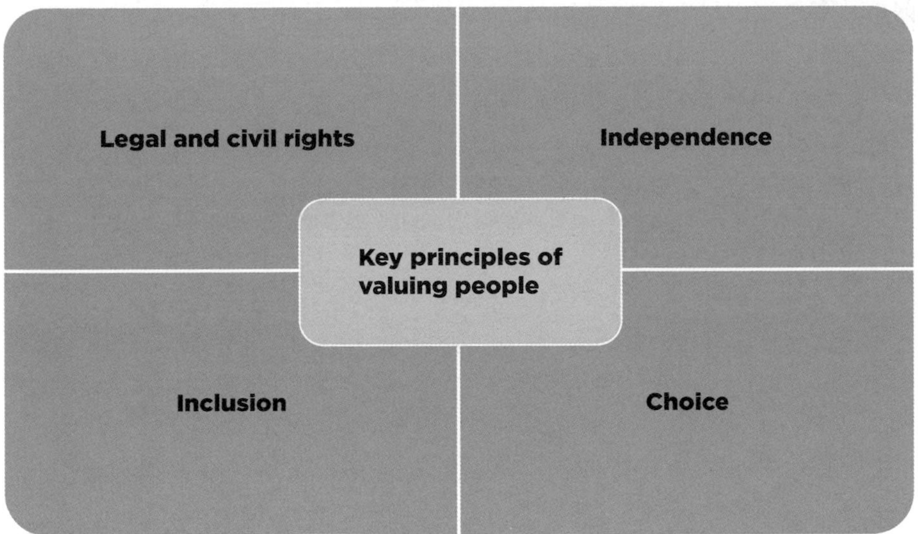

- *Legal and civil rights*. These include the right to vote; to marry and have a family; to express opinion and to have the support to enjoy these rights where necessary.
- *Independence*. People with learning disabilities are to be supported to enjoy the maximum level of independence possible.
- *Choice*. People with learning disabilities should have a real say in their lives about such things as where they live, what work they should do, and who looks after them. This includes supporting people with severe and profound learning disabilities to make important choices and express preferences about their day-to-day lives.
- *Inclusion*. We take for granted an ordinary life. We go to work, look after our families, visit our GP, use transport and go to the swimming pool or cinema, for example. People with learning disabilities should be supported to enjoy all the aspects of an ordinary life and be included in the local community.

When considering the service users you support you may well feel that they already enjoy their legal and civil rights; already live as independently as possible; already exercise choice; and are already fully included in their community. If you do feel that, it is likely that the people with learning disabilities you support enjoy their rights only relatively to other people with learning disabilities. When compared with people in the general population, what is striking is how deep the gulf still is.

For example, few adults with learning disabilities cohabit with romantic partners (or are married), live in their own homes (either as mortgage payers or tenants) or have paid jobs.

VALUING PEOPLE NOW (DEPARTMENT OF HEALTH 2009B)

A number of *Valuing People Now* implementation plans build on the foundation of *Valuing People*, and reflect the changing priorities based on the progress made against the targets set in the original white paper and on feedback from people with learning disabilities and their carers.

The key messages within *Valuing People Now* are connected with the following:

- The need to take account of the personalisation agenda in social care. In particular, this agenda is about people being able to decide for themselves how they want their own care to look, and being supported to purchase their own care in the way that they want.
- The need for inclusion and better approaches to address the needs of people with complex needs and those from minority groups.
- Addressing the health needs of people with learning disabilities, including people's access to health services, and their rights to dignity and respect.
- Increasing the housing options that people can access.
- Improving access to education and employment opportunities, as well as social, cultural and leisure activities.
- The right of people with learning disabilities to have relationships and families.
- Improving access to advocacy services.
- Addressing transport as a key issue for people.
- Safeguarding, and people's right not to be abused, and to feel safe in their community.

PRINCIPLES AND PRACTICE IN CONTEMPORARY SERVICES

A number of underlying principles now impact on contemporary practice in learning disability services.

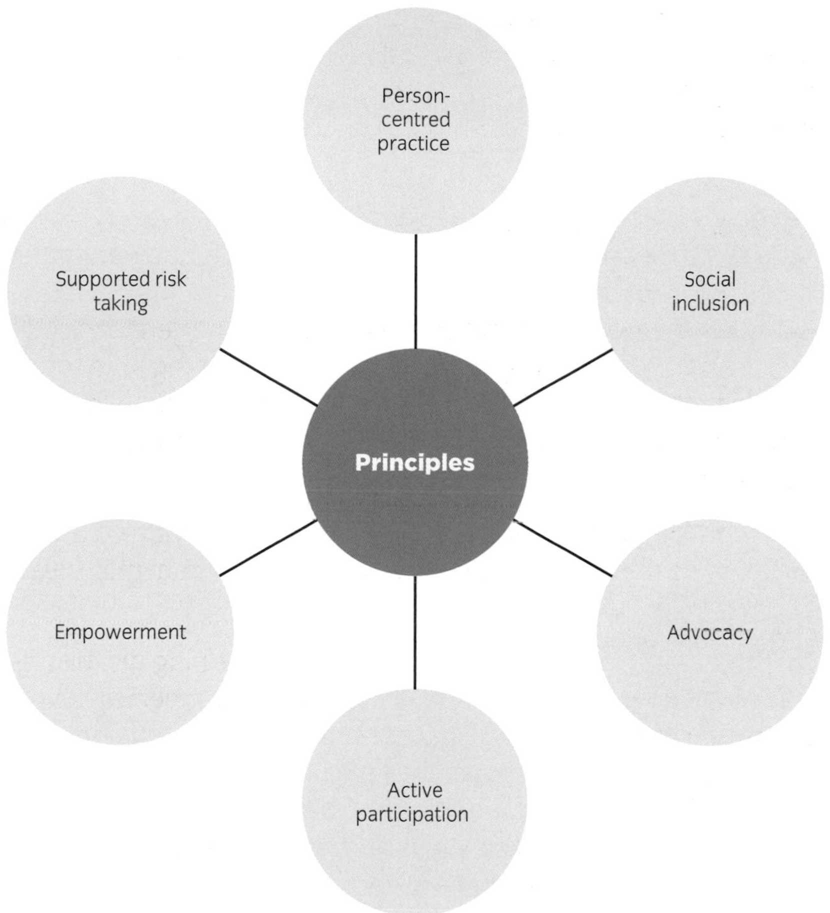

Although many of these principles were effectively 'born' in learning disability services, they have now significantly influenced other areas of health and social care practice. Many of these issues have therefore been covered in other chapters of this book. This chapter will now cover some of the key issues for learning disabilities connected with advocacy, empowerment and social inclusion.

ADVOCACY

Mencap (2008) defines advocacy as 'taking action to help people:

- say what they want
- secure their rights
- represent their interests
- get services they need
- represent their views and wishes'.

There are several different kinds of advocacy.

Self-advocacy

Self-advocacy is about people speaking up for themselves. A commitment to self-advocacy entails enabling and empowering people to act on their own behalf.

There is no doubt that this is a powerful way of helping people achieve independence, although it might not be feasible for all service users. Generally speaking, assertiveness training is needed as this can help people to raise their confidence and sense of self-worth and teach them the skills necessary to make other people listen to them.

Often self-advocacy sessions are set up by service user-led groups, which focus on groups of people supporting each other to be assertive about their own needs and wishes.

Many services now have links with self-advocacy groups. However, if managers and health and social care teams limit their understanding of self-advocacy to these groups, they misunderstand the aim of the whole advocacy movement. People should be listened to on a day-to-day basis as they express their views and make decisions about their own lives and the services they receive.

It is the failure of health and social care workers and services to listen to people that has resulted in the rise of the organised self-advocacy movement.

Peer advocacy

In peer advocacy the advocate shares a similar perspective to the person being represented. For example, a person with a learning disability may support another person with a learning disability to get their views across. Peer advocacy is often arranged through advocacy groups.

Representative (or citizen) advocacy

People may have difficulty in putting across their points of view. This can be because they have communication difficulties, because they lack confidence, because ill-health or disability makes it difficult for them to put their opinions across or because they lack the capacity to be able to make decisions for themselves. Although health and social care workers are expected to support service users to express their views, it can be difficult or impossible for them to do this if the person wishes to raise concerns about the service they are receiving. One option which may be appropriate in these circumstances is to use the services of an independent advocate to represent the service user.

The role of an advocate demands skill and is different from that of a support worker. Advocates can help in situations where:

- it is difficult for others to understand the person's means of communicating
- the person is not happy with the service they are receiving and wishes to complain
- supporters such as family, friends, paid carers or health and social care workers disagree about how to support the person or with the individual's point of view
- when a significant change has taken place in relation to the individual. This may be in relation to the person's health or social wellbeing, or a major life change.

An advocate will initially work with the person to understand the way they communicate and to find out what is important to them so that they can represent them in a variety of situations. They will usually go to a meeting alongside the person they are supporting, and must always be clear about representing the person's point of view even if the advocate believes that this may not be in the person's interests. The aim of the advocate is to empower the person by making sure that their views and interests are heard. The advocate will try to obtain permission from the person to represent their views and to contact others who may be able to help. Effectively, an independent advocate is simply a 'mouthpiece' for the service user. They ensure that the service user's views and wishes are heard by others.

Non-instructed advocacy

This is employed where someone is unable to put their views across, perhaps because of profound disability, and they lack the capacity to make decisions. Just as with the various forms of instructed advocacy, the advocate will work hard to form a strong relationship with the person they are representing, to learn about their preferences and to do their best to represent their interests. Sometimes non-instructed advocates work to what they call a 'watching brief' – essentially this means the advocate is working towards the principles of person-centred values and representing these in advocating on behalf of the individual.

Independent mental capacity advocates (IMCAs)

Sometimes referred to as an IMCA, this is a specific role which came about as a result of the Mental Capacity Act 2005. This Act established a role for IMCAs to work with individuals who:

- have no social support network
- have to make significant decisions
- lack capacity.

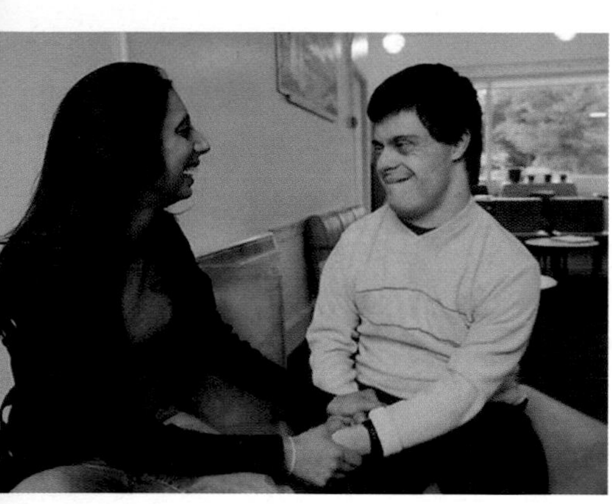

For example, where an NHS body is going to provide serious medical treatment or provide accommodation for such an individual, they must appoint an IMCA to speak on their behalf. If a Local Authority is to provide accommodation for more than eight weeks or arrange a change in accommodation, then they must appoint an IMCA where relevant for the individual.

IMCAs are expected to:

- support the person who lacks capacity to be as involved as fully as possible in decision making
- gather relevant information
- identify what the person's wishes and feelings would most likely be
- identify alternative forms of action
- where medical treatment is proposed, obtain a further medical opinion if it is felt necessary.

IMCAs are not decision makers but represent the individual's views in decision-making processes. They are also given the option to challenge any relevant decisions.

Staff advocacy

Health and social care workers, social workers and other professionals often talk about advocating on behalf of service users. They may well do so on some occasions. However, it is often difficult, if not inappropriate, for health and social care workers to advocate on behalf of service users, as this often involves challenging the organisation they are employed by.

DEVELOPING ADVOCACY SERVICES

The white paper *Valuing People* (Department of Health 2001) made it clear that the government wants a range of advocacy services (self-advocacy and citizen advocacy) to be available in every local area. The white paper highlights the benefits of advocacy services, which include enabling people with learning disabilities to express their wishes and make real choices; enabling people with learning disabilities to make a real difference to service development and delivery; and acknowledging the views of people with complex needs through citizen advocates. *Valuing People Now* recognises that significant advances have been made in advocacy service provision, but that there is still some way to go in ensuring that people have access to advocacy services where necessary.

REFLECT

- Is there a self-advocacy group in your service? If there is, identify when it meets. Is it advertised? Are people supported to attend?
- More generally, how good is the service at supporting people to express themselves? How effective is the service at responding to people's stated choices?

RESEARCH

If there is a self-advocacy group, arrange to meet with some of the members to discuss how they have benefited from the work of the group. Have they discussed matters with managers? Have they seen changes in response to their comments?

SOCIAL INCLUSION

Social inclusion is about understanding the way that people can be excluded from society on a range of levels and challenging this to ensure that people are socially included. In many ways, social inclusion is an extension of what was previously referred to in learning disability services as 'community presence'.

The United Nations Expert Group (2008: 2) stated that social exclusion is about a lack of access to services, information and participation, rights being denied, etc. It is multi-dimensional in that it encompasses so many issues of disadvantage, while social inclusion is the process of promoting the values, relations and institutions that enable all people to participate in social, economic and political life on the basis of equality of rights, equity and dignity.

Working towards social inclusion is a key aspect of contemporary practice in learning disability services. To promote social inclusion, all of the principles of good practice in health and social care are vital.

To ensure social inclusion for people with learning disabilities, services need to empower people, promote active participation and adopt positive approaches to risk.

KEY COMPONENTS OF ACTIVE SUPPORT

- Service users are offered opportunities to take part in everyday activities and all care tasks – 'little and often' is the key.
- 'Graded assistance' is about putting in the right level of support for the individual – see below.
- Health and social care workers focus on helping service users take part in things minute by minute – every moment has potential. They find parts of even very complex tasks that all people can do and undertake other parts of the task themselves.
- Health and social care workers pay particular attention to working as a team and coordinating their approaches. Staff monitor carefully the degree to which service users are taking part in everyday activities using simple record-keeping procedures. Regular staff meetings allow for plans to be modified in the light of experience and learning. 'Choice and control' for service users are essential to effectiveness.

For more on active support, see Chapter 10.

EMPOWERMENT

Empowerment is an essential aspect of practice in all areas of health and social care. In working with people with learning disabilities, it is particularly important to be aware of empowerment, because people with a learning disability can be so 'disempowered' by those around them.

Empowerment is about a service user having choice and control in their own life. Empowerment recognises the need to address each of the following areas to give the service user a true chance of making decisions for themselves.

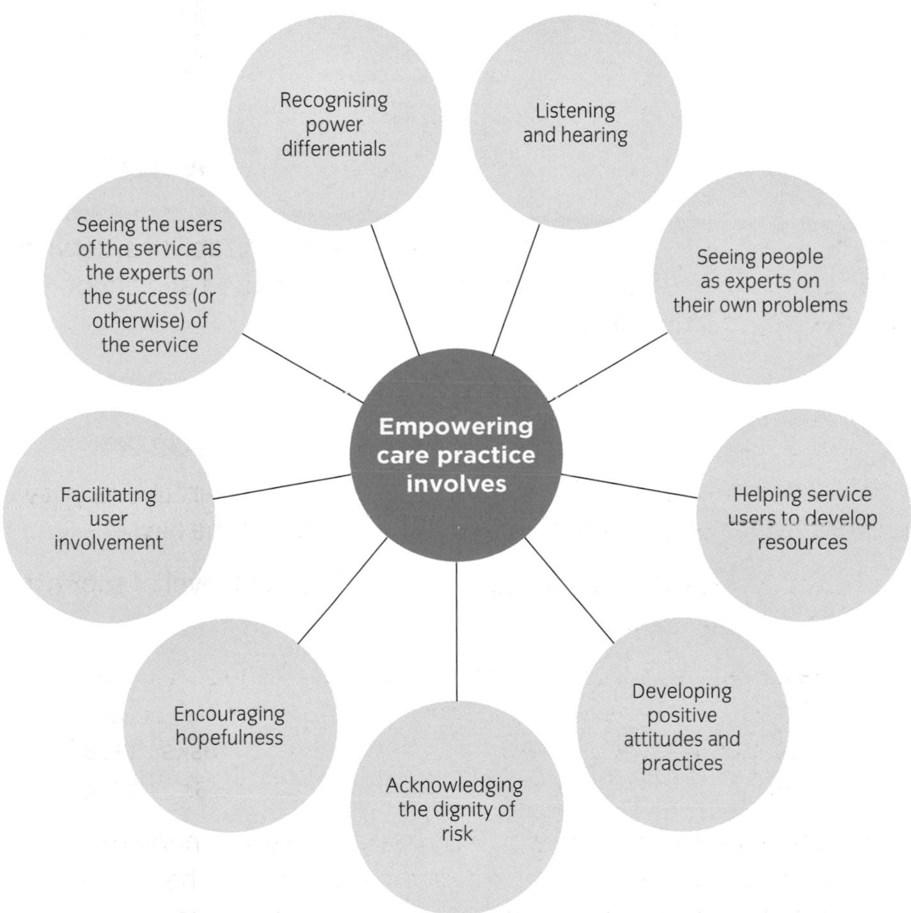

Helping service users develop resources

One of the starting points of empowerment is to acknowledge that the service user is the expert about their own life and what they want to achieve. From here, services need to support the person to develop a range of resources.

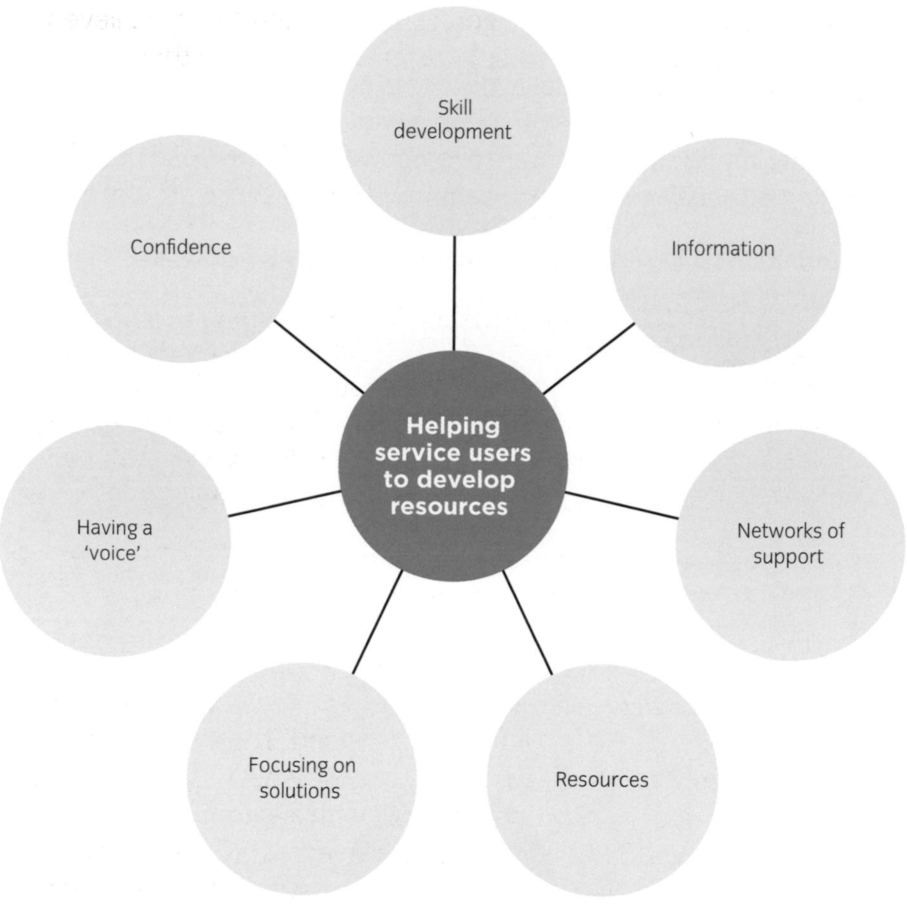

- *Information*. This should include information that is broader than simply what services are available. Information may need to be provided about the person's past, or their condition (if they have a condition). All information should be available to the service user in an accessible manner.
- *Networks of support*. Who is there to provide emotional and moral support? Who can the service user express their frustrations to, knowing that the listener will still help them renew their resolve and determination?
- *Skill development*. In a status- and class-conscious world, it's not always what we say but how we say it that counts. The service user may need to learn various social or technological skills (eg using email); or they may need to consider how to shape their argument and list points so that the person they are addressing is aware of why they need to listen to the service user.
- *Confidence*. Service users need to have confidence to express themselves. Confidence building can be a difficult and slow task. Ways to enhance confidence can include: joining with others who have had similar experiences and have successfully changed their lives positively; an individual choosing an aspect of their life they

want to change so there is a good chance of this being achieved; allowing a person to have a supporter present when they raise an issue of concern, etc.

- *Having a voice*. When a service user expresses something about their own life, services should listen. In the past, services were so poor at listening that the advocacy movement developed. Therefore having a voice may involve having an advocate.
- *Problem-solving/solution-focused approach*. The service user will need to recognise that practical difficulties could arise in seeking to change their own life in the way they would like to. To achieve their goal, they will need to adopt a solution-finding attitude. For every problem, there is a solution. Helping people focus on solutions rather than problems is a key aspect of empowerment.
- *Resources*. Most of life's achievers already have practical, financial and other resources. If a service user is to achieve their goals they will also need resources in some form. The idea is that services will provide the resources. When a service user has care needs but wants to continue their present lifestyle, established services can struggle to provide the flexibility needed. The introduction of direct payments and individualised care budgets has attempted to address this in providing service users with an amount of money that they can use flexibly to meet their needs. The money could be used for access to employment or housing support, for instance. Direct payments arguably represent one of the most practical tools for empowerment that are currently provided.

Risk and empowerment

One important aspect of empowerment is that it acknowledges the dignity of risk. In the past, opportunities for adult service users were restricted because of anxiety about risks to the service user. Supported risk taking is such a significant component of empowerment and a key principle of contemporary practice in learning disability services that it is covered in more detail on pages 492–3.

User involvement

Organisational structures that facilitate service user and carer involvement are vital in terms of empowerment. Social care services need to build service user and carer involvement into their structure and decision-making process. Services need to evaluate whether they are doing a good job and a key aspect of this is what the service users think. Therefore, services need to regularly find out from service users how they experience the service.

All services need a comments and complaints procedure, and this is one aspect of gaining some sense of service users' views, but on its own it is not enough.

Services need to have regular, planned involvement of service users. This can take various forms, including the following:

- managers having regular meetings with a self-advocacy group or service user group
- if there is a management board, then service users and carers should sit on this board
- if there are plans to develop or alter a service, then service users and/or carers should sit on the subcommittee or planning group
- the involvement of service users and carers in the training of new and existing health and social care workers.

SUPPORTED RISK TAKING

More information on risk issues is covered in Chapter 6. However, it is worth revisiting this here as a key principle in learning disability services.

It is widely recognised that services have in the past been too protective of service users with learning disabilities. Services have always sought to minimise or eliminate any risk of harm, be it emotional, mental or physical. It is now accepted that the attempt to eliminate all risk undermines service users' dignity (and, implicitly, workers' claims that they respect service users) and inhibits opportunities for personal development and growth. Often care environments that reduce risk as much as possible result in health and social care workers actively supervising everyone (having sight of service users all the time), or service users spending their time in impoverished environments.

The answer to over-protection is not to throw any sense of service responsibility to the wind and claim that service users should take unnecessary risks in the name of upholding their dignity. The aim should be for services to support service users to take measured risks, with the tasks being, at the time first initiated, at the top end of their present capability. If the task is successfully completed, the service user's sense of confidence and self-esteem should be notably enhanced. If the service user is not successful, while there is a risk that their confidence will be adversely affected there should be support to assist them through this. The service user will still have the sense that at least they tried it, even if it wasn't successful.

Examples of risk taking could apply to all aspects of a service. For example, instead of a health and social care worker actively assisting a service user to bathe, the service could seek to support them to bathe themselves. If this results in there being no need for a health and social care worker to be in the bathroom, this is a significant enhancement of the service user's dignity.

Another example would be supporting a service user to develop pedestrian skills. If a service user who formerly always needed a health and social care worker escort to go out could be given the opportunity to learn to cross roads on their own, safely, then this is a positive move towards increased independence.

At one level learning pedestrian skills represents a big risk, and health and social care workers may be tempted to say 'what if they get hit by a car?' It's always possible to point to the worst possible outcome, even in your own life. Anyone could be involved in a car crash, but people still drive.

In any programme intended to extend a service user's level of independence, but which involves risk, there must be planned steps that enhance the person's skills and control the level of risk. In essence services should actively use risk assessments in a constructive manner. As service users are supported to develop and extend their skills, the risks associated should be evaluated to see if they can extend their level of independence.

COMMUNICATING WITH PEOPLE WITH LEARNING DISABILITIES

Chapter 2 covers much of the knowledge that you will need to ensure that your communication is effective. However, there are some specific issues surrounding communication with people with learning disabilities that are worth covering here.

Everyone who has a learning disability is different and has different needs and desires, and as such the barriers that people face in communicating are very varied. Such barriers *may* include one or more of the following factors:

- inaccurate and dangerous assumptions about understanding
- lack of speech
- lack of anything of interest to communicate about
- sensory impairment
- mental health problems
- inappropriate environment, eg communication being impossible because there is too much noise, or because the person needs visual aids which are not available
- staff lack of understanding
- being supported as one of a group, rather than as an individual
- health and social care workers not taking time to listen.

Using age-appropriate and ability-appropriate language

The British Association of Learning Disabilities (2002) suggests that up to 90% of people with learning disabilities have issues with communication, and that 60% of people find symbolic techniques helpful in aiding communication. They argue that other people's unwillingness to learn the skills required to communicate with people who need different forms of communication is the primary cause of the frustration which many people with learning disabilities experience.

The language that you use is important, as this reflects to the service user and others how you perceive and value that person. It is appropriate to use language that enables understanding and relationship building with service users, but it is just as important not to infantilise people with the language that you use.

Choose language which is:

- *Age-appropriate*. In their twenties, service users do not want to be spoken to as if they are children. Likewise, an older adult would not wish to be spoken to in quite the same way as a younger adult
- *Ability-appropriate*. Communication is about interaction between two or more people. If the language used is too complex, too full of jargon or just too wordy, many of us switch off. If you were not interested in science or politics, you may struggle to concentrate on a lengthy article or a television programme that contained lots of specialised and verbose language. At the same time, you are unlikely to feel stimulated by the programmes or books you enjoyed as a young child. This is no different for the service users we work with. Language should stretch people, without excluding or boring them.

Adapting your verbal and non-verbal communication appropriately

As described, communication is a two-way process, which involves the sending of a message and the receiving of a message. It is important to be aware that a person with a learning disability may not understand what is said – because of the way the health and social care worker has said it.

Health and social care workers need to be conscious of the words and phrases they use. In essence it is important that the phrases are as concrete, simple and direct as possible. For example, instead of saying

'We won't be going out'

say

'We will stay in today'.

Time concepts can be difficult for a person with a learning disability. Health and social care workers need to be conscious to avoid references to times of the clock. However, to talk about 'after lunch' or 'this evening' may be more comprehensible.

For individuals with learning disabilities who do have verbal skills it is important not to assume from a couple of words they say that they understand you. Some people with learning disabilities repeat the last thing a person has said to them. Also, if a health and social care worker says to a service user, 'Do you understand what I've said?', the service user could well say, 'yes' even when they haven't understood. Try to ask more open questions, for example, 'Tell me what we have just agreed will happen?'

Where information is new or complex, visual representations of that information may be helpful. Also, non-verbal communication is critical (see Chapter 2).

Consider:

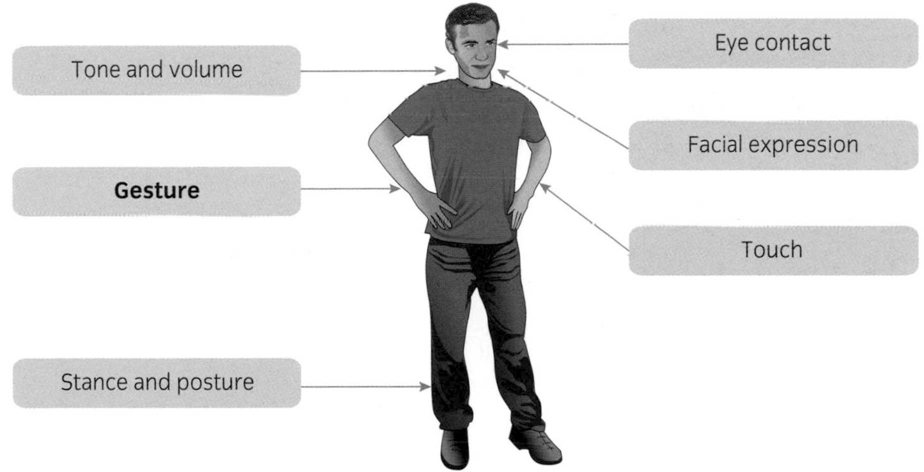

Key term

Gesture is a movement of part of the body, especially a hand or the head, used as a form of communication to express an idea or meaning.

Checking for understanding and addressing misunderstandings

The more significant a service user's learning disability is, the more likely it is that they may not understand all the words in a sentence. The words that are more concrete – nouns or proper nouns – may be recognised, but not other words.

For example,

'Don't drink your tea – it's hot'

may be understood as

'Drink your tea'.

Again, the simpler and more direct the language the better. In light of this, humour and especially sarcasm can be confusing. You should try to avoid the use of humour and sarcasm if you want to convey something, especially if it is important.

For some people with severe learning disabilities, information overload can occur after just two or three sentences. If the person can absorb only one piece of information at a time, you should recognise this and space out the presentation of information.

Remember, as explained in Chapter 2, to check that the person has understood you by:

- asking them to reflect back to you what has been said or agreed
- observing their non-verbal signs to see that they have understood you.

Chapter 2 also covers the main strategies to address misunderstandings. It is particularly relevant and important when working with service users with learning disabilities to:

- acknowledge, apologise and learn from misunderstandings
- observe any signs of distress or frustration displayed by the individual
- consider using other tools, accessing specialist advice and trying new ways to aid communication.

Recognising and respecting personal communication

Service users often use personal systems of communication, and you need to learn to recognise and value these. For example, a service user may convey the message that they want to use the toilet by rocking on their chair. Another may communicate their happiness by clapping. You need to ensure that you clearly recognise and respond to the various methods of communication that service users may use.

REFLECT

- How effective do you think your communication is?
- How could you improve your communication skills?

Before you conclude this chapter take some time to think about the following:

- What have you learnt about learning disabilities?
- In what ways have services for people with learning disabilities changed in the recent past?
- Key principles in working with people with learning disabilities reflect good practice in health and social care. What do these include? How do you promote them in your own practice?
- In the past people with learning disabilities have been over protected and have been denied opportunities to take risks. Why is supported risk taking important in working with people with learning disabilities?

Understanding the nature and characteristics of learning disabilities can be useful.However, recognising people as unique individuals and challenging any oppression they may face is vital. People with learning disabilities and their families may share some common experiences but it is vital to recognise that people are all unique individuals.

GLOSSARY

active listening is a key skill in health and social care, and involves ensuring that the service user knows you are working to understand what they are communicating. Active listening can be conveyed by your body language, nodding, eye contact, and by your summarising what the service user has said to check that you have fully understood them.

active participation is about people being involved in their own care, as opposed to being a 'recipient' of that care (ie it is about something being done *with* someone rather than something being done *to* someone). Active participation also means that people take part in the activities of daily and independent life as much as possible.

active support is a person-centred model of how to interact with service users, combined with a daily planning system that promotes participation and enhances quality of life.

advocacy is speaking for or on behalf of someone.

aim in this context is about finding a direction or purpose.

antibiotic is a substance from a micro-organism that is used to destroy other micro-organisms or prevent their growth.

axon is the main body of the neuron cell.

bacteria are microscopic organisms, some types of which are pathogenic. Bacteria are made up of just one cell and are capable of reproducing by themselves.

capacity is about whether someone is physically or mentally able to do something.

chaperone means to accompany. Most commonly a chaperone accompanies a person doing a medical treatment or examination.

cognitive means relating to thinking and understanding.

commission is where something is done where the person understands the implications of what they are doing. For example, hitting someone would be an act of commission.

consent is when a person agrees to something when they are making an informed decision or giving informed permission.

cross-contamination means the process by which bacteria or other micro-organisms are unintentionally transferred from one substance or object to another, with harmful effect.

cross-infection is when an infection spreads from one person to another.

culture refers to what people do and why they do it. All individuals have a culture which is shaped by their beliefs, their background and any groups which they belong to. Organisations also have a culture which is often shaped by the organization's leaders.

decontamination is removing contamination from somebody or something; to remove unwanted chemical, radioactive or biological impurities or toxins from a person, object or place.

de-escalation refers to techniques used to calm people down.

diagnosis is the identification of a medical condition.

discrimination is where someone is treated less favourably than another person.

disengagement is where a service user is not doing any constructive or meaningful activity, and can include aimlessly wandering about, pacing, staring, sitting, lying down, purposelessly fiddling with items and so on, with no social contact.

diversity refers to difference. Everyone is unique and different in some way. There is a wide range of diversity in every population.

domiciliary care worker is a person who provides care to people who live independently.

drug is any substance which when taken into the body affects the way that the body functions.

equality is about treating people in a way that ensures that they are not placed at a disadvantage to others.

endogenous means originating from within.

ethics are about how we see right and wrong, but ethics are generally drawn from our understanding of responsibilities and so are closely linked with professional standards, codes of conduct and legislation. Ethics are closely related to the duty of care in health and social care.

exclusion describes a situation where people face discrimination on many levels and are effectively 'excluded from society' – that is where they have no voice and are not recognised in their society.

exogenous means originating from an external source.

gesture is a movement of part of the body, especially a hand or the head, used as a form of communication to express an idea or meaning.

hazard is a possible source of harm.

holistic means looking at the whole picture.

holistic approach considers the service user as an individual, and all of the factors which make up their life, instead of focusing only on their support needs.

hotel model refers to institutional-style settings organised mainly around staffing needs. They are not person-centred and offer a poor quality of life to service users. For example, where health and social care workers undertake all the domestic tasks, and do not provide opportunities for service users to participate in constructive activities.

hygiene is keeping yourself and your environment clean to maintain health.

immune means resistant to a particular infection or toxin.

immunocompromised is where a person has impaired immunity due to disease (eg cancer) or treatment (eg corticosteroids or radiotherapy).

inclusion is the word used to describe the opposite of social exclusion. It is where action is taken to address the effects of discrimination, and to strive towards preventing or ideally eliminating oppression.

induction is training to introduce an employee to a new role or organisation.

infantilise or **infantilisation** relates to the way in which adults who have disabilities can be treated as though they were children.

informed choice means a choice is based on an understanding of its implications.

intersectional multiple discrimination is where a person experiences discrimination because they belong to a number of groups which may be treated less favourably than others. Where discrimination is 'intersectional', this means that the person's different identities interact in such a way that it is impossible to separate them out from each other. The person's whole experience of being treated differently is not because of one aspect of their uniqueness, but it is about how their *differences* (plural) intersect with each other.

IQ means intelligence quota.

job description is a written outline of the role and responsibilities of a specific job.

leading question is one which gives the person being asked a clear indication about the expected answer. For example 'He hit you, didn't he?'

levels of help refers to graduated levels of assistance, from simple verbal reminders providing the lowest level of support to actual physical guidance providing the highest level. Assistance should be given flexibly according to the individual service user's need for help, and should be focused on encouraging as much independence as possible.

liability is a legal responsibility. Employers can be legally responsible for action carried out by an employee. Individuals can also have legal responsibilities.

Local Authorities are local government organisations which operate local services such as schools and refuge collection.

Local Government Ombudsman is an official who has been appointed to look into complaints about councils and other organisations.

macerator is a pump which reduces solids to small pieces.

mediator is a person who intervenes in situations of conflict.

medicine is a drug that is used to diagnose, prevent or treat an illness.

micro-organisms are living organisms so small that they cannot be seen without the use of a very powerful microscope.

microscopic means so small as to be visible only with a microscope.

minimal sufficiency refers to providing the minimal prompt (or support) to someone – just sufficient – not too much and not too little. It is all about getting the balance right between supporting someone but not doing too much for them. It is a key principle in active support and in promoting independence in support work.

monitoring means keeping an eye on how something is working. Monitoring can either be done formally (on documentation, such as those prepared for review meetings), or informally (via conversation and observation).

morals are about our belief in what is right and wrong, and are often associated with faith and our personal values.

multiple discrimination is discrimination against someone on the basis of two or more characteristics at the same time. People can belong to more than one or two groups who experience discrimination, and people can experience 'double disadvantage' or 'multiple disadvantage'.

neuron is a nerve cell. Most of the cells in the human brain are neurons.

neurotransmitters are the chemicals that carry information in the brain.

objective refers to the point to which operations are directed; the point to be reached; the goal.

omission is where something is not done (accidentally or on purpose). For example, not providing an adequate standard of care for a service user would be an act of omission.

operant conditioning is a term used to describe the way that behaviours are very often linked to some kind of stimulus or event. It also refers to the way that behaviours lead to a consequence which can reinforce the behaviour. This idea has been very influential in theories about behaviour.

oppression refers to negative treatment of people. The word comes from the Latin 'opprinere' which means to flatten or to squash out of shape.

outcomes are what people want to achieve.

parasites are organisms that live on other organisms.

pathogen is a bacterium, virus, or other micro-organism that can cause disease. Not all bacteria, viruses or other micro-organisms are pathogenic; they will not all cause disease in humans.

pathogenic fungi are yeasts and moulds which can infect humans.

patient-identifiable information is any personal or sensitive information that can identify a patient.

person specification is a written outline of the qualities a person needs to have for a particular job – this will include the experience they should have, the skills they should hold, the knowledge they need, the qualifications they need and so on.

personal protective equipment (PPE) most commonly includes gloves and aprons.

personal values are what is important to an individual. See also *professional values*.

policy in health and social care is a written statement explaining the service or agency's expected approach to an issue, area of practice, or key aspect of people's work. Policies can be local and/or national.

positive interaction refers to supportive interaction using the levels of assistance, task analysis and positive reinforcement that help a service user to participate in constructive activity.

positive reinforcement refers to what a service user gains from undertaking a specific task. It can include naturally occurring rewards (eg drinking a cup of tea the service user has just made) or other things that the service user particularly likes (eg praise and attention or a preferred activity) as an encouragement or reward for participating in a specified activity.

prejudice is where an individual makes a judgement based on either inadequate or inaccurate information that leads to the development of irrational preferences. One of the main features of prejudice is rigidity or inflexibility of ideas. This means that new information may not have an impact on prejudicial views.

procedure is an agreed and understood way or order of doing something in work.

professional boundaries, in work settings, determine what we will and will not do, and what is appropriate in our relationships with service users and other people – and what is not.

professional values are what is important in a particular profession. See also *personal values*.

prognosis is the likely outcome of a medical condition.

reflecting on experiences is essential to good practice and professional development. Reflecting is about reviewing events and experiences, analysing information, using knowledge and supervision to consider issues and concerns, and taking a proactive stance in how you take responsibility for the development of your own learning and practices. In terms of communication within health and social care, reflecting also has another very significant meaning. Reflecting involves repeating the important things that are being said back to the speaker. This can encourage the speaker to say more. However, the listener shouldn't interrupt the speaker but simply reflect things back to show that they have understood and to encourage the speaker to say more. Reflecting is important to demonstrate that you are listening to someone, and to check that you have heard correctly. When you repeat key words it tells the person speaking that you are hearing them correctly and that what they are saying is important.

reflective practice involves thinking about work experiences specifically on what went well and what could be done differently next time.

resilience is best defined as a person's ability to 'bounce back'.

resistance is the ability of a micro-organism to withstand an antimicrobial agent.

risk is the likelihood that a hazard will actually cause harm.

safeguarding is defined by the government as 'a range of activity aimed at upholding an adult's fundamental right to be safe. Being or feeling unsafe undermines our relationships and self-belief, our ability to participate freely in communities and contribute to society. Safeguarding is of particular importance to people who, because of their situation or circumstances, are unable to keep themselves safe' (Department of Health 2010).

sanitise means to make clean or hygienic for example by using a preparatory hand sanitising gel.

self-esteem is about how we feel about or value ourselves.

self-image is about how we see or describe ourselves.

single equality duty was introduced by the Equality Act 2010. It is imposed on all public bodies when they are making plans and strategic decisions. The single equality duty means that services need to be targeted at people who are disadvantaged, instead of at groups who have specific characteristics in common. This focuses the duty of those planning services on to the goal of equality itself. The single equality duty tasks public bodies to:

- eliminate discrimination
- advance equality of opportunity
- foster good relations.

sputum is mucus that is sometimes coughed up from the lower airways.
stereotype is a generalised idea about a group of people.
sterile means free from bacteria or other living organisms.
synapse is the space between the neuron cells.
task-centred care practice focuses on what tasks need to be done. This can mean that workers lose sight of the fact that they are assisting people.
transmission means passing an infectious disease from one person to another.
valued lifestyle and **valued range of activities** refer to the balance of activities that contribute to a good quality of life for individual service users, and incorporates vocational, domestic, personal, leisure, educational and social activities.
values are what is seen as important.
vector is an organism, typically a biting insect or parasite, that transmits a disease.
virus is a pathogenic microscopic organism. Viruses cannot multiply on their own, so they have to invade a 'host' cell.
whistleblowing policy is where a colleague raises a concern about another person's work or wider practices in an organisation.

USEFUL WEBSITES

Age UK
http://www.ageuk.org.uk/documents/en-gb/factsheets/fs24_self-directed_support-direct_payments_and_personal_budgets_fcs.pdf?dtrk=true
An age UK guide to self-directed support

Alzheimer's Society
www.alzheimers.org.uk
A membership organisation which works to improve the quality of life of people affected by dementia

Alzheimer's Research UK
www.alzheimersresearchuk.org
The UK's leading dementia research charity specialising in finding preventions, causes, treatments and a cure for dementia

Beat
www.b-eat.co.uk
Provides information for people affected by eating disorders

British Institute of Learning Disabilities
www.bild.org.uk
An organisation that works to improve the quality of life of people with learning disabilities

British National Formulary
http://www.bnf.org/bnf/index.htm
Provides UK healthcare professionals with information on the selection and clinical use of medicines

Care Quality Commission
http://www.cqc.org.uk
The independent regulator of all health and social care services in England

Change
www.changepeople.co.uk/
A leading national human rights organisation led by disabled people

Communication Matters
http://www.communicationmatters.org.uk
A UK organisation supporting people who find communication difficult

Department for Education
http://www.education.gov.uk/childrenandyoungpeople/strategy/integratedworking/a0072915/information-sharing
Guides for practitioners and managers around sharing information

Department of Health
https://www.gov.uk/government/uploads/system/uploads/attachment_data/file/153462/dh_119973.pdf.pdf
Essence of Care 2010 guide to best practice in communication

Economic and Social Research Council (ESRC)
www.esrcsocietytoday.ac.uk
The UK's largest organisation for funding research on economic and social issues

Health & Safety Executive
www.hse.gov.uk
Health and Safety publications as well as a useful Health and Safety in health and social care services section

Improving Access to Psychological Therapies (IAPT)
www.iapt.nhs.uk
National Institute for Health and Clinical Excellence (NICE) guidelines

International Stress Management Association
www.isma.org.uk
Provides information on promoting wellbeing and performance

Joseph Rowntree Foundation
http://www.jrf.org.uk/publications/transforming-social-care-person-centred-support
Research from the Joseph Rowntree Foundation into person centred support

Local Government Association
http://www.local.gov.uk/adult-social-care
Provides updates and local and regional responses to government policy

London Deanery Faculty Development
http://www.faculty.londondeanery.ac.uk/e-learning/feedback/giving-feedback
Provides information on the principles of giving effective feedback

Mencap
www.mencap.org.uk
Website for valuing and supporting people with learning disabilities

http://www.mencap.org.uk/sites/default/files/documents/2008-04/make%20it%20clear%20apr09.pdf
Make It Clear guide from MENCAP

Mind
www.mind.org.uk
Provides advice and support on mental health problems and campaigns to improve services, raise awareness and promote understanding

Mind Tools
http://www.mindtools.com/pages/article/newLDR_81.htm
Information on conflict resolution

National Institute for Health and Care Excellence (NICE)
http://www.nice.org.uk/nicemedia/live/10998/30320/30320.pdf
NICE & SCIE guidelines on supporting people with dementia and their carers in health and social care

National Centre for Social Research (NATCEN)
www.natcen.ac.uk
UK's leading independent social research institute

National Institute on Deafness and Other Communication Disorders (NIDCD)
http://www.nidcd.nih.gov/health/hearing/Pages/Assistive-Devices.aspx#7
A guide to assistive devices for people with hearing, voice, speech, or language disorders

Patient.co.uk
www.patient.co.uk
Information on health, lifestyle, disease and other medical related topics

People First
http://peoplefirstltd.com
An organisation, run by, and for people with learning difficulties

Personal Health Budgets NHS England
http://www.personalhealthbudgets.dh.gov.uk
A website providing information and news about the Department of Health's personal health budgets policy

Plain English Campaign
www.plainenglish.co.uk
An independent campaign against misleading public information

Research in Practice for Adults
www.ripfa.org.uk
A charity that uses evidence from research and people's experience to help understand adult social care and improve how it works

Royal College of Speech and Language Therapists
www.rcslt.org
The professional body for speech and language therapists in the UK, providing leadership and setting professional standards

Royal Pharmaceutical Society of Great Britain
www.rpharms.com/support-pdfs/handling-medicines-socialcare-guidance.pdf
A guide to handling medication in social care work

SCOPE
http://www.scope.org.uk/help-and-information/communication/no-voice-no-choice
No Voice No Choice research from the UK disability charity that supports disabled people and their families

Skills for Care
http://www.skillsforcare.org.uk/developing_skills/e-learning/e-learning.aspx
Provides a range of e-learning resources from Skills for Care

http://www.skillsforcare.org.uk/developing_skills/leadership_and_management/providing_effective_supervision.aspx
Guide to effective supervision in social care

Skills for Health
www.skillsforhealth.org.uk
The Sector Skills Council for health

Social Care Institute for Excellence (SCIE)
www.scie.org.uk
An independent charity working with adults, families and children's social care and social work services across the UK

http://www.scie.org.uk/adults/safeguarding
SCIE website has a range of useful information and resources in relation to adult safegaurding

http://www.scie.org.uk/publications/elearning/communicationskills
E-learning resources on the principles of good communication skills and how to apply these to practice

http://www.scie.org.uk/publications/guides/guide23/messages/mean.asp
SCIE knowledge review into partnership work

http://www.scie.org.uk/publications/reports/report36/index.asp
SCIE research into self-directed support

www.scie-peoplemanagement.org.uk
A people management website which will be particularly relevant for managers

www.scie-socialcareonline.org.uk
SCIE also operate social care online – a fantastic website for research information

Social Policy and Social Work Subject Centre
www.swap.ac.uk
Provides updates and has a number of research articles on its site

The Equality & Human Rights Commission
http://www.equalityhumanrights.com
Provides information and guidance to individuals on equality, discrimination and human rights issues

The National Archives Department of Health
http://webarchive.nationalarchives.gov.uk/20130107105354/http://www.dh.gov.uk/en/Publichealth/Scientificdevelopmentgeneticsandbioethics/Consent/index.htm
Department of Health guidance on consent

Think Local Act Personal
www.thinklocalactpersonal.org.uk
A national, cross sector leadership partnership, promoting work with personalisation, community-based social care

University of Kent
http://www.kent.ac.uk/tizard/active
Information on person-centred active support

World Health Organization
http://www.who.int/features/qa/62/en/index.html
World Health Organization guide to mental health

Write Enough
www.writeenough.org.uk
Information on effective recording in children's services

BIBLIOGRAPHY

Alzheimer's Research UK (2013) 'Dementia Statistics.' Available online at http://www.alzheimersresearchuk.org/dementia-statistics/ (accessed 4 February 2013).

Ashman, B. and Beadle-Bown, J. (2006) *A Valued Life: Developing Person-centred Approaches so People can be More Included*. London: United Response.

Association for Real Change (2012) 'Research: Active Support.' Available online at http://arcuk.org.uk/activesupport/2012/04/05/research (accessed 4 January 2013).

Association of Directors of Social Services (2005) *Safeguarding Adults: A National Framework of Standards for Good Practice and Outcomes in Adult Protection Work*. London: ADSS. Available online at www.adass.org.uk/images/stories/Publications/Guidance/safeguarding.pdf (accessed 7 May 2013).

Russell, Hugo and Ayliffe (2013) *Principles and Practice of Disinfection, Preservation & Sterilization*. Oxford: Wiley-Blackwell.

Basnett, F. and Maclean, S. (2000) *The Value Base in Practice: An NVQ Related Reference Guide for Staff Working with Older People*. Rugeley: Kirwin Maclean Associates.

BBC (2012) 'Winterbourne View Patients in New Care Safety Alerts.' Available online at http://www.bbc.co.uk/news/uk-20070437 (accessed 29 October 2012).

British Institute of Learning Disabilities (2002) 'Factsheet: communication'. Kidderminster: British Institute of Learning Disabilities. Available online at file://cgli/user/Home/prodev/CLAIREO/Downloads/Communication%2002.pdf (accessed 3 May 2013).

Calderstones Partnership NHS Trust (2013) 'Learning Disabilities Facts and Figures.' Available online at http://www.calderstones.nhs.uk/about-us/learningdisabilities.php (accessed 23 January 2013).

Care Quality Commission (2010) *Guidance about compliance: Summary of regulations, outcomes and judgement framework*. Available online at http://www.cqc.org.uk/sites/default/files/documents/guidance_about_compliance_summary.pdf (accessed 20.06.2014).

Carer UK (2012) 'Policy Briefing: Facts about Carers.' www.carersuk.org/media/k2/attachments/Facts_about_carers_Dec_2012.pdf (accessed 2 April 2014).

Department for Education (2008) *Information Sharing: Guidance for Practitioners and Managers*. Available online at www.education.gov.uk/chilrdenandyoungpeople/strategy/integratedworking/a0072915/information-sharing (accessed 19 March 2013).

Department of Health (2001) *Valuing People: A New Strategy for Learning Disability for the 21st Century*. London: Department of Health. Available online at http://www.dh.gov.uk/en/Publicationsandstatistics/Publications/PublicationsPolicyAndGuidance/DH_4009153 (accessed 29 January 2013).

Department of Health (2007) *Independence, Choice and Risk: A Guide to Best Practice in Supporting Decision Making*. London: Department of Health. Available online at www.worcestershire.gov.uk/cms/PDF/Independence,%20choice%20and%20risk.pdf (accessed 17 April 2013).

Department of Health (2009a) *Safeguarding Adults: Report on the Consultation on the Review of* No Secrets: *Guidance on Developing and Implementing Multi-agency Policies and Procedures to Protect Vulnerable Adults from Abuse*. London: Department of Health.

Department of Health (2009b) *Valuing People Now: A New Three-year Strategy for People with Learning Disabilities*. London: Department of Health. Available online at: http://www.dh.gov.uk/en/Publicationsandstatistics/Publications/PublicationsPolicyAndGuidance/DH_093377 (accessed 29 January 2013).

Department of Health (2010) *Practical Approaches to Safeguarding and Personalisation*. London: Department of Health. Available online at www.communitylivingbc.ca/wp-content/uploads/Practicalapproaches-to-safeguarding-and-personalisation.pdf (accessed 23 April 2013).

Department of Health (2012) *Compassion in Practice: Nursing, Midwifery and Care Staff. Our Vision and Strategy*. Leeds: Nursing, Midwifery and Care Workers Team. Available online at www.commissioningboard.nhs.uk/wpcontent/uploads/2012/12/compassion-in-practice.pdf (accessed 18 March 2013).

Department of Health and Home Office (2000) *No Secrets: Guidance on Developing and Implementing Multi-agency Policies and Procedures to Protect Vulnerable Adults from Abuse*. London: Department of Health. Available online at www.elderabuse.org.uk/Documents/Other%20Orgs/No%20Secrets.pdf (accessed 23 4 April 2013).

Department of Health (2011) *Statement of Government Policy on Adult Safeguarding*. London: Department of Health. Available online at https://www.gov.uk/government/uploads/system/uploads/attachment_data/file/197402/Statement_of_Gov_Policy.pdf

Equality and Human Rights Commission (2009), *Equality Measurement Framework*. Available online at http://www.equalityhumanrights.com/about-us/our-work/key-projects/equality-measurement-framework

Food Standards Agency (2011), *The second study of infectious intestinal disease in the community (IID2 Study)*. Available online at http://www.foodbase.org.uk//admintools/reportdocuments/711-1-1393_IID2_FINAL_REPORT.pdf (accessed 12 June 14).

Foodlink, Food and Drink Federation, *Hygiene Fact File*. Available online at http://www.sustainweb.org/pdf2/Hygienefactfile.pdf (accessed 13 June 14).

Flynn, M. (2012) *South Gloucestershire Safeguarding Adults Board: Winterbourne View: A Serious Case Review*. South Gloucestershire Council. Available online at http://hosted.southglos.gov.uk/wv/summary.pdf (accessed 29 October 12).

Francis, R. (2013) *The Mid Staffordshire NHS Foundation Trust Public Inquiry: Executive Summary*. London: The Stationery Office.

Gillen, S. (2011) 'Breaking the Silence.' *Professional Social Work,* November, pp. 20–22.

Guardian (2012) 'Neglect and Indignity: Stafford Hospital Inquiry Damns NHS Failings.' Available online at http://www.guardian.co.uk/society/2011/dec/01/stafford-hospital-inquiry-nhs-failings (accessed 29 October 2012).

Health and Safety Executive (2006) 'Five Steps to Risk Assessment.' Available online www.hse.gov.uk/pubns/raindex.htm (accessed 26 October 2012).

Health and Safety Executive, 'Risk Factors Associated with Pushing and Pulling Loads.' Available online at http://www.hse.gov.uk/msd/pushpull/risks.htm (accessed 8 June 2014).

Health and Safety Executive, (2004) 'What are the Management Standards.' Available online at http://www.hse.gov.uk/stress/standards/ (accessed 20 June 2014).

Health and Safety Executive, Advisory Committee on Dangerous Pathogens (2003) *Infection at Work: Controlling the Risks – A Guide for Employers and the Self Employed on Identifying, Assessing and Controlling the Risks of Infection in the Workplace*. London: The Stationery Office. Available online at http://www.hse.gov.uk/pubns/infection.pdf (accessed 8 June 2014).

Health and Safety Executive (1998) *Safe use of lifting equipment: Lifting Operations and Lifting Equipment Regulations 1998*. London: The Stationery Office. Available online at http://www.hse.gov.uk/pubns/books/l113.htm

Holland, K. (2011) *Factsheet: Learning Disabilities.* Kidderminster: British Institute of Learning Disabilities.

International Stress Management Association (2009) 'Top Ten Stress Busting Tips.' Available online at www.isma.org.uk (accessed 29 December 2010).

Local Government Ombudsman (2009) *Six Lives: The Provision of Public Services to People with Learning Disabilities.* London: Department of Health. Available online at www.ombudsman.org.uk/improving-public-service/reports-andconsultations/reports/health/six-lives-the-provisionof-public-services-to-people-with-learning-disabilities. (accessed 15 April 2013).

Luengo-Fernandez, R., Leal, J. and Gray, A. (2010) *Dementia 2010: The Economic Burden of Dementia and Associated Research Funding in the United Kingdom*. Cambridge: Alzheimer's Research Trust. Available online at http://www.dementia2010.org (accessed 19 January 2013).

Mcgraw Hill, 'Skin Infections.' Available online at http://highered.mcgraw-hill.com/sites/dl/free/0072919248/64775/nester4ech22.pdf. Accessed 8.6.2014.

Mencap (2008) 'Advocacy.' Available online at www.mencap.org.uk/document.asp?id=2113 (accessed 21 September 2008).

Milczarek, M. Schneider, E. and Gonzalez, E (2009) *European Risk Observatory Report. OSH in Figures: Stress at Work – Facts and Figures*. Luxembourg: European Agency for Safety and Health at Work.

NHS (2014) 'The Eat Well Plate.' Available online at www.nhs.uk/Livewell/Goodfood/Pages/eatwell-plate.aspx (accessed 8 March 2014).

NHS Choices (2013) 'Meat in your diet.' Available online at http://www.nhs.uk/Livewell/Goodfood/Pages/meat.aspx. (accessed 20 June 2014)

NHS Knowledge Network Scotland (2013a) 'Genetics and Learning Disabilities: An Introduction.' Available online at http://www.knowledge.scot.nhs.uk/home/portals-and-topics/learning-disabilities-portal/topics--glossary/managing-physical-health--well-being/genetics--learning-disability---introduction.aspx. (accessed 22 January 2013).

NHS Knowledge Network Scotland (2013b) 'Communication and Learning Disability: An

Introduction.' Available online at http://www.knowledge.scot.nhs.uk/home/portals-and-topics/learning-disabilities-portal/topics--glossary/communication/communication--learning-disability---an-introduction.aspx (accessed 10 February 2013).

NICE, 'Infection: Prevention and Control of Healthcare-associated Infections in Primary and Community Care.' Available online at http://publications.nice.org.uk/infection-cg139/guidance (accessed 8 June 2014).

Office for Disability Issues (2010) *Public Perceptions of Disabled People: Evidence from the British Social Attitudes Survey 2009.* London: The Stationery Office.

Parliamentary and Health Service Ombudsman (2011) *Care and Compassion? Report of the Health Service Ombudsman on Ten Investigations.* London: The Stationery Office.

Public Health England, 'Infectious Diseases.' Accessed online at http://www.hpa.org.uk/Topics/InfectiousDiseases/InfectionsAZ/. Accessed 8.6.2014.

Royal College of General Practitioners, 'TARGET Antibiotics toolkit.' Available online at http://www.rcgp.org.uk/TARGETantibiotics/ (accessed 8 June 2014). http://www.schulke-mayr.co.uk/cic/Personal%20Protection/howshouldiclean.html (accessed 8 June 2014).

Skills for Care (2012) *The State of the Adult Social Care Sector and Workforce in England 2012: From the National Minimum Dataset for Social Care (NMDS-SC).* Leeds: Skills for Care.

Skinner, B.F (1971) *Beyond Freedom and Dignity.* Indianapolis: Hackett Publishing.

Social Care Institute for Excellence (2011a) *The Governance of Adult Safeguarding: Findings from Research into Safeguarding Adults Boards.* London: SCIE.

UNISON (2012) *UNISON Duty of Care Handbook: For Members Working in Health and Social Care.* London: Unison. Available online at www.unison.org.uk/acrobat/19786_Duty%20of%20care%20rev4.pdf (accessed 17 April 2013).

United Nations Department of Economic and Social Affairs (2008) 'Promoting Social Integration.' Expert group meeting held 8–10 July 2008, Helsinki, Finland. Convened in preparation for the 47th session of the Commission for Social Development. Available online at www.un.org/esa/socdev/social/meetings/egm6_social_integration/documents/AIDEMEMOIRE_REVISED.pdf (accessed 17 April 2013).

World Health Organization (2013) '10 Facts on Dementia.' Available online at http://www.who.int/features/factfiles/dementia/en/index.html (accessed 4 February 2013).

INDEX